Virtual Community Building and the Information Society:

Current and Future Directions

Christo El Morr
American University of Kuwait, Kuwait

Pierre Maret
Université de Lyon, France

Information Science
REFERENCE

Senior Editorial Director:	Kristin Klinger
Director of Book Publications:	Julia Mosemann
Editorial Director:	Lindsay Johnston
Acquisitions Editor:	Erika Carter
Development Editor:	Mike Killian
Production Editor:	Sean Woznicki
Typesetters:	Christen Croley, Adrienne Freeland
Print Coordinator:	Jamie Snavely
Cover Design:	Nick Newcomer

Published in the United States of America by
Information Science Reference (an imprint of IGI Global)
701 E. Chocolate Avenue
Hershey PA 17033
Tel: 717-533-8845
Fax: 717-533-8661
E-mail: cust@igi-global.com
Web site: http://www.igi-global.com

Library of Congress Cataloging-in-Publication Data

Virtual community building and the information society : current and future
directions / Christo El Morr and Pierre Maret, editors.
     p. cm.
  Includes bibliographical references and index.
  ISBN 978-1-60960-869-9 (hbk.) -- ISBN 978-1-60960-870-5 (ebook) -- ISBN 978-1-60960-871-2 (print & perpetual access) 1. Electronic villages (Computer networks) 2. Online social networks. 3. Information society. I. El Morr, Christo, 1966- II. Maret, Pierre, 1966-
  TK5105.83.V57 2011
  303.48'33--dc22
                              2011009281

British Cataloguing in Publication Data
A Cataloguing in Publication record for this book is available from the British Library.

All work contributed to this book is new, previously-unpublished material. The views expressed in this book are those of the authors, but not necessarily of the publisher.

Rajendra Akerkar, *Western Norway Research Institute, Norway*
Sabah Mohammed, *Lakehead University, Canada*
Stan Johann, *Jean Monnet University, France*
Xavier Boucher, *Ecole des Mines de Saint Etienne, France*

Table of Contents

Section 1
Creating Virtual Communities

Chapter 1

    Christo El Morr, American University of Kuwait, Kuwait
    Pierre Maret, Université de Lyon, France
    Mihaela Dinca-Panaitescu, York University, Canada
    Marcia Rioux, York University, Canada
    Julien Subercaze, Université de Lyon, France

Chapter 2

    Paola Falcone, University of Rome, Italy

Chapter 3

    Marianne Laurent, Orange Labs, Telecom Bretagne, France

Section 2
Monitoring Virtual Communities

Chapter 4

    Marco De Maggio, University of Salento (Lecce), Italy
    Francesca Grippa, University of Salento (Lecce), Italy

Section 3
Stimulating Virtual Communities: Participation and Awareness

Section 4
Responsive Communities: Semantics, Identity and Governance

Detailed Table of Contents

Section 1
Creating Virtual Communities

Community designers will find in this section knowledge for the development of their virtual communities. This task requires a good understanding of background information, and numerous criteria must be considered for the emergence of such communities. Analyses and relevant illustrations are given in the three chapters belonging to this section.

Chapter 1

Christo El Morr, American University of Kuwait, Kuwait
Pierre Maret, Université de Lyon, France
Mihaela Dinca-Panaitescu, York University, Canada
Marcia Rioux, York University, Canada
Julien Subercaze, Université de Lyon, France

Chapter 1 addresses the analysis, design and implementation of a virtual community for a group of users (such as researchers) that collaborate and have changing system requirements. Investigations into the life cycle model for the development of the virtual knowledge community have been conducted in the Disability Rights Promotion International Canada project and are presented in along this chapter.

Chapter 2

Paola Falcone, University of Rome, Italy

Chapter 2 intends to identify, describe and analyze the main issues concerning the creation and effective management of a specific type of virtual community: online brand communities. The chapter addresses a very contemporary and present topic with human, societal, marketing and economic dimensions.

Chapter 3

    Marianne Laurent, Orange Labs, Telecom Bretagne, France

Chapter 3 provides background information and analysis on virtual communities in the perspective of online environments for knowledge management. The MPOWERS framework illustrates the chapter with concrete examples, offering a comprehensive environment for the emergence of communities of practice and communities of interest.

Section 2
Monitoring Virtual Communities

Contents, structures and user's behavior within virtual communities constitute the raw material of the chapters in this section. Users are organized in networks and they share contents. Analysis on these emerging contents and structures provides additional knowledge that is useful to monitor the communities and to understand the sociology of formation online.

Chapter 4

    Marco De Maggio, University of Salento (Lecce), Italy
    Francesca Grippa, University of Salento (Lecce), Italy

Chapter 4 proposes and evaluates a methodology for the analysis of virtual communities operating in an organizational context. Structural and content analysis are combined to detect virtual communities' overall composition, evolution and social structure. The methodology helps understanding the way new ideas spread within and across networks, and recognizing the emergence of informal roles.

Chapter 5

    Constanta-Nicoleta Bodea, Academy of Economic Studies, Romania
    Radu Ioan Mogos, Academy of Economic Studies, Romania
    Maria-Iuliana Dascalu, Academy of Economic Studies, Romania

Chapter 5 presents an empirical study that has been carried out to establish a correlation between the experience with e-learning environments and the presence in communities of practice. Results were obtained by use of questionnaires, statistics and data mining techniques. Authors prove, for instance, that the online activities with colleagues depend -much more than in classical learning situations- on the ones with the trainers.

In Chapter 6 the author takes his point of departure in traditional sociological understandings and definitions of a community. He proposes a historical view and a discussion of ideas and practices of online social relationships featured with the specific affordances and limitations of Internet. It is argued that the social formation online should not be analyzed in the light of traditional, sociological understandings of traditional communities, but rather on a framework encompassing logics of networks.

Section 3
Stimulating Virtual Communities: Participation and Awareness

The reader will find in this section three chapters related to the development of functionalities for domain-specific virtual communities. These chapters describe and generalize advanced frameworks in collaborative on line laboratories, collaborative cultural text translation and collaborative design and simulation.

Chapter 7 deals with group awareness in the context of collaborative online laboratories. Classifications, facets, features and metaphors of several virtual, remote and hybrid laboratories are presented and discussed. Two case studies are presented in detail and conduct the authors to discuss about their practical experience and contribution on this specific field of Computer-Supported Collaborative Learning (CSCL).

Chapter 8 presents -and discuss about- a participative web platform designed as a collaboration and debate place for the confrontation of different points of view around texts. Authors demonstrate that virtual communities constitute a good paradigm to help human translators with both interpretative translation features and participation features.

Chapter 9 discusses how teams of innovators in the telecommunication companies form multidisciplinary design communities focusing on so-called service systems dedicated to end-users. These actors share some knowledge, visions, scenarios, etc. The authors propose a theoretical framework and a semi-formal semantic method for communities of innovators to co-describe, co-model and simulate the targeted services systems.

Section 4
Responsive Communities: Semantics, Identity and Governance

Collaboration in virtual communities requires an environment where a semantic is clarified, a definition of identity is shared, and governance is well understood. These topics are discussed in the next chapters: semantic models are used to link virtual communities; identification and self-verification are deeply discussed and impact the design of virtual communities; and governance aspects are depicted, showing the tension between freedom and control in communities.

Chapter 10

Chapter 10 aims to give a background on the semantic modeling issues involved in linking virtual communities. The authors discuss the various approaches, techniques and standards that have to be dealt with when addressing this topic. A model semantically rich enough to accommodate the linking of virtual communities is proposed, clearly emphasizing the advantages for community members ensued.

Chapter 11

Chapter 11 gives an in depth description of identity-related concepts and theories. It provides a comprehensive review of the literature, comparing and reconciling the two theoretical perspectives in VC participation: identification and self-verification. Interesting areas for future research in this field are discussed, as well as practical implications for VC design.

Chapter 12

Chapter 12 aims to develop a better understanding of the governance of Internet in order for the virtual communities' members to be aware of technical and governance aspects to manage their communities. It is shown that the community governance is very much dependent from the trust the users have among them. Authors also clearly depict the tensions in-between freedom and control in the web, and between the horizontal and vertical control in the networks. The Botnets example illustrates the discourse.

Foreword

I remember someone once said that if you put two people in a room and tell them not to speak with one another, they will sooner or later always "disobey this order" and start talking. Humans have a basic desire to communicate with one another, a desire that cannot be controlled by others. And now with the multitude of internet devices no further than an arm's length away, the walls of the room have disintegrated. Individuals are pouring online – interacting effortlessly with anyone, anywhere, and anytime, as is evidenced by the popularity of numerous social media sites. The most well-known example today is Facebook, with more than 500 million active users who are connected on average to 130 friends and 80 community pages, groups, and events, and whose founder just received the Time Magazine 2010 Person of the Year award.[1]

It is through this interaction among individuals that communities arise. Communities have always been at the center of human interaction and as such have been the focus of attention of both researchers and practitioners alike through time. While the number of definitions of community abound, communities tend to have two characteristics: 1) a web of affect-laden relationships among a group of individuals and 2) a commitment to a set of shared values, norms, and meanings, along with a shared history and identity.[2] There is a feeling of "we-ness in a community; one is a member"[3] and community is generally thought of as being in direct contrast to society, in which self-interest, individualism, and competition reign[4] (Tönnies, 1887; Durkheim, 1893; Weber, 1978, von Krogh 2002).

These community characteristics extend as well to the online environments of both 2D and 3D virtual worlds where virtual communities, also known under names such as electronic communities, online communities, electronic networks, and webs of knowledge, have experienced unprecedented growth. These communities take all forms: from local interest groups to global professional communities and from customer communities to user innovation communities to open source communities. As the list of different virtual communities grows, so, too, do the questions related to them. Some of the more fundamental questions relate to how online communities differ from communities based on physical co-presence and face-to-face interactions as well as does participation in online communities create positive change in people's lives or foster a decline in social capital[5] (Quan-Haase & Wellman, 2002). Other questions relate to community dynamics such as how online communities are created and sustained and to member issues such as identity and why do members voluntarily contribute their own time and resources to the community. Firms and organizations are also interested in understanding how they can leverage online communities for their own value creation, such as through design, innovation, brand, and service communities. Finally, there are a number of technological questions such as what do mobility, participative web services, and pervasive computing mean for virtual communities as well as methodological questions related to how can we observe and study virtual communities.

While previous publications on virtual communities have touched on one or more of the above issues, few publications have brought together a set of contributions that cater to a wider audience. Not only does this book enable its readers to gain a clear understanding of virtual communities and their related advantages and challenges from a variety of applications and viewpoints, but it also provides a practical understanding of the tools with which to implement and observe these communities.

We are quickly moving into a time in which a) internet devices are becoming increasingly cheaper and just as accessible to people in developing countries as in developed countries and b) communication technologies are advancing our ability to interact with others regardless of differences in language and culture in both 2D as well as 3D worlds. As a result, virtual communities promise to change much of society, politics, and the economy as we know it. This book is of importance as it provides its readers with an understanding of this phenomenon, and my hope is that it will both enable and inspire these readers to leverage virtual communities in such a way that society, politics, and the economy will be positively shaped for future generations.

This book provides a state of the art *holistic coverage* of virtual communities that discusses the different facets of virtual communities, from technology (e.g. infrastructure, modeling) to social impact (e.g. participation, identity, governance) passing by different aspects and applications.

Robin Teigland
Stockholm School of Economics, Sweden

ENDNOTES

[1]   http://www.facebook.com/press/info.php?statistics, accessed on December 29, 2010.

[2]   Etzioni, A. 1996. The responsive community: A communitarian perspective. *American Sociological Review,* 61,1: 1-11.

[3]   Bender, T. 1982. *Community and Social Change in America.* New Brunswick, NJ: Rutgers University Press, p.7.

[4]   Tönnies, F. 1887, translated 1957. Gemeinschaft und Gesellschaft (Community and Society). East Lansing, MI: Michigan State University Press; Durkheim, E. 1893 (translated 1933, 1960). *The Division of Labor in Society.* New York: Macmillan; Weber, M. 1978 (German edition 1922). *Economy and Society (Wirtschaft und Gesellschaft).* Berkeley: University of California;von Krogh, G. 2002. The communal resource and information systems. *Journal of Strategic Information Systems,* 11: 85-107.

[5]   Quan-Haase, A., & Wellman, B. (2002). How does the Internet affect social capital? In M.H. Huysman & V. Wulf (eds.) *Information Technology and Social Capital.* Boston: Kluwer Academic Publishers.

Preface

Humans gather to form groups or communities in order to accomplish certain individual or collective objectives. At the beginning of the 1990's., the Internet provided the infrastructure for the formation of similar communities, the difference being that the meeting place is not physical but virtual: the Virtual Communities (VCs). People form virtual communities in order to achieve a certain aim, e.g. playing, chatting, discussing, researching, collaborating, etc. Chat rooms, bulletin boards, and email groups can be considered as virtual communities that allow people to gather and bond.

Virtual Communities vary in the technologies they use and their wide domain of applications. In the 1990's mobility emerged in the telecommunication industry and had a remarkable impact of VC research; particularly on the design, the infrastructure to use, the services to offer, the user interface, the security as well as the privacy of the users.

With the growth of communication technology, the emergence of multi-partner global organizations, the increase in dynamic teams formation, the rise of teleworking, and the pervasive or ubiquitous nature of computing, Virtual Communities are to play an significant role in organizations and will undoubtedly change the way people communicate and collaborate; indeed, the information society we live in depends, in a great part, on the way the information is exchanged between collaborating groups and individuals.

In this context, Virtual Communities appears to be one of the main aspects of the information society, and there is a need to define the technologies, methodologies, and tools for the collection, management, exchange and use of information within Virtual Communities and to understand the social and political aspects involved in them.

In the recent years, Virtual Communities received a visible level of attention from the research community in many disciplines: Computer Science, Sociology, Psychology, and other disciplines. Today Virtual Communities are a well-recognized emergent domain of research and development. Its research scope is broad it covers different research domains (e.g. computer science, psychology, sociology) and applications (e.g. leisure, tourism, education, health). This book addresses the latest issues involved in *creating*, *monitoring*, *stimulating* Virtual Communities as well as studying some of *cresponsiveness*.

Traditionally, books that addressed the virtual communities' topic are either an (obsolete) overview of the subject matter, or present a theoretical investigation and reflection on the topic. The books lend themselves to a more practical approach focus on one particular application of virtual communities, such as education, knowledge management, communities of practice, or information technology infrastructure. Other books focus on the social aspect of virtual communities or the possible business models that Virtual Communities offer.

Though, to the best of our knowledge, there are no books that deal with the different aspects of virtual communities theoretical and practical way, and that provides a solid knowledgeable introduction to this field of research and development, and provide at the same time a cutting edge insight into the latest aspects in research and development that reflect on the technology side as well as on the human side of virtual communities.

This book offers researchers interested in the Virtual Communities field, novice or experts, a place where they can find integrated knowledge about the different aspects of Virtual Communities, relieving them from seeking disparate scattered knowledge distributed among several books.

This book gives the reader an insight into the latest challenges and opportunities involved in Virtual Communities allowing a swift and concentrated overview of technical and societal aspects of the domain.

This book addresses two kinds of audiences:

1. On one side the researchers, Masters and PhD students, who are *interested in the Virtual Communities domain* and would like to have an in depth introduction to Virtual Communities. These can be academic or professionals from different disciplines and that have interest in pursuing research connected to Virtual Communities and that would like to get a *knowledgeable introduction* to the domain. To those the current book provides more than just a mere "introduction", instead it gives them an overview of the different issues, revolving around Virtual Communities, related to both technical and social, such as computer infrastructure, community monitoring, information systems, security, privacy, identity, awareness, participation.

2. On the other side expert researchers in the domain, who would like to have an in depth analysis of the latest research findings and perspectives, as well as to the *state-of-the-art know-how* on the different Virtual Communities facets. For those expert researchers the current book does give them a holistic view of the Virtual Communities research field that allows them to broaden their understanding of the different factors (technical and societal) involved.

This book is a collection of chapters centered on the concept of virtual communities. We have grouped these chapters in 4 sections dealing respectively with Virtual Communities *Creation, Monitoring, Stimulation* (Participation and awareness), and *Responsiveness* (Semantic, Identity and governance).

Section 1: Creating Virtual Communities

Community designers will find in this section knowledge for the development of their virtual communities. This task requires a good understanding of background information, and numerous criteria must be considered for the emergence of such communities. Analyses and relevant illustrations are given in the three chapters belonging to this section.

Chapter 1 is titled *Virtual Community Building and the Information Society: Current and Future Directions*. Authors are El Morr, Maret, Dinca-Panaitescu, Rioux and Subercaze. This chapter addresses the analysis, design and implementation of a virtual community for a group of users (such as researchers) that collaborate and have changing system requirements. Investigations into the life cycle model for the development of the virtual knowledge community have been conducted in the Disability Rights Promotion International Canada project and are presented in along this chapter.

Chapter 2 is titled *The Creation and Management of Online Brand Communities*, authored by Paola Falcone. The chapter intends to identify, describe and analyse the main issues concerning the creation and effective management of a specific type of virtual community: online brand communities. The chapter addresses a very contemporary and present topic with human, societal, marketing and economic dimensions.

Chapter 3 is written by Marianne Laurent and is titled *Coordinating Nomadic Evaluation Practices by Supporting the Emergence of Virtual Communities*. The chapter provides background information and analysis on virtual communities in the perspective of online environments for knowledge management. The MPOWERS framework illustrates the chapter with concrete examples, offering a comprehensive environment for the emergence of communities of practice and communities of interest.

Section 2: Monitoring Virtual Communities

Contents, structures and user's behavior within virtual communities constitute the raw material of the chapters in this section. Users are organized in networks and they share contents. Analysis on these emerging contents and structures provides additional knowledge that is useful to monitor the communities and to understand the sociology of formation online.

Chapter 4 is written by De Maggio and Grippa; It is titled *An Integrated Methodology to Detect the Evolution of Virtual Organizational Communities*. Authors propose and evaluate a methodology for the analysis of virtual communities operating in an organizational context. Structural and content analysis are combined to detect virtual communities' overall composition, evolution and social structure. The methodology helps understanding the way new ideas spread within and across networks, and recognizing the emergence of informal roles.

Chapter 5 is called *How E-Learning Experience Enhances the Social Presence in Community of Practice: An Empirical Analysis*. It has been written by Bodea, Mogos and Dascalu. This chapter presents an empirical study that has been carried out to establish a correlation between the experience with e-learning environments and the presence in communities of practice. Results were obtained by use of questionnaires, statistics and data mining techniques. Authors prove, for instance, that the online activities with colleagues depend -much more than in classical learning situations- on the ones with the trainers.

Chapter 6 is written by Jensen and is titled *Online Communities: A Historically Based Examination of How Social Formations Online Fulfill Criteria for Community*. The author takes his point of departure in traditional sociological understandings and definitions of a community. He proposes a historical view and a discussion of ideas and practices of online social relationships featured with the specific affordances and limitations of Internet. It is argued that the social formation online should not be analyzed in the light of traditional, sociological understandings of traditional communities, but rather on a framework encompassing logics of networks.

Section 3: Stimulating Virtual Communities: Participation and Awareness

The reader will find in this section three chapters related to the development of functionalities for domain-specific virtual communities. These chapters describe and generalize advanced frameworks in collaborative on line laboratories, collaborative cultural text translation and collaborative design and simulation.

Chapter 7 is titled *Functionalities and Facets of Group Awareness in Collaborative Online Laboratories* and it is written by Gravier and Callaghan. This chapter deals with group awareness in the context of collaborative online laboratories. Classifications, facets, features and metaphors of several virtual, remote and hybrid laboratories are presented and discussed. Two case studies are presented in detail and conduct the authors to discuss about their practical experience and contribution on this specific field of Computer-Supported Collaborative Learning (CSCL).

Chapter 8 is written by Bénel and Lacour. It is titled *Towards a Participative Platform for Cultural Texts Translators* and presents -and discuss about- a participative web platform designed as a collaboration and debate place for the confrontation of different points of view around texts. Authors demonstrate that virtual communities constitute a good paradigm to help human translators with both interpretative translation features and participation features.

Chapter 9 is titled *Virtual Communities in a Services Innovation Context: A Service Science and Mereotopology Based Method and Tool,* authored by Bugeaud and Soulier. Teams of innovators in the telecommunication companies form multidisciplinary design communities focusing on so-called service systems dedicated to end-users. These actors share some knowledge, visions, scenarios, etc. The authors propose a theoretical framework and a semi-formal semantic method for communities of innovators to co-describe, co-model and simulate the targeted services systems.

Section 4: Responsive Communities: Semantic, Identity and Governance

Collaboration in virtual communities requires an environment where a semantic is clarified, a definition of identity is shared, and governance is well understood. These topics are discussed in the next chapters: semantic models are used to link virtual communities; identification and self-verification are deeply discussed and impact the design of virtual communities; and governance aspects are depicted, showing the tension between freedom and control in communities.

Chapter 10 is titled *Semantically Linking Virtual Communities* authored by Akerkar and Terje Aaberge. The aim of this chapter is to give a background on the semantic modeling issues involved in linking virtual communities. The authors discuss the various approaches, techniques and standards that have to be dealt with when addressing this topic. A model semantically rich enough to accommodate the linking of virtual communities is proposed, clearly emphasizing the advantages for community members ensued.

Chapter 11 is written by Shen and is titled *Identification vs. Self-Verification in Virtual Communities (VC): Theoretical Gaps and Design Implications*. This chapter describes in depth identity-related concepts and theories. It provides a comprehensive review of the literature, comparing and reconciling the two theoretical perspectives in VC participation: identification and self-verification. Interesting areas for future research in this field are discussed, as well as practical implications for VC design.

Chapter 12, *Freedom, Control, Security: Current and Future Implications for Internet Governance* is written by Knahl and Cox. This chapter aims to develop a better understanding of the governance of Internet in order for the virtual communities' members to be aware of technical and governance aspects to manage their communities. It is shown that the community governance is very much dependent from the trust the users have among them. Authors also clearly depict the tensions in-between freedom and control in the web, and between the horizontal and vertical control in the networks. The Botnets example illustrates the discourse.

Christo El Morr
American University of Kuwait, Kuwait

Pierre Maret
Université de Lyon, France

Acknowledgment

We would like to acknowledge Mrs. Valentina Al Hamouche and Mrs. Esther Wieland-Maret for their immense support and encouragement during the work towards the accomplishment of this book.

Christo El Morr
American University of Kuwait, Kuwait

Pierre Maret
Université de Lyon, France

Section 1
Creating Virtual Communities

Community designers will find in this section knowledge for the development of their virtual communities. This task requires a good understanding of background information, and numerous criteria must be considered for the emergence of such communities. Analyses and relevant illustrations are given in the three chapters belonging to this section.

Chapter 1
Virtual Community Building and the Information Society:
Current and Future Directions

Christo El Morr
American University of Kuwait, Kuwait

Pierre Maret
Université de Lyon, France

Mihaela Dinca-Panaitescu
York University, Canada

Marcia Rioux
York University, Canada

Julien Subercaze
Université de Lyon, France

ABSTRACT

This paper reports the results of an investigation into the life cycle model needed to develop information systems for groups of people with fluid requirements. For this purpose, we developed a modified spiral model and applied it to the analysis, design and implementation of a virtual community for a group of researchers and organizations that collaborated in a research project and had changing system requirements. The virtual knowledge community was dedicated to support mobilization and dissemination of evidence-based knowledge produced by the Disability Rights Promotion International Canada (DRPI-Canada) project.

DOI: 10.4018/978-1-60960-869-9.ch001

INTRODUCTION

Virtual communities (VCs) have drawn attention of researchers since the inception of the web. Health Virtual Communities (Health VCs) started to take shape in the mid of 1990's. Nevertheless, even though Health VCs share advantages and challenges with other types of VCs some of the advantages they present and the challenges they face are health care specific. Therefore, there is a need to conduct a *Health VCs assessment*. People form virtual communities in order to achieve a certain aim, e.g. playing, chatting, discussing, researching, collaborating, etc. Chat rooms, bulletin boards, and email groups can be considered as virtual communities that allow people to gather and bond. VCs received a visible level of attention from the research community in many disciplines: Computer Science, Sociology, Psychology, and other disciplines. Preece (Preece, 2000) suggests that a virtual community is shaped of: (a) socially interacting *people*, performing special roles or satisfying their needs, (b) a *purpose*, which is the reason behind the community, (c) *policies* to govern people interaction, and (d) a *Computer Systems* that support social interaction.

The Problem

While Virtual Communities are well defined and virtual communities modeling has been giving fair attention it is by definition assumed that the *purpose,* aims and objectives of a community members are well defined in advance; it follows that the inherent assumption - from an information systems perspective - is that existing development life cycles can be followed when developing any virtual community. Though, in a fluid environment, such as a situations where participants can change their role/situation/position in their participation, in multidisciplinary research and collaborative teams, or when the environment is evolving with the time (some external parameters are changing), little – if any - concrete systems

objectives, other than the general 'purpose' of collaboration, are defined in advance. Indeed, the concrete requirement needs are revealed as the project progresses or even during the community's life. To the best of our knowledge, there has not been an attempt to explore the system development life cycle model needed in projects where requirements are not only not well defined but also fluid and changing in nature. This paper is an attempt to draw the first sketches of such model in the context of a multidisciplinary collaborative virtual knowledge community. Our approach is general and is based on our experience in virtual communities for Human rights monitoring and for health prevention. Most of our examples will be taken from this first domain of application; however some requirements cited will illustrate our second domain of application which contains some additional characteristics (for instance information gathering based on sensed data).

Virtual Communities for Human Rights Monitoring

Framework of Disability

Disability activists and scholars refer to disability rights as "…the equal effective enjoyment of all human rights by people with disabilities" (Disability Rights Promotion International (DRPI), 2003). The majority consensus is that "disability" is a consequence of negative social conditions rather than an individual's specific medical impairment (Barnes, Mercer, & Shakespeare, 1999; Fougeyrollas, Cloutier, Bergeron, Côté, & Michel, 1999; Rioux, 1997, 2001; Shakespeare, 1999; Thomas, 2002).

A review of international human rights literature shows that, unlike areas such as women's rights (Callamard, 1999a, 1999b), disability rights monitoring is relatively underdeveloped (International Disability Rights Monitor, 2004). Mobilization and dissemination of evidence-based knowledge produced through monitoring processes represent the keystone of a holistic approach to monitoring; though integrating different facets of monitoring requires collaboration among a broad range of individuals (including people with disabilities) and organizations. This paper proposes an operational tool that enables dynamic collaboration among project's participants and knowledge creation and sharing.

Systemic human rights violations against people with disabilities are usually interpreted as issues of service provision rather than being recognized as fundamental rights in order to achieve a society in which people with disabilities are free to fully and equally participate. This requires a conceptualization of disability within a human rights framework that looks at how society marginalizes people, and what strategies are needed to address existing inequalities. It involves moving away from viewing people with disabilities as anomalies towards viewing them as rights holders and equal citizens (Quinn & Degener, 2002).

Rights monitoring is the first step in making this shift possible. While there are a number of international and Canadian human rights commitments and rights monitoring initiatives in the international arena(Disability Rights Promotion International (DRPI), 2003; International Disability Rights Monitor (IDRM), 2004), Canada lacks comprehensive and multi-level analysis of disability rights violations. *DRPI*-Canada project takes a significant step forward in developing a system to monitor the human rights situation of people with disabilities.

Mobilization and Dissemination of Evidence-Based Knowledge

Holistic disability rights monitoring is grounded in on-going communication and sharing of resources, training and methodological approaches among four themes (Policy and Law Monitoring, Individual Experiences Monitoring, Media Monitoring, Statistics Monitoring). Furthermore, it is essential to build capacity, leadership and knowledge development within the disability community in order to promote greater awareness of disability discrimination and to enable people with disabilities themselves to take ownership of disability rights monitoring. In this context, a complex system is required to facilitate the collaboration of a full range of project participants – researchers, representatives of disability community, policy makers, and general public – and support capacity building within disability community through access to online tools and training resources.

THE VIRTUAL KNOWLEDGE COMMUNITY

This section describes the design and development process of a Virtual Knowledge Community (VKC) to support, in this case, the holistic disability rights monitoring.

Virtual Communities

VCs received a visible level of attention from the research community in Computer Science, Sociology, Psychology and other disciplines (Preece, 2000). A virtual community is a form of social system; it inherits some of the social system's characteristics (Weissman, 2000) such as causal reciprocity, purpose, design, roles, circumstances, officers, passion, needs, loyalty, and access. There are different perspectives and different classifications of VCs (El Morr, 2007; El Morr & Kawash, 2007; Stein, Hawking, & Sharma, 2005); though, VCs can be constructed to form a knowledge network. Virtual knowledge Communities are communities where participants capture, access, use, create, and define knowledge (Merali & Davies, 2001), and/or where information is automatically captured to be accessed and shared in-between participants. Our purpose is to design and implement a VC for Knowledge Mobilization, i.e. for knowledge generation, dissemination and use, in the contexts of DRPI and health prevention.

While several virtual communities platform exist, none are general enouth to be adapted to our research team objectives in terms of creating dynamic relations among team members, enabling particularly each member (and not only administrators) to create folders and upload/download documents, to co-edit documents and to share files across communities in different levels of granularity: share with one person, one group of people and a whole community. Besides, none of these sites is fully accessible to people with visual disabilities or with limited abilities in the use of computers systems, while accessibility is an essential objective that we strive for in our projects. The VKC is described in detail in the next sections of the paper.

Platform Design and Implementation

Community Design

In the field of disability, tools and training resources for evidence-based data collection are scarce as are tools and methods for multiple levels of analysis (i.e. individual, systemic. Development and dissemination of these tools incorporating an e-learning component to a virtual knowledge community in order to support continuous training to develop monitoring skills (online manuals, course guides, books, tools...). Internally, the VKC finally consists of data/document base with links and interactions in-between participants. It should enable participants such as researchers (who are supposed to access and work on this great amount of data) and practitioners (who are supposed to assist concerned people), to *communicate* and *cross-check* their findings, and to *collaborate* around subjects of interest during the research activities. Therefore, members will need a component allowing collaboration to facilitate knowledge creation. Finally, the VKC needs to facilitate the search for information for

communities' members. Consequently the VKC was designed into four components allowing (1) knowledge *creation*, (2) knowledge *discovery*, (3) knowledge dissemination and (4) VKC management. The VKC platform was designed to comprise functionalities that support all four components.

Community Platform Implementation

This section presents the implementation choices we have made for the implementation of communities. Open source material has been used throughout the development of the model. The VC platform allows two major *roles* to be played: *Administrator* and *Member*; the members can play three possible roles: *consumer, producer* and consumer/producer of information. In the domain of human rights monitoring, information stored and exchanged materializes into documents (in different formats). In the domain of health prevention, information may also consist of raw data captured on or around the patient, or on aggregated data combining several data sources.

The administrator is concerned with the maintenance of the VKC (community and member management), such as creating a new community (Figure 2). Several communities can created, and members can belong to more than one community. Access to a community can be public or controlled. The application portal allows a person to connect and to create his/her own profile. In order to simplify information dissemination, we decided that a *public community* allows people to join without administrator approval since it is designed to disseminate knowledge (research findings, articles, reports, etc.) to the public in the society at large. Members of the *public community* can play the role of *information consumers.* Members of communities, other than the public, are both information producer (e.g. upload documents) and information consumers of information exchanged inside their community (e.g. download documents, consult data).

Figure 1. A high level view of the components of the collaborative platform

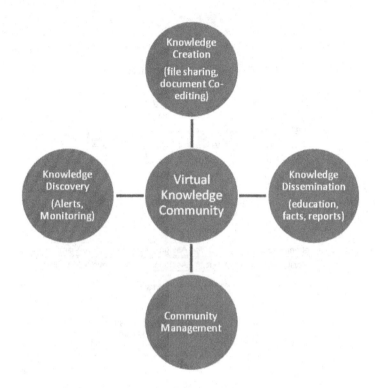

Figure 2. Creating a new community

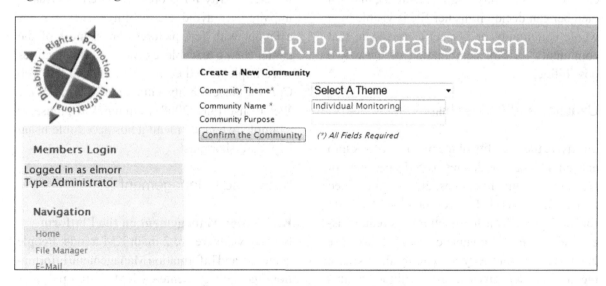

Figure 3. A member assigning "visibility" right (i.e. access rights) to other specific members and/or while communities

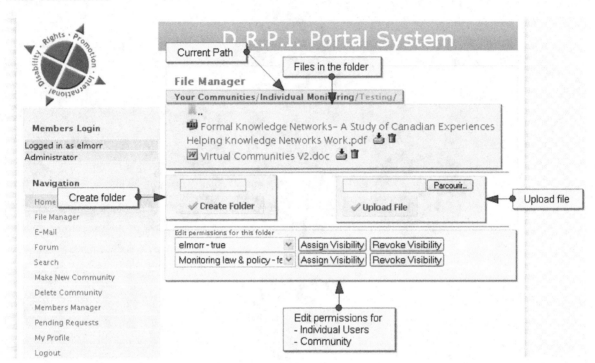

Administrators and members of the themes communities can upload and assign each file or each data a "visibility" right (Figure 3); that is a member can decide if his/her file is visible by a whole community or a specific person in that community, or any combination of these two possibilities.

Usability and Accessibility

To ensure the usability of the portal, we took into account relevant guidelines (U.S. Department of Health and Human Services, 2008) and decided to use a light XHTML W3C compliant template for the layout, with few pictures, to reduce users waiting time and enhance accessibility. The layout is light and easy to scan by the users, a menu on the left gives access to all the features of the portal in one click. The navigation was designed to minimize users' interaction to access information. Fonts and colors have been chosen for their clarity for people who are not visually impaired. To avoid accessibility issues, we use a layout with few pictures. Thus, most of the content being readable text, accessibility features were implemented easily. We followed the Web Content Accessibility Guidelines (World Wide Web Consortium, 2008) from the W3C; thus, for example, we made menu items accessible using keyboard shortcuts.

Knowledge Management

Knowledge Management on the Platform
Nowadays, there are 2 main KM trends: People centered, and Information Management/Information Technology Centered KM. Using previous experiences (Davenport, De Long, & Beers, 1998),

we used several relevant guidelines to develop our approach in our healthcare related platforms. As our initiative focuses more on the technical purpose than on a human approach, guidelines regarding technical support were taken in account. Flexible knowledge structure and good usability are important for the success of the initiative. During the development of our platform, those basic guidelines were taken in account, from early specification to late implementation.

Within the platform, numerous users, i.e. producers, will share large amount of documents within and between the communities for consumers. We identified two major issues and defined features to address them. First, searching through a *large* number of documents; therefore, finding relevant documents in the platform regarding to the users interest is identified as of utmost importance. Second, as the information producers are mainly researchers, this platform offers a great opportunity to create cross-theme synergies, open new collaborations or enforce the existing ones. Besides, the platform is designed for the public, and other researchers and organizations at a later stage. The large number of potential contributors will make the discovery of potential common interests between members difficult. Consequently, it is important to facilitate this discovery process.

To address these two issues, we designed a matching feature that enables the system to describe users and documents using metadata in order to (1) notify the user when relevant information has been added to the platform and (2) match users having a "similar" profile. We identified four sequential steps in the process: Information gathering, information extraction, matching, and push mechanism.

During information gathering we gather all the information concerning each member. While during information extraction, keywords are extracted from documents using a text-mining library: RapidMiner (rapid-i.com, 2008). These keywords will complete the documents metadata. These extraction will take place for both docu-

ments uploaded by users and the publications they entered to complete their profile. Navigation will also be mined to extract relevant topic of interest (Widyantoro, Loerger, & Yen, 2001; Xiaobin, Jay Budzik, & Kristian, 2000). We trained the Rapid-Miner model with more than 50 documents related to healthcare. Using this healthcare dedicated text-mining model gives impressive results for keyword extraction. Once the keywords automatically extracted, the owner of the file can decide to manually edit, add or remove keywords from this list (Figure 4).

Afterword, matching algorithms allowed us to provide a user to document and user to user matching. Both matching algorithms follow the same principle of computing a distance between the gathered metadata. Yu et al. (Yu, Al-Jadir, & Spaccapietra, 2005) presented an algorithm for matching demands and supplies of profiles using a description logic based approach, a similar approach can be used for the user/documents matching.

Multiplying channels of exchanges enhance the global performance of knowledge dissemination; therefore, we've build a forum and a mail system for users. Those communication channels are complementary. Users interaction is thus enhanced, discussion on a paper uploaded in the repository can start and lead to a better understanding or constructive critics.

Content Management: A Human Rights Monitoring Tool

The last aspect of the platform is the management of the content, i.e. human rights monitoring as such. Researchers and NGO (Non-Governmental Organizations) needed a way to collate data from different geographically dispersed sources and then to use it anywhere. Also they were in favor of creating a public community for the dissemination of knowledge to the people. Administrators decided then to create five communities: a public one and four dealing with the four substantive

Figure 4. Keyword editing after extraction

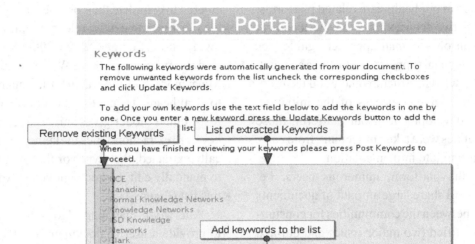

themes of research identified as such for the monitoring of disabilities:

1. **Policy and Law Monitoring:** involves the collection of legislation, policy and program data specific to disability rights in. A template is designed to gather data addressing all categories of rights (civil, cultural, economic, political and social). The template serves as an assessment tool, allowing the identification of gaps in legislation and policy and includes cross-references to the relevant provisions of key international human rights treaties. The community members of this theme investigate the policies and laws that are related to disability, on the provincial and federal levels. Researchers in this community are interested in looking into analyzing to which extent the Canadian laws and policies follow the International conventions related to disabilities. This is done through a survey that is designed to look into each article in an international convention that is related to disability and to see if there are policies and laws and case laws in the provinces and the federation that accommodate that article or that on the contrary hinder its application or simply do not acknowledge it.

2. **Individual Experiences Monitoring:** Monitoring of disability rights obligations should include a way to assess the actual situation of people with disabilities in a given country or area. Individual experiences monitoring involves the collection of data through surveys and collect the individual experiences of people with disabilities.

3. **Media Monitoring:** The media plays an important role in reflecting and influencing public opinion. Given the role that public opinion and attitudes play in facilitating or hampering the enjoyment of human rights by people with disabilities, a holistic approach to disability rights monitoring also examines the nature and extent of media coverage on

Figure 5. A partial View of the database

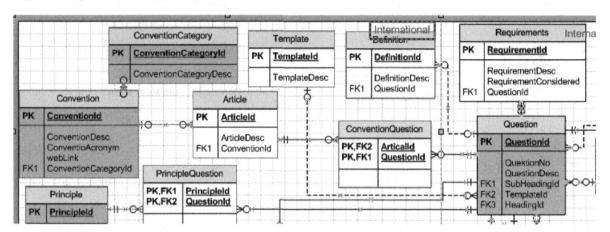

disability issues. The media monitoring team monitors the depiction and coverage of disability in the media. The analysis of media stories will take place on two levels - one quantitative (analyzing media coverage) and one qualitative (analyzing the context of media reporting).

4. **Statistics Monitoring:** that analyzed governmental statistical data to unveil the kind of data that can be used to draw a picture about the life of people with disabilities.

We've built a tool that organizes the different kinds of data and connects them together. The tool is built around a database designed to gather information from the different communities and to enable searching for data collected from the different communities. At this moment the tool has been used since several months to enter data. Researchers are currently formulating the criteria to be used to search for information; once these criteria are set search capacity will be added online to allow for researchers and later NGOs to use it to produce report about the state of disability rights in Canada. Researchers and disability institutions from around the globe have showed interest in using this tool (we expect it will be used in USA, Sweden, Portugal, Kenya, Cameroon, India, Croatia, and Australia).

THE MODEL

Requirements Elicitation During the Project

The Virtual Knowledge Community that we've presented before replies to a tangible need, i.e. to monitor the application of human rights treaties and international conventions in the Canadian context. This approach is based on a versatile model extensible to other situations.

After each requirement elicitation phase the development team went into analysis, design and prototyping of the virtual knowledge community based on those elicited requirements. In a later stage, community members assessed the prototype together with the changing environment and injected the team with changed or new requirements that were deemed essential in the next step of their collaborative work.

At the end of the development we've noticed that the requirements that were thought to be the most important at the beginning of the project (i.e. file sharing and searching capability) were given less priority and important in a later stage. Community members found that the e-library and the especially the content management tools (the human rights monitoring tools) are the most useful and the most potent to have a tangible impact on

Figure 6. Part of a form to enter law and policy monitoring data

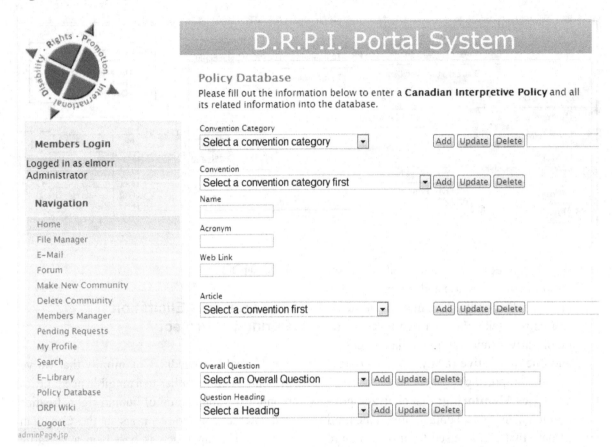

their collaborative work. Indeed, users used occasionally the VKC to store files and share them, and disregarded almost completely the email and forum facilities (at least at this stage), they expressed their preference not to have too many login passwords and too many email systems to use at the same time. On the other hand, the e-library and the monitoring tool were enthusiastically welcomed by the researchers and organization partners. Data entry has already started and search criteria are under development.

Model Development

Models for system development life cycle already exist.

The traditional 'waterfall' model requires all requirements to be gathered and clarified in order for the design to start, and the implementation to take place (after the design). This model obviously does not fit projects with fluid requirements.

The spiral model (Boehmm, 1986) is a more subtle model that relies on iterative prototyping in order to develop a system. This model gives more flexibility in terms of development and input/output tuning, though it needs that the requirements/objectives be defined in advance (at least in terms of processes); indeed, "each cycle of the spiral begins with the identification of the objectives of the portion of the product being elaborated (performance, functionality, ability to accommodate change, etc.)" (Boehmm, 1986).

Figure 7. A partial view of the spiral model that shows how requirements are to be elicited at the beginning of the life cycle

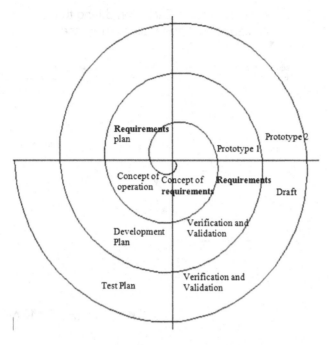

In a fluid environment, where the needs are changing during the progress of work, functionalities are defined and re-defined, and some may be relegated altogether at the end. The spiral model doesn't seem to explicitly accommodate this situation since the requirements are defined clearly at the beginning of the life cycle. We suggest a modified version of the Spiral Model that takes into consideration the requirements elicitation in a fluid environment. Our model involves a prototyping approach like the spiral model with one difference: at every cycle the requirement may change based on environmental changes (e.g. changes in the community members need) and therefore the Verification and Validation after each phase should involve not only the prototype but also the requirements, which permits to detect arising new needs, or fading former needs (once believed to be important) (Figure 8).

Once requirements are detected they are communicated to the development team that goes into *analysis and design* and *prototyping*, while the requirements may evolve in parallel due to *environmental changes*. Once a prototype is ready an *assessment* meeting gathers the development team with the community members in order to:

- Assess the prototype (interface, functionality, etc.)
- Elicit new requirements and tune former requirements

Then the process starts all over.

Since iterations end with "verification and validation", we suggest that the requirements elicitation process, shown in Figure 8, be part of the Verification and Validation phase.

We believe that this updated Spiral Model is flexible enough to allow development in a fluid environment where requirements change during the System Development Life Cycle (SDLC).

Figure 8. Requirements elicitation in a fluid environment

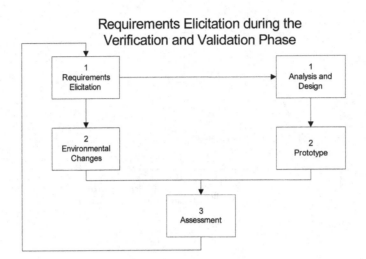

CONCLUSION

We have proposed in this paper the description of a life-cycle of community based applications. Our methodology has been mainly illustrated by the example of a system implementing Virtual Knowledge Communities for the monitoring of human rights. Communities are the right tool to support the creation of information and the exchange of information in-between participants such as researchers and partners, and to mobilize community members, academics, students, as well as the media and policy makers around disability rights. We've observed during the project development that some of the formerly believed important requirements were relegated while other requirements appeared to be more important at a later stage in the project and were included in a subsequent Verification and Validation phase. We have then suggested a modified Spiral Model for information system development in a fluid environment to take into consideration changes in requirements during SDLC. More work should be done to observe if this modified spiral model can be applied in similar contexts.

ACKNOWLEDGMENT

We would like to acknowledge the SSHRC (CURA, Social Sciences and Humanities Research Council of Canada) for funding this research project as part of a larger initiative on Disability Rights Monitoring.

REFERENCES

Barnes, C., Mercer, G., & Shakespeare, T. (1999). *Exploring Disability: A Sociological Introduction*. Cambridge, UK: Blackwell Publishers.

Callamard, A. (1999a). *Documenting Human Rights Violations by State Agents*. Montreal, Canada: Amnesty International and Canadian Human Rights Foundation.

Callamard, A. (1999b). *A methodology for Gender-Sensitive Research*. Montreal, Canada: Amnesty International and Canadian Human Rights Foundation.

Davenport, T., H., De Long, D., W., & Beers, M., C. (1998). Successful Knowledge Management Projects. *Sloan Management Review*, *39*(2), 43–57.

Disability Rights Promotion International (DRPI). (2003). *Phase 1 report: Opportunities, methodologies, and training resources for disability rights monitoring*. Toronto, Canada: Disability Rights Promotion International.

El Morr, C. (Ed.). (2007). *Encyclopedia in Mobile Computing & Commerce*. Hershey, PA: Information Science Reference.

El Morr, C., & Kawash, J. (2007). Mobile virtual communities research: A synthesis of current trends and a look at future perspectives. *International Journal for Web Based Communities, 3*.

Fougeyrollas, P., Cloutier, R., Bergeron, H., Côté, J., & Michel, G. S. (1999). *The Quebec classification: Disability creation process*. Québec, Canada: International Network on the Disability Creation Process.

International Disability Rights Monitor. (2004). *International disability rights monitor*. Chicago, IL: Center for International Rehabilitation.

International Disability Rights Monitor (IDRM). (2004). *International disability rights monitor*. Chicago, IL: Center for International Rehabilitation.

Merali, Y., & Davies, J. (2001). *Knowledge capture and utilization in virtual communities*. Paper presented at the proceedings of the 1st International Conference on Knowledge Capture.

Preece, J. (2000). *Online communities: Designing usability supporting sociability*. USA: John Wiley & Sons Ltd.

Quinn, G., & Degener, T. (Eds.). (2002). *Human rights and disability: The current use and future potential of United Nations human rights instruments in the context of disability*. Geneva, Switzerland: United Nations, Office of the High Commissioner for Human Rights.

Rapid-i.com. (2008). *Rapid-i*: Rapid Intelligence, Rapid Solutions. Retrieved on June 10, 2008

Rioux, M. (1997). Disability: The place of judgment in a world of fact. *Journal of Intellectual Disability Research*, *4*(1), 102–111. doi:10.1111/j.1365-2788.1997.tb00686.x

Rioux, M. (2001). Bending towards justice. In Barton, L. (Ed.), *Disability, politics and the struggle for change*. London, UK: David Fulton Publishers.

Shakespeare, T. (1999). What is a Disabled Person? In Jones, M., & Marks, L. B. (Eds.), *Disabilty, diversAbility and legal change* (pp. 25–35). The Hague, Netherlands: Martinus Nijhoff Publishers.

Stein, A., Hawking, P., & Sharma, P. (2005). *A classification of u-commerce location based tourism applications*. Paper presented at the 11th Australasian World Wide Web Conference (AUSWeb05).

Thomas, C. (2002). Disability theory: Key ideas, issues and thinkers. In Barnes, C., Oliver, M., & Barton, L. (Eds.), *Disability studies today* (pp. 38–57). Cambridge, UK: Polity Press.

U.S. Department of Health and Human Services. (2008). Research-based Web design & usability guidelines. Retrieved June 13, 2008, from http://www.usability.gov /pdfs/guidelines.html

Weissman, D. (2000). *A social ontology*. New Haven, CT: Yale University Press.

Widyantoro, D. H., Loerger, T. R., & Yen, J. (2001). Learning user interest dynamics with a three-descriptor representation. *Journal of the American Society for Information Science and Technology*, *52*(3), 212–225. doi:10.1002/1532-2890(2000)9999:9999<::AID-ASI1615>3.0.CO;2-O

World Wide Web Consortium. (2008). Web content accessibility guidelines. Retrieved on June 13, 2008, from http://www.w3.org/TR/WCAG20/

Xiaobin, F., Jay Budzik, H., & Kristian, J. (2000). *Mining navigation history for recommendation.* Paper presented at the International Conference on Intelligent User Interfaces.

Yu, S., Al-Jadir, L., & Spaccapietra, S. (May 9, 2005). *Matching user's semantics with data semantics in location-based services.* Paper presented at the 1st Workshop on Semantics in Mobile Environments (SME 05) in conjunction with MDM 2005, Ayia Napa, Cyprus.

Chapter 2
The Creation and Management of Online Brand Communities

Paola Falcone
University of Rome, Italy

ABSTRACT

Online brand communities are a specific type of virtual community, which gather admirers and consumers of a given brand on the web. Their captivating nature, plus their marketing effectiveness compared to their costs are attracting the interest of both researchers and marketing/brand managers.

This chapter intends to identify, describe and analyse the main issues concerning their creation and effective management.

INTRODUCTION

During the last decade online brand communities have received a lot of attention from both academics and marketing professionals.

In times of complexity, with demanding consumers and intense global competition, the Web has given marketing and communication managers new tools and new opportunities to improve the effectiveness of their action. Online brand communities provide one of the most interesting and powerful examples.

This is mostly for their ability to establish and enhance relationships between companies and markets, reinforcing the brand image of their products, as well as customers' brand awareness and loyalty. In doing so -not irrelevant in times of scarce financial resources given the economic downturn- they are a rather low cost solution.

Several companies have endowed themselves with a brand community, each revealing different functional or strategic aspects.

DOI: 10.4018/978-1-60960-869-9.ch002

This chapter intends to identify and describe specific characteristics of online brand communities and to analyse creation and valorization strategies.

ONLINE BRAND COMMUNITIES

Online brand communities (Muniz and O'Guinn 2001; Cova and Cova, 2002) are a specific type of virtual community (Rheingold, 1993; Hagel and Armstrong, 1997; Bagozzi and Dholakia, 2002), characterized by the fact that different people with the common trait of being "admirers of a brand" are gathered together (Muniz and O'Guinn, 2001).

As for any other online community, they base themselves upon relations, resulting from three basic elements (see Prykop and Heitman, 2006):

- people (community members);
- a shared interest (in the brand);
- a common space of interaction (the platform).

So, they are marketing tribes (Cova and Cova, 2002), made up of different people, either customers or not, coming from different countries, with different socio-demographic features, who have in common an interest in the brand (Kapferer, 1992; Fournier, 1998) and want to interact with both the firm and their peers.

The brand is the mediator for this online interaction, and benefits foremost from the positive social interaction within the community. Brands tell stories (Semprini, 1992) and the most truthful and strongest are those that people recognize some common, personal traits in. This recognition process helps customers to accept these stories, to make them their own.

As "passionate consumers want their brands to become a form of self-expression" (Brady, 2004), brands acquire much more sense beyond a simple positive reputation. This way, in fact, they enter the customers' imagery, generate some

identification processes, becoming "lovemarks" (Roberts, 2006).

Online brand communities are good places to carry on the process of social construction. Within online brand communities this process is co-managed by both marketers and brand admirers (see among others Muniz and O'Guinn, 2005); in fact, the latter help the former to transform and enrich the brand sense through a co-construction process.

The consequence, in the brand value system, is that its identity is not just "the brand concept from the brand's owner's perspective" (Aaker and Joachimsthaler, 2000), but the synthesis of its original identity with the customer's experience, which is both functional and emotional, within the brand community context. Through the brand community's constant re-actualisation, customer participation and interest is renewed. What happens to consumers is something similar to being called to co-create an open work, a plurality of meanings, co-existing all together, within a single significant (Eco, 1962).

The brand community acts as a multiplier of meaning (Musso, 2005): in fact, it is the perfect place for brand sense and meaning co-creation.

In this virtual space people can experience the brand, feel part of its world (identity, culture, values, image) and share opinions. In doing so, they develop "a shared consciousness, rituals and traditions, and a sense of moral responsibility" (Muniz and O'Guinn, 2002, p. 412) in the exchange.

ADVANTAGES FOR FIRMS FROM ONLINE BRAND COMMUNITIES

Firms can get several advantages from the creation, be it spontaneous or planned, of an online brand community.

First of all, they help companies to get closer to their markets and to learn more about their actual and potential customers, in order to understand their tastes, evolution, define their trends and preferences, see how their products are perceived.

A brand community, in fact, can be assimilated to a huge focus group, whose panellists' thoughts, attitudes, orientations can be monitored day by day at very low costs, lower than any other investigation tool. In this focus group aggregates of people interact, discuss, make opinions, can reward or destroy a brand. And are free to do it without the limits of the focus group, as they are free to manage conversations and take them where they want.

Through a community, a firm opens up a listening and dialoguing channel with its customers; it develops an archive of information day by day, which goes to feed a capital of knowledge (Bagozzi and Dholakia, 2002).

Firms also have the chance to activate a regular low-cost customer profiling program, through the submission of an entry questionnaire; this has a very relevant informative value in terms of marketing knowledge management and informative CRM.

It allows firms to increase their competitiveness, as this information can help them to improve products and services, to customize them in order to meet customers' needs better than competitors do, to verify their strategic positioning on the markets.

As a two way channel, a brand community has a listening function and also offers firms a space to communicate, inform the markets on news, events, new product launches, promotions at a very low cost per contact.

Communication within communities is both rational and emotional. The latter is particularly important in reinforcing customers' tie with the brand, its imagery, identity and value system (Musso, 2005).

The customers' own storytelling increase the level of engagement in the brand and help the company to be closer to their markets.

This way brands are kept alive, evolve and are enhanced (Brady, 2004; Fournier and Lee, 2009).

The 2004 annual ranking of the most valuable global brands, reported a very high performance for Samsung; its global marketing chief did not hesitate to attribute it to the ability of "building communities around our brand" (in Brady, 2004).

This is because it helps companies to have a regular interaction with their markets.

Interactivity has become the "must have imperative" for companies in recent years, bringing companies to modify their websites, in order to favour both the communication between the company and its customers, and among customers. Tools such as chats, forums, newsgroups, are always more present in company websites as they enhance their interactivity. The brand community is an extension of this process, but it is much more, as it helps companies to get more from their markets than an interactive website (Fournier and Lee, 2009).

Fostering communication induces relationship enhancement. A brand community is a tool of communication, as well as of relationship marketing (see among others Dwyer et al., 1987), as it cultivates and maintains alive the relationship between the company and the brand on the one hand, and consumers on the other (Musso, 2005). Established relationships are also economically valorized, as companies can make cross-selling or up-selling actions, and also start strategies of online collaborative marketing.

Online brand communities also help companies to start new relationships with new potential customers, who can meet the brand community in their online navigation during the information search stage. Jeff Bezos, founder of Amazon. com, defines the brand community as "neighbours helping neighbours make purchase decisions" (in Brady, 2004) and so expresses the value of the exchange in the community, able to orient new customers or established customers willing to upgrade their products towards the brand products.

Figure 1. The set of players which can be met in an online brand community, according to their status

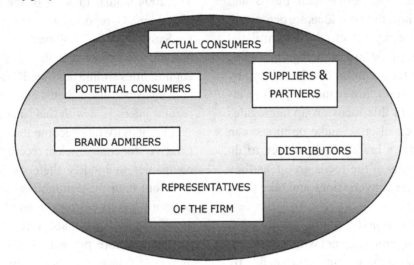

A FOCUS ON MEMBERSHIP

Members and Behaviours

The community gathers people with different engagements and different levels of participation, from those who have a starting interest to those who are truly enthusiasts of the brand (Kalman, 2009).

Different kinds of players can be interested in joining an online brand community. According to their status, they are (Figure 1):

- actual product consumers who aim at exchanging opinions and experiences regarding their products use, or willing to get information on new upgraded products in the firm's selection;
- potential customers, who are searching for information from established consumers. They are analytical buyers, willing to maximise the effectiveness of the information search and evaluation analysis in their buying behaviour;
- brand admirers, appreciating the brand, but actually unable to buy or not really convinced to buy. They stay at the window,

talk and most of all read others' community members opinions about products;
- employees or managers of the firm, who can decide to:
  - participate in community discussions, declaring their own real status. This can inhibit participants from developing discussions, declaring and explaining their point of view, feeling more controlled. It is harder to express a poor evaluation of something in presence of those who have made it. This is why detractors usually express their opinions in public discussion forums, which are not oriented as brand communities are. This has positive consequences in managing the community but limits the possibility to elicit this critical information, necessary for product improvements.
  - participate in community discussions choosing not to declare their own real status, pretending to be a customer. This gives members a higher comfort in participating, but is a violation of an etiquette principle concerning identity. If identified, such as from

less credible postings, this undermines trust relationships;

○ watch the community evolution only reading posted messages, without taking direct part into it, acting as lurkers;

- other players in the productive value chain, which, in the case of a non-exclusively demand-oriented community, can be stably involved in it, like suppliers, co-partners, or distributors.

Other interesting behavioural parameters are the intensity and frequency of member attendance (Rheingold, 1993). Some regularly read, write and live the community following its development. Others do this on an occasional basis (Preece, 2000); they come and go according to their commitment, time or even mood. Also the durable identification as community members is variable. Kozinets (1999) identifies two influencing factors:

- the relation with the specific consumption activity;
- the relation with other community members.

In online brand communities there is a third variable to add: the relation with the company and with the brand (the process of anthropomorphization of the brands which allows to conceive a relationship between customers and brands has been largely studied; see for a review Patterson & O'Malley, 2006).

Different levels of the three above described variables define different types of members. Strong relations with consumption, the brand and other members identify potentially highly committed members.

A regular, durable participation is necessary for community relations as well as for company information tracking, and so has to be encouraged through an effective community management. This is why an effective brand communities man-

agement will enhance the three above reported types of relations, and most of all the one with other community members and the one with the company and the brand.

Roles Members Assume

Within an online brand community members can play, as in any other community, different roles.

Fournier and Lee (2009) identify eighteen different roles: mentors, learners, back-ups (reassure members experiencing new products), partners, storytellers, historians (preserving community identity and collective memory), heroes, celebrities, decision makers (they define some community government issues) providers (sustain other members), greeter (as hosts, they welcome new members), guides, catalysts (they capture others' interest and drive the change), performers, supporters, ambassadors, accountants (registering interactions), talent scouts (find new members).

Some of them (decision makers) are leading players. Rheingold, 1993 and Preece, 2000, also identify as special figures in online communities:

- moderators: they guide discussions and orient the community; they manage the list, help to avoid spamming and inappropriate messages, raise questions in order to keep discussions going, answer questions etc. They can focus members' attention and so suggest new product uses, focus members' attention on specific product issues, establish new priorities in product evaluation scales;
- mediators: they can intervene to calm disputes and flaming;
- professional commentators; they are experts of the product and take part in discussions; their presence is occasional in chats on specific days and times.

MOTIVATIONS TO PARTICIPATE

Brand community management has to be informed to take a better look at their members' motivations to participate.

Entering and participating in a brand community, as for any kind of virtual community, is a form of "intentional social action" (Bagozzi and Dholakia, 2002, p.4), resulting from an integrated mix of both personal motives, such as interests, desires, etc. and social ones (Bagozzi and Dholakia, 2002).

Community members are conscious of their participation and that they "strive to achieve mutual goals" (Bagozzi and Dholakia, 2002); moved by the common passion for a brand, mutual goals can be can be functional, hedonic, social and psychological.

Online brand communities give members the chance to talk, listen, give and take useful information -sometimes not found in any other website or specialized magazine- about products and their use, exchange ideas, opinions and experiences, find answers to specific problems, through a direct question or reading answers to similar problems.

A brand community is a sort of open archive of knowledge, which can be accessed by anyone entering the community.

In some cases, members of a brand community can get specific facilitations, given by the firm in order to reward the devotion to the brand.

The participation in an online brand community can also give members the chance to spend some free time enjoying (Musso, 2005) and most of all experiencing the brand beyond consumption and actively participate to its construction.

In addition to the functional value, brand communities also have a relevant psychological and social value for their members, by effect of the social interaction with others with the same interest and identification in the brand and its core values. This gives them social recognition and makes them establish weak ties (Granovetter, 1973).

This set of values is in some cases elevated to a lifestyle for customers and produces a sense of reciprocal cohesion and social identity, defining "an attractive group-identity" (Brady, 2004): the brand aggregates its admirers/consumers, who stand apart from admirers/consumers of other brands, who are non-members (Wellman and Gulia, 1999). An example of a strong brand image and connected identification power is the social identity of Mac users, who feel different from PC users (Muniz and O'Guinn, 2001).

The higher the brand identity and its related image, the higher its identification effect. The spirit of the Harley Davidson has raised a high commitment in its community members "who wear the Harley-branded gear to feel more like rugged individualists and outlaws when they hit the road on weekends" (Brady, 2004).

Over time, the community can even become a relevant reference group for its members (Bagozzi and Dholakia, 2002).

The group social identity is reinforced by a specific jargon, social norms, rituals, slang, symbols, stories (Muniz and O'Guinn, 2001; 2005; Cova and Cova, 2002) aiming at inducing reactions, which "are always the same, amazement and affirmation" (Muniz and O'Guinn, 2005), able to solve cognitive dissonance problems and keep together community members under the same brand umbrella. It is interesting to read car owners' postings, who often tell "saved my life stories" (Muniz and O'Guinn, 2005), aiming at giving evidence of the functional qualities of the product, sometimes with animistic connotations.

Possible symbols are the first prototype, the progenitor of successive products, the first location of the firm or persons, such as the founder of the firm or the community founders. They are part of the brand mythology, and their photos appear on the community website.

Sometimes the self-identification and the loyalty to the brand are so strong to even determine in more involved members the conviction that "their interest in the brand may surpass those of the marketer and that they may be better aware of the realities in which the product is used" who can tend to "regard marketers not as owners of the brands, but as temporary stewards" (Muniz and O'Guinn, 2005).

The motivation to participate in a brand community is volatile, as it can vanish through time, together with the interest in the brand. Two are the main reasons why. The first is in case of a very negatively perceived customer product experience: a cognitive dissonance resulting from an unsatisfying experience can induce disaffection towards the brand. The tie of trust between the customer and the brand breaks and so for them there is no more sense of belonging to the brand community.

The other case is not due to a specific fact, or accident, but is physiological: motivation to participate can vanish simply as a result of a lack of commitment on the part of both the brand and the community. A weak tie with the brand, the search for new stimuli, the redundancy of messages and contents can be boring for participants in the long run: they can be less motivated to participate in the community and desire to spend their time on the Internet in other ways.

For the above briefly reported reasons, a great attention to effective community building and management is required.

To build a brand community, it takes (Kalman, 2009) a brand with a strong identity able to make consumers "feel different", the knowledge of one's own markets and some "mechanisms" (p.1) to make them live a shared online experience of the brand. These mechanisms concern both the design and the management stage.

BUILDING AND MANAGING ONLINE BRAND COMMUNITIES

Designing the Community: Some Possible Erroneous Approaches

There are some possible approaches to the creation of an online brand communities which can be erroneous, and can negatively affect its management. They are briefly described below.

1. *Online brand communities are just a marginal, operational tool*: The first mistake in community design is to underestimate the potential of a brand community, considering it marginal in marketing plan implementation. On the contrary it is something really important as a connector to customers. Fournier and Lee (2009) report the case of Harley Davidson, which is a prime example in this sense. In 1985 Harley Davidson "completely reformulated the competitive strategy and business model around a brand community philosophy" (p. 106). Managers chose a "community-centric positioning" (Fournier and Lee, 2009, p. 106), accepting to get closer to their motor-bikers community, sharing their vales, being guided by them and serving them, meeting their needs. In this case the brand community is central to the company business strategy. This can be an extraordinary case of business innovation. But if not in the business strategy, a brand community can be a relevant part of a marketing strategy. This happens through the identification of specific goals for the brand community. Fostering relationships with their customers is the first implicit goal of building an online brand community. Besides, a brand community can help to reinforce the brand market perception, awareness, memory; to operate a repositioning of the brand or favour its enhancement; to improve customer loyalty; to improve

market knowledge and more. A clear definition of this set of goals is fundamental. A poor strategy about communities, without previously identified goals makes the tool lose some of its effectiveness. So, community goals are to be aligned with the overall marketing ones, and the community is to be integrated in the overall marketing strategy.

2. *The problem is just building the community: then it goes by itself*: The third mistake is thinking that the creation of an infrastructure is enough and that community members will organize themselves and autonomously do something. But this is not so. Interaction does not come by itself, but has to be facilitated (Fournier and Lee, 2009). This implicates both a proper promotion and management. In fact, without a proper promotion, members will not find it, nor join. Without a proper management, they will not come nor stay long in the community.

3. *A strong brand is everything*: The brand is the glue for interactions, and the stronger it is, the higher the commitment. But interpersonal interaction desire has to be taken into account. Members adhere to beliefs and ideas, but want to socially interact with other people, be they company managers or peers. In fact, a poor social gratification (e.g. unkind, cold messages), or too dominant opinion leaders can make people disaffect from the brand community and this risk is higher for those communities organized in the form of a pool (Fournier and Lee, 2009). This is why the social, interactive dimension has to always be enhanced.

4. *Technology is not so important:* Another possible mistake is to underestimate the importance of technological interface. It marks members' virtual space of interaction and so mediates relationships. This is why it has to be easy to access and use, enabling members to post and manage multimedial UGCs (user generated contents) and other digital contents and be adequate and stimulating to members. One of the advantages companies have in choosing to locate their community using actual social network platforms is the easy, well known interface. The diffusion of mobile devices (e.g. smartphones) has enabled people to multiply their daily internet connections. So, both communities and social networks (e.g. Twitter) welcomed wireless solutions becoming mobile (Prykop and Heitman, 2006; El Morr and Kawash, 2007), and so more accessible to their members.

5. *An online brand community is just a virtual matter*: An online brand community lives in the Web space, but it is not just a virtual matter. It has to be strategically integrated through the offline dimension of the company's relationship marketing strategy, through events, communication and so on. The offline environment can be helpful in recruiting new members.

Defining Core Aspects of the Community Functioning

Several decisions are to be taken in the design stage.

The first one concerns the target of the community. It is easy for newbies to understand where they are, if discussions are high level, for experts, or it does not require specific skills. Obviously, the more specialized the community, the smaller it will be.

This target decision has to be explicated on the entering welcome page.

In case of non-selective communities, it is necessary for firms to check the number of members, which can influence the quality of interaction and communication (Hagel and Armstrong, 1997). A sudden growth can transform the shape of the community and make communication more fragmented. If the community dimension gets too high, the management will better decide to divide it in smaller and more targeted groups (Preece, 2000). Group clustering can be done on the basis of member status and personal characteristics or type of interest. Managers also have to decide both entry and status requirements in order to join a brand community. Most communities are filtered entry ones, as they ask members prior registration. The same decision concerns exit mechanisms: member exclusion in case of inappropriate messages, as well as membership lapsing as a result of non- participation for a certain period of time.

Managers can also define what can be done or not in the community (e.g. name concurrent products, offend competitors, post flaming messages and so on) and also the communication style (e.g. allowing a more or less formal style; promoting a positive communication, with a tone of voice coherent with the target and the brand values conveyed; a serious tone vs. a playful one and so on).

Managers also have to take into account the number and relevance of possible communication channels, both vertical and horizontal, within the community, in order to favour interexchange.

The other relevant aspect is the set up of the community: a friendly and easy to use interface, with full accessibility of different sections and a flexible structure is important as it can enable different communication and exchange options.

A nice graphic can be attractive in capturing the interest of new potential members. The graphic has to be in line with the brand image and the company integrated communication.

Resources to Take

Building and managing a brand community requires some resources which are technological, human, financial.

Technological resources are those needed to create the space of interaction for community members. Companies can choose to create a new platform or rather use an already existing one, creating a group on a social network. The latter solution allows companies to cut costs and to better reach their members, who have maybe already opened a personal profile in the social network and know the platform perfectly well.

A brand community also needs human resources to follow its activities, stimulate postings and monitor them. The number of necessary guiding people grows as the number of members increases. These people are to be technologically, but also relationally competent and motivated to follow the community.

The two needs described require some financial resources. Supporting the community economically is usually not a problem for communities created for consumers by firms, because it is a part of the communication budget. Maybe some companies can find it more difficult to dedicate one or more staff components just to follow this project.

In the case of communities created by consumers, sustaining them economically can be much more demanding, but it can be guaranteed by:

- self-financing carried out by community founders;
- special memberships, which give special benefits to members in exchange for an annual fee, such as a club;
- advertising revenue coming from the selling of space to put banners, pop ups and so on.

The first solution is frequent in early stages, in order to make the first investments.

The second has to be carefully designed, in order to let members perceive and find joining the community attractive as special members. Benefits can be the chance to be invited to special events (e.g. gala dinners or concerts), to receive publications, gadgets and so on. Clearly, these benefits have to be consistent with the target of the community, the brand imagery and its value system.

The third solution, of advertising, is useful as it doesn't require founders, nor members to contribute in order to sustain the community. But it has to be carefully selected. In fact, the strong relational potential between members and the brand can make members feel any other brand eventually present as an undesired stranger. On the contrary selling online advertising spaces to firms selling related complementary products can become a sort of information service to community members and so preferable.

Managing the Community: Main Issues

The Need for Attention and Care

As remarked before, communities need attention and care. Discussions and moods are to be actively and regularly monitored, never neglected. The community needs to be monitored in real time, in order not to go adrift. In fact, online brand communities can "evolve in ways that the head office can't often control. Newly empowered consumers can appropriate and manipulate the brand in whatever way they want" (Brady, 2004, p.2). This is a collateral effect of the previously cited high commitment effect, which can induce expert consumers belonging to a brand community to "regard marketers (...) as temporary stewards" (Muniz and O'Guinn, 2005) of the brand. In fact, as customers feel to be responsible for their favourite brand, they will evaluate any action carried out by managers with severity.

Communities need to be observed and known in detail, in their ways, rituals, slang, especially those created by customers, in order to follow how brands develop, respect the peculiarities of the community and leverage its knowledge. Few standard indications are valid for brand communities, and only through field observation is it possible to manage them effectively.

Specific care must be taken for each single stage in the community lifetime, as it first needs to take on shape, then consolidate it by managing member turnover and possible changes.

The care is for the whole community, but also, possibly, for each member. From their welcome (Shau et al., 2009), it is important to help members feel relevant and not just an anonymous contact. Besides, as Shau et al. 2009 notice, feeling considered can encourage the "customer's willingness to engage in creating value for the brand and the firm" (p.37). This is especially true for opinions: the firm caring for its customers, listening to them and taking their opinions into consideration, stimulates them to share their ideas and points of view.

The Need for Stimuli

Another aspect which is relevant to consider in managing an online brand community is giving members regular stimuli.

They can be successfully differentiated, being targeted to different segments of members.

Stimuli can be functional information, gossips or firsthand news, the launch of discussions on certain topics, event organization, benefits (see infra), but also contests and calls to action (e.g. Saab owners community asks its members to post a picture of them close to their own car).

They keep the community alive and are useful to encourage member participation, as they can increase their motivation to connect to the community and actively take part in it. Active members post more, talk more, and, in doing so, give more useful information and feedbacks to the company.

The Need for Trust

Last, but not least, brand community management must be informed to trust. Trust is the first element in interpersonal relationships, as it is in the relationship between customers and firms, mediating the ones customers have with brands (Dall'Olmo and de Chernatony, 2000). According to Hiscock (2001, p.1) "the ultimate goal of marketing is to generate an intense bond between the consumer and the brand, and the main ingredient of this bond is trust". It is related to the customers' expectations of the brand (Morgan and Hunt, 1994). If the firm pursues its objectives without fulfilling member expectations, it can put their trust at risk.

Managing a brand community in order to maintain and develop trust means to take care of any aspect which is important to customers, in managing privacy, using information, accepting advertising through more or less invasive modalities (banners, pop ups, etc.), promotional activities, and so on.

The firm must be prepared at all times to evaluate the expected perception of each action by community members, in consideration of unwritten rules of their participation. Members ask firms coherence, severely evaluate novelties and changes, sometimes seen with suspicion, always in the name of the beloved brand. So new stimuli described above must always be consistent with the company's accepted conduct.

The Set of Benefits to Customers

In line with the social exchange theory, a successful key factor in managing an online brand community is to give members specific benefits responding to their needs, in order to encourage their permanence in the community.

Benefits are to be identified and clearly communicated to members, as they reinforce the motivation to take part in the community.

Membership can allow participants to get information, gain access to something exclusive, economic facilities or even something tangible.

Informative benefits are:

- rich and updated information about new products and their characteristics;
- online problem solving regarding product use, thanks to an online expert, etc., intervening on specific days and times in chat and through the F.A.Q.;

- information about anything surrounding a product (e.g. a brand community of a firm producing clothes and toys for children, a session dedicated to paediatric themes can be interesting for community members).

Members of a community can take part in special online or offline events, meeting each other live and meeting firms representatives; these events can be concerts, or meetings in specific locations and have a strong social value for members. For example these are used a lot by communities gathering Museum friends and sustainers.

Members can also get economic facilities, such as the possibility to buy products of the company or complementary products at special prices (e.g. consumption materials). Benefits can also be gifts, such as a free ticket for a première.

Or benefits can be tangible products such as gadgets (e.g. pens and stickers), ID personalized cards, or exclusive branded products such as t-shirts, caps, mugs and so on, which can be bought on the brand community website. These products can feed both identity needs and wants of collections (Belk et al, 1988) from community members.

Lastly, as said in advance, the company can organize specific initiatives for its community members, such as awards and contests for their members. This meets the social needs of their members.

CONCLUSION

Online brand communities are the core of a marketing strategy oriented towards the development of relationships. In the era of Web 2.0, with the diffusion of participation in social networks and the increase of virtual interactions, they meet a specific need for interaction and offer companies several benefits. In fact, it can help firms to reinforce relationships with their customers and so improve their market position and enhance their brands.

Building a community requires first of all a careful strategic design, in terms of objectives, targets, interface. Then careful management is required, respectful of the brand identity and meeting the expectations of its members.

Several aspects are to be taken into account in the different stages of the community's development, and resources are needed in order to start and maintain them.

A lot has still to be known about them, and the research has to study their applications, processes, results.

But there are few doubts that brand communities and all forms of interactions around the brands are going to be the future in relationship marketing. In fact, if effectively managed, online brand communities can be a very powerful tool for firms and a crucial element in their approach to markets.

REFERENCES

Bagozzi, R.P., & Dholakia, U.M. (2002, Spring). Intentional social action in virtual communities, *Journal of Interactive Marketing*.

Belk, Russell W., Wallendorf, M., Sherry, J., Holbrook, M., & Roberts, S. (1988). Collectors and collecting. [Ed. Michael J. Houston, TX.]. *Advances in Consumer Research. Association for Consumer Research (U. S.)*, 15.

Brady, D. (2004, August 2). Cult brands, *Business Week*. New York, NY: Bloomberg L.P.

Cova, B., & Cova, V. (2002). Tribal marketing: The tribalization of society and its impact on the conduct of marketing . *European Journal of Marketing*, 36.

Dall'Olmo Riley, F., & De Chernatony, L. (2000). The service brand as relationship builder. *British Journal of Management*, *11*(2), 137–150. doi:10.1111/1467-8551.t01-1-00156

Dwyer, F. R., Schurr, P. H., & Oh, S. (1987). Developing buyer-seller relationships. *Journal of Marketing*, *51*(2), 11–27. doi:10.2307/1251126

El Morr, C., & Kawash, J. (2007). Mobile virtual communities research: A synthesis of current trends and a look at future perspectives. *International Journal of Web Based Communities*, *3*(4), 386–403. doi:10.1504/IJWBC.2007.015865

Fournier, S. (1998). Consumers and their brands: Developing relationship theory in consumer research . *The Journal of Consumer Research*, *24*(March), 343–373. doi:10.1086/209515

Fournier, S., & Lee, L. (2009). Getting brand communities right. *Harvard Business Review*, 105–111.

Granovetter, M. (1973, May). The strength of weak ties. *American Journal of Sociology*, *78*(6), 1360–1380. doi:10.1086/225469

Hagel, J., & Armstrong, A. G. (1997). *Net gain: Expanding markets through virtual communities*. Boston, MA: Harvard Business School Press.

Hiscock, J. (2001, March 1). Most trusted brands, *Marketing*, 32-3.

Kalman, D. M. (2009). Brand communities, marketing, and media, *Terrella Media*. From http://www.terrella.com.

Kapferer, J.-N. (1992). *Strategic brand management*. New York, NY: Free Press.

Kozinets, R. (1999). E-tribalized marketing?: The strategic implications of virtual communities of consumption. *European Management Journal*, *17*(3), 252–264. doi:10.1016/S0263-2373(99)00004-3

Morgan, R. M., & Hunt, S. D. (1994). The commitment trust theory of relationship marketing . *Journal of Marketing*, *58*, 20–38. doi:10.2307/1252308

Muniz, A., & O'Guinn, T. (2001, March). Brand community. *The Journal of Consumer Research,* 412–432. doi:10.1086/319618

Muniz, A., & O'Guinn, T. (2005). Communal consumption and the brand . In Ratneshwar, S., & Mick, D. G. (Eds.), *Inside consumption. Consumer motives, goals, and desires*. New York, NY: Routledge.

Patterson, M., & O'Malley, L. (2006). Brands, consumers and relationships: A review. *Irish Marketing Review, 18*(1&2).

Preece, J. (2000). *Online communities. Designing usability, suporting sociability*. Chichester West Sussex, UK: John Wiley and Sons Ltd Baffins Lane.

Prykop, C., & Heitman, M. (2006). Designing mobile brand communities: Concept and empirical illustration. *Journal of Organizational Computing and Electronic Commerce, 16*(3/4), 301–323.

Rheingold, H. (1993). *The virtual community: Homesteading on the electronic frontier*. Reading, Massachusetts: MIT Press.

Roberts, K. (2006). *Lovemarks. The future beyond brands. Saatchi & Saatchi Designer Edition*. Brooklyn, NY: Powerhouse Books.

Schau, H. J., Muniz, A. M. Jr, & Arnould, E. J. (2009). How brand community practices create value. *Journal of Marketing, 73*, 30–51. doi:10.1509/jmkg.73.5.30

Semprini, A. (1992). *Le marketing de la marque*. Parigi, Liaisons.

ADDITIONAL READING

Aaker, D. A. (1997). Dimensions of Brand Personality. *JMR, Journal of Marketing Research, 34*(2), 347–356. doi:10.2307/3151897

Algesheimer, R., Dholakia, U. M., Herrmann, Andreas (2005). The Social Influence of Brand Community: Evidence from European Car Clubs. *Journal of Marketing, 69(*3), July.

Bagozzi, R. P., & Dholakia, U. M. (2001). Consumer behaviour in digital environments . In *Wind J., Mahajan V., Digital Marketing*. Wiley.

Baudrillard, J. (1998). *The Consumer Society; Myths and Structure*. London, UK: Sage Publications.

Benedikt, M. (Ed.). (1991). *Cyberspace: First Steps*. Cambridge, UK: MIT Press.

Dowling, B. (2004). Rise of the cult brand, *Business Week*, August 9, 2004.

Jones, S. (1995). *Cybersociety*. Thousand Oaks, California: Sage.

Sheth, J. N., & Parvatiyar, A. (1995). Relationship marketing in consumer markets: Antecedents and consequences . *Journal of the Academy of Marketing Science, 23*(4). doi:10.1177/009207039502300405

Tapscott D. (2002). *Rethinking strategy in a networked world, business strategy, 24*.

Wallace, P. (1999). *The psychology of the Internet*. Cambridge, UK: Cambridge University Press.

Wellman, B., & Gulia, M. (1999). Net-surfers don't ride alone: Virtual communities as communities . In Wellman, B. (Ed.), *Networks in the global village*. Bouder, CO: Westview Press.

KEY TERMS AND DEFINITIONS

Brand: The set of information able to identify a product, a service, a product/service line. It is made up of a name, a logo and other visual cues.

Community: A group of people characterized by affiliation, collective identity, membership, intimacy, shared values, experiences, rituals and moral obligations. (Muniz and O'Guinn, 2002).

Flaming: The negative practice to post hostile, offensive messages, in order to provoke a reaction in community members.

Interactivity: The ability of a system to modify its behavior on the basis of user's input (e.g. information).

Lovemark: A brand which is able to get both respect and love from its audiences.

Online Brand Communities: Type of virtual community made of "admirers of the brand" (Muniz and O'Guinn, 2001).

Virtual Communities: "Social aggregations that emerge from the Net" (Rheingold, 1993, p.6), by the effect of online repeated public discussions among some persons on certain topics.

Chapter 3
Coordinating Nomadic Evaluation Practices by Supporting the Emergence of Virtual Communities

Marianne Laurent
Orange Labs, Telecom Bretagne, France

ABSTRACT

The research and development on spoken dialog systems embraces technical, user-centered and business-related perspectives. It brings together stakeholders belonging to distinct job families, therefore prone to different traditions and practices. When assessing their contributions, as well as the final solution, they conduct very nomadic evaluation protocols. As a result, the field is eager to set up norms for evaluation. Contributions abound in this way. However, despite standardization exercises, we believe that the absence of common conceptual foundations and dedicated "knowledge creation spaces" frustrates the effort of convergence. The chapter therefore presents an application framework meant to rationalize the design of evaluation protocols inside and across project teams. This Multi Point Of VieW Evaluation Refine Studio (MPOWERS) enforces common models for the design of evaluation protocols. It aims at facilitating, on the one hand, the individual evaluator-users task and, on the second hand, the emergence of (first virtual, then maybe real) communities of practice and multidisciplinary communities of interest. It illustrates how implementing shared knowledge frameworks and vocabulary for non-ambiguous asynchronous discussions can support the emergence of such virtual communities.

DOI: 10.4018/978-1-60960-869-9.ch003

INTRODUCTION

Need for a Convergence of Evaluation Practices

The success of a product or service design generally cannot rely on the sole accumulation of elementary isolated contributions. In his analysis of the Renault Twingo's groundbreaking project, Midler (1995) illustrates that exterior and interior designers are solely responsible for success. However the latter provided key ingredients for the car's personality, the various engineers and stylists, the purchasers and providers implicated in the design-to-cost operation and the industrials and commercials that came up with original production and distribution processes are also accountable for the successful outcome. As a matter of fact, the design of products and services impanels stakeholders with various expertise, roles and therefore points of view on the project. They need to measure their contribution to the system design, both between versions and with competing solutions. They process instrumented evaluations (for e.g., noise and consumption are measured and confronted to requirements) in parallel to experimental setups and questionnaires enabling the expression of the stakeholder's subjectivity (e.g. presentation of models, prototypes trials, project reviews). Methods encompass technical-oriented, user-centered and business-related outlooks. Accordingly, Midler alerts that this diversity of coexisting evaluation practices may deceive the one looking for a straightforward recipe for project evaluation.

Multidisciplinary projects bring together very different dictates of evaluation inferred and generalized from the team members' past experience. Contrary to traditional hierarchical working organizations, transverse project groups cannot abide by established rules, inherited from the silo relative job family. On the contrary, they combine and accommodate various traditions. This requires recognizing the coexistent norms and policies, understanding why they are endorsed and to what extent they can be negotiated.

Meanwhile, such nomadism of practices leads to the poor reusability of evaluation protocols from a project to another, the difficult comparison of performance across projects and a lack of credence for communication on the systems' performances. The domain therefore claims for a convergence of practices toward more transparent and prevailing metrics that would both make authority for service commensurability and lower evaluation efforts so as to concentrate on the service design.

Lack of "Knowledge Creation Spaces"

Such an effort of convergence compels the evaluators to share their expertise and to debate the benefit of their practice. Nevertheless, Pfeffer and Hinds (2003) inventory both organizational and cognitive factors that inhibit such incentives.

Organizational Related Issue

Traditional organizational trees sketch out a functional division of activity with clear separations between job families. They engage vertical flows of information: instructions going down the organization chart, while reports on activity being escalated. This fosters intergroup competition that tends to refrain stakeholders from sharing their knowledge (Argote, 1999).

In contrast, the transversal project teams get together stakeholders from various job families. These temporary groups tend to reinvent new working procedures and organizations over projects. Ad hoc evaluation methods are defined and processed on a case-by-case basis. Rapid taking up of positions, fast project pace and focus on immediate objectives do no encourage stakeholders to dedicate special time to project feedback so as identify best practices and lessons learnt. Moreover, teams are regularly reshaped over projects. They constitute new working contexts together with consequent methodological adjustments. Longer-term relationships, on the contrary, would spare opportunities for stakeholders to refine methodologies and enhance their mutual trust and willing to build a stable common working framework.

Difficulty to Share Knowledge

First, *knowledge is power*. Retaining knowledge comes to conserving control within the organization. This goes against the stakeholders' self-motivation to contribute to the methods' improvement effort. Consequently, only relationships truly based on reciprocal trust, within an organization that lays emphasis on the group performance (as opposed to the individual one), can predispose the effective knowledge sharing.

Second, both the explicit and the tacit components of expertise lead to cognitive issues for sharing. On the one hand, the explicit knowledge requires conventions to be described and communicated. On the other hand, the tacit knowledge, not always manipulated consciously, is intrinsically difficult to share (Polanyi, 1966). Consequently, when describing their practice, experts tend to focus on the salient aspects of their modus operandi and pass over these unconscious facets of their practice (Pfeffer and Hinds, 2003). This embedded "know-how", strongly context-dependent and associated to past experiences, is difficult to articulate and share without an effort of de-contextualization. Yet, even if embedded in individuals, people diffuse this knowledge informally when co-involved in activities and for example relating stories.

The chapter however addresses a knowledge-based activity where working processes are out of sight. If evaluation campaigns involve several people to define the experimental setup and to carry on evaluation campaigns, there is no real sharing between silo teams when it comes to define evaluation metrics. With a view to trigger the convergence of evaluation practices, we

therefore believe that even before addressing the knowledge sharing issue, we should think about adequate social conditions for sharing.

Brown and Duguid (1991) highlight that the explicit knowledge depicted in job descriptions and displayed in training programs is not as useful as the one informally shared by practitioners. They lean upon the work led on Xerox copiers service technicians by Orr (1991). However working alone at the customer's premises, technicians regularly meet and discuss of their experience and unusual problems solving. In addition to initial training, this tacit knowledge enriches the organization's expertise socially distributed across the technicians. While studying how knowledge is produced and disseminated within organizations, Lave and Wenger (1991) introduced the concept of Communities of Practice (CoP), *"groups of people who share a concern, a set of problems, or a passion about a topic, and who deepen their knowledge and expertise in this area by interacting on an ongoing basis"* (Wenger et al., 2002). They advocate that these communities provide practitioners with a rich context of learning and apprenticeship inside which a common knowledge is co-produced by a "legitimate peripheral participation" in joint activities. In a similar fashion, we aspire to promote the emergence of knowledge communities to support the dissemination of the evaluators' expertise.

Online Environments for Virtual Communities

We introduced that bringing knowledge owners together is not always an easy task. First, because the project stakeholders may belong to distinct job families. Second, because the knowledge communities should be extended across dedicated projects' frontiers. Discussions on evaluation methods should involve individuals participating to various evaluation campaigns, themselves relative to different products or services. Therefore, as we need to settle knowledge-sharing spaces

Figure 1. High-level architecture for spoken dialog systems

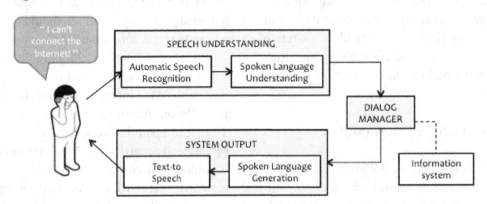

that cut across time and geographical barriers, we opted for an online environment encouraging project stakeholders to interact on their practices of evaluation. We present an online platform that allows users to make their methodologies explicit with respect to conventional concepts and language, and to browse within contributions. It also encourages them to interact for a better mutual understanding of each other's approach and a cooperative refinement of evaluation protocols. As a result, bringing transparency to the nomadic practices, we support the emergence of rich interactions among actors, somehow regrouped into knowledge communities.

It touches on the notion of *virtual communities,* made popular with the spread of social networking services over the World Wide Web. According to Rheingold (1993), virtual communities spring up *"when people carry on public discussions long enough, with sufficient human feeling, to form webs of personal relationships".* Their members interact on subjects of common interest via online applications like forums, groupware and social networks. This definition mostly focuses on the people being connected to each other, but eludes the idea of implication into common activities and practices. We therefore opt for the definition proposed by Kim et al. (2003): *"self-organizing groups whose members might live or work in dispersed geographical settings but who still possess common interests, share knowledge, and*

take part in unified learning experiences". Our platform intends to support knowledge-based activities for which real-world communities of practice are missing by fostering the emergence of online communities.

CASE STUDY

Evaluating Spoken Dialog Systems

Jokinen and McTear (2009) define Spoken Dialog Systems (SDS) as solutions enabling *"a human user to access information and services that are available on a computer or over the Internet using spoken language as the medium of interaction."* These solutions are nowadays commonly used to automate customer services such as yellow-page services, transport information and banking. They also help to automatically qualify the callers' motive for their direction to the adequate service. They involve three main components (see Figure 1).

To begin with, the *Speech Understanding* component characterizes the user input to make it manageable by the system. It includes *Automatic Speech Recognition* (ASR) that converts the user utterances' acoustic signal into textual estimates, and *Spoken Language Understanding* (SLU) that statistically interprets this text into "meaningful" alternatives for the *Dialog Manager*. The latter decides of the next step in the interaction. As a central component of the dialog system, it controls the interaction by producing output messages for the user in accordance with both the interpreted user inputs and the information retrieved from third-party sources of information. Last, the system's output involves a *Natural Language Generation* (NLU) component that provides a string of words to a *Text-to-Speech* (TTS) module that synthesizes the text into an acoustic response to the user. This architecture allows for structured "ping-pong" conversations respecting distinct successive dialog turns.

The technologies involved in the development of SDS have reached a level of maturity that allows focusing attention on the interaction design itself. Actually, high performances of vocal synthesis and vocal recognition components taken individually do not guarantee the service's adequacy to the end-users' needs. Consequently, within a perspective of service enhancement, a 360-degree evaluation is essential where stakeholders measure the adequacy of the solution according to their criteria along the service's development and lifecycle. For over two decades now, the evaluation issue has been addressed differently by industry and academia.

On the one hand, evaluation in commercial projects mainly supports iterative development and monitoring of live systems. Project teams bring together, for a limited period of time, contributors dedicated to various facets of the service, such as technical development, usability, user experience, marketing and hosting. They gather abide by implicit modus operandi inherited from the different traditions, and thus a variety of ad hoc evaluation protocols tailored to local decision-making processes (Laurent, Bretier and Manquillet, 2010). This nomadism, augmented with a lack of formalism, inevitably causes difficulties for sharing, return on experience, reuse and cross-evaluation between services. Consequently, the whole idea of cooperation and collaboration between stakeholders is at stake since neither

common vocabulary nor process exists to ease the communication.

On the other hand, in academia, evaluation mostly stands behind solution benchmarking and research communications. Contributors, therefore, strongly recommend converging towards a standardized evaluation procedure to be used across research laboratories. Contributions proposing evaluation protocols abound in this way, relying on very different approaches, such as:

- Servqual compares a priori user expectations with their perception on systems (Hartikainen, Salonen and Turunen, 2004),
- Paradise predicts a measure of the user satisfaction from a linear regression of task success and dialog cost metrics collected from the interaction logs (Walker, Litman, Kamm and Abella, 1997),
- and the WOZ Gold Standard compares WOZ-generated interactions with the ones generated with the evaluated systems (Paek, 2001).

In a similar fashion, each contribution of the fifty evaluation methodologies we studied is tailored to a local decision-making framework and inevitably discloses the evaluator's subjectivity.

A Twofold Expectation Toward the ICTs

The above-mentioned individualization and normalization are antagonist requirements that echo with the twofold expectations on the Information and Communication Technologies (ICTs). On the one hand, we invoke them to support the standardization of processes and automate the flow of information among companies. They are of great use from small project teams to paramount multi-site organizations. Just as the standardization of technical infrastructures supports software integration, standardizing processes facilitates sharing and enables business alignment, combined reporting and comparison across teams (which might also put brakes to the users' involvement). On the other hand, we expect these systems, geared with mass-customization features, to support the expression of our individuality. Without customization, a given solution may be put in jeopardy. In the working environment, it might only be seen as an additional burden with no real chance to substitute the existing bespoke solutions. Many are the unproductive examples of corporate accounting applications, held mandatory but populated before each monthly deadline by a copy/paste of the results obtained by locally maintained spreadsheets.

The iPhone, as a clearly standard but customizable device, well illustrates these opposite expectations. 24 million iPhones were sold in 2009, representing 14% of the global mobile phone market (Gartner, 2009). Just as for our project stakeholders regarding evaluation methods, every smartphone user has specific needs and expectations. The device is sold in a standard version worldwide, but the users can personalize it with protection/decoration cases and, most of all, install applications among the thousands available for download on the Itunes Store. The 2009 commercials advert advocated that, no matter what your need is, "there is an application for that". Users therefore tailor their personal device so that they fit to their practice, but without the overload of irrelevant features. Therefore, faced with a catalog of thousands of applications, iPhone owners may opt for several strategies. First, they may explore the catalog by themselves, a time-consuming exercise that demands them to download, test and compare various applications to select the fittest one. It also entail that they discern their needs and preferences. Second, they may browse blogs and forums for recommendations and best lists. Yet, depending on the contributors' objectives, the suggestions may be either very general, consisting in the must-haves for every iPhone owner, or on the contrary, too specific. Third, considering the extended community of iPhone owners, users

sharing common concerns should be easy to find for users to mutualize their experience of functionalities testing, catalog exploring and web browsing. Such intercourses might be repeated with various individuals to cover a matter of concern (e.g. applications related to transportation services, accountability, sport practice, games). As a matter of fact, it happens that users mostly mix the three alternatives, as in every knowledge-based activity. They combine individual initiatives, reference to best practices and interactions with similar users to validate, refine and adjust both strategies.

Finally, as irreconcilable as they may seem, the *standardization* and *customization* objectives may be associated into a unique initiative. Standardization supports interoperability between processes and relative information to be shared (for evaluation, the description models and relative sets of indicators), while personalization ensures that every user come up to their needs thanks to a self-suitable tool.

A Multi-Viewpoints Evaluation Platform

As mentioned above, evaluating SDS encompasses opposite needs: the convergence of evaluation practices and the respect of the various stakeholders' points of view. In this context, we launched a project towards the rationalization – not the standardization – of evaluation efforts. By rationalization, we refer to the definition of common norms for the description of processes, common thinking models and vocabulary, for evaluators to make their procedures explicit. Our multi-profile evaluation platform facilitates the design, from a unique corpus of parameters, of personalized evaluations adapted to the particular decision-making contexts.

The application, called MPOWERS for *Multi Point Of vieW Evaluation Refine Studio* (Laurent and Bretier, 2010c), relies on the SpagoBI 2.6 open source solution. It abides by a classical Business Intelligence (BI) architecture (see Figure 2). BI

Figure 2. MPOWERS high-level architecture

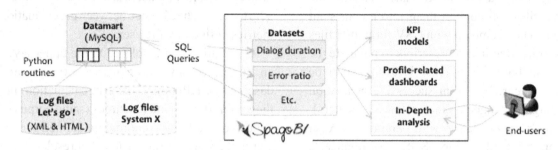

solutions support decision-makers by providing them with ready to interpret sets of relevant information retrieved from the enterprise data. They notably implement an ETL (Extract, Transform and Load) module that extracts data from heterogeneous provenances and then clean and load them into data warehouses. Last, query-based analysis tools display dashboards and operational reports relevant to the decision-making needs.

MPOWERS is an anthropocentric solution that supports the evaluator-users in their evaluation process. The definition of KPIs, and thus the information retrieved for evaluation purposes, depend both on (i) the content of the input corpora that limits the parameters possibly calculated and (ii) the decision-making context, i.e. the information needed for decision-making purposes and the evaluators' practices. The solution does not automate the evaluation task, but supports both evaluation design (definition and choice of KPIs) and automated data processing. As a result, the evaluator-users only deal with the creative evaluation design and the interpretation of results, while the system offloads them from the tractable tasks.

End-users, i.e. the evaluators, are limited to display the results and carry out in-depth queries. An administrator access allows for prior data processing and the configuration of datasets, KPIs and dashboards. With collaborative enhancement purposes, the application supports communication between users with built-in discussion threads and shared to-do-lists that suggest future configurations.

The evaluation process supported by the platform is slightly modified from the one defined by Stufflebeam (1980): *"a process through which one defines, obtains and delivers useful pieces of information that enable to settle between the alternative possible decisions"*. To better locate our solution's added value, we sketched the major steps of the evaluation process in Figure 3.

Data collection: SDS evaluation generally involves three types of data: interaction logs automatically collected from the SDS solutions platforms, user questionnaires and third-party annotations relative to recorded interactions. As data may originate from diverse sources, they array in different formats and often display different parameters. We use custom-made Python

Figure 3. Evaluation process as for Stufflebeam (1980). Grey tinted stages are supported by MPOWERS.

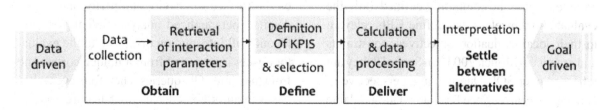

routines to extract the appropriate data from the source files and convert them into a consistent format. They come up with CSV formatted files to be converted into SQL scripts to populate the data warehouse. The latter is designed to be gradually enriched from successive evaluation campaigns arranged on the evaluated system(s).

Database population with parameters: A set of parameters describing SDS performance is pre-parameterized for evaluator-users within the application. We define them according to the ITU-T Recommendation P.Sup24 (2005). This way, we ensure that the metrics used across teams and projects are specified, calculated and maintained only once and in the same place. Yet, unless input corpora are defined accordingly we can only implement an extract of the recommendation's parameters.

We use the *Let's Go!* corpus (Eskenazi, 2008). The Carnegie Mellon University shares, since 2003, log files generated from the Pittsburgh's telephone-based bus information system. It allows the calculation of a satisfying number of parameters to support the system development and refinement. Examples are: the dialog duration, the number of system and user turns, the number of interruptions by the user (barge-ins), the ratio between user and system turn number, the number of help requests and of no-matches per call and the number of successful interactions.

KPIs definition and reports design: Key Performance Indicators (KPIs) are aggregated from the above parameters. They describe the SDS's performance and behavior. Examples of KPIs are: vocal recognition error ratio, average number of dialog turns for dialog achieving task completion, percentage of satisfied users with call duration exceeding 90 seconds. Whereas parameters may be commonly defined, only the evaluators themselves can define KPIs relevant to their local evaluation objectives, constraints and practices (Möller, 2005). In SpagoBI they are retrieved over SQL-Queries. In a perspective of convergence, all defined KPIs are made available

to all evaluators for reuse. Such cooperation might help to reduce the distance between the evaluation metrics defined by the users.

Calculation and display: On the upper layer, an engine retrieves personalized reports and dashboards. KPIs may differ in calculation, but they refer to the same resources (same corpus of data) and vocabulary (commonly defined parameters). It ensures the consistency of results across the project stakeholders when comparing their results. Nevertheless, as for KPIs definition and selection, their interpretation depends on both the evaluation's needs and context, and the evaluators' expectations. Therefore, we do not pre-define acceptance thresholds for KPIs retrieved by the system. Evaluators can chose among three models to display their evaluation reports:

- High-level KPIs can be combined to provide a general view on the evaluated system. "Red-light indicators" may provide warnings, notably when the application is used for monitoring purposes. Links to more detailed charts or analysis tools are displayed next to each of them (see Figure 4).
- Visual dashboards are displayed according to pre-defined evaluation profiles (see Figure 5).
- Tools for in-depth individual analysis permit evaluators to individually adjust their analysis according to local evaluation objectives. Queries can be stored for later use or saved in PDF documents for distribution to non-MPOWERS users.

These distinct outlooks on the corpus are complementary. They combine a high-level view on the service's behavior and performance with detailed personalized analysis. Whatever their layouts, all information displayed to the evaluators-users is retrieved from a unique corpus and from the same SQL-queries. Therefore, even when all evaluators consider distinct features on the

Figure 4. High-level KPIs with link to trends and more detailed documents

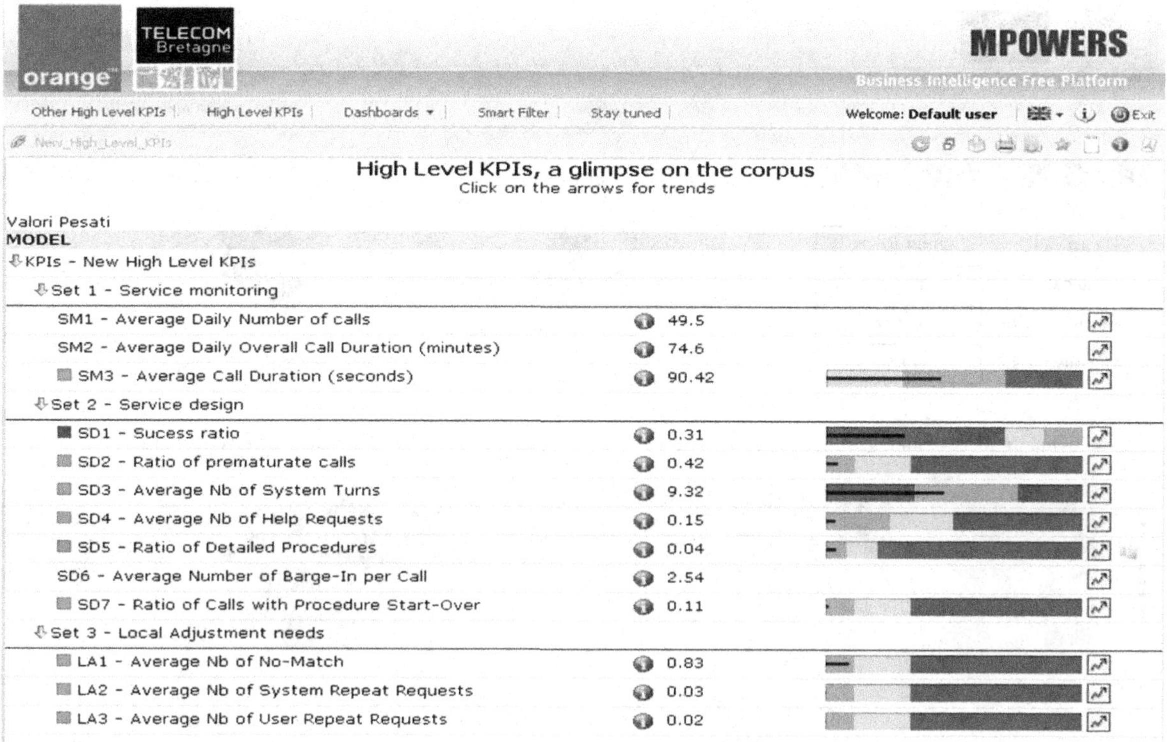

evaluated service, our framework brings consistency to their evaluation practices.

In this context, the project constitutes a response for varied issues we expressed above: a common vocabulary to describe practices, a memory for individual evaluators and a place for sharing. By bringing dispatched practices together in a single collaborative tool, we target an enhanced mutual understanding, commitment and trust between evaluator-users.

A Bottom-Up Knowledge Management Based Approach

By targeting a rationalization of evaluation practices that allows for the expression of individual points of view, the project meets both the instrumental and the process-oriented approaches of Knowledge Management Hildreth and Kimble (2002) refer to.

On the one hand, we consider evaluations as objects that can be codified, memorized and reused. From the application's point of view, evaluation comes down to the retrieval of aggregated performance indicators describing the interactions led by a system. Providing a common framework to define evaluations brings consistency among individual contributions. It calls for both conventions to represent this structured knowledge (e.g. data format and database design) and an effort of conceptualization from evaluator-users. The latter have to convert their unstructured tacit evaluation knowledge into an explicit description of their modus operandi, which compels them to step back from their practice and conceptualize it according to the application framework. This codification permits to "capitalize" knowledge, a first step toward cooperation. However, characterizing one's practice and the tacit reasons motivating evaluation strategies is not an easy task.

Figure 5. Dashboard dedicated to a high-level view on usability performance

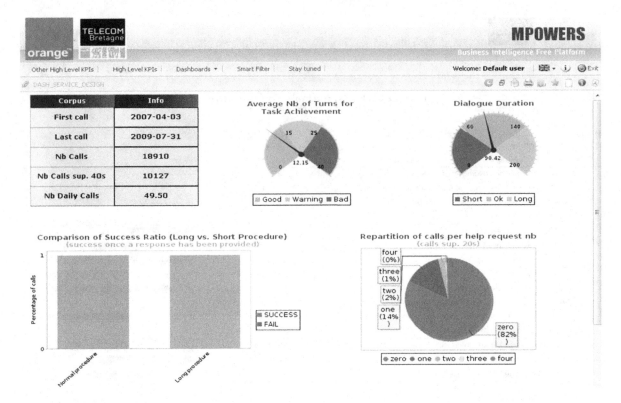

This approach corresponds to classical top-down information system projects. Enterprise Resource Planning (ERP) solutions, for example, are business-integrated solutions that link various functions within an organization (e.g. sale, accounting, billing, human resources and logistics). The coordination and synchronization of the activities relies on both a centralized information system that assures real time updates across the organization and a set of normalized processes. ERP projects involve, upstream, the definition of one-size-fits-all operation procedures and, downstream, change management campaigns. The latter include communication, training and incitation to support the costly deployments. These top-down projects bet on the alignment of end-users to standard processes, aspiring to ease both intra and inter professions' interactions. The chosen standard can either be the most popular one within the company, the one implemented in a subsidiary

that already handled standardization or even the one supported by the most influencing decision-maker. No matter the choice, there will always be some left-behinds unsatisfied with the standard. Armies of change management consultants will not free such standardization project from the threat to be seen as burdens and to never take over the bespoke solutions developed and maintained in-house. Therefore, ERP projects have to focus on situations where the targeted user profiles are appropriate to such streamlining (e.g. HR, invoicing, cost control) since they would be at risk when many fields of competence collaborate.

On the second hand, in order to avoid such a pitfall, our solution also aspires to build "knowledge creation spaces" (Nonaka and Takeuchi, 1995) where knowledge is not seen as a *product* anymore, but as a process supported by the participation of diverse stakeholders in joint activities. Getting together thanks to the application, evaluator-users may: browse already defined evaluation methodologies for inspiration, receive feedbacks from other users that may have faced similar issues and generally discuss on evaluation methods. Outcomes are: an improved self-knowledge on one's evaluation practices, a shared knowledge of disseminated ones and their potential future convergence.

ERP solutions are better suitable to routine tasks (both individual and collaborative) in well-structured hierarchical organizations. In contrast, evaluation is a complex knowledge activity, for which ad hoc problem-solving situations may involve networks of interrelations. Davenport (2007) specifies that the only tools that may support the iterative non-structured activities in which small groups of stakeholders cooperate are *"knowledge repositories and collaborative aids, which are used voluntary"*. Our approach is bottom-up and relies on two notions: a knowledge repository to which users cooperate individually and a support to collaboration among contributors. By delivering common methods for evaluation design to isolated stakeholders, nomadic practices are better understood. This should trigger positive group dynamics required for the complex knowledge-based activities.

Sharing Practice and Experience through the System: The Spiral of Knowledge

Our solution places the evaluator-user as a mediator between the interpreted situation of evaluation and the information system in charge of automating the tractable tasks (Laurent, Kanellos and Bretier, 2010). However dedicated to support custom-made individual approaches, MPOWERS also supports the transfer of knowledge within communities. The tacit component of knowledge related to the evaluation task includes the way evaluators choose and associate the metrics so that they provide relevant information for decision-making. The explicit part resides in the

Figure 6. The spiral of knowledge (adapted from Nonaka and Takeuchi, 1995)

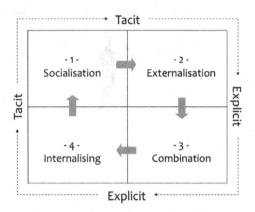

outcome of the evaluation design, *i.e.* the list of KPIs arranged individually by each stakeholder in response to their local decision needs. We depict them using Nonaka (1991)'s spiral of knowledge that considers both tacit and explicit components of knowledge into a continuous learning process (see Figure 6).

1. The socialization stage refers to the situation we observed within our SDS development projects (Laurent, Bretier and Manquillet, 2010). The various SDS stakeholders share their knowledge through informal interactions and involvement in joint activities. Problem is, in our case, that agents have neither time dedicated to knowledge sharing nor common vocabulary to interact, which limits the collaborative learning.

2. Externalization is correlated to the individual description of protocols within the application framework. Evaluator-users make their often-tacit practice explicit thanks to conventional formalization tools. Stepping back from their practice, they can better spell out their operating methods.

3. The combination stage consists in the dissemination of the explicit knowledge within and across working groups. The previous stage supplied transparency on each other

Figure 7. Repartition of individual and community activities

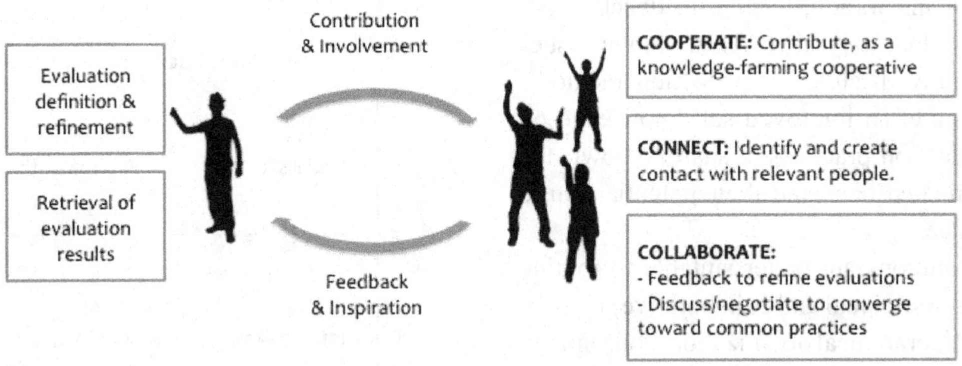

practice. This one promotes the dissemination, reuse of protocols and inspiration for new protocols design from scratch. It fosters the discussion, comparison, negotiation and adaptation, thanks to a shared description format. Dialogs and feedbacks between agents ease the dissemination of their *know-how*.

4. The internalization phase deals with *learning-by-practice*, i.e. the process of converting explicit knowledge into a tacit embedded one. The tasks' descriptions are integrated into personal tacit knowledge. This is similar to the way chiefs emancipate from the cookbooks (know-what), when they unconsciously internalize the gestures (know-how) without even being able, after a while, to explain and decompose them.

5. Finally, the spiral gets back to the first stage. The first loop granted actors with the ability to collaborate, and even share tacit knowledge as it is rooted on common baselines, explicit procedures and objects. Then, they continue to gradually learn and create new knowledge through successive refinement loops.

Michel Grundstein (2004) summarizes this continual learning process by both the involvement in the practice and the contact with community members into the concept of "axis of progress". It

supposes an endogenous definition of knowledge as created by a personal and organizational learning loop. This axis advocates for the production of individual knowledge and its conversion from being "non-formalized and private" to being "formalized and disseminated".

The Individual vs. Community Dichotomy

Davenport (2007) considers that the most rational approach to implement a knowledge sharing solution is to *"embed it into the technology that knowledge workers use to do their jobs. When knowledge supports the primary technology-enabled transactions used in day-to-day work, it is no longer a separate activity requiring slack time and the motivation to seek knowledge."* Likewise, while our solution allows evaluator-users to individually define and process their evaluation, it nurtures three of the main community assets (see Figure 7).

Cooperation is a *one-to-many* activity where isolated evaluator-users share their practices as if the application was a *knowledge-farming cooperative*. It mostly consists in selecting KPIs relevant to their decision-making needs, however they need to render the evaluation methods explicit thanks to the application's framework. Individually, evaluators contribute to develop a shared repository of resources, points of reference to discuss the methodologies. Rending the practice explicit is a prerequisite to any further discussion and collaboration.

The second step is the *one-to-one* connection between evaluator-users. Connection may result either from their co-participation into a joint activity in real life projects or from their similar evaluation practices.

Once contacts are set up and discussions initiated, a *many-to-many* collaboration may take place. Based on both the sharing and the co-creation of information, collaboration is the subsequent purpose of our framework. By pooling their modus operandi, individual users are both invited to step back on their practice and prompt to better apprehend alternative methodologies. This installs a baseline for debate toward conventional practices and evaluation refinements.

Anticipated Outcomes for Both the Individual and Group Levels

Individual Level

At the individual level, MPOWERS offloads the user from low added-value computable tasks (data collection, cleaning, transformation and aggregation into key performance indicators). It enables isolated evaluators to concentrate on the creative aspects of evaluation and the ongoing decision-making. Making the methodology explicit thanks to a prescribed framework, they gain on reusability over projects. Thus, by reusing the evaluation protocols described in the application over evaluation campaigns and SDS projects, evaluators are predisposed to pay more attention to lessons learnt. Serial refinements over evaluation campaigns and projects should lead to methodological enhancement, leading to more accurate information, more efficiently, for their decision-making.

Emergence of Communities

The solution intends to serve collaborative initiatives by creating an environment that facilitates social and intellectual interactions, notably around the sharing of knowledge, best practices and feelings. Nevertheless, stakeholders may be reluctant to contribute online. The online support tool must therefore ensure to bring rewarding virtual communities with something more than the *real-life* face-to-face synchronous communication (Kim et al., 2003). We address virtual communities of two different natures: the divisional communities of practice and the transverse communities of interest.

Community of Practice

Pierre Lévy states that the best thing enabled by emergent technologies is not *Artificial Intelligence* but *Collective Intelligence, i.e.* computers not imitating humans beings but helping them to evolve their ideas collectively (Lévy, 2002). Similarly, MPOWERS do not take over the evaluators' role, but supports the transfer of knowledge within the community. The tacit knowledge made explicit at the individual level allows the community to share, discuss and potentially converge towards debated best practices. This co-creation of shared resources and processes fosters cooperation and collaboration. However, the real life job families associated with SDS development projects generally do not suit Wenger's definition of communities of practice. As a matter of fact, SDS-project dedicated teams are defined top-down and they do not often endorse time neither dedicated to feedback nor to lessons-learned when projects and evaluation campaigns finish. On that account, our system targets the renewal of collaboration within the community.

Knowledge co-creation and learning inside the group needs a balance between interaction and formal ingredients. When describing their evaluation protocols, evaluator-users follow a capture-store-codify approach. They however do not articulate the know-how involved in the evaluation design, i.e. the heuristics summoned to render a decision-making context into an evaluation protocol. Our anthropocentric framework only endeavors the tractable tasks from computable data. The "hard knowledge" may be captured within the system, providing explicit sharable methodological elements. But the "soft" one, the know-how, requires a personal involvement including trial-and-error refinement cycles along with successive evaluation campaigns. In the framework developed by Wenger, learning comes out social interactions among stakeholders involved in a shared activity. Talking permits to render explicit past experiences that will be used as points of reference for future discussions. However, embedded skills relies more on practice than on activity-related discourse. Whereas projects are temporary and geographically limited organizations, practice is persistent and a-temporal.

Still, the explicit descriptions of evaluation protocols within MPOWERS, a shared artifact, provide reference baselines for discussion. It enforces conventional concepts and wordings to prevent, as much as possible, misunderstandings between stakeholders.

Community of Inquiry or Interest: Constellations of Communities of Practice

As mentioned, SDS projects involve participants belonging to distinct communities of practice. These "communities of communities" (Brown and Duguid, 1991), organizations centered on the task achievement and not on common practices, refer to two analogous notions. Lorino (2007) names Communities of Inquiry (CoI) the groups of individuals whose cooperation converges around a conjoint activity, i.e. an *"activity that is not characterized by similar practices but their heterogeneous complementarities"*. Similarly, Fischer (2001) alludes to Communities of Interest that *"bring together stakeholders from different communities*

of practice to solve a particular (design) problem of common concern" and which *"are characterized by their shared interest in the framing and resolution of a design problem"*. Wenger (1998) calls them *"constellations of interconnected communities of practice"*. They gather communities co-involved in projects, belonging to the same institution, sharing a few members and artifacts, interacting and somehow competing for shared resources. Finally, Haas (1992) calls epistemic communities these *"networks of professionals with recognized expertise and competence in particular domain or issue-area"*. They get together professionals, from a variety of disciplines and backgrounds, but attempting to build a legitimate knowledge in the dedicated area.

No matter the designation, this concept drives a reflection on the temporal and geographical consistency of practice within the organization. For more transparency and mutual understanding inside the project group, stakeholders would benefit from apprehending the mechanisms that govern each other's practice, i.e. which criteria they favor when opting for an alternative. Actually, stakeholders often only have a vague glimpse on each other's roles, motivations and contributions to the global project. Fischer (2001) highlights that design-related projects combine the knowledge tacitly distributed among the stakeholders, *"each of whom possess an important and yet incomplete understanding of the problem"*. Actors embrace diverse cultures and traditions and are inclined to consider their own point of view as the *one best way*, occasionally leading to sterile monologues confrontations. Learning in a community of interest is consequently more complicated than the *"legitimate peripheral participation"* (Lave and Wenger, 1991) in homogeneous communities of practice. The practice delimitates frontiers between communities governed by different conceptual frameworks and modus operandi.

Yet, Wenger (1998) introduces the role of "frontier objects" that bound communities with shared significations. However "reified", they concentrate tacit knowledge. They enable various different social groups to involve into common practices, just like a contract signed by both providers and customers. Similarly, documents bring *"people from different groups together to negotiate and coordinate common practices"* (Brown and Duguid, 1995). They provide common references for disambiguated interactions between distinct communities of practice. Accordingly, MPOWERS constitutes a frontier artifact for stakeholders belonging to distinct communities. It supports the communities of interest by creating shared understanding of the task at hand. It implements the ITU-T recommendation P. Sup. 24 (ITU-T, 2005) that provides a common vocabulary for evaluation definition and also constitutes a shared repertory of resources, *i.e.* an interface between projects and a capitalization of evaluation methods independently to the project timeline. The practices thus made transparent, stakeholders should better understand each other's points of interest, objectives and methods; a cross understanding that promotes the trust and respect needed for cooperation.

At a knowledge dissemination point of view, it backs the hierarchical organization divided into functional silos, with an alternative network of interactions in which all actors can interact. Knowledge and practices may therefore be distributed transversely across the organization. However participation and reification must be balanced.

Alignment requires specific forms of participation and reification to support the required co-ordination... With insufficient participation, our relations to broader enterprises tend to remain literal and procedural: our co-ordination tends to be based on compliance rather than participation in meaning... With insufficient reification, coordination across time and space may depend too much on the partiality of specific participants, or it may simply be too vague, illusory or contentious to create alignment. (Wenger, 1998)

The cohabitation of communities of practice and the description of each other's practice on the application aim the reciprocal consciousness of complementary duties toward the joint objective. In fact, the different cohabitating strategies only display the diversity of points of view on a given task. The evaluation platform enables to make explicit, and thus sharable and modifiable, the collective activity that would otherwise be seen as a constraint by isolated stakeholders. Transforming "foreigners" into team players.

The issue is about the balance between the compulsory framework and the structure emerging from the user practice. We must therefore fine-tune between elements to institutionalize and practice for which participation is more adequate. However MPOWERS offers a repertory of evaluation parameters to build evaluations, all stakeholders and their belonging communities must assimilate this artifact in their own practice.

ROUND-UP AND FUTURE RESEARCH DIRECTIONS

Knowledge creation and knowledge sharing within an organization is a complex issue. As per Morin (1990), this is due to notably the cohabitation of actors absorbed by distinct objectives and sharing complex interactions, the abundance of sources of information, the untold procedures and the tacit knowledge for resolution of problems.

We could call upon the theory of systems to address the issue, a system being understood as a group of elements in dynamic crossed interactions organized according to a goal. For example, whereas children of the same age form a group of elements, the same children considered as class constitute a system (Narbonne, 2005). As classmates, they are individuals in interaction pursuing one or several common goals. The functioning of a class cannot be apprehended as the sum of individual behaviors since both individual and collective behaviors are determined by the whole

Figure 8. Convergence vs. customization as implemented in MPOWERS

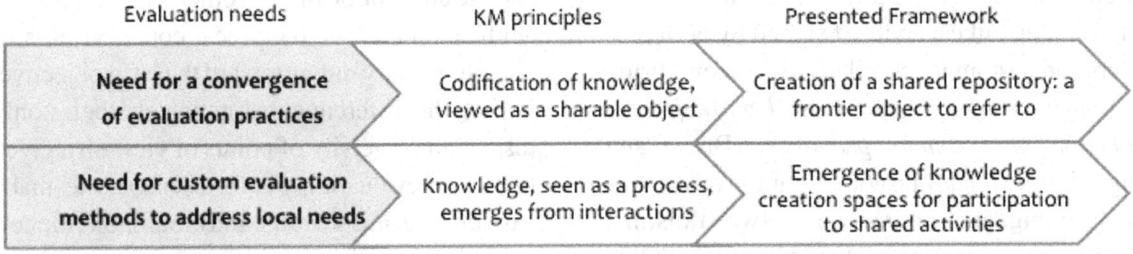

Evaluation needs	KM principles	Presented Framework
Need for a convergence of evaluation practices	Codification of knowledge, viewed as a sharable object	Creation of a shared repository: a frontier object to refer to
Need for custom evaluation methods to address local needs	Knowledge, seen as a process, emerges from interactions	Emergence of knowledge creation spaces for participation to shared activities

system. Considering the community of actors involved in the project as a system, the project team's outcome should be considered beyond the sum of the individuals' contributions as well.

Tackling such complex environments requires conceptual models that restrain the working framework to a limited number of interconnected components. We therefore restrict our definition of evaluation to the retrieval of Key Performance Indicators from various types of data collected over the evaluated SDSs. Thus, the implementation framework disregards the leading motivations and the various implicit components, real sources of complexity.

We oscillate between two opposite needs. On the one hand, we need a framework to permit individual evaluators to collaborate on protocol definition and refinement. For that purpose, we implemented a common vocabulary to disambiguate interactions and frontier objects for actors to refer to. On the other hand, the framework should be flexible enough for the actors to express their individual point of view. A balance should be found between an established imposed structure and a structure that emerges spontaneously from recurring practices (Soulier, 2004). Therefore, while contributing to the organization consistency, frameworks should remain discrete enough so that emerging practices can surface.

Our tool imposes concepts and vocabulary for the evaluators to define their practice but it leaves them the latitude to express their points of view. Contrary to skeptical authors about the

role of technology in facilitating the knowledge sharing (e.g. Pfeffer and Hinds, 2003), we believe in its support function. We do not focus on the management of expertise itself, but in the way a given tool may provide boundary objects for the discussion between actors. The Figure 8 illustrates the approach we detailed in the chapter.

For the time being, the application focuses on the definition of evaluation protocols and the relative retrieval of Key Performance Indicators. It would beneficiate from further developments to support the localization of experts and social networking features.

"I don't want raw data, I don't even want information, I want the judgment of people I trust." Boone (2001) illustrates how the location of the organization expertise is becoming a big issue. Knowledge repositories are extensively used to grant access to information, but giving access to the people who developed this knowledge from their experience is another stake. We should therefore add features to ease both the tracking of the users' activities and the online communication to support interconnection between community members. This includes search engines to browse contributions and user profiles, connection support, automatic notification of connected users' updates on methodologies' description, possibility to comment on the latter and the support to discussion threads. Erickson and Kellogg (2003), for example, developed an online multi-user environment to support the communication aspect among knowledge communities.

The issue of evaluation cannot be separated from the design of service or product, and therefore its monitoring exercise. We aim at fostering more collective and comprehensive outlooks on project evaluation. Where stakeholders now evaluate individually their contribution, projects would beneficiate from a coordination of local judgments, enriched with a common consciousness on the projects' essence, priorities and constraints.

CONCLUSION

This chapter presented an original approach to knowledge management (KM) for complex projects in the context of two-dimensional organization models (one dimension for communities of practices and the other for communities of interest). By supporting individual agents in a *rational* definition of their practices, we want to foster the cooperation and collaboration within the various types of communities they belong to. We however bear in mind that even if the ICTs are sine qua non elements for such a KM-tainted project, they only are technical supports to a profound redefinition of collaboration.

The solution not only supports the sharing of methodological resources but also the development of both social and intellectual behaviors. This way, it encourages the development of interpersonal networks inducing the stakeholders' confidence, commitment and liability to the common enterprise. However the *"organic, spontaneous, and informal nature"* that makes communities of practice resistant to regulation, a few companies successfully nurtured them (Wenger and Snyder, 2000). Their success relied on the managers' ability to both bring the right people together and provide an infrastructure in which communities can thrive. Above that, communities of interest tend to create congruence into silo organizations. By putting together distinct job families and cutting across knowledge systems, they foster direct and transverse interactions. Such approach instruments

the transformation of mutual incomprehension of stakeholders into "knowledge creation space" based on collaboration and creative exchanges.

The chapter articulated the rationalization aspects of implementing a socio-technical system that fosters emerging social practices within the organization. It is a starting point for aspiring researches about the social, organizational and managerial ingredients that may stimulate the communities' emergence and welfare.

REFERENCES

Argote, L. (1999). *Organizational learning: Creating, retaining c transferring knowledge*. Norwell, MA, USA: Kluwer Academic Publishers.

Boone, M. E. (2001). *Managing inter@ctivity*. New York, NY: McGraw-Hill.

Brown, J. S., & Duguid, P. (1991). Organizational learning and communities-of-practice: Toward a unified view of working, learning, and innovation. *Organization Science*, *2*(1), 40–57. doi:10.1287/orsc.2.1.40

Brown J. S., & Duguid, P. (1995, October 11). *The Social Life of Documents. EDventure Holdings*, (1-18). New York, NY.

Davenport, T. H. (2005). *Thinking for a living: How to get better performance and results from knowledge workers*. Boston, MA: Harvard Business School Press.

Davenport, T. H. (2007). Information technologies for knowledge management . In Ichijo, K., & Nonaka, I. (Eds.), *Knowledge creation and management. New challenges for managers* (pp. 97–109). New York, NY: Oxford University Press.

Erickson, T., & Kellogg, W. A. (2003). Knowledge Communities: Online Environments for Supporting Knowledge Management and its Social Context. In M. Ackerman, V. Pipek, & V Wulf (Eds.), *Beyond knowledge management: Sharing expertise* (299-325). Cambridge, MA.: MIT Press.

Eskenazi, M., Black, A. W., Raux, A., & Langner, B. (2008). *Let's go lab: A platform for evaluation of spoken dialogue systems with real world users*. Brisbane, Australia: Interspeech.

Fernandez, V., & Rivard, S. (2007). KM: Knowledge networks. *Annals of Telecommunications, 62*(7/8: *Knowledge Management: Knowledge Networks*), 723-733.

Fischer, G. (2001). Communities of interest: Learning through the interaction of multiple knowledge systems. In *24th Annual Information Systems Research Seminar in Scandinavia* (IRIS'24). Ulvik, Norway.

Gartner (2009). De La Vergne, H. J., Milanesi, C., Zimmermann, A., Cozza, R., Nguyen, T. H., Gupta, A., & CK Lu (in press). *Competitive Landscape: Mobile Devices, Worldwide, 4Q09 and 2009*.

Grundstein, M. (2004). De la capitalisation des connaissances au management des connaissances dans l'entreprise. In Imed Boughzala and Jean-Louis Ermine (Eds.), *Management des connaissances en entreprise* (25-54). Paris, France: Lavoisier.

Haas, P. M. (1992). Introduction: Epistemic communities and international policy coordination. *International Organization, 46*(1), 1–35. doi:10.1017/S0020818300001442

Hartikainen, M., Salonen, E., & Turunen, M. (2004). Subjective evaluation of spoken dialogue systems using SERVQUAL method. In *Proceedings of the Eighth International Conference on Spoken Language Processing (INTERSPEECH 2004-ICSLP)*. Jeju Island, Korea.

Hildreth, P. M., & Kimble, C. (2002). The duality of knowledge. *Information Research, 8*,(1).

Hutchins, E. (1995). *Cognition in the wild*. Cambridge, MA: The MIT Press.

Jokinen, K., & McTear, M. (2009). *Spoken dialogue systems*. San Rafael, CA: Morgan & Claypool Publishers.

Laurent, M., & Bretier, P. (2010). MPOWERS: A multi points of view evaluation refinement studio. In *SIGDIAL 2010, The 11th Annual SIGdial Meeting on Discourse and Dialogue*. Tokyo, Japan.

Laurent, M., Bretier, P., & Manquillet, C. (2010). Ad-hoc evaluations along the lifecycle of industrial spoken dialogue systems: Heading to harmonisation? In *LREC 2010: 7th International Conference on Language Resources and Evaluation*. Malta.

Laurent, M., Kanellos, I., & Bretier, P. (2010). Considering the subjectivity to rationalise evaluation approaches: The example of spoken dialogue systems. In *QoMEx'10, Second International Workshop on Quality of Multimedia Experience*. Trondheim, Norway.

Lave, J., & Wenger, E. (1991). *Situated learning: Legitimate peripheral participation*. Cambridge, MA: Cambridge University Press.

Lévy, P. (2002). *Cyberdémocratie*. Paris, France: Odile Jacob.

Lorino, P. (2007). Communities of inquiry and knowledge creation in organizations: The process model in management. *Annals of Telecommunications, 62* (7/8: *Knowledge Management: Knowledge Networks)*, 753-771.

Midler, C. (1995). *L'auto qui n'existait pas, management des projets et transformation de l'entreprise*. Paris, France: InterEditions.

Möller, S. (2005). *Quality of telephone-based spoken dialogue systems*. New York, NY: Springer-Verlag New York, Inc.

Morin, E. (1990). *Introduction à la pensée complexe, Communication et complexité*. Paris, France: ESF éditions.

Narbonne, Y. (2005). *Complexité et systémique*. London, UK; Paris, France: Hermès - Lavoisier.

Nonaka, I. (1991). The knowledge creating company. *Harvard Business Review, 69*, 96–104.

Nonaka, I., & Takeuchi, H. (1995). *The knowledge-creating company: How Japanese companies create the dynamics of Innovation*. New York, NY: Oxford University Press.

Orr, J. E. (1991). *Talking about machines: An ethnography of a modern job*. Ithaca, NY: Cornell University Press.

Paek, T. (2001). Empirical methods for evaluating dialog systems. In *Proceedings of the Second SIGdial Workshop on Discourse and Dialogue*. Aalborg, Denmark.

Pfeffer, J., & Hinds, P. J. (2003). Why organizations don't "know what they know": Cognitive and motivational factors affecting the transfer of expertise. In M. Ackerman, V. Pipek, & V Wulf (Eds.), *Sharing expertise: Beyond knowledge management* (3-26). Cambridge, MA: MIT Press.

Polanyi, M. (1966). *The tacit dimension*. London, UK: Routledge & Kegan.

Prax, J.-Y. (2003). *Le manuel du knowledge management: Une approche de 2e génération*. Dunod.

Rheingold, H. (1993). *The virtual community*. Reading, MA: Addison-Wesley Pub. Co.

Sawhney, M., & Prandelli, E. (2000, Summer). Communities of creation: Managing distributed innovation in turbulent markets. *California Management Review, 42*(4).

Soulier, E. (2004). Les communautés de pratique pour la gestion des connaissances. In *Management des connaisances en entreprise*, 149-179. Paris, France: Lavoisier.

Stufflebeam, D. I. (1980). *L'évaluation en éducation et la prise de décision*. Ottawa, Canada: Edition NHP.

Walker, M. A., Litman, D. J., Kamm, C. A., & Abella, A. (1997). PARADISE: A framework for evaluating spoken dialogue agents. In *Proceedings of the 35th Annual Meeting of the Association for Computational Linguistics* (ACL-97), 271–280. Madrid, Spain.

Wenger, E. (1998). *Communities of practice: Learning, meaning, and identity*. New York, NY: Cambridge University Press.

Wenger, E., McDermott, R., & Snyder, W. M. (2002). *Cultivating communities of practice: A guide to managing knowledge, 1 edition*. Boston, MA: Harvard Business Press.

Wenger, E., & Snyder, W. (2000). Communities of Practice: The Organizational Frontier. *Harvard Business Review*, (January-February): 139–145.

KEY TERMS AND DEFINITIONS

Collaboration: "Working together". Collaboration is the common elaboration of a negotiated enterprise. Participants are more implicated in the enterprise and develop more interactions than in cooperative approaches, since the responsibility of the success is global and collective. Collaborative work stands on the idea that the organization knowledge is not separately embedded in individuals but disseminated in the whole organization.

Cooperation: "Operating together". The cooperation is the sharing out of tasks between the various stakeholders of a shared enterprise. All the contributions are pooled and juxtaposed as in a farming cooperative. The contributors' responsibility is often limited to their task realization. Therefore interactions between them are often limited to organization and monitoring.

Key Performance Indicators (KPIs): KPIs are business-related metrics used to track performance within a company. They are used in the presentation of monitoring dashboard used to help decision-makers in their daily exercise. For us, KPIs refer to the evaluation metrics aggregated from the basic parameters retrieved to describe the interaction with spoken dialogue systems.

Knowledge Management: Knowledge management consists the implementation and the exploitation of a destined socio-technical system that modifies the modalities of managing information and knowledge in a way to enhance the knowledge workers' activity.

Practice: A practice is a custom, a tradition, a modus operandi that ritualizes the belonging to a given community. It marks the observance of the norms and conventions that regulates the community. Evaluation practices embrace the way given evaluators apprehend their decision-making situations so as to translate them into experimental set-ups and evaluation metrics.

Spoken Dialog Systems (SDS): A spoken dialog system is a computer-based solution enabling callers to access information or process transactions over their telephone. It also enables to identify callers, to qualify their call according to their motive and to dispatch them to adequate services or human operators. They are widely used by insurance and banking companies, telecommunication operators, as well as yellow page services.

Section 2
Monitoring Virtual Communities

Contents, structures and user's behavior within virtual communities constitute the raw material of the chapters in this section. Users are organized in networks and they share contents. Analysis on these emerging contents and structures provides additional knowledge that is useful to monitor the communities and to understand the sociology of formation online.

Chapter 4
An Integrated Methodology to Detect the Evolution of Virtual Organizational Communities

Marco De Maggio
University of Salento (Lecce), Italy

Francesca Grippa
University of Salento (Lecce), Italy

ABSTRACT

This chapter describes an integrated methodology developed to combine two analytical approaches, social network analysis and content analysis, to investigate the organizational mechanisms responsible for the emergence of social capital within virtual communities. This integration is proposed to overcome the main limitation of social network analysis: the analysis of the content of the information flows and the organizational and cultural aspects of their exchanges.

We propose a methodology applied to virtual communities operating in an organizational context. We aim to demonstrate how such an integrated approach may help understanding the way new ideas spread within and across networks, helping to recognize the emergence of informal roles, community phases and the network structure.

The proposed methodology has the potential to enable the analysis of virtual communities' overall composition, evolution and social structure, characteristics and organizational behavior of the "project related sub-communities", informal members' roles and their contribution to the development of project's task.

DOI: 10.4018/978-1-60960-869-9.ch004

INTRODUCTION

As the focus of competition moves from the firm to the network, and from rigid organizational structures to informal networks, communities are presented in literature as the most flexible governance model to build a value-creating organization. New organizational forms – such as communities of practice, communities of innovation, industry consortia, knowledge-sharing networks - are now emerging in response to new environmental forces that call for new organizational and managerial capabilities (Dyer, 2000). The success of these new organizational forms depends on the ability to behave as integrated networks, where different stakeholders gather in an open and flexible interaction, inside and outside the company boundaries (Ghoshal and Bartlett, 1997).

The diffusion of the Internet allowed communities to benefit from virtual networking, and delocalization, and to become more capable to afford the challenges of a more complex business environment (Cothrel and Williams, 1999; Hildreth et al., 2000). The effectiveness of these new forms of collaboration and knowledge creation explains the growing interest of scholars and managers to understand how communities really work, how they organize internally, how they produce value (Schultz et al., 2003; Mitchell, 2002; Burt, 2000).

The main contribution of the present work is to map the subject matter of the information flows within virtual communities, to match the community's social structure with the emerging ideas or topics. It also provides empirical evidence from the application of the integrated methodology to a "longitudinal study" looking for the organizational facets of a global, dispersed community.

A case study analysis has been conducted on a large Virtual Community developed at a global scale, involving a high number of members and a wide range of different organizations located all over the world.

The achievement of the presented goal has been conducted under the guide of the following question: *How to detect the evolutionary structure of a virtual community by following the diffusion pattern of a new project idea?*

The main limitation of the Social Network Analysis, that is to treat all the connections in the same way, without differentiating the topics of discussion, might represent an obstacle in the analysis of large communities. It would be hard to understand communications referred to friendly personal ties or projects-related ones. This can prevent the development of a more comprehensive picture of the community, making it difficult to disentangle the web of many interactions, 5431 in our case, that can provide no meaning and possibly lead to misinterpretations.

While SNA was able to point the "who" and the "how" of the social capital structural dimension, the integration with the Content Analysis revealed the "who", "how" and "what" of the social capital overall dimensions, structural, cognitive and relational. The integrated methodology provided a more complete picture of the Community, useful to improve the understanding and the monitoring of such "hidden organizations", and to offer useful insights for their management.

The main managerial implications of the outcomes of this research can be classified following some key managerial processes, related to the organizations' capability to better:

1. Understand Communities: the application of the integrated methodology showed its suitability to describe the main characteristics of a project-oriented community, identifying several aspects such as: the topics associated to emergent sub-communities, the role of the original core group in leading all the projects; the impact of a strong leadership built around few coordinators.

2. Analyze and Monitor Communities: the use of the methodology as a monitoring system able to detect and map:
    a. the most involved actors, the way in which they interact with the others and the spontaneous emerging of unpredicted roles;
    b. the trend in organizational behaviour, in density level, and centralization dynamics and the involvement of task-related subgroups, in the "operative" phase of the lifecycle.
3. Manage Communities: the application of the integrated methodology and the use of the frameworks and tools used to present results might be useful as a managerial tool for identifying step by step the areas of intervention for each project, helping to avoid the failure of project development activities. They can also support the activity of recognition of the best contributions to be rewarded, and the identification of knowledge experts who play a crucial role in speeding up the process of innovation.

THEORETICAL BACKGROUND

The emerging phenomenon of Virtual Communities finds its roots in the concept of Community of Practice (CoP) introduced in 1991 by J. Lave and E. Wenger in the book "Situated Learning: Legitimate Peripheral Participation." This concept was further developed by E. Wenger in 1998 in the book "Community of Practice: Learning, Meaning and Identity" and then elaborated with W. Snyder in 2000 in the Harvard Business Review. Communities of Practice are considered groups of people informally bound together by shared expertise and passion for a joint enterprise. People in Communities of Practice share their experiences and knowledge in free-flowing, creative ways that foster new approaches to problems (E. Wenger & W. Snyder, 2000). Sawhney and Prandelli (2000)

propose a similar concept, *communities of creation*, representing the governance mechanism particularly crucial for the organizations operating within knowledge intensive industries.

Over time this concept was further developed and assumed different connotations depending on the properties of the groups involved. New concepts were introduced such as "Knowledge Community", "Community of Interest", "Learning Community", "Communities of Creation". Simultaneously, the explosive development of information and communication technologies and their pervasiveness in the organizational and managerial processes of the community, have enabled the introduction of a virtual dimension within the traditional mechanisms of functioning of an Organizational Community.

The diffusion of Information and Communication Technologies had a deep impact on several community features. We propose eight dimensions to characterize the nature of virtual communities in an organizational context, highlighting the main differences between virtual and physical communities.

Purpose: virtual communities, similarly to the physical ones, may emerge for several reasons, having different characteristics based on the rate of environmental uncertainty, strategy or operation management goals. Virtuality represents an important advantage when the community is formed in emergency conditions, when rapid organizational changes are required following unpredicted alteration of the business environment.

Size: Community size is widely variable, in physical as well as in virtual settings. The more the number of people increases, the more evident is the distinction between the intellectual organizational *core* of the community and the periphery, or extended community (Wenger and Snyder, 2000; McDermott, 2000). The main distinction between physical and virtual communities is that the latter grow easily and fast, facilitated by web connection and the rapid diffusion of aggregative movements on the web-sphere. They can reach very large dimensions and high dispersion, which might introduce the risk to neglect the common goals and reduce internal motivation (Van Krogh, 2000).

Physical Proximity: in virtual communities the employment of information technology to communicate and to exchange content allows people to interact in an ubiquitous way. Although their voluntary nature that defies managerial intrusion, Virtual Communities need a strong management commitment to encourage interaction, and to coordinate common actions toward the achievement of the community's goals.

Membership: in virtual communities membership is more critical than in physical contexts, provided the low level of control exerted on the community. Selection principles can be initially shared, but they can change as the community grows. When membership is almost mandatory, the organization can establish requirements for the access. When the process is free and voluntary, a sort of natural selection may emerge making potential entrants aware of the "entrance rules" (Mitchell, 2002). Being virtual communities more fluid, membership might vary quicker than in situation of physical co-location.

Leadership: leadership creation and distribution throughout community's life cycle can change according to different factors: evolution of the community, organizational dynamics, management intrusion in the community life. Although it is common for virtual communities to have a flexible not hierarchical organizational structure, some scholars suggest to create the conditions for a more stable leadership, to provide members with the required recognition of their contribution and a precise landmark for the community identity (Lesser, Storck, 2001; Fontaine, 2001; Gretchko et al., 2002).

Diversity: The degree of diversity in the community represents the primary source of innovativeness and one of the main sources of competitive advantage created for the organization (Aral and Van Alstyne, 2007, Hofstede, 1993).

The community diversity may be attributed to the individual background and idiosyncrasies of each member (e.g. cultural differences and geographical origin that shape collaboration and relationships). Another source of diversity comes from different organizational behaviours and corporate culture, which can create suspicion and difficulty of collaboration (Hesselbein and Johnston, 2002). A third source of diversity comes from the individual professional background, which helps avoid the "groupthink effect", but can create problems in interpreting individual contribution.

Lifecycle: Virtual communities have no definite boundaries, both in time and space, but they can change in composition and goals (Gloor, 2006). Though they are generally considered constant settings of knowledge sharing and collaborative work, when created for strategic purpose or to face unpredictable events, they can be planned to have a short duration to concentrate energy and efforts (Wenger et al, 2000). While several models have been developed to describe the hypothesis of lifecycle of a community (Tuckman, 1956, Wenger and Snyder, 2000) virtual communities show a high rate of variability in phases of development, depending on their vision, size, cohesiveness and goals (Gongla and Rizzuto, 2001).

Sponsorship and Institutionalization: the last feature of virtual communities regards the relationship with the organization, one of the most critical issues related to the creation and evolution of a virtual community (Brown and Duguid, 2001). Because of their voluntary and open nature, factors like the involvement of management, the dependence on the organizational structure, culture and practices may represent strong constraints to creativity and innovativeness for virtual communities (McDermott, 1999). This relationship can assume different shapes (Wenger et al., 2000), from total independence, to some degree of organizational support, until the total institutionalization of the community as an operative program within the organization structure.

Figure 1. Components of collaborative knowledge networks (adapted from Gloor, 2006)

Community Type	Category	Focus	Mode of Participation	Example
COIN	Innovation	Fundamentally new insights	Peer group of Innovators	Linux kernel developers, creators of Web
CLN	Best-practice knowledge stewarding	Shared Knowledge	Active sharers of knowledge as experts; active seekers of knowledge as students	Xerox repair technicians, oneFish, Web masters
CIN	Helping	Shared Interest	Few sharers of knowledge as experts, many silent seekers of knowledge, lurkers	The Motley Fool, Internet Users

VIRTUAL COMMUNITIES: A SYSTEMATIC TAXONOMY

In the attempt to define a systematic taxonomy of virtual communities that interact at a global scale, Peter Gloor (2006) proposed in the book *"Swarm Creativity"* three types of networks (see Figure 1):

1. Collaborative Innovation Networks (COINs): made of self motivated people that share a common vision, meeting on the web to exchange ideas, knowledge, experiences and to work in a collaborative way to achieve a common goal.
2. Collaborative Interest Networks (CINs): composed by people sharing the same interests who do not perform a common task in the virtual team; this kind of community is very frequent on the web, has a lot of silent members, who collect information from web sites, forums, and a few active members who are keen to share their knowledge and experiences within the community.

3. Collaborative Learning Networks (CLNs): a community made of people inclined to share knowledge and practice to benefit reciprocally from personal mastery and the collective knowledge accumulation of experiences.

These three types of virtual communities are intended to form what is called Collaborative Knowledge Network (CKN), a *"high-speed feed-back loop in which the innovative results of COINs are immediately taken up and tested, refined or rejected by Learning and Interest Networks, and fed back to the originating COINs"* (Gloor, 2006, p.128).

COINs are the creative base of the CKN, the enabling factor for the creation of fluid organizations, characterized by organizational creativity, productivity and efficiency because of its key principles of "creative collaboration, knowledge sharing and social networking". Generally, a COIN is formed around a new interesting idea absorbed outside organizations, brought inside and discussed in a "swarm" collaborative and creative way to improve individual knowledge, capabilities and organizations' performance.

Virtual Communities and Social Capital

Communities began to be observed as the natural expression of employees seeking time and place to connect with others, to exchange opinions and ideas about common work, and to built a sense of identity to praise the human dimension of organizations. Over time they have been recognized as actual organizational assets (Lesser and Stork, 2001), able to:

- exploit the potential of the issues linked to the crucial passage from the slow and linear traditional hierarchies to the new fast, unpredictable and complex global economy;
- positively affect the organizational performance;
- handle unstructured problems;
- share knowledge outside traditional organizational boundaries;
- develop and maintain the organizational memory.

The difficulty in assessing their contribution is that communities are often hidden assets, appearing neither on the organizational chart, nor on a balance sheet. To understand how communities create organizational value, we suggest thinking of them as engines for the development of "social capital". Some studies indicate how social capital developed within virtual communities leads to behavioural change, change that results in greater knowledge sharing, which then positively influences business performance (Lesser and Stork, 2001, p.2).

Central to the Social Capital theory is to recognize the importance of "networks of relationships" considered valuable resources to support social business, able to provide the community members with "*the collectivity, owned capital, a credential which entitles them to credit, in the various senses of the word*" (Bourdieu, 1986, p.249).

One of the most widely recognized contributions to the theory on Social Capital is represented by the work of Naphiet and Ghoshal (1998). They move from the work of Bourdieu (1980, 1993) and Putnam (1995), accepting a comprehensive concept of Social Capital including the actual or potential resources becoming accessible through networks of relationships. Accordingly they define Social Capital as "*the sum of the actual and potential resources embedded within, available through, and derived from the network of relationships possessed by an individual or social unit. Social capital thus comprises both the network and the assets that may be mobilized through that network*" (Naphiet and Ghoshal, 1998, p.248). They propose a model of Social Capital based on three key dimensions:

1. Structural Dimension: it is related to the individual capability to connect with other people; the value that derives from exploiting this capability is represented by the opportunity to reduce time and costs related to have access to new information, avoiding redundancy and dispersion.

2. Relational Dimension: another aspect related to the attitude to build connections is the personal human management of interpersonal relationships, that create trust and reinforcement in community networks; this dimension is intended to be based on four factors: obligations, norms, trust and identification, that affect the network behaviour, building rules and standards that give the group a deep sense of identity.

3. Cognitive Dimension: it regards the process of sharing information and knowledge, that create a common context, with common codes and a "common language" (Naphiet,

Ghoshal, 1998, p.253), intended to be a virtuous cycle of shared practices and models that grows over time.

To avoid confusion in the wide range of definitions of Social Capital available in literature, Lesser and Storck (2001) provided a first classification of the positive impact of Communities on organizational performance. Their work has been based on the study of seven companies in which Communities had been recognized as value creating mechanisms for the organizations (Lesser, Stork, 2001). Among these benefits we recall the following:

1. Decreasing the learning curve of new employees
2. Responding more rapidly to customer needs and inquiries
3. Reducing rework and preventing "reinvention of the wheel
4. Spawning new ideas for products and services

After discussing the nature and the importance of virtual communities for organizations, it is important to answer an important managerial question: "how to monitor the evolution of social capital within virtual communities inside and across organizations?". Next paragraph refers to Social Network Analysis (SNA) as a possible first answer to address this question.

SOCIAL NETWORK ANALYSIS: AN ANALYTICAL APPROACH TO INVESTIGATE SOCIAL CAPITAL CREATION

Social Network Analysis has been defined as *"the disciplined inquiry into the patterning of relations among social actors, as well as the patterning of relationships among actors at different levels of analysis"* (Breiger, 2004). This methodology was widely employed since the 1960s to highlight the link between the network structure of communities and the creation of social capital, represented by organizations' competitive advantage.

The application of Social Network methods and tools within organizations had a great impact on the diffusion of SNA theories. Today, many scholars and practitioners refer to the field of Organization Network Analysis (ONA) as a tool that enables companies to map the information exchanges among employees and determine how to support information brokers, gatekeepers and boundary spanners, and to integrate isolated groups (Foster and Falkowski, 1999).

In general, social network analysis focuses on the relationships between people, rather than on actors' characteristics and attributes. These relationships may comprise the feelings people have for each other, the exchange of information, or more tangible exchanges such as goods and money. By mapping these relationships, network analysis helps to uncover the emergent and informal communication patterns present in an organization, which may then be compared to the formal communication structures. These emergent patterns can be used to explain several organizational phenomena (Burt, 2000). Since the patterns of relationships bring employees into contact with the attitudes and behaviors of other organizational members, these relationships may also help to explain why employees develop certain attitudes toward organizational events or job-related matters.

Network analysis techniques focus on the informal structure of an organization, which can be operationalized into various aspects. Structural features that can be distinguished and analyzed through the use of network analysis techniques include the formal and informal communication patterns in an organization and the identification of groups within an organization (cliques or functional groups). Moreover, communication-related roles of employees can be determined (e.g., stars, gatekeepers, and isolates). Special attention may be given to specific aspects of communication patterns: communication channels and media used by employees, the relationship between information types and the resulting communication networks, and the amount and possibilities of bottom-up communication. Additional characteristics that could, in principle, be investigated using network analysis techniques are the communication load as perceived by employees, the communication styles used, and the effectiveness of the information flows.

The main benefits of applying Social Network Analysis within organizations can be summarized as follows (Cross, Borgatti, Parker, 2002, Wellman, 1996, Cumming and Cross, 2003)):

- Supporting strategic partnerships (e.g., joint venture, alliances, consortia).
- Assessing strategy execution (e.g., core competencies or market strategies).
- Improving information and decision-making in top leadership networks.
- Integrating networks across core processes (e.g., commercial lending or software development).
- Improving innovation (e.g., new product development, research and development).
- Finding and supporting communities of practice (e.g., promoting connectivity or finding opinion leaders).
- Ensuring integration post-merger or large scale change (e.g., targeting collaboration and correcting over time).

As scholars and practitioners have pointed out, social network analysis is applied in a lot of application scenarios:

- Bridging strategically important disconnects between departments or organizations
- Improving a network's ability to sense and respond to opportunities
- Aligning the organizational context to energize and support networks

- Identifying overburdened employees and redistributing workloads
- Identifying and eliminating information bottlenecks
- Recognizing and supporting key "connectors"

All the previous benefits might be merged into the unifying goal of reaching a suitable level of collaboration among people. With reference to this specific aspect, it is essential to distinguish between collaboration and interaction, since our study will often refer to the way people interact using different channels and creating different kinds of ties. According to Ramesh and Tiwana (1999), interaction refers to formal, transactional communication links, while collaboration refers to informal, cooperative relationships that build a shared vision around common objectives. In the context of this research, we will refer to "communication ties" as a concept bonding the ones we have previously mentioned: people communicate by continuous interactions trying to establish contacts functional to collaboration, so to reach a mutual benefit.

According to Burt (2000), *closure* and *brokerage* are the foundation of the Social Capital research, and the starting point for every empirical research on the organizational mechanisms responsible for Social Capital creation. If *closure* is operationalized with the social network indicator "density", *brokerage* is a concept connected to the advantage provided by the presence of "structural holes" within social structures. Structural holes are an opportunity to broker the information flow between people, and manage the project that brings together people from opposite sides of the hole (Coleman, 1988).

The great contribution given by Burt (2000) is in that his work points of the correlation between network measures and performance: although several contingency factors usually affect the network evolution and behaviour and the organizational performance, his study was able to outline the main network conditions that explain a positive performance. The *three-dimension model* of social capital was considered as composed by the structural capital, representing the connections among members, the relational capital, embracing cultural aspect and motivation of the relationships, and the cognitive capital, regarding the content of the information flows (Naphiet and Ghoshal, 1998).

As Goodwin and Emirbayer (1999) pointed out, Social Network Analysis is a framework useful to investigate the information structure of groups. In their work, they stress how SNA is able to understand only the "structural dimension" of social capital or the connections developed, disregarding the content of relationships and neglecting the other social capital dimensions. It considers all the ties in a network as comparable, indistinguishable and homogeneous in content. In this perspective, members of large, dispersed communities, monitored over time while performing different activities, can only be observed in their interaction without differentiation of content-related clusters.

Stinchcombe (1990) expressed the need to articulate a systematic theory of social network relying on both quantitative aspects, based on SNA metrics, and qualitative aspects, in terms of content of ties or discussion topics. This perspective provides meaning to the "relational" and "cognitive" dimensions of social capital, explaining what people are doing, what they are working for, how much they are involved in a specific activity, who decides for what and who proposes a new idea.

SEARCHING FOR A VIABLE CONCEPTUAL FRAMEWORK FOR THE METHODOLOGICAL INTERGRATION

In this theoretical perspective, the proposal of a methodological combination of two different approaches aims to advance our understanding of the relationship between communities implementa-tion and organizational performance, by detecting the organizational behavior of community members with reference to the "topic" of the ties.

To describe the content of the ties and propose an integrated methodology, we mined an email database to approximate the organizational ties within a global virtual community. In this context, different opinions emerged during the last years about the use of email datasets as unit of analysis to represent a network. Email has been established to be a reliable indicator of collaboration and knowledge exchange (Wellman, 2002, Whittaker, Snider, 1996). As argued by Tyler et al. (2003) it is a tantalizing medium for research as it provides plentiful data on personal communication in an electronic form. Different insights come from Ducheneaut and Bellotti (2002), who conducted an in-depth field study of email behavior and found that membership in email communities is quite fluid, but depends mostly on organizational context.

A recent study on Social Networks inside research and business communities (Grippa et al., 2006) identified some biases of e-mail mining methods when applied to monitor a community with a strong physical proximity. According to Aral and Van Alstyne (2007) the network study based on email databases is advisable to address a "methodological puzzle" that historically troubled network research: the trade-off between comprehensive observation of whole networks and the accuracy of respondents' recall might create a bias that impacts the research validity. (Kumbasar et al., 1994).

Finally, in the perspective of the Content Analysis, email messages seem to satisfy the seven criteria proposed by Beaugrande and Dressler to define the text to analyze: cohesion, coherence, intentionality, acceptability, informativity, situationality, intertextuality (Beaugrande, Dressler, 1981).

The case study described in this paper is an "embedded" case study, that is particularly suitable for analysis in organizational field, since it involves different ontological dimensions: the community as whole, especially in the definition of lifecycle, and trends detectable through group centrality metrics; the different sub-communities related to the development of a project; the single members of the community observed in their role evolution and level of involvement in each project.

This study is based on the following assumptions:

- **Assumption 1:** The social structure of a community is detectable applying *Social Network Analysis* methods, by mapping the community members' interactions and applying the centrality and contribution metrics.

- **Assumption 2:** The email database is a reliable source of data to approximate a community's network characterized by a low physical proximity (highly dispersed community).

- **Assumption 3:** The *Content Analysis* of the exchanged messages can track the diffusion of an idea and its lifecycle within a project-based community.

- **Assumption 4:** The combination of a *Social Network Analysis* and of a *Content Analysis* of the email database of a dispersed project-oriented community allows to identify the individual role of the community members in developing each project, defining the community members that cover the central roles for the development of each project in a stated period of time analysis

- **Assumption 5:** the application of *Social Network Analysis* and of *Content Analysis* to a dispersed project-oriented community allows to define its characteristics and evolution, as well as lifecycle, organizational behaviour and informally defined roles. Based on these assumptions we propose the conceptual model represented in Figure 2.

COMBINING CONTENT ANALYSIS AND SOCIAL NETWORK ANALYSIS

Content Analysis (CA) is "a research technique for making replicable and valid inferences from

Figure 2. Conceptual model

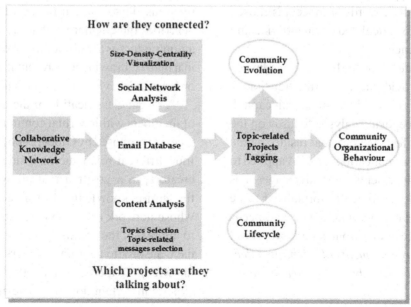

texts or other meaningful matter to the context of their use" (Krippendorff, 2004).

Highly flexible methodology diffused in library and information science, it is conceived to identify the presence of certain words or concepts within texts or group of texts, following the basic communication model "sender/message/receiver". The concept of *Inference* is a fundamental component of the methodology: the researcher uses analytical constructs or rule of inference to move from the text to the answer to the research question (Marsh and White, 2006).

Different CA typologies are described in literature; a research developed within the project of the Writing Center at Colorado State University, clarifies the differences between two fundamental categories of CA, the Conceptual and the Relational Analysis. Both kinds of research start with the identification of concepts present in a text or a set of texts; the fundamental difference is that Relational CA, also known as Semantic Analysis, focuses on the semantic, meaningful relationships between concepts: concepts individually are considered without any inherent meaning. Indeed Conceptual Analysis, also known as thematic analysis, is designed to recognize the existence and frequency of concepts, generally represented by single words: a concept is chosen and the analysis is articulated on quantifying and tallying its presence.

To differentiate ties on the basis of their discussion topic, and provide meaning to the "relational" and "cognitive" dimensions of social capital, we chose a Conceptual Analysis, focused on the analysis of Manifest Content, that resides on the surface of the communication. The CA applied to Manifest Content presents some advantages: it is easily observable, sufficiently formalized to be operationalized in an automatic way, and needs few interpretative efforts from coders (Rourke et al., 2000). "*The requirements of scientific objectivity dictate that coding be restricted to manifest content*" (Holsti, 1969).

In 1979 Tichy, Tushman and Fombrun stated that Network Analysis represents an underutilized framework for analysing and conceptualizing organizations. In the last two decades, an increasing interest towards application of SNA application to study inter and intra organizational relationships followed the identification of the community dimension of actors working in a collaborative way for reaching common goals (Wenger and Snyder, 2000; Gloor, 2006).

Some important measures at a Group level like distance and density (Wassermann and Faust, 1994), as Betweenness, Closeness and Degree Centrality (Borgatti and Everett, 1999) give a quantitative description of the social network structure, while the same measures of centrality at the Individual level identify the most prominent actors, extensively involved in relationships with other network members. Using these measures and a network representation, (Krackhardt, 1994) is a reliable way to obtain the identification of the network structure. As for the representation, Social Network Analysis rests upon the development of the Graph Theory, a complex framework able to translate in formal language the characteristics, dimensions and peculiarities of a network. The main elements that form a graph are nodes, representing actors, and the lines, or edges, representing their relations; the sociogram, or the graph of networks, describes the qualitative patterns of connections among actors as a translation of the data contained in a matrix, drawing a representation of each row or column in a visually simple and intuitive way.

A recent classification of the individual roles of members within virtual communities has been recently proposed by Gloor (2006) who identified four different role patterns inside the networks: creators, in a position that allows them to see the entire knowledge flows; communicators, whose network role is to link external members to the rest of the community; collaborators, who have the task to coordinate others' activities; and knowledge experts, usually the subject matter experts in certain domains. The author suggests this classification by utilizing a social network metric defined Contribution Index (Gloor, 2006).

The contribution index is +1, if somebody only sends messages and does not receive any message. It is −1, if somebody only receives messages, and never sends any message, and 0 if somebody has a balanced communication behavior, sending and receiving the same number of messages.

Recently the concept of density has been associated to the concept of cohesion (White, Harary, 2001): a group is intended to be cohesive "*to the extent that the members are pulled together when confronted with disruptive forces*" (Kadushin, 2004). To evaluate the level of cohesiveness of a network it is sufficient to remove one or more members and to report the emerging dynamics in terms of disconnectedness.

Density is a core concept and metric to the objective of the present study. Following the findings of Burt's research (2000), the identification of the clear negative correlation between density and performance makes its evolution a relevant indicator of the performance evolution of the network.

In our contribution, we referred to the trend in density evolution to discover the organizational change in the community as related to the most evident change in density value. The assumption that "as density decreases the community performance improves" might drive the observation of the periods in which the network assumes a clear and effective organizational structure.

THE METHODOLOGICAL INTEGRATION

The proposed methodology is articulated in three main phases:

1. Initial audit to acquire contextual information on the case study. It may consist of an interview to a community member, preferably in a strategic network position to behave as a key informant. This information must be integrated with other documents and data, to guarantee the differentiation in terms of sources of evidence.

2. Content analysis of the exchanged messages within the community, with the general goal to divide large communities in sub-groups, differentiated on the basis of the project they are working on. It consists of processing the overall messages stored in a database to associate each project to a unique word, or a set of words, unequivocally representative of the project itself. The final goal is to "tag" the communication flow for each project.

3. Social Network Analysis: Starting from the results of the content analysis, each "project-related sub-community" can be observed under the Social Network Analysis view. The outcome of this process is twofold:

   - Identify each sub-community boundaries, by investigating the network structure (i.e. network size, number of organizations involved, overall density/cohesiveness, core-periphery structure); the project Initiative features (i.e. project idea appearing date, promoters, project development temporal length); the emerging characters and positions for each project, mainly through the application of the actors contribution index.

   - Recognize the sub-community evolution over time, choosing a temporal unit, based on both the quantitative evidence (i.e. network growth, number of organizations involved and density/cohesiveness evolution by month) and the qualitative visualization (i.e. actors positions, centrality; emerging roles and hierarchies; organizational dynamics).

The application of both Content and Social Network Analysis required the support of an automated system. For the purpose of the study we adopted the Condor software, formerly known as TeCFlow, a tool developed over the last 5 years at the MIT Center for Collective Intelligence and the Dartmouth Tuck Center for Digital Strategies (Gloor and Zhao, 2006).

This research posed the challenge to use the applications of Condor software in an original way, rather different from its original use. Our study helped refine and improve the functionalities of a software tool designed to observe only the information flow emerging from the network position of actors exchanging emails. Our research was able to illustrate the benefits of implementing improved functionalities within the Condor software in order to integrate structural and semantic observation of the network.

Consistently with the construct validation strategy, the present work relies on the convergence of multiple sources of evidence (Patton, 1987): archival records, that is the email database; documentation, such as articles, deliverables and reports about the community events.

The use of open-ended systematic *interviews* to a key informant, who was one of the leading coordinators in the community, allowed tracking a path of evidence during the development of the study and the design of the methodology. The final audit with this strategic member was the final test of the study.

THE CASE STUDY

The described methodology was applied to a large virtual Community, shaped as a Collaborative Knowledge Network (Gloor, 2006), created in 2001 by a global consulting firm. This organization is composed of 70 firms distributed in 140 Countries, providing professional services in several areas of expertise, like accounting, consulting and other professional services. Today it is one of the Big Four auditor firms, and a very important advisory company. With a strong culture

of cooperation, it employs about 95.000 people, has customers in about 150 Countries, and a large number of partners with whom it develops consulting services, IT solutions, methodologies and products to maximize shareholder value.

In October 2007 the company reported a record financial performance on a global scale, showing a general growth in all the service fields, in all the geographic areas. Consulting services, that are the core areas of the Company overall services offer, recorded a growth of 16.5 percent, suggesting the CEO to plan and increase in the number of employees of a whole 50.000 units, in four years, recruiting them in 140 Countries. This positive trend started in 2002, a crucial phase of changes within the Company life, marked by important international awards like:

- *SAP America Services*, leader in business software solutions, awarded the Company with the "*Partner Award of Excellence*";
- *Workforce Magazine*, leading US human resource publication, awarded the Company with the "*Workforce Optimas Award for the Global Outlook Category*";
- *Fortune*'s ranking included the Company in the prestigious list of "*100 Best Companies to Work For*".

The Company performance during the period 2000 – 2002 was the result of a Company project aiming to create a cross-boundary community, recognized as a good practice to support their customers and partnering organizations.

The company's top management considered the "Collaborative Knowledge Network" the most suitable shape for a community to be developed: a very large group spanning geographical and organizational boundaries to embrace several communities of practice linked electronically in the same circuit.

The idea to create and support a CKN was shared among two promoters, namely the key informant and a colleague in the same Company, who met while working on a new service development.

Emails, and rarely virtual meetings, were the main channels of communication within the virtual community. The language was primarily English, sometimes German.

CKN could count on a Knowledge Management Portal and a repository, that constituted the basic infrastructure to make it possible to store data, and to provide an "organizational memory" for all the production of the community.

Some relevant positions and roles naturally formed during the CKN life cycle: for each service, product or practice developed, at least one coordinator, one consulting manager and a group of volunteers emerged. None was ever appointed for any role.

This community was a suitable setting for testing the methodology because of the following features:

- the actual amount of messages: 5431
- the size of the community: 1141 actors
- the diverse involved organizations: 85
- the wide geographical distribution: 100 different countries
- the length of the period of observation: 19 months
- the availability of a key informant to test step by step the reliability of the research findings

The Content Analysis Phase was articulated as follows:

1. Direct observation of the sample messages: 30 messages over 5431 were read to understand the main characteristics of the language used in the email exchange, and to facilitate the developing of "inference rules" aimed to identify project-representative words.
2. Development of "Inference Rules": the "coding schema" derived from the recognition that in the exchanged messages the projects

were identified always by their "proper names" or "titles" and by the recurrent common features of these terms: never common words; always expressed in English independently from the conversation languages, English or German; generally composed by two terms merged; sometimes composed by a letter (e.g. "e") and a common word (e.g. "ehome").

3. Coding process: It was the result of a semi-automated process, consisting of two phases:
   ◦ Data collection and refining through the Condor software
   ◦ "Preview terms" selection through the human involvement

The use of the two "stopword lists" in the automated data processing let us to extract from 5135 messages 3807 words to be analyzed. The analysis was conducted "by hand" on the basis of the developed Inference Rules, and articulated in an iterative process. Five iterations were made, with a continuous further selection, obtaining a gradual reduction from 3807 to 652, 141, 62, 27, 11 words. The extracted 11 words were supposed to be the "topics" representative of the projects, products, services, methodologies, that the community had developed during the period of observation. From a second interview it resulted that 9 out of the 11 terms were the searched tags, that is to say that each tag was unequivocally representative of a project.

The Social Network Analysis was used to monitor the large community composed of the 9 sub-communities, each one represented by the topics extracted through the Content Analysis. These topics were employed as "tags" to differentiate in the software aided analysis the community in subgroups.

The Condor software was used to select the communication flows related to each topic, to highlight the network nodes "talking about" the chosen project. To each of these sub-communities the intended set of measurements and visualiza-

Figure 3. Monthly distribution of actors per project (actor-projects table)

Months	Project 1	Project 2	Project 3	Project 4	Project 5	Project 6	Project 7	Project 8	Project 9
1	0	0	0	0	0	0	0	0	0
2	0	0	0	0	0	0	0	0	0
3	5	8	4	5	0	0	0	0	0
4	2	4	8	6	0	0	0	0	0
5	26	2	50	24	12	0	0	0	0
6	8	4	36	16	9	0	0	0	0
7	23	10	116	31	7	28	21	0	0
8	11	13	95	83	41	32	25	6	0
9	19	11	91	99	24	34	24	18	0
10	151	25	86	97	33	171	194	12	3
11	13	9	102	78	21	57	50	15	2
12	14	17	85	189	28	77	34	5	12
13	4	13	218	111	184	96	26	9	9
14	3	36	135	119	58	116	20	18	2
15	0	3	146	127	55	102	13	19	0
16	0	0	52	23	31	20	0	24	0
17	0	0	0	8	4	0	0	0	0
18	0	0	3	0	4	0	0	0	0
19	0	0	19	19	0	0	0	0	0

tions of the analytic approach were applied, on a monthly scale, to give an approximation of the development of each project.

While the only application of Social Network Analysis would have provided the picture of the community evolution and its network structure as a whole, the integrated methodology allowed us to discover the 9 sub-communities, and to analyse each of them separately and in comparison with the others.

The analysis of each "project-related sub-community" and the cross-project analysis comparison allows to recognize the overall community evolution in terms of four dimensions: size, organizational chart, project initiative and organizational dynamics.

Size: the overall community made of 1141 actors carried on 9 projects over a period of 19 months. The 9 project-related sub-communities varied in size from 16 to 605 actor. Project 3 with 605 actors was the most participated, involving more than half of the overall community's mem-

bers. It has been defined by the key informant "the most complex and important one". The monthly distribution of actors per project is summarized in a "Actor–Projects Table" (Figure 3).

Organizational Chart: while the application of SNA could have provided only the identification of the most central actors, through the application of indices like Betweenness Centrality and Contribution Index (Gloor, 2006), the integrated methodology allowed a segmentation of the community in 9 sub-communities associated to 9 projects. This helped to recognize an emergent "organizational chart" of the community, a hidden organizational structure of the Collaborative Knowledge Network, with the localization of the central actors across all the projects, and those central only in few projects. Combining CA and SNA brought to define a five levels organizational structure, as represented in Figure 4.

Project initiative: the first five projects were the most important ones, and also the most successful, as showed by the density trend of the

Figure 4. The hidden organizational structure of the CKN

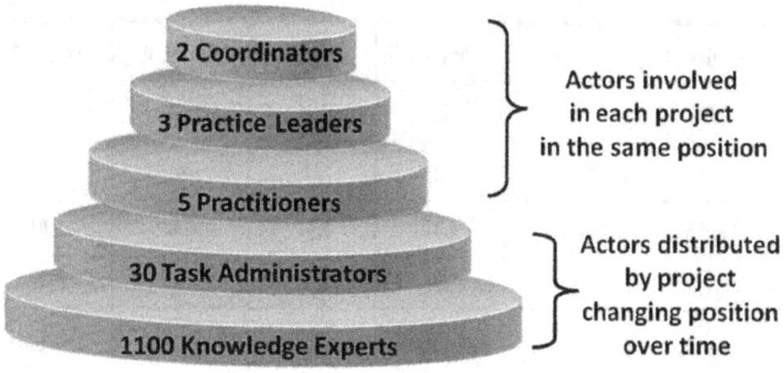

study. They were developed under the proposal of the two leading coordinators, probably because of their relevance for the leading organization, and the temporal distribution of the proposals. The first four projects are attributed to the same month, August 2001, the fifth one to October, two months later. The others came out from the contribution of other actors but always within the 10 most central ones.

Figure 5 shows in detail the Cross Project Analysis Matrix, where the nine projects conducted by the community and identified through the Content Analysis are matched with cross-project factors like Network Structure, Project Initiative and Network Evolution and behaviour.

Organizational dynamics: the community showed evidences of a clear trend in maintaining a fixed core group of actors, coordinating the CKN, and a wide variety of consultants, engineers, researchers, marketing experts who contributed in different ways to the projects' development, justifying the *high rate of turnover* of the different groups. When the goal was clear to the whole community and the project activities started, the involvement of new resources was generally concentrated in few months. This has been observed by the trend in *size* and *density* values, by analyzing for each project the months in which it decreased under the value of 0.1. Figure 6 provides an example of organizational dynamics in a low density month.

The Community Lifecycle

The SNA implemented through the utilization of the Condor software makes it possible to draw the Community lifecycle starting from the evaluation of the trend in *centrality metrics for the overall Network*; the result is a sort of "structural" lifecycle, based on the shifts in the structural features of the network, but without any further investigation on the reasons that could give meaning to the identified structural shift.

Applying the integrated methodology we have been able to recognize what changed in the community evolution when the trend in the *Group Betweenness Centrality, Group Degree Centrality, Average Weighted Contribution Index Value* indicated a shift.

The information flows detected through the application of Social Network Analysis indicated a cycle in the CKN life: it was evident from the evolution of the community size, launch and ending with no more than 10 actors (see Figure 7 and 8).

As illustrated in Figure 9, four stages of development have been recognized thanks to the application of the integrated methodology:

- Stage A: the period from June to August 2001 was an *introductory phase*, where no project was proposed, started or carried on.
- Stage B: from August to December 2001 it was a period of intense interaction, marked

Figure 5. Cross project analysis matrix

Cross Projects Analysis		Project 1	Project 2	Project 3	Project 4	Project 5	Project 6	Project 7	Project 8	Project 9
Network Structure	Size	206	86	605	437	295	281	268	71	16
	Organizations	4	2	18	9	11	6	9	4	1
	Density	0,01	0,05	0,01	0,01	0,01	0,02	0,01	0,05	0,22
	Core-Periphery	N	N	N	N	N	N	N	N	N
Project Initiative	Project idea starting date	Aug 2001	Aug 2001	Aug 2001	Aug 2001	Oct 2001	Dec 2001	Dec 2001	Jan 2002	Marc 2002
	Project idea promoters	Char 1 Char 2	Char 1 Char 2	Char 1 Char 2	Char 1 Char 2	Char 1 Char 2	Char 2	Char 5	Char 1 Char 5	Char 1 Char 2 Char 3
	Project length	12 months	13 months	17 months	17 months	14 months	10 months	10 months	9 months	5 months
Network evolution and behaviour	Not operative months	1,2 15,16,17,18, 19	1,2 16,17,18,19	1,2 17	1,2 18	1, 2, 3, 4 19	1,2,3,4,5,6 17,18,19	1,2,3,4,5,6 16,17,18,19	1,2,3,4,5,6,7 17,18,19	1 – 9 15 – 19
	Max centralization months	5, 9, 10, 12	8, 10, 14	From 5 To 16	From 8 To 15	8, 13, 14, 15	From 10 To 15	10	9, 14,15,16	12,13
	Average actors	11	10	45	48	25	44	26	14	2
	Max actors	151	36	218	189	184	171	194	24	12
	Subgroups	2	0	5	2	2	1	1	0	0
	Central secondary organizations	N	N	Y	N	Y	Y	N	N	N

Figure 6. Project 2 community sociogram (Month 13)

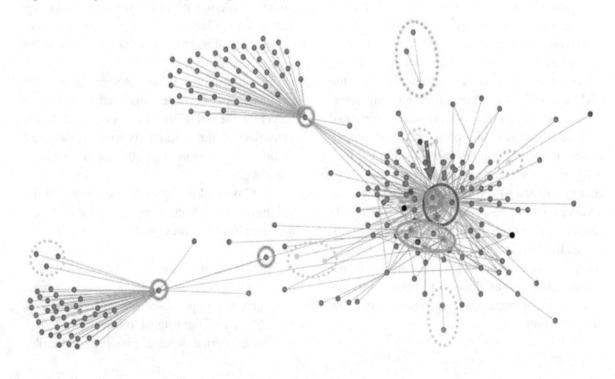

Figure 7. Cross project analysis: average size

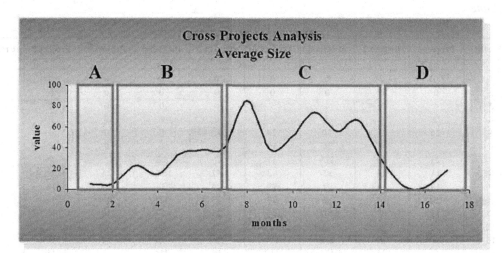

Figure 8. Cross project analysis: average density

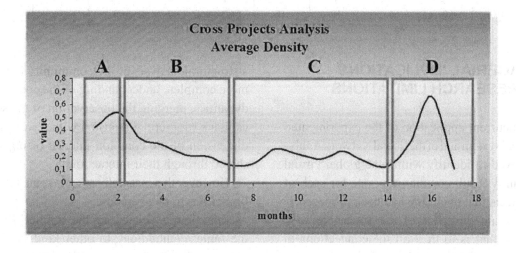

by an *"idea generating"* activity: it saw the emerging of almost all the project-ideas and the launch of the most important projects (i.e. projects 1, 2, 3, 4, 5, 6, 7).

- Stage C: from January to July 2002 the group changed completely in shape and organization, working on different topics, realizing the first results of the first projects. We called this the *"operating"* phase. March 2002 was the most intense month: all the projects were activated, and

the CKN core group decided to start with a marketing campaign to launch the services and products that the community was developing.

- Stage D: from August to December 2002 was the *"organizational memory"* period; all the projects came to their conclusion, the results were evaluated, best practices were collected and knowledge for the organizational memory of the community was stored.

Figure 9. Community lifecycle compared with cross projects average size and density, and with actors-projects table

	Months	Project 1	Project 2	Project 3	Project 4	Project 5	Project 6	Project 7	Project 8	Project 9
A	1	0	0	0	0	0	0	0	0	0
	2	0	0	0	0	0	0	0	0	0
B	3	5	8	4	5	0	0	0	0	0
	4	2	4	8	6	0	0	0	0	0
	5	26	2	50	24	12	0	0	0	0
	6	8	4	36	16	9	0	0	0	0
	7	23	10	116	31	7	28	21	0	0
C	8	11	13	95	83	41	32	25	6	0
	9	19	11	91	99	24	34	24	18	0
	10	151	25	86	97	33	171	194	12	5
	11	13	9	102	78	21	57	50	15	2
	12	14	17	85	189	28	77	34	5	12
	13	4	13	218	111	184	96	26	9	9
	14	3	36	135	119	58	116	20	18	2
D	15	0	3	146	127	55	102	13	19	0
	16	0	0	52	23	31	20	0	24	0
	17	0	0	0	8	4	0	0	0	0
	18	0	0	3	0	4	0	0	0	0
	19	0	0	19	19	0	0	0	0	0

MANAGERIAL IMPLICATIONS AND RESEARCH LIMITATIONS

The concurrent application of the experimented "tagging" system and of the Social Network Analysis allowed to identify within the global virtual community 9 sub-communities, one for each of the projects that over time had been proposed.

The main limitation of the Social Network Analysis, that is to treat all the connections in the same way, without differentiating the topics of discussion, might represent an obstacle in the analysis of large communities. It would be hard to understand communications referred to friendly personal ties or projects-related ones. This can prevent the development of a more comprehensive picture of the community, making it difficult to disentangle the web of many interactions, 5431 in our case, that can provide no meaning and possibly lead to misinterpretations.

The application of the integrated methodology represents a useful attempt to evolve from a structural analysis of the community toward a more complete understanding of the community dynamics, merging the observation of the social capital's structural dimension with the cognitive dimension of the common interest or objective shared through their interaction

However this research presents some relevant limitations to be overcome.

The first is related to the applicability of the same methodology to other kind of virtual communities. The successful application of the presented methodology relies in some parts on the features of what we have defined a "virtual community operating in organizational context", by which we can identify different project-oriented activities and groups, and count on the email as the main kind of message to be analyzed. In particular the email message is particularly suitable to be the unit of the Content Analysis, since it presents characteristics like directionality, timeline, clear definition of sender and receiver, and structured text content. Other kinds of virtual online communities, as the community of interest developed around a common and abstract focus changing over time, made of ever new people, and interacting through different kind of media are a different context to which this methodology could be hardly applied.

Secondly, the application of this methodology to this kind of communities requires the intervention of an analyst for the observation and the interpretation of the elaborated data.

The third limitation to take into consideration is related to the cognitive and relational dimensions of the social capital analysis. The application at the document-level or at the sentence-level of a sentiment analysis (Wilson et al., 2005) could improve the quality of the findings of this research helping to identify positive and negative opinions, emotions, and evaluations, and to map the learning path of the community during the development of the project-based activities.

Another critical point of the research is related to the application of the Content Analysis, as it is a very flexible and inferential approach. Since the *direct observation* of the sample messages could be affected by some degree of subjectivity, it is recommended to involve multiple researchers in this phase. Moreover, the analysis of the social capital of a community requires attention to the cultural, relational and organizational context, which means the involvement of an internal actor, preferably one of the central members, to better frame the dynamics and emerging behaviour of the community.

Managing Communities is a peculiar task, and a strange game: the self-organization principle, the spontaneity of their nature, their being non-hierarchical structures make them something difficult to be mandated into action until they are not effective, traditional approaches to implementation and deployment don't work with them (Gloor et al., 2002).

Understanding and recognizing the emerging communication dynamics represented an impor-tant element for the observed virtual community. These dynamics, with all the managerial implications that might follow, were still in the "black box" for the sponsoring companies, hidden in a large, spontaneous flow of information exchange among the actors.

REFERENCES

Aral, S., & Van Alstyne, M. (2007). *Network structure and information advantage*: Structural Determinants of Access to Novel Information and their Performance Implications, MIT, Retrieved June 28, 2010, from http://ssrn.com/abstract=958158

Beaugrande, R. D., & Dressler, W. U. (1981). *Einfuhrung in die textlinguistik*. Tubingen: Niemeyer.

Bellotti, V., Ducheneaut, N., Howard, M. A., & Smith, I. E. (2002). Taskmaster: Recasting email as task management. *CSCW workshop on re-designing e-mail for the 21st century*. New Orleans, LA.

Borgatti, S. P., & Everett, M. G. (1999). Models of core periphery structures. *Social Networks, 21*(4), 375–395. doi:10.1016/S0378-8733(99)00019-2

Bourdieu, P. (1980). Le capital social: Notes provisoires. *Actes de la Recherche en Sciences Sociales, 3*(31), 2–3.

Bourdieu, P. (1986). The forms of capital. In Richardson, J. G. (Ed.), *Handbook of theory and research for the sociology of education* (pp. 241–258). Greenwood, New York.

Bourdieu, P. (1993). *Sociology in question*. London, UK: Sage.

Breiger, R. L. (2004). The Analysis of Social Network. In Hardy, M., & Bryman, A. (Eds.), *Handbook of Data Analysis (505)*. London, UK: Sage.

Brown, J. S., & Duguid, P. (1991). Organizational learning and communities of practice: Toward a unified view of working, learning and innovation. *Organization Science, 2*(1), 40–57. doi:10.1287/orsc.2.1.40

Burt, R. S. (2000). The network structure of social capital. In R. I. Sutton & B. M. Staw (Eds.), *Research in Organizational Behavior (pp.* 345-423). Greenwich, CT: Jai Press.

Coleman, J. S. (1988). Social capital in the creation of human capital. *American Journal of Sociology, 94*, 95–121. doi:10.1086/228943

Cothrel, J., & Williams, R. L. (1999). On-line communities: Helping them form and grow. *Journal of Knowledge Management, 31*, 54–60. doi:10.1108/13673279910259394

Cross, R., Borgatti, S. P., & Parker, A. (2002). Making Invisible work visible: Using social network analysis to support strategic collaboration. *California Management Review, 44*(2), 25–46.

Cummings, J., & Cross, R. (2003). Structural properties of work groups and their consequences for performance. *Social Networks, 25*(3), 197–210. doi:10.1016/S0378-8733(02)00049-7

Dyer, H. J. (2000). *Collaborative advantage: Winning through extended enterprise supplier networks.* New York, NY: Oxford University Press.

Foster, F., & Falkowski, G. (1999). Organization network analysis: A tool for building a learning organization. *Knowledge and Process Management, 6*(1), 53–60. doi:10.1002/(SICI)1099-1441(199903)6:1<53::AID-KPM38>3.0.CO;2-Y

Ghoshal, S., & Bartlett, C. A. (1997). *The individualized corporation.* New York, NY: Harper Business.

Gloor, P. (2006). *Swarm creativity. Competitive advantage through collaborative innovation networks.* New York, NY: Oxford University Press.

Gloor, P., & Zhao, Y. (2006). Analyzing actors and their discussion topics by semantic social network analysis, *Proceedings of 10th IEEE International Conference on Information Visualization IV06.* London, UK.

Gongla, P., & Rizzuto, C.R. (2001). Evolving communities of practice: IBM global service experience, *IBM System Journals, 40.*

Goodwin, J., & Emirbayer, M. (1999). Network analysis, culture, and the problem of agency. *American Journal of Sociology, 99*(1), 1411–1454.

Gretchko, S., Gloor, P., Taylor, A., & Kleinert, R. (2002). *Collaborative knowledge network.* Deloitte Research.

Grippa, F., Zilli, A., Laubacher, R., & Gloor, P. (2006). Email may not reflect the social network, *Proceedings Annual Conference of the North American Association for Computational Social and Organizational Sciences Conference,* Indiana, USA.

Hesselbein, F., & Johnston, R. (2002). *On leading change.* San Francisco: Jossey-Bass.

Hildreth, P. M., Kimble, C., & Wright, P. (1998). Computer mediated communications and international communities of practice [Erasmus University, The Netherlands]. *Proceedings of Ethicomp, 98*, 275–286.

Holsti, O. (1969). *Content analysis for the social sciences and humanities.* Reading, MA: Addison-Wesley.

Kadushin, C. (2004). Basic network concepts: *Introduction to social network theory.* Retrieved on June 28, 2010, from http://home.earthlink.net/~ckadushin/.

Krackhardt, D. (1994). Graph theoretical dimension of informal organizations. In Carley, K., & Prietula, M. (Eds.), *Computational organizational theories.* Hillsdale, NJ: Lawrence Erlbaum Associaties, Inc.

Krippendorff, K. (2004). *Content analysis: An introduction to its methodology*. Thousand Oaks, CA: Sage.

Kumbasar, E., Romney, A. K., & Batchelder, W. H. (1994). Systematic biases in social perception. *American Journal of Sociology, 100*(2), 477–505. doi:10.1086/230544

Lave, J., & Wenger, E. (1991). *Situated learning. Legitimate peripheral participation*. New York, NY: Cambridge University Press.

Lesser, E. L., & Storck, J. (2001). *Communities of practice and organizational performance*. Retrieved June 28, 2010, from http://research.ibm.com/journals/sj/404/lesser.html

Marsh, E. E., & White, M. D. (2006). Content analysis: A flexible methodology. *Library and Information Science, 55*(1), 22–45.

Mitchell, J. (2002). *The potential for communities of practice to underpin the National Training Framework*. Melbourne, Australia: Australian National Training Authority.

Naphiet, J., & Ghoshal, S. (1998). Social capital, intellectual capital and the organizational advantage. *Academy of Management Review, 23*(2), 242–266.

Patton, M. Q. (1987). *How to use qualitative methods in evaluation*. Newbury Park, CA: Sage.

Putnam, R. D. (1995). Bowling alone: America's declining social capital. *Journal of Democracy, 6*(1), 65–78. doi:10.1353/jod.1995.0002

Ramesh, B., & Tiwana, A. (1999). Supporting collaborative process knowledge management in new product development teams. *Decision Support Systems, 27*(1-2), 213–235. doi:10.1016/S0167-9236(99)00045-7

Rourke, L., Anderson, T., Garrison, D. R., & Archer, W. (2001). Methodological issues in the content analysis of computer conference transcripts. *International Journal of Artificial Intelligence in Education, 12*(1), 8–22.

Sawhney, M., & Prandelli, E. (2000). Communities of creation: Managing distributed innovation in turbulent markets. *California Management Review, 42*(4), 24–54.

Schultz, F., & Pucher, H. F. (2003). Wissensmanagement bei Wolkswagen. *Industrie Management, 19*(3), 64–66.

Stinchcombe, A. L. (1990). *Information and Organizations*. Berkley, CA: University of California Press.

Tichy, N., Tushman, M., & Fombrun, L. (1979). Social network analysis for organizations. *Academy of Management Review, 4*(4), 507–519.

Tuckman, B. (1965). Developmental sequence in small groups. *Psychological Bulletin, 63*(6), 384–399. doi:10.1037/h0022100

Tyler, J., Wilkinson, D., & Huberman, B. (2003). *Email as spectroscopy: Automated discovery of community structure within organizations*. Palo Alto, CA: HP Laboratories.

Wassermann, S., & Faust, K. (1994). *Social network analysis: Methods and applications*. New York, NY: Cambridge University Press.

Wellman, B. (1996). Computer networks as social networks: Collaborative work, telework, and virtual community. *Annual Review of Sociology, 22*(8), 213–238. doi:10.1146/annurev.soc.22.1.213

Wenger, E. C., & Snyder, W. M. (2000). Communities of practice: The organizational frontier. *Harvard Business Review, 78*(1), 139–145.

White, D. R., & Harary, F. (2001). The cohesiveness of blocks in social networks: Node connectivity and conditional density. *Sociological Methodology, 31*(1), 305–359. doi:10.1111/0081-1750.00098

Whittaker, S., & Sidner, C. (1996). Email overload: Exploring personal information management of email, *Proceedings of CHI* (276-283). ACM Press

Wilson, T., Wiebe, J., & Hoffmann, P. (2005). Recognizing contextual polarity in phrase-level sentiment analysis, *Proceedings of the 2005 Conference on Empirical Methods in Natural Language Processing (EMNLP)*, (pp. 347–354).

ADDITIONAL READING

Allee, V. (2000). The value evolution. Addressing larger implications of an intellectual capital and intangibles perspectives. *Journal of Intellectual Capital, 1*(1), 17–32. doi:10.1108/14691930010371627

Bresnena, M., Edelmanb, L., Newell, S., Scarbroug, H., & Swan, J. (2003). Social practices and the management of knowledge in project environments. *International Journal of Project Management, 21*, 157–166. doi:10.1016/S0263-7863(02)00090-X

Castells, M. (2000). *The rising of the network society*. Oxford, UK: Blackwell Publishers Ltd.

Chen, A. P., & Chen, M. Y. (2005). A review of survey research in knowledge management performance measurement: 1995-2004. *Journal of Universal Knowledge Management, 1*, 4–12.

Cohen, W. M., & Levinthal, D. A. (1990). Absorptive capacity: A new perspective on learning and innovation. *Administrative Science Quarterly, 35*.

Freeman, L. C. (1980). The gatekeeper, pair dependency and structural centrality. *Quality & Quantity, 14*.

Gladwell, M. (2000). *The tipping point: How little things can make a big difference*. New York, NY: Little Brown & Company.

Granovetter, M. S. (1978). The strengths of weak ties. *American Journal of Sociology*, 1360–1380.

Granovetter, M. S., & Soong, R. (1983). Threshold models of diffusion and collective Behavior. *The Journal of Mathematical Sociology*, 9165–9179.

Hansen, M. (1999). The search-transfer problem: The role of weak ties in sharing knowledge across organization subunits. *Administrative Science Quarterly, 44*(1), 82–11. doi:10.2307/2667032

Kogut, B., & Zander, U. (1992). Knowledge of the firm and the replication of technology. *Organization Science, 3*(3), 383–397. doi:10.1287/orsc.3.3.383

Lorrain, F., & White, H. C. (1971). Structural equivalence of individuals in social networks. *The Journal of Mathematical Sociology, 1*.

Malone, T., Laubacher, R., & Scott, M. S. (2003). *Inventing the organizations of the 21st Century*. MIT Press.

Marsden, P. V. (1993). The reliability of network density and composition measures. *Social Networks, 15*, 1993. doi:10.1016/0378-8733(93)90014-C

McEvily, B., & Zaheer, A. (1999). Bridging ties: a source of firm heterogeneity in competitive capabilities. *Strategic Management Journal, 20*.

Neuendorf, K. A. (2002). *The content analysis guidebook*. Thousand Oaks, CA: Sage.

Pawlowsky, P. (2001). *The treatment of Organizational Learning in Management Science, Handbook of Organizational Learning and Knowledge*. Oxford University Press.

Rizova, P. (2006). Are you Networked for Successful Innovation? *MIT Sloan Management Review*, *47*(3), 49–55.

Sawhney, M., & Prandelli, E. (2000). Communities of Creation: Managing Distributed Innovation in Turbulent Markets. *California Management Review*, *42*(4), 24–54.

Scott, J. (2003). *Social Networks Analysis* (2nd ed.). London: Sage Publications.

Storck, J., & Hill, P. A. (2000). Knowledge diffusion through "strategic communities". *Sloan Management Review*, *41*, 63–74.

Tushman, M., & Katz, R. (1980). External communication and project performance: an investigation into the role of gatekeepers. *Management Science*, 26.

Varghese, G. & Allen, T. (1993), Relational Data in Organizational Settings: An Introductory Note for Using AGNI and Netgraphs to Analyze Nodes, Relationships, Partitions and Boundaries, *Connections*, 16 (1, 2).

KEY TERMS AND DEFINITIONS

Collaborative Innovation Networks (COIN): Networks created from the interaction of like-minded, self-motivated individuals who share the same vision. An innovative idea is pushed forward by charismatic leaders, who assemble a group of highly motivated collaborators. These people share a common vision, and want to be part of the innovation that "will change the world." They typically bring a broad range of skills and expertise to the COIN and are not necessarily related in terms of the corporate hierarchy, as they work outside of the formal organization.

Collaborative Knowledge Network (CKN): According to the taxonomy provided by Peter Gloor (2001) it is an ecosystem of interconnected communities that shaped as COIN (COllaborative Innovation Networks), CLN (Collaborative Learning Networks), and CIN (Collaborative Interest Networks).

Community Lifecycle: The sequence of the phases of evolution of a community, whose map is based on the shifts in the structural features of the network according to the change in the values of the centrality and density measures. This research considers the lifecycle of the community as a four stages development: an introductory phase, an idea generating phase, an operating phase, and an organizational memory phase.

Content Analysis: Methodology in the social sciences for studying the content of communication. It is generally referred to as the study of recorded human communications, such as books, websites, paintings and laws; it is also considered a scholarly methodology in the humanities by which texts are studied as to authorship, authenticity, or meaning.

Social Capital: Sociological concept, which refers to connections within and between social networks. For this research, it is followed the definition provided by Naphiet and Ghoshal in 1998, by which it is considered as the sum of the actual and potential resources embedded within, available through, and derived from the network of relationships possessed by an individual or social unit. Social capital thus comprises both the network and the assets that may be mobilized through that network". They propose a model of Social Capital based on three key dimensions, Structural, Relational and Cognitive.

Social Network Analysis: Analytic methodology that views social relationships in terms of network theory consisting of nodes and ties (also called edges, links, or connections): nodes are the individual actors within the networks, and ties are the relationships between the actors. Social networks operate on many levels, from families up to the level of nations, and play a critical role in determining the way problems are solved, organizations are run, and the degree to which individuals succeed in achieving their goals.

Virtual Organizational Community: Virtual community developed within or across the boundaries of an organization, characterized by a mission, objectives and organizational culture.

Chapter 5
How E-Learning Experience Enhances the Social Presence in Community of Practice:
An Empirical Analysis

Constanta-Nicoleta Bodea
Academy of Economic Studies, Romania

Radu Ioan Mogos
Academy of Economic Studies, Romania

Maria-Iuliana Dascalu
Academy of Economic Studies, Romania

ABSTRACT

The chapter presents a study made in order to find out how the e-learning experience enhances the social presence in the community of practice. The study was carried out for the online master degree programme in project management, delivered by the Academy of Economic Studies, Bucharest. The main research method was a survey and the research instrument was a questionnaire. Statistics and data mining were applied. Statistics was applied to check hypothesis and quantify the correlation significance. Due to the large number of the variables and the indirect relationships, the analysis paths become very complex and it would be extremely difficult to manage the analysis workflow. So, the data mining approach was chosen. As a theoretical framework and analytical perspective for this research, Wenger's theories of learning in Community of practice (CoP), and the social presence model of Garisson et al., are applied. The study revealed that the characteristics of the online social presence in learning environments enhanced the students' interest for CoPs. Another finding of this study is that for project management area there is not a significant correlation between the learning domain and that of the CoPs chosen to get involved. The reason is that most of the project personnel hold a first degree in an area other than project management.

DOI: 10.4018/978-1-60960-869-9.ch005

INTRODUCTION

Wenger defines a community of practice as a "group of people who share a concern or a passion for something they do and learn how to do it better as they interact regularly" (Wenger, 2006). Members of a community of practice (CoP) are engaged in common activities and discussions, sharing knowledge. They are united by confidence, trust and common identity (Kimble, Hildreth, & Wright, 2001). Learning and interaction are the necessary characteristics, in order to call a group as CoP. The interactions act as learning enablers. These two elements are very much related. The CoP members build relationships, interact and thus, learn together. They share experiences, stories, solutions to real problems, in other words, they share practices. Practice is, according to Wenger, about meaning as an experience of everyday life (Wenger, 1998). The primary interest of a CoP's members is apprenticeship, as Wenger noticed (Kimble, Hildreth, & Wright, 2001). Apprenticeship means learning from the other more experimented members of CoP: "novices learn how to become professionals by being mentored by and appreciated to more experiences mentors" (Hara & Kling, 2002), they come into contact the expert ways of knowing, thinking and reasoning (Zimitat, 2007). New learners are learning through interactions with experienced members of the CoP, but the interesting aspect is that these more experienced members also learn by teaching.

Online learning communities and CoPs are close concepts. Every CoPs is a learning community, not necessarily online, but not every learning community is a CoPs. Online (or distance) education community is a learning community (Fredskild, 2008). When the learning approach is a combination of experience and theories and techniques exploration, conducted by a problem-based learning curriculum (PBL), then the community could act as a CoP (Zimitat, 2007). The characteristics of a learning community (Ragan & Tello, 2005) are: safety and trust, openness, respect – members feel valued and respected, responsiveness –moderated by facilitator, collaboration- in both creation and consultation, relevance – relationship to participants academic life, challenge – high expectations for quality of outcomes, enjoyment - activities must include social opportunities, capacity of sharing individual and community outcomes with colleagues, empowerment - a sense that activity is focused around a crucial element and a desired outcome. The members of a learning community are engaged in joint activities and discussions, as CoPs' members are, too. The common features of learning communities and CoPs are the stress put on domain experience, shared knowledge, shared knowing, the way in which time is managed, the way in which users' needs are addressed and in which these needs emerge. The main difference between learning communities and CoPs are the formalization degree (Ragan & Tello, 2005): learning communities are formal, institutionally created, and CoPs are informal, self-generated. There are authors who mix the both concepts, of learning communities and communities of practice, when talking about a community in which certain professionals are trained. Baran and Çağıltay (2006) describe the relationship between teachers' professional development and online communities of practice. They classify the communities of practice in task based learning communities ("produce a product or outcome and their members know each other. These are generally temporary groups whose members try to accomplish well-specified tasks"), knowledge based learning communities ("compose knowledge based on a specific area. Members of it may or may not know each other personally. There is a long-term commitment to construct knowledge base") and practice based learning communities (these communities "differ from task based community mainly by voluntary participation. There is a shared activity among members of the community to produce knowledge. Tacit knowledge is shared amongmembers.") (Baran & Çağıltay, 2006)

The chapter argues that there is a formal difference from between learning community and community of practice, but the social relationships developed within a learning community can induce to a community of practice, which has a more obvious effect on development professional skills and competences.

In online learning environments, an important concept related to the interaction is *social presence*. Students need to interact with their peers and want to be perceived as being "there" and being "real." According to Tu & McIsaac (2002), the social presence influences online interaction and the learning process as well. They consider that the quantity or frequency of online participation did not necessarily mean a high social presence; rather, it is the quality of online interactions that make the difference. Perceptions of social presence and the corresponding adjustments are more important than the objective quality of the communication medium. Learner's perceptions of social presence are related to their satisfaction with the course, the trainer, and learning environment. Social presence is one of the most important instruments for determining the level if interaction and the effectiveness of learning in an online learning environment (Mykota & Duncan, 2007).The measurement of social presence focuses on the observable behaviors used by the students to project themselves as "real" people (Bulu & Yildirim,2008). Rourke et al.(2001) identified three categories (affective, interactive and cohesive) and the following twelve indicators to measure social presence:

1. Expression of emotions, Use of humor, Self-Disclosure (related to the affective category)
2. Continuing a thread, Quoting from other messages, Referring explicitly to other messages, Asking questions, Complimenting, expressing appreciation (related to the interactive category)
3. Agreement Vocatives Addresses or refers to the group using inclusive pronouns and Phatics / Salutations (related to the cohesive category)

Mykota and Duncan (2007) said that learners' characteristics are predictors for online social presence: this finding is the starting point for our chapter, as well. The chapter presents a study where the aim is to establish a correlation between the experience (presence) with e-learning environments during the scholarship and the presence in Communities of practice, as a professional or personal involvement. Mykota and Duncan (2007) analyzed number of online courses taken, the capacity of instructors to structure interaction in order to overcome the potential lack of social presence (it is more difficult to be social present in an online environment than in a real-life one), the influence of the age to social presence (are younger people more social present in online learning environments than older people). Hara and Kling (2002) investigated whether the people who used IT most intensively are capable of developing a better CoP. Hanewald (2009) studies the social influence of online mailing list to the development of a CoP. Having these studies as a model, the authors of the chapter tried to set their own set of indicators for the social presence.

There are researchers regarding the learning communities of practice in many proffesions, especially in educators' learning (Hanewald, 2009), in PhD and master students (Van Brakel, 2010), attorneys' learning (Hara & Kling, 2002), but we focus on project management domain. Current research aims at finding out how e-learning experience enhanced the social presence in the project management community of practice. The chapter is structured, as follows: first section presents the research context – what e-learning community is observed, the next sections highlight the research objectives and methodologies, then the actual study, based on a survey is described. In the end, the authors try to underline what indicators of

Table 1. AES Education & Training portfolio for 2009-2010

AES Education &Training Programs	Total Number	Online Programs
Bachelor's degree in Economics	13	0
Continuing education (Courses)	75	16
Scientific Master's degree	29	0
Professional Master's degree	56	10
International Master's degree	9	0
Doctor's degree	10	0
Total	**192**	**26**

social presence are important in an online learning community and what indicators can transform this community in an efficient community of practice for project management domain.

THE RESEARCH CONTEXT

The Academy of Economic Studies (AES) is a national university. The education and training programs are delivered based on a public budget, coming from the Education and Research Ministry, and also on its own resources. It also has freedom and autonomy according to the law. AES is considered a remarkable representative of superior economic studies in Romania. The university has 10 faculties, over 49.000 students and course attendants; 35500 - graduation cycle, 9400 - master programs, 2500 - PhD enrolled, over 1600 in academic schools and post-graduation courses and 2000 didactical staff and technical and administrative personnel. In 2009-2010, AES has delivered more than 192 education & training programs, 26 delivered as online programs (see Table 1).

More than 5000 master students attend the AES online master programmes. Several e-learning platforms are used, but Moodle is preferred by the majority of programmes' organizers. Moodle (http://moodle.org/) is a Course Management System (CMS), also known as a Learning Management System (LMS) or a Virtual Learning Environment (VLE). Twelve educational programmes have Project Management (PM) as main topic. AES delivered 5 master programmes and 7 courses in project management. More than 80% of the education & training programmes have PM topic included as disciplines or modules.

The research was done for an online master programme in project management, with more than 300 students enrolled every year. The programme has two years duration and 120 ETCs. 23 courses are included, which are sequentially delivered, in a modular format. Each course has two weeks as duration. A face-to-face meeting is organized every month. Participants of the meeting are the enrolled students, trainers having activities scheduled in that month, and the programme organizers. The project management programme was chosen as the empirical area of this study because the programme is one of the first master programmes in project management in Romania (it was set up in 2000), with a good stability regarding the number of attendees, with a national representation and very good relationships with national and international professional associations in project management. In addition, a lot of interest was rising around CoPs in project management domain (PM CoPs).

THE RESEARCH QUESTIONS

The main research objective is to find out how the e-learning experience enhanced the social presence in communities of practice. The research is based on the following findings from previous studies (Eom & Arbaugh, 2011), (Mykota & Duncan, 2007):

1. The e-learning experience changes the students' social presence in the online communities, enhancing or diminishing different characteristics of the social presence.
2. The impact of e-learning experience on social presence depends on student's satisfaction.
3. The characteristics of social presence have a significant inertia; therefore changing the social presence characteristics represents a quite long process.

The research questions of the study are the following:

1. What is the profile of the students interested, but not involved in PM CoPs and which are the characteristics of their social presence in the online community?
2. How e-learning experience could be a predictor for further involvement in a CoP?
3. What is the profile of the students belonging to a PM CoP and which are the characteristics of their social presence in the online community?
4. What is the profile of the students belonging to a CoP in another domain than project management and which are the characteristics of their social presence in the online community?

The research hypotheses are the following:

1. There is a relationship between the social presence in online learning community and the students' interest for CoPs, with a significant impact on the decision to get involved in a CoP.
2. There is not a significant relationship between project management, as a learning domain and the domanin of the CoP in which the student is involved.

THE RESEARCH METHODOLOGY

The research was done using the data gathered from students enrolled in an online master programme in project management, delivered by the Academy of Economic Studies, the biggest Romanian university in economics and business administration. The research was part of a larger study, aiming at finding out the performance factors for online students, their behavioral patterns, including the PM CoP involvement (Eom & Arbaugh, 2011).

The main research method was a survey and the research instrument was a questionnaire. The questionnaire is structured into six main parts:

1. Organization aspects and technical platform;
2. Motivation to participate into an online education programme;
3. Commitment of the students towards the project management educational programme;
4. Expectations on syllabus and training providers;
5. Trainers involvement;
6. Student involvement in communities of practice;

Both open and multiple-choice questions were addressed. The questionnaire was filled out by 181 students, from 1st year and 2nd year of master. The collected data was processed and recorded, for further analysis. Data about students' activities in online environment and students' performance (homework grades, exam grade, project scores at each course) were gathered from the e-learning platform.

Statistics and data mining were used to perform the data analysis. *Statistics* is applied to check hypothesis and quantify the correlation significance, as other researchers used it, too (McDonald, Dorn & McDonald, 2004). Due to the large number of the variables and the indirect relationships, the analysis paths become very complex and it would be extremely difficult to manage the analysis workflow. So, the *data mining* approach was chosen (Talavera & Gaudioso, 2004), (Waiyamai, 2004). Data mining facilitates the analysis of data when the amount of is huge or when the analysis workflow is becoming very complex (Chapman, Clinton & Kerber, 2005), (Witten & Frank, 2005).

Usually, significant amount of data should be explored in the e-learning related studies. Most of the e-learning platforms have the ability to collect data about the student activities, tracking navigational pathways through educational resources, time spent on various topics, or number of visits. Also, the e-learning systems capture data about the amount and type of resources usage. By data mining, it is possible to discover patterns to be used in predicting student behavior and efficient allocation of resources. Many case studies on data mining techniques in education are cited in the literature (Luan, 2002), (Ma & al, 2000), (Barros & Verdejo, 2000), (Ranjan & Malik, 2007). These case studies aim at predictions of student performance, mainly through cluster analysis to identify relevant types of students. Delavari & al (2004, 2005) proposed a model for the application

of data mining in higher education. Shyamala & Rajagopalan (2006) developed a model to find similar patterns from the data gathered and to make predication about students' performance.

As a theoretical framework and analytical perspective for this research, Wenger's theories of learning in CoPs, and the social presence model of Garisson et al., are applied.

General Information About Students

Table 2 presents the survey items, related to the student's general characteristics

The students distribution was analyzed from the following point of views (see Figure 1).

Practical experience in project management: 43% were juniors in project management activities (less than 3 years of experience), 21% had between 3 and 5 years of experience, just 2% of them were seniors (over 5 years of working in project management) and the rest of respondents didn't specify their level of expertise;

Experience in project management educational programmes (whether they attended or not other project management courses): just 13% of them were engaged in previous forms of project management education (occasional workshops, trainings at work, shorter project management courses organized by well-known institutions), but 61% of them were already in the second year of project management master;

Table 2. The general student's characteristics

PROFILE_INFORMATION_Age	Age of student
PROFILE_INFORMATION_Experience	Experience in the work field
PROFILE_INFORMATION_OtherTrainings	I participated at other types of communities of practice, too, like: workshops, courses, master programmes.
PROFILE_INFORMATION_OrganisationPosition	Position in the organization held by the respondent
PROFILE_INFORMATION_ActivityField	Field of activity of the respondent (IT, Accounting, Assurance, Advertising, Banking and so on)
PROFILE_INFORMATION_MontlyIncome	I have a considerable /enough monthly income
PROFILE_INFORMATION_DailyActivityVirtual	Number of hours spent per day in front of the computer

Figure 1. The distribution of students by general characteristics

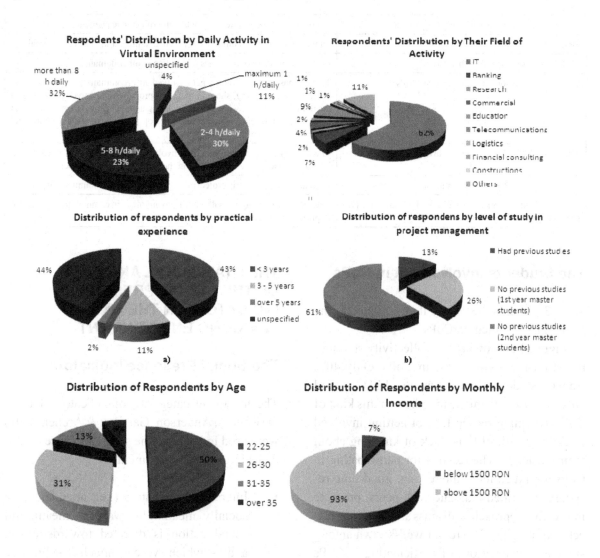

Age: most of our respondents were below 30 years old (50% of them were between 22-25, 31% were between 26-30, 13% were between 31-35 and just 6% were above 35 years old);

Monthly income: 93% of online students have a considerable monthly income;

Daily activity in virtual environments: 23% spend between 5 and 8 hours in average per day and 32% spend over 8 hours per day in front of the computer; besides work, they use the virtual environments for documentation, communica-tion, forums, e-mailing, personal or professional improving, entertainment;

Their field of activity: most of our respon-dents come from IT (62%), others come from telecommunications, banking, research, educa-tion, commercial, logistics, financial consulting, constructions; the most common jobs among our students are: software developer, IT analyst, business analyst, consultant, engineer, researcher, team leader, project manager;

Table 3. The main variable related to the student involvement in CoPs

PRACTICE_Knowing_CoPs_in_PM_domain	I know other communities of practice in project management domain.
PRACTICE_Member_of_PM_CoPs	I am a member of communities of practice in project management domain.
PRACTICE_Member_of_other_CoPs	I am a member of communities of practice in other domains.
PRACTICE_Reason_get_involved_in_CoPs	The reasons for someone to get involved in a community of practice are: quick problem solving, share knowledge, promote innovative approaches in the domain by debating key issues, planning and reporting on sessions held at conferences, introduce, discuss, and develop projects, develop, capture, and share promising practices, others
PRACTICE_Reason_not_get_involved_in_CoPs	The reasons for someone not to get involved in communities of practice are: lake of knowledge and experience in the field, lake of time, others.
PRACTICE_ MIP_online_programme_is_a_CoPs	The master programme in project management is/is not a community of practice.
PRACTICE_Involvement_in_CoPs_in_PM_after_the_programme_graduation	After master graduation I will/ won't stay involved in communities of practice in project management.

The Students Involvement in CoPs

Table 3 presents the survey items, related to the student involvement in CoPs.

Figure 2 is showing the collectivity structure based on the involvement in CoPs. Only 40% from the students know about other PM CoPs and only 15% from them are members in this kind of CoPs The main reason for not getting involved in CoPs is lack of time, lack of knowing about their existence. The reasons for participating in CoPs are much more interesting: good time response, informed dialogue with peers, promote innovative approaches, discuss and develop projects. Although CoPs are not well-known among students, their reasons of participating in CoPs are constructive reasons, which announce, in a way, that CoPs will become in the near future active environments for MIP students.

As we can observe from Figure 2, there is not a relationship between the learning domain (project management) and that of the CoPs chosen to get involved. The reason is that most project personnel hold a first degree in an area other than project management (Turner & Huemann, 2000) and project management education is commonly achieved through postgraduate studies.

THE STATISTICAL ANALYSIS OF THE SOCIAL PRESENCE INDICATORS IN THE ONLINE LEARNING ENVIRONMENT

The Social Presence Indicators

The following categories of indicators defined in (Rourke, Anderson, Garrison & Archer, 2001) were used to evaluate the social presence of students in virtual environment:

- Interactive indicators (i.e., attending in a socially meaningful way). A meaningful social action is directed towards others and to which we can attach a subjective meaning.
- Affective indicators (i.e., values, beliefs, feelings, and emotions)
- Cohesive indicators (i.e. group presence and commitment): The number of platform accesses in the 1st year of study (BEHAVIOR_Platform_access_total_number_Teaching_area_1st_year)

The chosen indicators were similar to the ones from other related studies (Serrano Núñez, 2005). The measures for them are described below and those measures and indicators were chosen, be-

Figure 2. The collectivity structure based on the involvement in CoPs

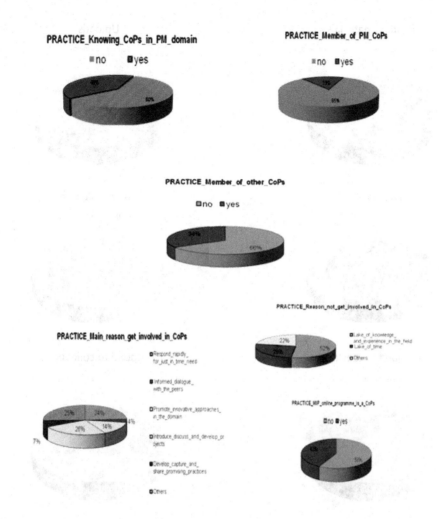

cause the information provided by them could be extracted from a questionnaire. For more aquarate measures or indicators, face-to-face interviews should be applied.

The Interactive Indicators

The Figure 3 presents the favorite types of actions in virtual environment

As one can see from the graphics, the favourite types of actions are:

- *reading materials:* 57% from the students read the materials between 1 and 100

times, 39% do this type of actions between 100 and 130 times and the rest do it more than 130 times;

- *uploading materials*: 36% make less than 10 uploads and the rest between 10 and 20 uploads, in the whole learning programme; of course the number of uploads increases as the students progress with their studies;

- *ask and respond to teachers:* 75% of the students ask the teachers more than 10 times, but just 19% of them respond to the teachers' request more than 10 times;

- *propose to teachers:* just 4% of the students make more than 10 proposals during

Figure 3. Favorite types of actions in virtual environment

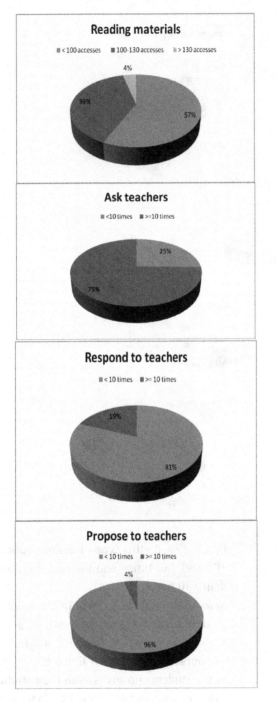

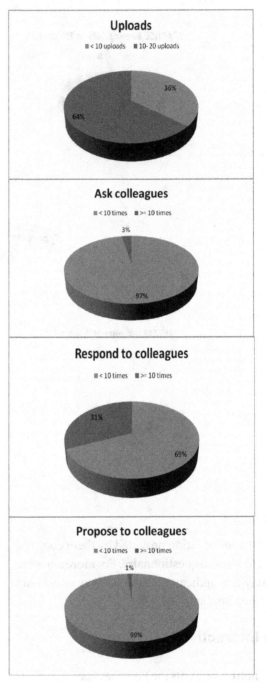

the entire master; the rest of them limit to less than 10 proposals;

- *ask and respond to colleagues' requests:* just 3% of the students ask the colleagues more than 10 times, the rest ask them less than 10 times; 31% of them answer the colleagues more than 10 times, to the online students have a collaborative attitude;
- *propose to colleagues:* just 1% make more than 10 proposals; most of them make no proposals;

According to R square, which has a big enough value (close to 1), the correlation model between the activities with the teachers and the activities with the colleague seems valid: the activities with colleagues depend very much on the ones with the trainers (Table 4), they are explained in 67% by the ones with the teachers.

Other results from the questionnaire revealed that the main reasons for choosing an e-learning programme are the interest towards the domain (49%) and professionally improving (46%). A few of the respondents said that they considered the training to be useful (3%) and the programme to be more accessible than a traditional one (2%). These reasons dictate also the behavior in online environments. 65% of the students prefer interac-

tive activities and just 27% of them said they didn't like interactivity (see Figure 4). More than 50% of them consider that homework is very important. Just 5% are convinced that homework doesn't really matter. The fact that most of them consider homework an important aspect in an e-learning environment proves the fact that they are serious when doing their projects at home.

The Affective Indicators

Table 5 presents the affective indicators (i.e., values, beliefs, feelings, and emotions) used in this research.

Analyzing the correlation between the reasons not to get involved in a community of practice and the age and experience of the respondents, we noticed that there is no correlation between those data sets, R square being very low value (Tables 6 and 7). So, although the reasons for not getting involved are sometimes peculiar (lack of time), they are not influenced by individuals' experience or age. The same result was obtained when analyzing the reasons for getting involved in a community of practice.

According to R square from Table 8 and 9, the expectations of the students before enrolling to the project management master programme influ-

Table 4. Correlation between the activities with trainers and colleagues

Dependent Variable: ACTIVITIES_WITH_COLLEAGU				
Sample: 1 181				
Included observations: 181				
Variable	Coefficient	Std. Error	t-Statistic	Prob.
ACTIVITIES_WITH_TEACHERS	0.723584	0.037289	19.40455	0.0000
C	-3.956399	0.951461	-4.158234	0.0000
R-squared	0.677789	Mean dependent var		12.60221
Adjusted R-squared	0.675989	S.D. dependent var		9.946345
S.E. of regression	5.661655	Akaike info criterion		6.316298
Sum squared resid	5737.727	Schwarz criterion		6.351640
Log likelihood	-569.6250	F-statistic		376.5366
Durbin-Watson stat	1.532010	Prob(F-statistic)		0.000000

Figure 4. Preference regarding interactivity and homework

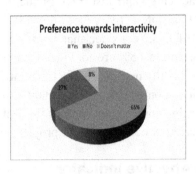 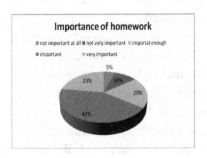

ence more their implications to a project management community of practice than their implications to a community of practice from other domains: R square from Table 8 is bigger than the one from Table 9.

The fact that students know about other communities of practice is explained, in a proportion of 19%, by their participation at discussions from forums (see Table 10).

The importance given to candidate selection mechanism does not influence their reasons for participating at online communities (Table 11).

The cohesive indicators are not addressed by this study.

EXPLORATORY DATA ANALYSIS USING DATA MINING

The Workflow in the Exploratory Analysis

The analysis was done in Weka, a Java-based data mining environment (Bouckaert, et al., 2010). The designed workflow, including the main processes and data mining algorithms to be used on each phase is illustrated in the Figure 5. According to the designed workflow, the following processes have to be executed:

1. The collected data are converted from .xls format to "arff" and "csv" format, in order to be loaded and processed in Weka environment.

2. Using the visualization facilities and the descriptive statistic methods, data are checked for consistency and completeness, before being saved for future usage.

3. The most relevant attributes are selected for the exploratory analysis. *AttributeSelection* algorithm, *Gain Ratio* evaluator (for attribute filtering), *AttributeRanking* evaluation method and *Ranker* ordering method (for selecting attributes) are used. The most important six attributes will be used on the next phases of the analysis.

4. The relevant associations of attributes are discovered, using *APRIORI* algorithm. This algorithm iteratively reduces the minimum support until a required number of rules with a given minimum confidence are identified. The algorithm has an option to mine class association rules.

5. Clusters models are developed, using the *Simple K-Means* algorithm. A cluster assignment can be done and a visualisation of this assignment (Graph viewer). Based on the cluster assignment a new attribute is add in order be used as a class attribute in further analysis.

6. Classification models (decision trees and decision rules) are developed, using *J48, J48Graft, ID3* algorithms. *PART* algorithm was also used to discover classification rules. Finally, the analysis results are visualized.

Table 5. Summary of survey items related to the affective indicators

No	Name	Explanation
1	MOTIVATION_NEEDS_Reason	The reason to participate in an online master programme was: the desire to improve professionally, the interest in project management, the fact that an online educational programme is easier than a classical one, the fact that I have time and I believe that any training is useful.
2	MOTIVATION_NEEDS_Benefits	The benefits of participating at an online educational programme lie in: the easy access to information, without going to class, the fact that I am integrated in a community of practice, others.
3	MOTIVATION_NEEDS_PreviousOnlineProgrammes	I took/ I didn't take other online programmes.
4	SATISFACTION_SYLLABUS_Interactivity	My favorite subject has a higher degree of interactivity. / I don't have time for interactivity. / Interactivity doesn't matter for me.
5	SATISFACTION_SYLLABUS_ProjectsRelevancy	I consider the projects to be relevant for the training, as a method of interaction in a community of practice.
6	SATISFACTION_SYLLABUS_ProjectRelevancyInGrade	I consider that projects have a proper weight in the final grade.
7	SATISFACTION_PLATFORM_Forums	The importance of online discussions with other members from the learning community
8	SATISFACTION_PLATFORM_ForumsParticipation	The density of participation at online discussions (often enough, not very often, now and then, never)
9	BEHAVIOR_COMMITMENT_CandidatesSelection	I consider that anyone could register for an online master programme. / I consider that an initial test is required./ I consider that an initial check of CV or other documents is required for registration.
10	BEHAVIOR_COMMITMENT_TeamWork	The attitude towards team work, as a performing method in online learning communities
11	SATISFACTION_INSTRUCTORS_IdealInstructor	I consider that the ideal instructor in online communities should be involved/ not involved/ doesn't matter.
12	SATISFACTION_INSTRUCTORS_Role	I consider that, in online communities, an instructor should moderate communication/ monitor the master students' participation/ promote the collaborative learning/ offer support for learning activities/ other.
13	BEHAVIOR_INSTRUCTORS_CommunicationMethod	My favorite way of communication is: on forums/ using online meetings/ by e-mail/ face-to-face.
14	SATISFACTION_INSTRUCTORS_InteractivityTechniques	Techniques which should be used to ensure interactivity in online communities are: feedback on the quality of learning (Brew, 2008), creative and open questions, team work, others.

Table 6. Correlation between the reasons not to get involved in a community of practice and respondents' age and experience

Dependent Variable: PRACTICE_REASON_NOT_GET_				
Method: Least Squares				
Sample: 1 181				
Included observations: 181				
Variable	Coefficient	Std. Error	t-Statistic	Prob.
PROFILE_INFORMATION_AGE	-0.014518	0.014186	-1.023431	0.3075
PROFILE_INFORMATION_EXPE	0.001281	0.039109	0.032744	0.9739
C	2.655596	0.382704	6.939040	0.0000
R-squared	0.006511			

The first two processes are considered as pre-processing phases, while the next processes are the modeling phases.

THE PROFILE OF THE STUDENTS INTERESTED IN THE PM COMMUNITIES OF PRACTICE; THE MOST RELEVANT CHARACTERISTICS OF THEIR SOCIAL PRESENCE

In the following, we will present how the first research question (R1) was address in the exploratory analysis.

Selection of the Most Relevant Attributes

Attribute ranking method was applied and the results are shown below in Box 1. Attribute ranking algorithm is based on selecting the attributes which provide the most gained information based on ranker search.

The attribute *6_5_PROFILE_INFORMA-TION_OrganisationPosition* has the biggest gain ratio with 0.13677 as relevancy, meaning that this attribute has the great impact on the attribute *7_1_PRACTICE_Knowing_CoPs_in_PM_domain*. The second attribute, as relevancy, is *BE-HAVIOR_Platform_access_total_number_Ad-*

Table 7. Correlation between the reasons to get involved in a community of practice and respondents' age and experience

Dependent Variable: PRACTICE_REASON_GET_INVO				
Method: Least Squares				
Sample: 1 181				
Included observations: 181				
Variable	Coefficient	Std. Error	t-Statistic	Prob.
PROFILE_INFORMATION_AGE	-0.021775	0.024894	-0.874711	0.3829
PROFILE_INFORMATION_EXPE	0.012771	0.068632	0.186082	0.8526
C	3.694927	0.671602	5.501660	0.0000
R-squared	0.004369			

Table 8. Correlation between implication in project management communities of practice and their expectations from the master programme

Dependent Variable: PRACTICE_MEMBER_OF_PM_CO				
Method: Least Squares				
Sample: 1 181				
Included observations: 181				
Variable	Coefficient	Std. Error	t-Statistic	Prob.
MOTIVATION_NEEDS_BENEFIT	-0.023730	0.103816	-0.228582	0.8195
MOTIVATION_NEEDS_REASON	0.022362	0.042732	0.523299	0.6014
C	1.144273	0.138584	8.256892	0.0000
R-squared	0.002053			

ministrative_area_Class_1st_year with a 0.12617 gain ration. (explain)

The method is based on the following algorithms:

- **GainRatio**: It is an attribute evaluator which estimates the worth of an attribute by measuring the gain ratio with respect to the class. In this case, the class attribute is *7_1_PRACTICE_Knowing_ CoPs_in_*

Table 9. Correlation between implication in other domains communities of practice and their expectations from the master programme

Dependent Variable: PRACTICE_MEMBER_OF_OTHER				
Method: Least Squares				
Sample: 1 181				
Included observations: 181				
Variable	**Coefficient**	**Std. Error**	**t-Statistic**	**Prob.**
MOTIVATION_NEEDS_BENEFIT	0.004773	0.135785	0.035149	0.9720
MOTIVATION_NEEDS_REASON	0.022047	0.055891	0.394459	0.6937
C	1.297170	0.181259	7.156442	0.0000
R-squared	0.000876			

Table 10. Correlation between knowing other communities of practice in project management domain and the importance given to platform forums

Dependent Variable: PRACTICE_KNOWING_COPS_IN				
Method: Least Squares				
Sample: 1 181				
Included observations: 181				
Variable	**Coefficient**	**Std. Error**	**t-Statistic**	**Prob.**
SATISFACTION_PLATFORM_FO	0.016852	0.038016	-0.443274	0.6581
C	1.432363	0.075082	19.07735	0.0000
R-squared	0.197000			

Table 11. Correlation between the reasons of participating at a community of practice and the importance given to candidate selection mechanism

Dependent Variable: PRACTICE_REASON_GET_INVO				
Method: Least Squares				
Sample: 1 181				
Included observations: 181				
Variable	**Coefficient**	**Std. Error**	**t-Statistic**	**Prob.**
BEVAVIOR_COMMITMENT_CAND	0.078456	0.120705	0.649977	0.5165
C	2.960955	0.255189	11.60300	0.0000
R-squared	0.235500			

Figure 5. The workflow in the exploratory analysis through data mining

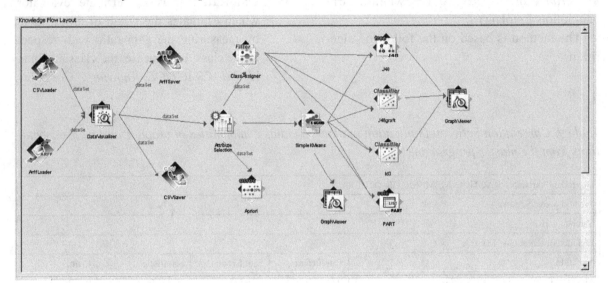

PM_domain. It has the option *missing-Merge,* having two values: *True* meaning that the evaluator distributes counts for missing values (counts are distributed across other values in proportion to their frequency). *False* means that the missing values are treated as a separate value. The parameter setup window is presented in Figure 6.

- **Ranker**: It is a search algorithm which ranks attribute by its individual evaluations. It can be used in conjunction with attribute evaluators (such as: GainRatio). The parameters are the following: *generateRanking* (ranker is capable of generating only attribute rankings), *numToSelect* (specify the number of retain attributes; the default value (-1) indicates that all attributes has to be retained; use either this option or a threshold to reduce the attribute set), *startSet* (specify a set of attributes to be ignored, meaning that when the ranking is generated, Ranker will not evaluate the attributes in this list), *threshold (*threshold for attributes discarding). The parameter setup window is presented in Figure 7.

Based on the results of the APRIORI Algorithm (a classic algorithm for learning association rules), the attributes seen in Box 2 were selected as being the most significant and used on the modelling processes.

Association Rules

Apriori algorithm, used to identify the most relevant association rules reduces iteratively the minimum support until it finds the required number of rules with the given minimum confidence. Given a set of *itemsets,* the algorithm attempts to find subsets which are common to at least a minimum number C of the itemsets. Apriori uses a "bottom up" approach, where frequent subsets are extended one item at a time (a step known as *candidate generation*), and groups of candidates are tested against the data. The algorithm terminates when no further successful extensions are found. The algorithm has an option to mine class association rules. The most important options are: **car** (class association rules are mined instead of general association rules), *classIndex* (index of the class attribute; when is -1, the last attribute will be taken as the class attribute), *delta* (sup-

Box 1. Attribute ranking method

```
Search Method: Attribute ranking.
Attribute Evaluator (supervised, Class (nominal): 23
7_1_PRACTICE_Knowing_CoPs_in_PM_domain): Information Gain Ranking Filter

Ranked attributes:
 0.13677    18 6_5_PROFILE_INFORMATION_OrganisationPosition
 0.12617    21 BEHAVIOR_Platform_access_total_number_Administrative_area_
Class_1st_year
 0.12204    22 BEHAVIOR_Platform_access_total_number_Teaching_area_Class_1st_
year
 0.08736    19 6_9_PROFILE_INFORMATION_ActivityField
 0.05519    17 6_4_2_PROFILE_INFORMATION_Experience_Class
 0.03355     9 4_1_BEVAVIOR_COMMITMENT_CandidatesSelection
 0.03346     1 1_1_MOTIVATION_NEEDS_Reason
 0.02427     6 2_9_SATISFACTION_SYLLABUS_ProjectRelevancyInGrade
 0.01489    20 PERFORMANCE_Class_1st_Semester
 0.01259    12 5_3_SATISFACTION_INSTRUCTORS_Role
```

Figure 6. The GainRatio setup window

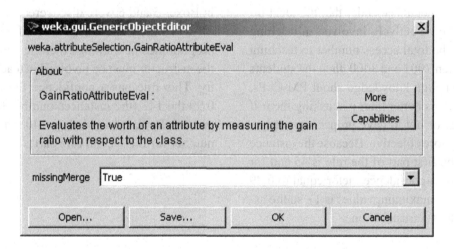

port decreasing factor; reduces support until min support is reached or required number of rules has been generated), *lowerBoundMinSupport* (lower limit for the support), *metricType* (set the type of rule ranking; confidence is the proportion of the examples covered by the premise that are also covered by the consequence; class association rules can only be mined using confidence), *minMetric* (minimum metric score; consider only rules with scores higher than this value), *numRules* (number of rules to be discovered), *upperBound-MinSupport* (upper bound for minimum support; minimum support will be iteratively decreased starting from this value).

For a confidence factor greater or equal than 0.5 (minMetric) and the "car – class association

Figure 7. The Ranker setup window

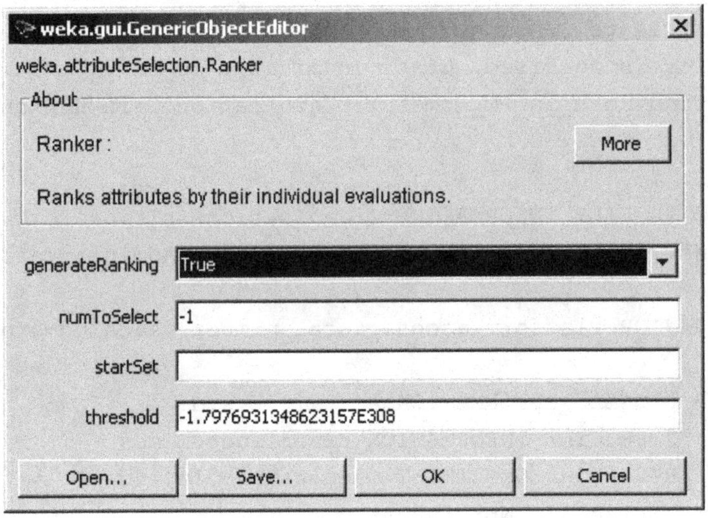

rules" parameter set as "True" (class association rules are mined instead of general association rules), the rules shown in Boxes 3 and 4 were discovered:

When the students consider that the ideal instructor has to be actively involved in teaching activity and the total access number to teaching area is between 1001 and 3000, then the students don't have enough knowledge about PM CoPs. This approach is better than just asking them if they consider or not to have proper knowledge, because it is more objective. Because the instance number of the first part of the rule is 45 and for the second 40, a confidence factor equal to 0,89 is obtained (its maximum values is 1), so the association rule is a trustable one.

For a confidence factor greater or equal than 0.75 and the "car – class association rules" parameter set as False (this means that general association rules are generated), the rules shown in Boxes 5 and 6 were discovered:

When the student didn't attend others online programmes or trainings then he considers that the instructor must be involved in teaching activity. This rule has a confidence factor equal to 0.99:the 142 (the instances number for the first part of the rule) divided to 140 (the instances number for the second rule part).

Box 2. Attributes used in modelling processes

```
6_5_PROFILE_INFORMATION_OrganisationPosition
BEHAVIOR_Platform_access_total_number_Administrative_area_Class_1st_year
BEHAVIOR_Platform_access_total_number_Teaching_area_Class_1st_year
6_9_PROFILE_INFORMATION_ActivityField
6_4_2_PROFILE_INFORMATION_Experience_Class
4_1_BEVAVIOR_COMMITMENT_CandidatesSelection
7_1_PRACTICE_Knowing_CoPs_in_PM_domain   (class)
```

Box 3. Best association rule for confidence factor greater than or equal to 0.5 and CAR parameter set as "True"

```
1. 5_2_SATISFACTION_INSTRUCTORS_IdealInstructor=Involved
BEHAVIOR_Platform_access_total_number_Teaching_area_Class_1st_year=1 45 ==>
7_1_PRACTICE_Knowing_CoPs_in_PM_domain=no 40    conf:(0.89)
```

Cluster Models

Through this cluster analysis, the authors tried to discover the students' profiles that have knowledge about Communities of Practice (CoPs) in Project Management Domain. The Simple K Means assigns each point from the set of analysed points to the cluster whose center (also called centroid) is nearest. The center is the average of all the points in the cluster—that is, its coordinates are the arithmetic mean for each dimension separately over all the points in the cluster. The Simple K Means used either Euclidean (as default) or Manhattan distance. If the Manhattan distance is used, then centroids are computed as the component-wise median rather than mean. Its options are: *displayStdDevs* (display standard deviations of numeric attributes and counts of nominal attributes), *distanceFunction* (the instances comparison function), *dontReplaceMissingValues* (replace missing values globally with mean/mode), *maxIterations* (the maximum number of iterations), *numClusters* (the number of clusters), *preserveInstancesOrder* (preserve order of instances), *seed* (the random number).

The algorithm has more steps:

- Choose the number of clusters, *k*.
- Randomly generate *k* clusters and determine the cluster centers, or directly generate *k* random points as cluster centers.
- Assign each point to the nearest cluster center, where "nearest" is defined with respect to one of the distance measures discussed above.
- Recompute the new cluster centers.

- Repeat the two previous steps until some convergence criterion is met (usually that the assignment hasn't changed).

After using the SimpleKMeans Algorithm, the following results were obtained (Table 12):

The profile of the *students not interested in PM CoPs* (the centroid of the Cluster 1) is:

- consider candidates selection as irrelevant;
- experience class is 0, meaning that the students have experience less than one year;
- position in organisation is IT Engineer and the activity field is IT;
- behavioural characteristics are: class (1) for the total access to the administrative area, meaning that the total access number is between 501 and 800; and class (1) for the platform access to the teaching area, meaning that the total access number is between 1001 and 3000.

The profile of the *students interested in PM CoPs* (the centroid of the Cluster 2) is:

- consider candidates selection as irrelevant;
- experience class is 0, meaning that the students have experience less than one year;
- position in organisation is Project Manager and the activity field is also IT;
- behavioural characteristics are: class (2) for the total access number to the administrative area, meaning that the total access number is between 801 and 1500; class (2) for the platform access number to the teaching area, meaning that the total access number is between 3001 and 4000.

Box 4. Other association rules for confidence factor greater than or equal to 0.5 and CAR parameter set as "True"

```
2. BEHAVIOR_Platform_access_total_number_Teaching_area_Class_1st_year=1 45 ==>
7_1_PRACTICE_Knowing_CoPs_in_PM_domain=no 40     conf:(0.89)


3. 6_3_PROFILE_INFORMATION_OtherTrainings=Is_not_the_case
BEHAVIOR_Platform_access_total_number_Teaching_area_Class_1st_year=1 43 ==>
7_1_PRACTICE_Knowing_CoPs_in_PM_domain=no 38     conf:(0.88)


4. 5_2_SATISFACTION_INSTRUCTORS_IdealInstructor=Involved
6_3_PROFILE_INFORMATION_OtherTrainings=Is_not_the_case
BEHAVIOR_Platform_access_total_number_Teaching_area_Class_1st_year=1 43 ==>
7_1_PRACTICE_Knowing_CoPs_in_PM_domain=no 38     conf:(0.88)


5. 1_1_MOTIVATION_NEEDS_Reason=Interested_in_PM
1_4_MOTIVATION_NEEDS_PreviousOnlineProgrammes=NO
5_4_BEHAVIOR_INSTRUCTORS_CommunicationMethod=Forums
6_4_2_PROFILE_INFORMATION_Experience_Class=0 52 ==>
7_1_PRACTICE_Knowing_CoPs_in_PM_domain=no 41     conf:(0.79)


6. 1_1_MOTIVATION_NEEDS_Reason=Interested_in_PM
1_4_MOTIVATION_NEEDS_PreviousOnlineProgrammes=NO
5_2_SATISFACTION_INSTRUCTORS_IdealInstructor=Involved
5_4_BEHAVIOR_INSTRUCTORS_CommunicationMethod=Forums
6_4_2_PROFILE_INFORMATION_Experience_Class=0 52 ==>
7_1_PRACTICE_Knowing_CoPs_in_PM_domain=no 41     conf:(0.79)


7. 1_1_MOTIVATION_NEEDS_Reason=Interested_in_PM
1_4_MOTIVATION_NEEDS_PreviousOnlineProgrammes=NO
5_4_BEHAVIOR_INSTRUCTORS_CommunicationMethod=Forums 56 ==>
7_1_PRACTICE_Knowing_CoPs_in_PM_domain=no 44     conf:(0.79)


8. 1_1_MOTIVATION_NEEDS_Reason=Interested_in_PM
1_4_MOTIVATION_NEEDS_PreviousOnlineProgrammes=NO
5_2_SATISFACTION_INSTRUCTORS_IdealInstructor=Involved
5_4_BEHAVIOR_INSTRUCTORS_CommunicationMethod=Forums 56 ==>
7_1_PRACTICE_Knowing_CoPs_in_PM_domain=no 44     conf:(0.79)


9. 5_2_SATISFACTION_INSTRUCTORS_IdealInstructor=Involved
BEHAVIOR_Platform_access_total_number_Administrative_area_Class_1st_year=1 50 ==>
7_1_PRACTICE_Knowing_CoPs_in_PM_domain=no 39     conf:(0.78)
```

continued on following page

Box 4. Continued

```
10. 1_1_MOTIVATION_NEEDS_Reason=Interested_in_PM
1_4_MOTIVATION_NEEDS_PreviousOnlineProgrammes=NO
5_4_BEHAVIOR_INSTRUCTORS_CommunicationMethod=Forums
6_3_PROFILE_INFORMATION_OtherTrainings=Is_not_the_case
6_4_2_PROFILE_INFORMATION_Experience_Class=0 50 ==>
7_1_PRACTICE_Knowing_CoPs_in_PM_domain=no 39    conf:(0.78)


 22. BEHAVIOR_Platform_access_total_number_Teaching_area_Class_1st_year=3 31 ==>
7_1_PRACTICE_Knowing_CoPs_in_PM_domain=yes 20    conf:(0.64)


 32. 6_9_PROFILE_INFORMATION_ActivityField=IT
BEHAVIOR_Platform_access_total_number_Teaching_area_Class_1st_year=2  42 ==>
7_1_PRACTICE_Knowing_CoPs_in_PM_domain=yes 23    conf:(0.54)
```

Box 5. Best association rule for confidence factor greater than or equal to 0.75 and CAR parameter set as "False"

```
1. 1_4_MOTIVATION_NEEDS_PreviousOnlineProgrammes=NO
6_3_PROFILE_INFORMATION_OtherTrainings=Is_not_the_case 142 ==>
5_2_SATISFACTION_INSTRUCTORS_IdealInstructor=Involved 140    conf:(0.99)
```

As we can see, the main difference between the described profiles lies in the organisational position and the amount of the activity of the student in the virtual environment. Cluster 1 includes 56% of students, meaning 101 instances out of 181 and cluster 2 has 44% of students (80 instances). The majority of the students enrolled on the master degree programme don't have knowledge about PM CoPs and the main reason is that they are not working in PM.

Figure 8 shows the resulting clusters. In order to visualize the clusters *7_1_PRACTICE_Knowing_CoPs_in_PM_domain* attribute was chosen.

After the cluster analysis, an additional attribute is added to the attribute list. The new attribute is *Custer_assignments_7_1_PRACTICE_Knowing_CPs_in_PM_domain* and it has the following values {cluster1_7_1,cluster2_7_1}

HOW E-LEARNING EXPERIENCE COULD BE A PREDICTOR FOR FURTHER INVOLVEMENT IN A COMMUNITY OF PRACTICE

In order to answer to the second research question of our study, the classification using *decision trees and decision rules* was applied. Let's consider the following objectives for the classification:

- How to classify students into two classes, one for each value of the attribute: *7_1_PRACTICE_Knowing_CoPs_in_PM_domain*.
- How to classify students into the clusters discovered during the clustering analysis (i.e. how to classify students into two classes, one for each value of the attribute *Custer_assignments_7_1_PRACTICE_Knowing_CPs_in_PM_domain*

Table 12. KMeans Algorithm results

Attributes	Cluster 1 (101 instances, 56%)	Cluster 2 (80 instances, 44%)
4_1_BEVAVIOR_COMMITMENT_CandidatesSelection	Anyone_could_register	Anyone_could_register
6_4_2_PROFILE_INFORMATION_Experience_Class	0	0
6_5_PROFILE_INFORMATION_OrganisationPosition	IT_Engineer	Project_Manager
6_9_PROFILE_INFORMATION_ActivityField	IT	IT
BEHAVIOR_Platform_access_total_number_Administrative_area_Class_1st_year	1	2
BEHAVIOR_Platform_access_total_number_Teaching_area_Class_1st_year	1	2
7_1_PRACTICE_Knowing_CoPs_in_PM_domain	no	yes

Box 6. Other association rules for confidence factor greater than or equal to 0.75 and CAR parameter set as "False"

```
2. 6_3_PROFILE_INFORMATION_OtherTrainings=Is_not_the_case 156 ==>
5_2_SATISFACTION_INSTRUCTORS_IdealInstructor=Involved 154    conf:(0.99)


3. 4_5_BEHAVIOR_COMMITMENT_TeamWork=Team_work_develops_collaboration 146 ==>
5_2_SATISFACTION_INSTRUCTORS_IdealInstructor=Involved 144    conf:(0.99)


  4. 1_4_MOTIVATION_NEEDS_PreviousOnlineProgrammes=NO 161 ==>
5_2_SATISFACTION_INSTRUCTORS_IdealInstructor=Involved 158    conf:(0.98)


5. 6_3_PROFILE_INFORMATION_OtherTrainings=Is_not_the_case 156 ==>
1_4_MOTIVATION_NEEDS_PreviousOnlineProgrammes=NO 142    conf:(0.91)


6. 5_2_SATISFACTION_INSTRUCTORS_IdealInstructor=Involved
6_3_PROFILE_INFORMATION_OtherTrainings=Is_not_the_case 154 ==>
1_4_MOTIVATION_NEEDS_PreviousOnlineProgrammes=NO 140    conf:(0.91)


7. 6_3_PROFILE_INFORMATION_OtherTrainings=Is_not_the_case 156 ==>
1_4_MOTIVATION_NEEDS_PreviousOnlineProgrammes=NO
5_2_SATISFACTION_INSTRUCTORS_IdealInstructor=Involved 140    conf:(0.9)


8. 5_2_SATISFACTION_INSTRUCTORS_IdealInstructor=Involved 178 ==>
1_4_MOTIVATION_NEEDS_PreviousOnlineProgrammes=NO 158    conf:(0.89)


9. 1_4_MOTIVATION_NEEDS_PreviousOnlineProgrammes=NO
5_2_SATISFACTION_INSTRUCTORS_IdealInstructor=Involved 158 ==>
6_3_PROFILE_INFORMATION_OtherTrainings=Is_not_the_case 140    conf:(0.89)


10. 1_4_MOTIVATION_NEEDS_PreviousOnlineProgrammes=NO 161 ==>
6_3_PROFILE_INFORMATION_OtherTrainings=Is_not_the_case 142    conf:(0.88)
```

Figure 8. Cluster visualization using the cluster number and the attribute 7_1_PRACTICE_Knowing_CoPs_in_PM_domain

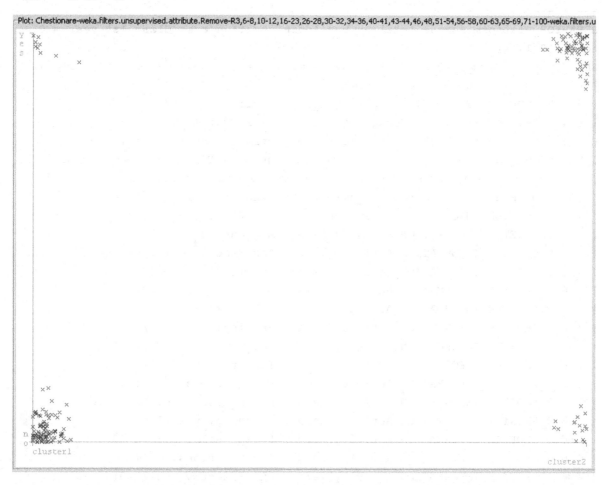

Box 7. 6 most important attributes in classification

```
6_5_PROFILE_INFORMATION_OrganisationPosition
BEHAVIOR_Platform_access_total_number_Administrative_area_Class_1st_year
BEHAVIOR_Platform_access_total_number_Teaching_area_Class_1st_year
6_9_PROFILE_INFORMATION_ActivityField
6_4_2_PROFILE_INFORMATION_Experience_Class
4_1_BEVAVIOR_COMMITMENT_CandidatesSelection
7_1_PRACTICE_Knowing_CoPs_in_PM_domain   (class)
```

Based on the APRIORI algorithm, 6 attributes were selected as being the most important in the classification (see Box 7).

Decision Trees

In order to induce decision trees, *J48 algorithm* was chosen. The parameters of the algorithm are: *binarySplits* (binary splits to be used for nominal attributes), *confidenceFactor (*the pruning depth),

Box 8. J48 pruned tree

```
------------------
BEHAVIOR_Platform_access_total_number_Administrative_area_Class_1st_year = 0:
no (42.0/14.0)
BEHAVIOR_Platform_access_total_number_Administrative_area_Class_1st_year = 1
| 6_4_2_PROFILE_INFORMATION_Experience_Class = 0: no (33.0/5.0)
| 6_4_2_PROFILE_INFORMATION_Experience_Class = 1: no (15.0/4.0)
| 6_4_2_PROFILE_INFORMATION_Experience_Class = 2: yes (3.0)
BEHAVIOR_Platform_access_total_number_Administrative_area_Class_1st_year = 2
| BEHAVIOR_Platform_access_total_number_Teaching_area_Class_1st_year = 0: no (0.0)
| BEHAVIOR_Platform_access_total_number_Teaching_area_Class_1st_year = 1: no (11.0)
| BEHAVIOR_Platform_access_total_number_Teaching_area_Class_1st_year = 2
| | 6_9_PROFILE_INFORMATION_ActivityField = IT: yes (25.0/12.0)
| | 6_9_PROFILE_INFORMATION_ActivityField = Accounting: no (0.0)
| | 6_9_PROFILE_INFORMATION_ActivityField = Assurance: no (0.0)
| | 6_9_PROFILE_INFORMATION_ActivityField = Advertising: no (0.0)
| | 6_9_PROFILE_INFORMATION_ActivityField = Logistics: no (0.0)
| | 6_9_PROFILE_INFORMATION_ActivityField = Commercial: no (0.0)
| | 6_9_PROFILE_INFORMATION_ActivityField = Banking: yes (5.0/1.0)
| | 6_9_PROFILE_INFORMATION_ActivityField = Research: no (0.0)
| | 6_9_PROFILE_INFORMATION_ActivityField = Industry: no (1.0)
| | 6_9_PROFILE_INFORMATION_ActivityField = Public_Sector: no (0.0)
| | 6_9_PROFILE_INFORMATION_ActivityField = Human_Resources: yes (1.0)
| | 6_9_PROFILE_INFORMATION_ActivityField = Teaching: yes (1.0)
| | 6_9_PROFILE_INFORMATION_ActivityField = Public_Relation: no (0.0)
| | 6_9_PROFILE_INFORMATION_ActivityField = Constructions: no (1.0)
| | 6_9_PROFILE_INFORMATION_ActivityField = Oil_Industry: no (0.0)
| | 6_9_PROFILE_INFORMATION_ActivityField = Public_Acquisitions: no (0.0)
| | 6_9_PROFILE_INFORMATION_ActivityField = Telecommunications: no (5.0)
| | 6_9_PROFILE_INFORMATION_ActivityField = Production: no (0.0)
| | 6_9_PROFILE_INFORMATION_ActivityField = ONG: no (0.0)
| | 6_9_PROFILE_INFORMATION_ActivityField = Other: no (0.0)
| BEHAVIOR_Platform_access_total_number_Teaching_area_Class_1st_year = 3: yes (20.0/9.0)
BEHAVIOR_Platform_access_total_number_Administrative_area_Class_1st_year = 3: yes (18.0/1.0)
Number of Leaves:        28
Size of the tree:        32
```

Box 9. Selected branch of J48 pruned tree

```
BEHAVIOR_Platform_access_total_number_Administrative_area_Class_1st_year = 1
|   6_4_2_PROFILE_INFORMATION_Experience_Class = 0: no (33.0/5.0)
```

debug (detailed information to the console), *minNumObj* (the minimum number of instances per leaf), *numFolds* (amount of data used for reduced-error pruning; one fold will be used for pruning, and the other part for growing the tree), *reducedErrorPruning* (reduced-error pruning will be used instead of C.4.5 pruning), *saveInstanceData* (to save the training data for visualization), *seed* (the seed used for randomizing the data when reduced-error pruning is used), *subtreeRaising* (during pruning, the sub-tree raising operation will be applied), *unpruned* (pruning will be performed or not), *useLaplace* (the counts at leaves are Laplace-based smoothing).

The induced decision tree can be seen in Box 8.

The significance of the part of the decision tree shown in Box 9 is the following: In the most cases when the student has the total access to the administrative area between 501 and 800 (class 1) and the experience less than one year (class 0) then the student doesn't have knowledge about PM CoPs (the attribute *7_1_PRACTICE_Knowing_CoPs_in_PM_domain* has value "no"). For

this example, 35 instances were correctly classified and 5 instances were not correctly classified.

The decision tree is presented in Figure 9.

The experiment quality indicators are presented in Figure 10:

Confusion matrix shows that for the first line, 85 instances were correctly classified in class a, 23 instances were incorrectly classified (class b instead of a).

Based on confusion matrix, some indicators are calculated, such as:

- *TP rate* (true Rate - positive); It represents the proportion of the examples classified in class x according to the whole number of examples that belong to that class. In our case, for class a we have 85/(85+23); It represents the proportion of the examples classified in class x according to the whole examples number that belong to another class.

- *Precision*, representing the proportion of instances that belong to class x from the whole number of instances and were clas-

Figure 9. Decision tree induce with the J48 Algorithm

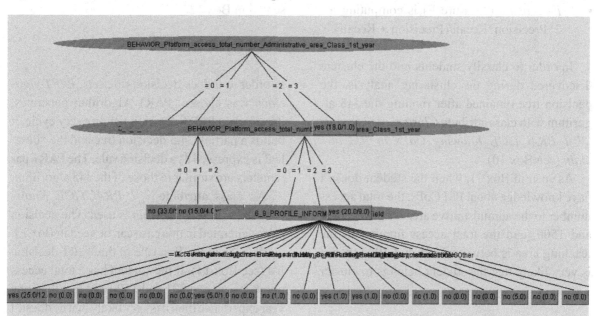

Figure 10. J48 Algorithm results

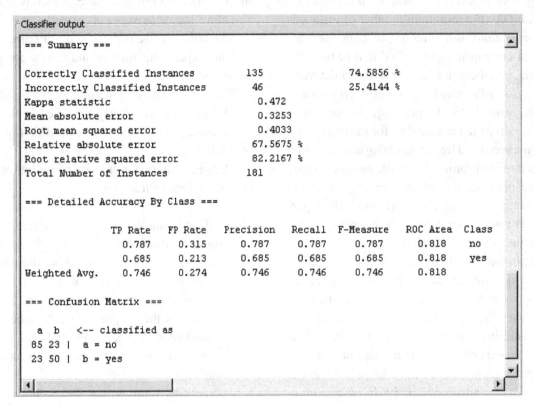

sified in class x. For class a, Precision = 0.787.

- *Recall* = TP rate
- *F-Measure* (Measure F) is computing as: 2*Precision*Recall/(Precision + Recall).

In order to classify students into the clusters discovered during the clustering analysis, the decision tree obtained after running the J48 algorithm with class attribute *Cluster_assignments_7_1_PRACTICE_Knowing_CoPs_in_PM_domain* (see Box 10).

As seen in Box 11, when the student doesn't have knowledge about PM CoPs, the total access number to the administrative area is between 801 and 1500, and the total access number to the teaching area is between 1001 and 3000 then it is very likely that the student belongs to cluster 1.

The experiment results are presented in Figure 11.

The experiment quality indicators are presented in Box 12.

Decision Rules

In order to induce decision rule sets, *PART algorithm* was chosen. PART Algorithm generates, iteratively a PART decision list. In every cycle, it builds a partial C4.5 decision tree and the "best" leaf is expressed as a decision rule. The PART parameters are similar to those of the J48 algorithm.

As class attribute *7_1_PRACTICE_Knowing_CoPs_in_PM_domain* is used. The decision rules generated in this case can be seen in Box 13.

As seen in the first rule of the PART decision list (see Box 14), if the student has a total access number between 801 and 1500 and less than one year experience then it is very likely that he doesn't

Box 10. J48 Pruned Tree using Class Attribute Cluster_assignments _7_1_PRACTICE_Knowing_CoPs_ in_PM_domain

```
J48 pruned tree
------------------
7_1_PRACTICE_Knowing_CoPs_in_PM_domain = no
| BEHAVIOR_Platform_access_total_number_Administrative_area_Class_1st_year=0:
cluster1_7_1 (28.0)
| BEHAVIOR_Platform_access_total_number_Administrative_area_Class_1st_year=1:
cluster1_7_1 (39.0)
| BEHAVIOR_Platform_access_total_number_Administrative_area_Class_1st_year=2
| | BEHAVIOR_Platform_access_total_number_Teaching_area_Class_1st_year=0:
cluster1_7_1 (0.0)
| | BEHAVIOR_Platform_access_total_number_Teaching_area_Class_1st_year=1:
cluster1_7_1 (11.0)
| | BEHAVIOR_Platform_access_total_number_Teaching_area_Class_1st_year=2:
cluster2_7_1 (20.0/6.0)
| | BEHAVIOR_Platform_access_total_number_Teaching_area_Class_1st_year=3:
cluster1_7_1 (9.0/2.0)
| BEHAVIOR_Platform_access_total_number_Administrative_area_Class_1st_year=3:
cluster1_7_1 (1.0)
7_1_PRACTICE_Knowing_CoPs_in_PM_domain = yes
| BEHAVIOR_Platform_access_total_number_Teaching_area_Class_1st_year=0:
cluster2_7_1 (14.0/2.0)
| BEHAVIOR_Platform_access_total_number_Teaching_area_Class_1st_year=1:
cluster1_7_1 (5.0)
| BEHAVIOR_Platform_access_total_number_Teaching_area_Class_1st_year=2:
cluster2_7_1 (34.0/1.0)
| BEHAVIOR_Platform_access_total_number_Teaching_area_Class_1st_year=3:
cluster2_7_1 (20.0/1.0)
Number of Leaves:          11
Size of the tree:          15
```

Box 11. Selected Branch of J48 Pruned Tree using Class Attribute Cluster_assignments _7_1_PRAC-TICE_Knowing_CoPs_in_PM_domain

```
7_1_PRACTICE_Knowing_CoPs_in_PM_domain = no
| BEHAVIOR_Platform_access_total_number_Administrative_area_Class_1st_year = 2
| | BEHAVIOR_Platform_access_total_number_Teaching_area_Class_1st_year = 1:
cluster1_7_1 (11.0)
```

Figure 11. Decision tree after running the J48 Algorithm

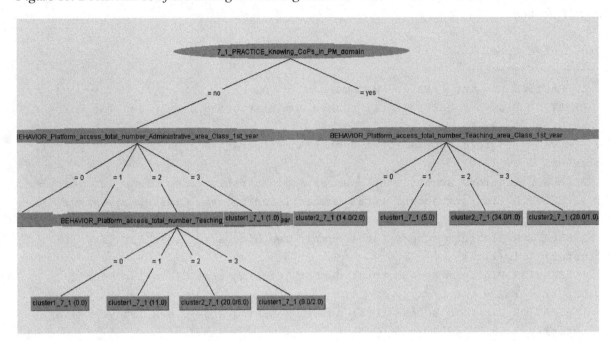

Box 12. J48 Algorithm experiment quality indicators

```
Correctly Classified Instances        162              89.5028%
Incorrectly Classified Instances       19              10.4972%
Kappa statistic                     0.788.  It is a good value (maximum is 1).
Mean absolute error                 0.1359
Root mean squared error             0.2938
Relative absolute error           27.5493%
Root relative squared error       59.1658%
Total Number of Instances             181
=== Detailed Accuracy By Class ===


            TP Rate   FP Rate  Precision   Recall  F-Measure  ROC Area        Class
             0.891      0.1      0.918     0.891     0.905      0.942 cluster1_7_1
             0.9       .109      0.867     0.9       0.883      0.942 cluster2_7_1
Weighted Avg. 0.895    0.104     0.896     0.895     0.895      0.942
=== Confusion Matrix ===
  a  b   <-- classified as
 90 11 |  a = cluster1_7_1
  8 72 |  b = cluster2_7_1
```

Box 13. Decision rules using PART algorithm

```
PART decision list
------------------
BEHAVIOR_Platform_access_total_number_Administrative_area_Class_1st_year = 1 AND
6_4_2_PROFILE_INFORMATION_Experience_Class = 0: no (33.0/5.0)
BEHAVIOR_Platform_access_total_number_Administrative_area_Class_1st_year = 0: no
(42.0/14.0)
BEHAVIOR_Platform_access_total_number_Administrative_area_Class_1st_year = 3:
yes (18.0/1.0)
6_9_PROFILE_INFORMATION_ActivityField = IT AND
6_4_2_PROFILE_INFORMATION_Experience_Class = 0: no (30.0/12.0)
6_5_PROFILE_INFORMATION_OrganisationPosition = Project_Manager AND
6_4_2_PROFILE_INFORMATION_Experience_Class = 1: no (14.0/6.0)
: no (44.0/19.0)
```

Box 14. First rule in PART decision list

```
BEHAVIOR_Platform_access_total_number_Administrative_area_Class_1st_year = 1 AND
6_4_2_PROFILE_INFORMATION_Experience_Class = 0: no (33.0/5.0)
```

know anything about Communities of Practice in Project Management domain.

The correctly classified instance is 35 and the incorrectly classified is 5 (35 instances have "no" as value for the class attribute and 5 have "yes" value instead of "no").

The experiment quality indicators can be found in Box 15.

The decision rules obtained based on the PART algorithm considering as class attribute *Cluster_assignments _7_1_PRACTICE_Knowing_ CoPs_in_PM_domain* (see Box 16).

The first rule (see Box 17) indicates that if a student has knowledge about PM CoPs and has total access number between 801 and 1500 then he belongs to cluster 2. This rule has a very high level of confidence because 34 instances are correctly classified and only one incorrectly classified.

The experiment quality indicators are presented in Box 18.

The main finding of the experiment is the following: it is very likely the student not to be interested and not to get involved in CoPs when he/she has not enough knowledge about PM CoPs, and its social presence in the online community is characterized by a weak interactivity (the total access number to the administrative area is between 801 and 1500, and the total access number to the teaching area is between 1001 and 3000).

THE PROFILE OF STUDENTS BELONGING TO A COMMUNITY OF PRACTICE IN ANOTHER DOMAIN THAN PM. THE PROFILE OF STUDENTS BELONGING TO A PM COMMUNITY OF PRACTICE

In this section, we are answering to the last two research questions of our study, using the cluster analysis approach. In order to do that, we should

Box 15. Decision rules experiment quality indicators

```
=== Summary ===
Correctly Classified Instances          124           68.5083%
Incorrectly Classified Instances         57           31.4917%
Kappa statistic                      0.2547
Mean absolute error                  0.3972
Root mean squared error              0.4456
Relative absolute error             82.4853%
Root relative squared error         90.8405%
Total Number of Instances               181
```

```
=== Detailed Accuracy By Class ===
              TP Rate   FP Rate   Precision   Recall   F-Measure   ROC Area   Class
                0.991     0.767       0.656    0.991        0.79      0.701      no
                0.233     0.009       0.944    0.233       0.374      0.701     yes
Weighted Avg.   0.685     0.461       0.773    0.685       0.622      0.701
```

```
=== Confusion Matrix ===
   a    b   <-- classified as
 107    1 |   a = no
  56   17 |   b = yes
```

identify the most relevant attributes, using the attribute ranking methods. The results are presented in Box 19.

The class attribute is *7_2_PRACTICE_Member_of_PM_CoPs*. The biggest gain ration is 0.154968 for the attribute *BEHAVIOR_Platform_access_total _number_Administrative_area_Class_1st_year*. The gain ration of the attribute *7_3_PRACTICE_Member_of_other_CoPs* is 0.017612, meaning that there is a poor correlation between the attributes: *7_2_PRACTICE_Member_of_PM_CoPs* and *7_3_PRACTICE_Member_of_other_CoPs*.

The experiment quality indicators are presented in Figure 12.

Based on the results of the APRIORI Algorithm, the following attributes highlighted in Box 20 were selected as being the most significant and used on the modelling processes.

The rules discovered for a confidence factor grater or equal than 0.60 and the "car – class association rules" parameter set as "True" (class association rules are mined instead of general association rules are presented in Box 21.

As seen in Box 22, when a student considers that the teacher has to be involved in teaching activity, its role being to offer support and he/she consider the Forums to be the most appropriate communication method and he/she is not a member of a PM CoPs, then the chances to be a member of other CoPs are very low.

The rules discovered for a confidence factor greater or equal than 0.9 and the "car – class association rules" parameter set as False (this means that general association rules are generated), are presented in Box 23.

Considering the first rule, the interpretation is the following: When a student finds a benefit of

Box 16. PART algorithm considering class attribute Cluster_assignments _7_1_PRACTICE_Knowing_CoPs_in_PM_domain

```
PART decision list
------------------
7_1_PRACTICE_Knowing_CoPs_in_PM_domain = yes AND
BEHAVIOR_Platform_access_total_number_Teaching_area_Class_1st_year = 2:
cluster2_7_1 (34.0/1.0)


7_1_PRACTICE_Knowing_CoPs_in_PM_domain = no AND
BEHAVIOR_Platform_access_total_number_Administrative_area_Class_1st_year = 1:
cluster1_7_1 (39.0)


7_1_PRACTICE_Knowing_CoPs_in_PM_domain = yes AND
BEHAVIOR_Platform_access_total_number_Teaching_area_Class_1st_year = 3:
cluster2_7_1 (20.0/1.0)
BEHAVIOR_Platform_access_total_number_Teaching_area_Class_1st_year = 0 AND

7_1_PRACTICE_Knowing_CoPs_in_PM_domain = no: cluster1_7_1 (26.0)
BEHAVIOR_Platform_access_total_number_Teaching_area_Class_1st_year = 2:
cluster2_7_1 (20.0/6.0)
BEHAVIOR_Platform_access_total_number_Teaching_area_Class_1st_year = 1:
cluster1_7_1 (18.0)
BEHAVIOR_Platform_access_total_number_Teaching_area_Class_1st_year = 0:
cluster2_7_1 (14.0/2.0)
: cluster1_7_1 (10.0/2.0)


Number of Rules:         8
```

Box 17. First Rule of PART algorithm considering class attribute Cluster_assignments _7_1_PRACTICE_Knowing_CoPs_in_PM_domain

```
7_1_PRACTICE_Knowing_CoPs_in_PM_domain = yes AND
BEHAVIOR_Platform_access_total_number_Teaching_area_Class_1st_year = 2:
cluster2_7_1 (34.0/1.0)
```

master programme in having access to information without going to class and he/she is neither a member of a PM CoP nor member of other CoP then he/she will consider the teachers' role as being very important and therefore the teachers has to be involved in current activities with students.

Cluster Models

Based on APRIORI Algorithm, the attributes selected as being the most significant are presented in Box 24.

Box 18. The experiment quality indicators for PART algorithm

```
=== Summary ===
Correctly Classified Instances          169             93.3702%
Incorrectly Classified Instances         12              6.6298%
Kappa statistic                       0.867
Mean absolute error                   0.0828
Root mean squared error               0.2185
Relative absolute error              16.7811%
Root relative squared error          43.9971%
Total Number of Instances               181

=== Detailed Accuracy By Class ===
           TP Rate  FP Rate  Precision  Recall  F-Measure  ROC Area      Class
           0.901    0.025    0.978      0.901   0.938      0.976    cluster1_7_1
           0.975    0.099    0.886      0.975   0.929      0.976    cluster2_7_1
Weighted Avg. 0.934  0.058   0.938      0.934   0.934      0.976

=== Confusion Matrix ===
  a  b    <-- classified as
 91 10 |  a = cluster1_7_1
  2 78 |  b = cluster2_7_1
```

The K Means Algorithm was used for the cluster modelling and the results are presented in Table 13.

The profile of the *students not belonging to a CoP* (the centroid of the *Cluster 1*) is:

- considers having access to information without going to class as the main benefit of the
- online master programme;
- forums participation is not very high, meaning that he/she focuses on the main events/activities;
- considers that the teacher has to be involved in the activities;
- not other online programmes/trainings were attended;
- organizational position is IT_Programme and the activity domains is IT;

- behavioural characteristics: class (2) for the total access number to the administrative area (the total access number is between 801 and 1500) and class (2) for the total access number in the teaching area (the total access number is between 3001 and 4000).

The profile of *the students belonging to a PM CoP* (the centroid of *the Cluster 2*) is very similar to the profile of the students not belonging to a CoPs (cluster 0). The main differences between cluster 1 and cluster 2 are:

- forums participation is higher than those of the students included in the cluster 0;
- consider that the teacher must facilitates communication
- position in organization is Project Manager

Box 19.Attribute ranking method using Gain Ration feature

```
Search Method:
        Attribute ranking.
Attribute Evaluator (supervised, Class (nominal): 23 7_2_PRACTICE_Member_of_
PM_CoPs):
        Gain Ratio feature evaluator
Ranked attributes:
 0.154968    21 BEHAVIOR_Platform_access_total_number_Administrative_area_
Class_1st_year
 0.09813     22 BEHAVIOR_Platform_access_total_number_Teaching_area_Class_1st_
year
 0.033309    11 5_2_SATISFACTION_INSTRUCTORS_IdealInstructor
 0.033043    16 6_3_PROFILE_INFORMATION_OtherTrainings
 0.027207     2 1_3_MOTIVATION_NEEDS_Benefits
 0.026129     8 3_4_SATISFACTION_PLATFORM_ForumsParticipation
 0.021919    19 6_9_PROFILE_INFORMATION_ActivityField
 0.020562    12 5_3_SATISFACTION_INSTRUCTORS_Role
 0.02032     18 6_5_PROFILE_INFORMATION_OrganisationPosition
 0.017612    24 7_3_PRACTICE_Member_of_other_CoPs
 0.01551     13 5_4_BEHAVIOR_INSTRUCTORS_CommunicationMethod
 0.007527     1 1_1_MOTIVATION_NEEDS_Reason
 0.006866     7 3_3_SATISFACTION_PLATFORM_Forums
```

Figure 12. The The GainRatio algorithm results

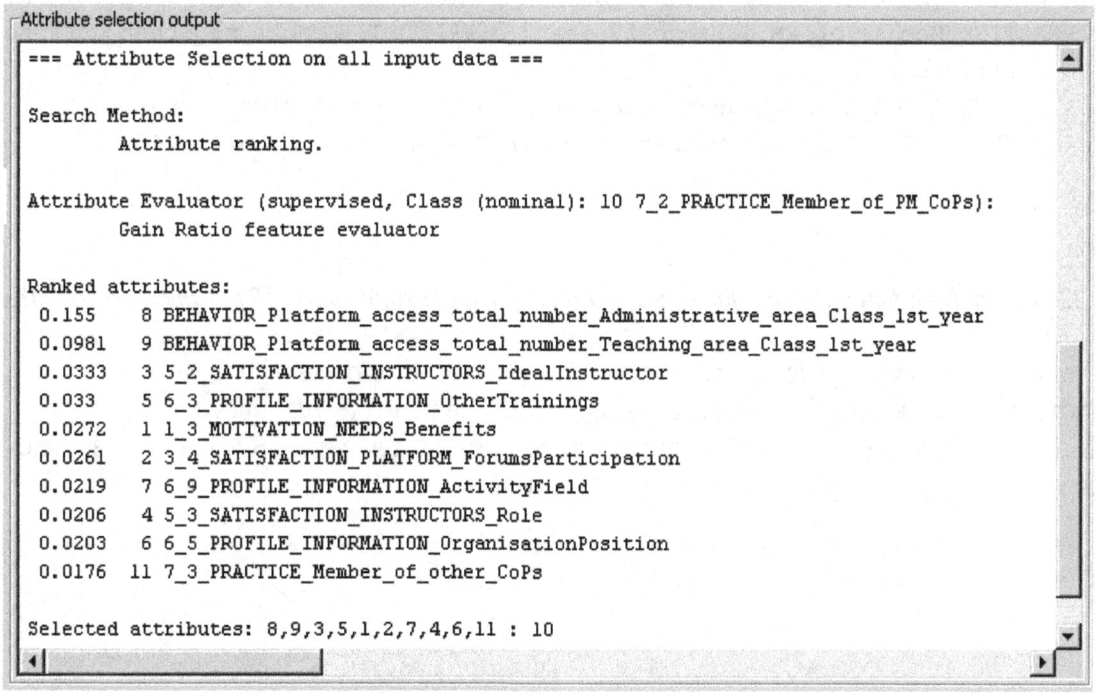

```
Attribute selection output
=== Attribute Selection on all input data ===

Search Method:
        Attribute ranking.

Attribute Evaluator (supervised, Class (nominal): 10 7_2_PRACTICE_Member_of_PM_CoPs):
        Gain Ratio feature evaluator

Ranked attributes:
 0.155     8 BEHAVIOR_Platform_access_total_number_Administrative_area_Class_1st_year
 0.0981    9 BEHAVIOR_Platform_access_total_number_Teaching_area_Class_1st_year
 0.0333    3 5_2_SATISFACTION_INSTRUCTORS_IdealInstructor
 0.033     5 6_3_PROFILE_INFORMATION_OtherTrainings
 0.0272    1 1_3_MOTIVATION_NEEDS_Benefits
 0.0261    2 3_4_SATISFACTION_PLATFORM_ForumsParticipation
 0.0219    7 6_9_PROFILE_INFORMATION_ActivityField
 0.0206    4 5_3_SATISFACTION_INSTRUCTORS_Role
 0.0203    6 6_5_PROFILE_INFORMATION_OrganisationPosition
 0.0176   11 7_3_PRACTICE_Member_of_other_CoPs

Selected attributes: 8,9,3,5,1,2,7,4,6,11 : 10
```

Box 20. Most significant attributes after using APRIORI algorithm

```
21 BEHAVIOR_Platform_access_total_number_Administrative_area_Class_1st_year
22 BEHAVIOR_Platform_access_total_number_Teaching_area_Class_1st_year
11 5_2_SATISFACTION_INSTRUCTORS_IdealInstructor
16 6_3_PROFILE_INFORMATION_OtherTrainings
2 1_3_MOTIVATION_NEEDS_Benefits
8 3_4_SATISFACTION_PLATFORM_ForumsParticipation
19 6_9_PROFILE_INFORMATION_ActivityField
12 5_3_SATISFACTION_INSTRUCTORS_Role
18 6_5_PROFILE_INFORMATION_OrganisationPosition
24 7_3_PRACTICE_Member_of_other_CoPs
```

Box 21. Discovered rules for confidence factor greater than or equal to 0.60 and CAR parameter set as "True"

```
53. 5_2_SATISFACTION_INSTRUCTORS_IdealInstructor=Involved 5_3_SAT-
ISFACTION_INSTRUCTORS_Role=Offers_support 5_4_BEHAVIOR_INSTRUCTORS_
CommunicationMethod=Forums 7_2_PRACTICE_Member_of_PM_CoPs=no 49 ==> 7_3_PRAC-
TICE_Member_of_other_CoPs=no 38    conf:(0.78)
63. 4_1_BEVAVIOR_COMMITMENT_CandidatesSelection=Anyone_could_register 5_2_
SATISFACTION_INSTRUCTORS_IdealInstructor=Involved 5_4_BEHAVIOR_INSTRUCTORS_
CommunicationMethod=Forums 6_3_PROFILE_INFORMATION_OtherTrainings=Is_not_the_
case 52 ==> 7_3_PRACTICE_Member_of_other_CoPs=no 40    conf:(0.77)
938. BEHAVIOR_Platform_access_total_number_Administrative_area_Class_1st_year=2
7_2_PRACTICE_Member_of_PM_CoPs=no 57 ==> 7_3_PRACTICE_Member_of_other_CoPs=no
38    conf:(0.67)
965.1_1_MOTIVATION_NEEDS_Reason=Interested_in_PM 7_2_PRACTICE_Member_of_PM_
CoPs=no 77 ==> 7_3_PRACTICE_Member_of_other_CoPs=no 51    conf:(0.66)
```

Box 22. Selected rule for confidence factor greater than or equal to 0.60 and CAR parameter set as "True"

```
53. 5_2_SATISFACTION_INSTRUCTORS_IdealInstructor=Involved 5_3_SAT-
ISFACTION_INSTRUCTORS_Role=Offers_support 5_4_BEHAVIOR_INSTRUCTORS_
CommunicationMethod=Forums 7_2_PRACTICE_Member_of_PM_CoPs=no 49 ==> 7_3_PRAC-
TICE_Member_of_other_CoPs=no 38    conf:(0.78)
```

Box 23. Discovered rules for confidence factor greater than or equal to 0.9 and CAR parameter set as "False"

```
124.1_3_MOTIVATION_NEEDS_Benefits=Access_to_info_without_going_to_class 7_2_
PRACTICE_Member_of_PM_CoPs=no 7_3_PRACTICE_Member_of_other_CoPs=no 96 ==> 5_2_
SATISFACTION_INSTRUCTORS_IdealInstructor=Involved 95     conf:(0.99)
229. 1_4_MOTIVATION_NEEDS_PreviousOnlineProgrammes=NO 6_3_PROFILE_INFORMATION_
OtherTrainings=Is_not_the_case 7_3_PRACTICE_Member_of_other_CoPs=no 95 ==>
1_3_MOTIVATION_NEEDS_Benefits=Access_to_info_without_going_to_class 5_2_SATIS-
FACTION_INSTRUCTORS_IdealInstructor=Involved 93     conf:(0.98)
253. 1_4_MOTIVATION_NEEDS_PreviousOnlineProgrammes=NO 7_2_PRACTICE_Mem-
ber_of_PM_CoPs=no 137 ==> 1_3_MOTIVATION_NEEDS_Benefits=Access_to_info_with-
out_going_to_class 5_2_SATISFACTION_INSTRUCTORS_IdealInstructor=Involved 133
conf:(0.97)
254. 2_3_SATISFACTION_SYLLABUS_Interactivity=YES 7_2_PRACTICE_Member_of_PM_
CoPs=no 99 ==> 1_3_MOTIVATION_NEEDS_Benefits=Access_to_info_without_going_to_
class 5_2_SATISFACTION_INSTRUCTORS_IdealInstructor=Involved 96     conf:(0.97)
```

Box 24. Most significant attributes for Cluster Models when using APRIORI algorithm

```
21 BEHAVIOR_Platform_access_total_number_Administrative_area_Class_1st_year
22 BEHAVIOR_Platform_access_total_number_Teaching_area_Class_1st_year
11 5_2_SATISFACTION_INSTRUCTORS_IdealInstructor
16 6_3_PROFILE_INFORMATION_OtherTrainings
2 1_3_MOTIVATION_NEEDS_Benefits
8 3_4_SATISFACTION_PLATFORM_ForumsParticipation
19 6_9_PROFILE_INFORMATION_ActivityField
12 5_3_SATISFACTION_INSTRUCTORS_Role
18 6_5_PROFILE_INFORMATION_OrganisationPosition
24 7_3_PRACTICE_Member_of_other_CoPs
```

- class (3) for the total activity in the platform teaching area (over 1301 platform access).

The profile of the *students belonging to a CoP not in PM domain* (the centroid of the *Cluster 3*) is:

- Like the students from cluster 1 and 2, he/she considers that the main benefit of online master programme is having access to information without going to class, teacher has to be involved in the activities,

he/she did not attend any previous online programmes/trainings,

- class (0) for the total activity in the administrative area (meaning that he has less that 500 accesses) and class (0) for the activity in teaching area (less that 1000 accesses);
- Activity domain is Commercial and position in organisation is IT_Engineer;

Cluster 1 has 71% of instances, meaning 101 instances. Cluster 2 has 15% of instances having 28 instances. Cluster 3 has 25% of instances having 25

Table 13. Cluster models based on SimpleKMeans Algorithm

Attributes	Cluster 1 (128 instances, 71%)	Cluster 2 (28 instances, 15%)	Cluster 3 (25 instances, 14%)
1_3_MOTIVATION_NEEDS_Benefits	Access_to_info_without_going_to_class	Access_to_info_without_going_to_class	Access_to_info_without_going_to_class
3_4_SATISFACTION_PLATFORM_ForumsParticipation	Not_very_often	Now_and_then	Not_very_often
5_2_SATISFACTION_INSTRUCTORS_IdealInstructor	Involved	Involved	Involved
5_3_SATISFACTION_INSTRUCTORS_Role	Offers_support	Facilitates_communication	Offers_support
6_3_PROFILE_INFORMATION_OtherTrainings	Is_not_the_case	Is_not_the_case	Is_not_the_case
6_5_PROFILE_INFORMATION_OrganisationPosition	IT_Programmer	Project_Manager	IT_Engineer
6_9_PROFILE_INFORMATION_ActivityField	IT	IT	Commercial
BEHAVIOR_Platform_access_total_number_Administrative_area_Class_1st_year	2	2	0
BEHAVIOR_Platform_access_total_number_Teaching_area_Class_1st_year	2	3	0
7_2_PRACTICE_Member_of_PM_CoPs	no	yes	no
7_3_PRACTICE_Member_of_other_CoPs	no	no	yes

instances. The profiles described by the centroids of the cluster 0 and cluster represent 86% of the entire group of students, we can consider that in near future, most of them will become member of a community of Practice in Project Management or at least, will have to deal with some CoPs.

The relationship between the most important factor *1_3_MOTIVATION_NEEDS_Benefits* and the attribute *7_2_PRACTICE_Member_of_PM_CoPs* is shown in Figure 13.

Classification Using Decision Tree

ID3 algorithm was used with 7_2_PRACTICE_Member_of_PM_CoPs as the class attribute. A fragment of the induced decision tree is presented in Box 25.

According to the decision tree branch highlighted in Box 26, if the class for the activity in administrative area is 2 (total access number is between 801 and 1500) and the position in organization is IT_Programmer and the forums par-

ticipation is not high and the trainer role has to be offering support and the class for the activity in the teaching area is 2 (the total access number is between 3001 and 4000) and the student is not a member of a CoP then the class attribute has the value "no".

The experiment quality indicators are presented in Box 27.

Confusion matrix shows that for the first line, 134 instances were correctly classified in class a, 12 instances were incorrectly classified in class b instead of a.

Classification Using Decision Rules

The PART algorithm was applied with the attribute *7_2_PRACTICE_Member_of_PM_CoPs* as class attribute. The decision rule set generated is presented in Box 28.

The first rule indicates that if the class for the activity in the administrative area is 3 (the total access number is over 1501) and the student is

Figure 13. Relation between the most important factor 1_3_MOTIVATION_NEEDS_Benefits and the 7_2_PRACTICE_Member_of_PM_CoPs

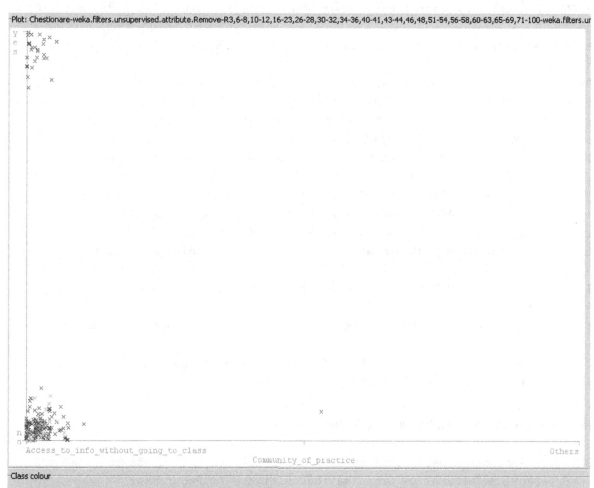

not a member of CoPs and the forum participation is not very high then the class attribute (7_2_PRACTICE_Member_of_PM_CoPs) has the value "yes" (the student is member of a PM CoPs).

The experiment quality indicators are presented in Box 29.

Confusion matrix shows in the first line that 141 instances were correctly classified in class a, 12 instances were incorrectly classified in class b instead of a. 9 instances were correctly classified in class b and 19 instances were incorrectly classified in class a instead of b.

FUTURE DEVELOPMENT

The study will be followed by another research, having as an objective to model the influence of the social presence characteristics on the students' engagement into the CoPs. Based on this model the authors will make predictions about the social presence of the students in the online master programme community. The model will then be checked, by applying it at other master programme communities, as

Arbaugh did. (Arbaugh, 2004) Also, the cooperation with the national association in project

Box 25. Fragment of induced decision tree using ID3 algorithm

```
BEHAVIOR_Platform_access_total_number_Administrative_area_Class_1st_year = 0:
no
BEHAVIOR_Platform_access_total_number_Administrative_area_Class_1st_year = 1:
no
BEHAVIOR_Platform_access_total_number_Administrative_area_Class_1st_year = 2
|   6_5_PROFILE_INFORMATION_OrganisationPosition = IT_Programmer
|   |   3_4_SATISFACTION_PLATFORM_ForumsParticipation = Often_enough: no
|   |   3_4_SATISFACTION_PLATFORM_ForumsParticipation = Not_very_often: no
|   |   3_4_SATISFACTION_PLATFORM_ForumsParticipation = Now_and_then
|   |   |   5_3_SATISFACTION_INSTRUCTORS_Role = Facilitates_communication: no
|   |   |   5_3_SATISFACTION_INSTRUCTORS_Role = Monitors_participation: null
|   |   |   5_3_SATISFACTION_INSTRUCTORS_Role = Promotes_collaboration: null
|   |   |   5_3_SATISFACTION_INSTRUCTORS_Role = Offers_support
|   |   |   |   BEHAVIOR_Platform_access_total_number_Teaching_area_Class_1st_year
= 0: null
|   |   |   |   BEHAVIOR_Platform_access_total_number_Teaching_area_Class_1st_year
= 1: null
|   |   |   |   BEHAVIOR_Platform_access_total_number_Teaching_area_Class_1st_year
= 2
|   |   |   |   |   7_3_PRACTICE_Member_of_other_CoPs = no: no
|   |   |   |   |   7_3_PRACTICE_Member_of_other_CoPs = yes: yes
```

Box 26. Decision tree branch with value of "no"

```
BEHAVIOR_Platform_access_total_number_Administrative_area_Class_1st_year = 2
|   6_5_PROFILE_INFORMATION_OrganisationPosition = IT_Programmer
|   |   3_4_SATISFACTION_PLATFORM_ForumsParticipation = Now_and_then
|   |   |   5_3_SATISFACTION_INSTRUCTORS_Role = Offers_support
|   |   |   |   BEHAVIOR_Platform_access_total_number_Teaching_area_Class_1st_year
= 2
|   |   |   |   |   7_3_PRACTICE_Member_of_other_CoPs = no: no
```

management will be proposed, to find solutions for increasing students' interest for engagement in networks of professionals in project management.

As Wegner (2006) said, "the perspective of communities of practice affects educational practices along three dimensions": internally, externally, and over the lifetime of students. Our aim is to enhance each of these dimensions, by:

- Internally: by offering the training and the help needed by the online students, to increase their social presence within the e-learning platform; these training will be guided by the indicators of social presence which seem to matter most for the students;
- Externally: connect the experience of students to actual practice in broader commu-

Box 27. Experiment quality indicators for classification using decision tree

```
Correctly Classified Instances        139          76.7956%
Incorrectly Classified Instances       28          15.4696%
Kappa statistic                    0.7697
Mean absolute error                0.1647
Root mean squared error            0.4039
Relative absolute error           72.9144%
Root relative squared erro       126.1544%
UnClassified Instances                 14           7.7348%
Total Number of Instances             181
```

```
=== Detailed Accuracy By Class ===
                TP Rate  FP Rate  Precision  Recall  F-Measure  ROC Area  Class
                0.918    0.762    0.893      0.918   0.905      0.668     no
                0.238    0.082    0.294      0.238   0.263      0.567     yes
Weighted Avg.   0.832    0.676    0.818      0.832   0.825      0.655
```

```
=== Confusion Matrix ===
   a    b   <-- classified as
 134   12 |   a = no
  16    5 |   b = yes
```

Box 28. Decision rule set generated using PART algorithm with class attribute of 7_2_PRACTICE_Member_of_PM_CoPs

```
BEHAVIOR_Platform_access_total_number_Administrative_area_Class_1st_year = 3 AND
7_3_PRACTICE_Member_of_other_CoPs = no AND
3_4_SATISFACTION_PLATFORM_ForumsParticipation = Not_very_often: yes (5.0)

BEHAVIOR_Platform_access_total_number_Teaching_area_Class_1st_year = 2 AND
6_9_PROFILE_INFORMATION_ActivityField = IT AND
7_3_PRACTICE_Member_of_other_CoPs = yes: no (6.0)

6_9_PROFILE_INFORMATION_ActivityField = IT AND
6_5_PROFILE_INFORMATION_OrganisationPosition = IT_Consultant AND
7_3_PRACTICE_Member_of_other_CoPs = no: yes (2.0)

6_9_PROFILE_INFORMATION_ActivityField = IT AND
7_3_PRACTICE_Member_of_other_CoPs = no AND
3_4_SATISFACTION_PLATFORM_ForumsParticipation = Not_very_often: no (2.0/1.0)
```

Box 29. Experiment quality indicators for classification using decision rules

```
Correctly Classified Instances          150              82.8729%
Incorrectly Classified Instances          31              17.1271%
Kappa statistic                       0.2706
Mean absolute error                   0.1607
Root mean squared error               0.3629
Relative absolute error              60.7432%
Root relative squared error         100.3133%
Total Number of Instances                181

=== Detailed Accuracy By Class ===
          TP Rate    FP Rate   Precision   Recall   F-Measure   ROC Area   Class
           0.922      0.679      0.881      0.922     0.901       0.742     no
           0.321      0.078      0.429      0.321     0.367       0.742     yes
Weighted Avg.0.829     0.586      0.811      0.829     0.818       0.742

=== Confusion Matrix ===
  a    b    <-- classified as
 141   12  |   a = no
  19    9  |   b = yes
```

nities, by establishing a continuous form of communication between the MIP students and the member of Romanian associations of project management;

• Over the lifetime of students: by keeping a forum, to which former students can have access and by giving access to former students to MIP resources;

CONCLUSION

The study reveals interesting correlations and patterns existing in data. Statistics analysis of the social presence shows that the activities with colleagues depend very much on the ones with the trainers. So the influence of trainers in online enviroments is even higher than in the classical ones, concearning the students' behaviour.

Analyzing the correlation between the reasons not to get involved in a community of practice and the age and experience of the respondents, we noticed that there is no correlation between those data sets. So, although the reasons for not getting involved are sometimes peculiar (lack of time), they are not influenced by individuals' experience or age. The same result was obtained when analyzing the reasons for getting involved in a community of practice. The expectations of the students before enrolling to the project management master programme influence more their implications to a project management community of practice than their implications to a community of practice from other domains. The fact that students know about other communities of practice is explained, in a proportion of 19%, by their participation at discussions from forums.

Based on data mining algorithms, the selection of the most important attribute for the profile of the students interested in PM CoPs was done. These attributes are: position in organization, activity volume in the first year in the administrative site area (showing the student interest for the administrative issues), and activity volume in the first year in the teaching site area, experience, knowing other CoPs in PM domain. These findings can be used when creating a new community of practice. Sometimes, the development of a CoP can fail, because the individuals invited to join the community aren't interested or don't have the right profile for it. The profiling of the students can be generalized and used as a pattern when searching for CoP followers.

Association rules and cluster models were developed. Based on that, the profile of the students being/not being interested in PM CoPs was defined. The student interested in PM CoPs considerss that the candidates' selection is irrelevant.. Regarding the behavioural characteristics, the student accessed the platform a lot (meaning that the total access number is between 801 and 1500) and especially the teaching area (total access number is between 3001 and 4000).

The profile of the students not belonging to a CoP is as following:

1. considers having access to information without going to class as the main benefit of the online master programme;
2. forums participation is not very high, meaning that he/she focuses on the main events/ activities;
3. considers that the teacher has to be involved in the activities;
4. not other online programmes/trainings were attended;
5. organizational position is IT_Programme and the activity domains is IT;
6. behavioural characteristics: he/she accesses the platform a lot area (the total access number is between 801 and 1500) and especially the teaching area (the total access number is between 3001 and 4000).

The profile of the students belonging only to a PM CoP is very similar to the profile of the students not belonging to a CoPs. The main differences are:

1. forums participation is higher than those of the students incnot belonging to a CoPs;
2. considers that the teacher must facilitates communication;
3. position in organization is Project Manager;
4. the total activity in the platform teaching area is high enough(over 1301 platform access).

The fact that the profile of the students who don't belong to any CoP is similar to the ones belonging to a PM CoP proves that the PM CoPs should be more developed in the future. So, collaboration to a project management association in developing a national PM CoP would be a nice follow-up for this study.

The profile of the students belonging to a CoP but not in project management is:

1. he/she considers that the main benefit of online master programme is having access to information without going to class, teacher has to be involved in the activities, he/she did not attend any previous online programmes/ trainings, not much total activity in the administrative area (meaning that he/she has less that 500 accesses) and less activity in the teaching area (less that 1000 accesses);
2. Activity domain is Commercial and position in organisation is IT Engineer;

The study revealed that the characteristics of the online social presence in learning environments enhanced the students' interest for CoPs. Also, the characteristics of the online social presence in learning environments have a significant correlation with the students' decision to get involved in CoPs. There is not a significant correlation between the learning domain and that of the CoPs chosen to get involved.

The Wenger' "legitimate peripheral participation", a feature of CoP, is present in MIP environment, this fact proving that MIP, as an online learning community, can be considered a solid base for developing a PM CoP. By analyzing the students' participation in forums, we noticed that students tend to ask each other first and then, they ask the tutor. This pattern of interaction was noticed by Zimitat (2007) also, in another case study, and it is a characteristic of an incipient CoP: "The less-experienced students tended to consult each other first, before asking the more experienced, already practicing midwives about the case study. In turn the midwives tended to consult each other first before asking the lecturer. The case study design and learning environment both modeled and facilitated learning as if in a CoP" (Zimitat, 2007).

REFERENCES

Arbaugh, J. B. (2004). Learning to learn online: A study of perceptual changes between multiple online course experiences. *The Internet and Higher Education*, *7*, 169–182. doi:10.1016/j.iheduc.2004.06.001

Baran, B., & Çağıltay, K. (2006). Knowledge management and online communities of practice in teacher education. *The Turkish Online Journal of Educational Technology – TOJE*, *V* (3), 12-19.

Barros, B., & Verdejo, M. F. (2000). Analyzing student interaction processes in order to improve collaboration: The degree approach. *International Journal of Artificial Intelligence in Education*, *Vol*, *11*, 221–241.

Bouckaert, R., Frank, E., Hall, M., Kirkby, R., Reutemann, P., Seewald, A., & Scuse, D. (2010). *WEKA Manual for Version 3-6-2*. Hamilton, New Zealand: University of Waikato.

Brew, L. S. (2008). The role of student feedback in evaluating and revising a blended learning course. *The Internet and Higher Education*, *11*, 98–105. doi:10.1016/j.iheduc.2008.06.002

Bulu, S. T., & Yildirim, Z. (2008). Communication behaviors and trust in collaborative online teams. *Journal of Educational Technology & Society*, *11*(1), 132–147.

Chapman C., Clinton J., & Kerber R (2005). *CRISP-DM 1.0, Step-by-step data mining guide.*

Delavari, N., Beikzadeh, M. R., & Amnuaisuk, S. K. (2005). Application of enhanced analysis model for data mining processes in higher educational system, *Proceedings of ITHET 6th Annual International Conference*. Juan Dolio, Dominican Republic.

Delavari, N., Beikzadeh, M. R., & Shirazi, M. R. A. (2004). A new model for using data mining in higher educational system, *Proceedings of 5th International Conference on Information Technology based Higher Education and Training: ITEHT '04*, Istanbul, Turkey.

Eom, S. B., & Arbaugh, J. B. (2011). *Student satisfaction and learning outcomes in e-learning: An introduction to empirical research*. Hershey, PA: Information Science Reference. doi:10.4018/978-1-60960-615-2

Fredskild, T. U. (2008). Distance learning students in communities of practice, *International Journal of Media, Technology and Lifelong Learning*, *3*(4). Available at: www.seminar.net

Garrison, D. R., Anderson, T., & Archer, W. (2000). *Critical enquiry in a text-based environment*: Computer conferencing in higher education. *The Internet and Higher Education*, *2*(2-3), 87–105. doi:10.1016/S1096-7516(00)00016-6

Guardado, M., & Shi, L. (2007). ESL students' experiences of online peer feedback. *Computers and Composition*, *24*, 443–461. doi:10.1016/j.compcom.2007.03.002

Hanewald, R. (2009). Sustainability in an online community of practice: The case study of a group of secondary school educators in Victoria. *Australian Journal of Teacher Education Group of Secondary School Educators in Victoria, 34*(5), 26–42.

Hara, N., & Kling, R. (2002). *IT supports for communities of practice: An empirically-based framework*. Bloomington, IN: Center for Social Informatics, Indiana University.

Kimble, C., Hildreth, P., & Wright, P. (2001). Communities of Practice: Going virtual. In Malhotra, Y. (Ed.), *Knowledge management and business model innovation* (pp. 220–234). Hershey, PA, USA: IGI Global.

Luan, J. (2002). Data mining and its applications in higher education. In Serban, A., & Luan, J. (Eds.), *Knowledge management: Building a competitive advantage for higher education. New Directions for Institutional Research, No. 113*. San Francisco, CA: Jossey Bass.

Ma, Y., Liu, B., Wong, C. K., Yu, P. S., & Lee, S. M. (2000). Targeting the right students using data mining, *Proceedings of the Sixth ACM SIGKDD International Conference on Knowledge Discovery and Data Mining (457-464)*, Boston, MA.

McDonald, M., Dorn, B., & McDonald, G. (2004). A statistical analysis of student performance in online computer science courses, Proceedings of the 35th SIGCSE Technical Symposium on Computer Science Education (71-74), Norfolk, Virginia.

Mykota, D., & Duncan, R. (2007). Learner characteristics ad predictors of online social presence. *Canadian Journal of Education, 30*(1), 157–170. doi:10.2307/20466630

Ragan, C. L., & Tello, S. (2005, November 17). Building the learning community community: The power of online learning. Orlando, Florida, USA: Sloan-C International Conference.

Ranjan, J., & Malik, K. (2007). Effective educational process: A Data Mining Approach. *Vine, 37*(4), 502–515. doi:10.1108/03055720710838551

Rourke, L., Anderson, T., Garrison, D. R., & Archer, W. (2001). Assessing social presence in screen text-based computer conferencing. *Journal of Distance Education, 14*. available at http://auspace.athabascau.ca: 8080/dspace/bitstream/2149/732/1/ Assessing%20Social%20 Presence%20In%20 Asynchronous%20Text-based%20Computer%20 Conferencing.pdf.

Serrano Núñez, Y. S. (2005). Assessing faculty's social presence indicators in online courses at the Inter American University of Puerto Rico, Bayamón Campus. *Focus (San Francisco, Calif.), 4*(1), 47–49.

Shyamala, K., & Rajagopalan, S. P. (2006). Data mining model for a better higher educational system. *Information Technology Journal, 5*(3), 560–564. doi:10.3923/itj.2006.560.564

Talavera, L., & Gaudioso, E. (2004). Mining student data to characterize similar behavior groups in unstructured collaboration spaces, *presented at Workshop on Artificial Intelligence in Computer Supported Collaborative Learning at European Conference on Artificial Intelligence,* Valencia, Spain, pp *17-23*.

Tu, C.-H., & McIsaac, M. (2002). The relationship of social presence and interaction in online classes. *American Journal of Distance Education, 16*(3), 131–150. doi:10.1207/S15389286AJDE1603_2

Van Brakel, P. S. (2010). Mentoring doctoral students within a virtual community of practice - With special reference to their information recording behaviour. *Proceedings of Informing Science & IT Education Conference* (pp. 439-448). InSITE.

Waiyamai, K. (2004). Improving quality of graduate students by data mining, Faculty of Engineering, Kasetsart University, *Frontiers of ICT Research International Symposium*.

Wenger, E. (1998). *Communities of practice. Learning, meaning and identity.* Cambridge, UK: Cambridge University Press.

Wenger, E. (2006). *Communities of practice - A brief introduction.* Available at: http://www. ewenger.com/ theory/ index.htm.

Witten, I., & Frank, E. (2005). *Data mining: practical machine learning tools and techniques.* Elsevier.

Zimitat, C. (2007). Capturing community of practice knowledge for student learning. *Innovations in Education and Teaching International, 44*(3), 321–330. doi:10.1080/14703290701486753

ADDITIONAL READING

Anjewierden, A., Kollöffel, B., & Hulshof, C. (2007). *Towards educational data mining: Using data mining methods for automated chat analysis to understand and support inquiry learning processes. ADML 2007* (pp. 27–36). Crete.

Bodea, C. (2007). An Innovative System for Learning Services in Project Management. In *Proceedings of 2007 IEEE/INFORMS International Conference on Service Operations and Logistics. And Informatics.* Philadelphia, USA, 2007. IEEE.

Bodea, V. (2003). *Standards for Data Mining Languages,* The Proceedings of the Sixth International Conference on Economic Informatics - Digital Economy, INFOREC Printing House, ISBN 973-8360-02-1, Bucureşti, pp. 502-506.

Bodea, V. (2007). *Application and Benefits of Knowledge Management in Universities – a Case Study on Student Performance Enhancement,* Informatics in Knowledge Society, The Proceedings of the Eight International Conference on Informatics in Economy, May 17-18, ASE Printing House, pp. 1033-1038.

Bodea, V. (2008). *Knowledge management systems, PhD thesis,* supervised by Prof. Ion Gh. Roşca, The Academy of Economic Studies, Bucharest.

Bodea V., & Roşca I. (2007). *Analiza performanţelor studenţilor cu tehnici de data mining: Studiu de caz în Academia de Studii Economice din Bucureşti,* în: C. Bodea, I. Andone (coordonatori) - *Managementul cunoaşterii în universitatea modernă,* Editura Academiei de Studii Economice din Bucureşti.

Castells, M., & Pekka, H. (2002). *The Information Society and the Welfare State. The Finnish Model.* Oxford, UK: Oxford University Press.

Charpentier, M., Lafrance, C., & Paquette, G. (2006). *International e-learning strategies: Key findings relevant to the Canadian context,* available at: http://www.ccl-cca.ca/ pdfs/CommissionedReports/ JohnBissInternationalELearningEN. pdf

CRoss Industry Standard Process for Data Mining, available at http://www.crisp-dm.org/

Demirel, M. (2009). Lifelong learning and schools in the twenty-first century. *Procedia Social and Behavioral Sciences, 1,* 1709–1716. doi:10.1016/j.sbspro.2009.01.303

European Commission. (2005). *Mobilizing the brainpower of Europe: Enabling universities to make their full contribution to the Lisbon Strategy,* Brussels, Communicate no. 152.

Eurostat (2009) The Bologna Process in Higher Education in Europe Key indicators on the social dimension and mobility, European Communities and IS, Hochschul-Informations-System G mbH, 2009, available at http://epp.eurostat.ec.europa.eu/ portal/page/portal/ education/ bologna_process

Garcia, A. C. B., Kunz, J., Ekstrom, M., & Kiviniemi, A. (2003). *Building a Project Ontology with Extreme Collaboration and VD&C. CIFE Technical Report #152*. Stanford University.

Gareis, R. (2007). *Happy Projects!* Romanian version (ed.). Bucharest, Romania: ASE Printing House.

Guardado, M., & Shi, L. (2007). ESL students' experiences of online peer feedback. *Computers and Composition*, *24*, 443–461. doi:10.1016/j.compcom.2007.03.002

Haddawy, P., & Hien, N. (2006). *A decision Support System for Evaluating International Student Applications, Computer Science and Information management program*. Asian Institute of Technology.

Kalathur, S. (2006) An Object-Oriented Framework for Predicting Student Competency Level in an Incoming Class, Proceedings of *SERP '06*, pp. 179-183, Las Vegas, NV, 2006.

Kanellopoulos, D., Kotsiantis, S., & Pintelas, P. 2006. Ontology-based learning applications: A development methodology. In *Proceedings of the 24th IASTED International Multi-Conference Software Engineering*. Innsbruck, Austria, 2006.

Luan, J., Zhai, M., Chen, J., Chow, T., Chang, L., & Zhao, C.-M. (2004). Concepts, myths, and case studies of data mining in higher education, *AIR 44th Forum*, Boston, MA.

Lytras, M. D., Carroll, J. M., Damiani, E., & Tennyson, R. D. (2008). Emerging technologies and Information Systems for the knowledge society. In *First World Summit on the Knowledge Society*. Athens, Greece: WSKS.

Markkula, M. (2006). Creating favourable conditions for knowledge society through knowledge management, e-gorvernance and e-learning. Budapest, Hungary, 2006. *FIG Workshop on E-governance*, Knowledge management and e-learning.

McFarland, D., & Hamilton, D. (2006). Factors affecting student performance and satisfaction: Online versus traditional course delivery. *Journal of Computer Information Systems*, *46*(2), 25–32.

Monolescu, D., & Schifter, C. (2000). Online Focus Group: A tool to evaluate online students' course experience. *The Internet and Higher Education*, *2*, 171–176. doi:10.1016/S1096-7516(00)00018-X

Teekaput, P., & Waiwanijchakij, P. (2006). E-learning and knowledge management, symptoms of a reality. In *Third International Conference on E-learning for Knowledge-Based Society*. Bangkok, Thailand, 2006.

Turner, R. J., & Huemann, M. (2000). Formal education in project management: Current and future trends, *PMI Annual Seminars & Symposium*, Houston, TX, USA. 7-16 September.

Turner, R. J., & Simister, S. J. (2004). *Gower handbook of project management*. Romanian version (ed.). Bucharest, Romania: Codecs Printing House.

Young, A., & Norgard, C. (2006). Assessing the quality of online courses from the students' perspective. *The Internet and Higher Education*, *9*, 107–115. doi:10.1016/j.iheduc.2006.03.001

KEY TERMS AND DEFINITIONS

Association Rule: An implication expression of the form X > Y where X and Y are disjoint conjunctions of attribute-value pairs. Strength of association rules can be measured in terms of support and confidence. Support determines how often a rule applies to a data set and confidence determines how frequently items appear in transactions that contain X. Association analysis has as objective to find hidden relationships in large sections of data.

Classification: The process consisting in learning function f, which assigns a predefined class label y to each set of attributes X. The function f is known as the model for classification. A classification model can serve as an explanatory tool to distinguish between instances of different classes. In this case, the classification is considered as a descriptive modeling. A classification model can also be used to predict the class label for the unknown instances. In this case, the classification is considered as a predictive modeling. Classification techniques are better suited for prediction or description of data sets for binary or nominal attributes.

Clustering: Technique by which similar instances are grouped together. All the instances grouped in the same cluster have a certain understanding, a certain utility, or both. Clusters capture the natural structure of data and so, the clustering process might be the starting point for other data handling processes such as summarization.

Community of Practice: A group of people who share a concern or a passion for something they do and learn how to do it better as they interact regularly.

Data Mining: The process of extracting previously unknown, valid, and operational patterns/models from large collection of data. Essential for data mining is the discovery of patterns without previous hypotheses. Data mining is not aimed to verify, confirm or refute hypothesis, but instead to discover "unexpected" patterns, completely unknown at the time of the data mining process take place, which may even contradict the intuitive perception. For this reason, the results are truly valuables.

Decision Tree: A diagrammatic representation of the possible outcomes and events used in decision analysis. A decision tree with a range of discrete (symbolic) class labels is called a classification tree, whereas a decision tree with a range of continuous (numeric) values is called a regression tree. Decision trees are attractive because they show clearly how to reach a decision, and because they are easy to construct automatically from labeled instances. Two well known programs for constructing decision trees are C4.5 and CART (Classification and Regression Tree).

E-Learning: A type of distance education in teaching-learning interaction is mediated by an environment set up by new information and communication technologies in particular the Internet. Internet is both the material environment, as well as the communication channel between the actors involved.

Educational Data Mining: An emerging discipline: concerned with developing methods for exploring the unique types of data that come from educational settings, and using those methods to better understand students, and the settings which they learn in.

Social Presence: Represents the ability of learners to project themselves socially and emotionally in a community of inquiry. The function of this element is to support the cognitive and affective objectives of learning. It supports affective objectives by making the group interactions appealing, engaging, and thus intrinsically rewarding, leading to an increase in academic, social, and institutional integration and resulting in increased persistence and course completion.

Chapter 6
Online Communities:
A Historically Based Examination of How Social Formations Online Fulfill Criteria for Community

Jakob Linaa Jensen
University of Aarhus, Denmark

ABSTRACT

The metaphor of "community" has been among the most widely used when describing the Internet in political and sociological terms. It has dominated public and scholarly discourses at the expense of other early metaphors like "the information highway" (Parks, 2011: 105). This chapter discusses the concept of online communities from a historical and theoretical perspective. It is argued that the possibility and quality of online community formations online, widely discussed in literature, must be seen in the light of traditional, sociological understandings of social formations and community, taking onto consideration the specific affordances and limitations of Internet based communication. It is argued that communities online do not resemble traditional close-knit, geographically bound communities but that they allow for valuable interactions and genuine passions and emotions anyway.

I will take the point of departure in traditional sociological understandings and definitions of community. Next, I will give a brief summary of the history of online social phenomena, major debates and attempts to define community online. It is followed by a thematic discussion of ideas and practices of online social relationships. I will argue that the traditional focus on community as the dominant metaphor in understanding social formation online might be somehow mistaken as the Internet, although not necessarily unable to foster genuine social relations, is materially different from the realm in which traditional communities were shaped. It is claimed, in the end, that a framework encompassing logics of network might be appropriate in understanding online communities.

DOI: 10.4018/978-1-60960-869-9.ch006

THE CONCEPT OF COMMUNITY

The concept of community is basically what Connolly (1974) has called an essentially contested concept: there are no clear, undisputed definitions and defining community often bears strong normative implications. In fact, community is among the most widely-used and heavily debated concepts within the social sciences. The word "community" is derived from the Old French "communité" which is derived from the Latin "communitas", meaning fellowship or organism (Wikipedia, 2010). Community is often understood in connection with some kind of social bonding or social structure, like the tribe, the family or the city. Since the peace of Westphalia in 1648 the word has been widely used as the raison d'etre for the emerging nation states: a certain country's citizens share some interests and values and thus they have to participate in and contribute to the national community. Compulsory army service and schooling as well as flags and national hymns have been among the mechanisms to strengthen community. It is clear, however, that community traditionally has been connected to a sharing of a certain location, contrary to today's "virtual" communities

One of the classic community theorists is the German sociologist Ferdinand Tönnies (1887) who distinguished between community (*gemeinschaft*) and society (*gesellschaft*). He claimed that in modern life the former has been replaced by the latter. Traditional close-knit communities based on kinship and physical proximity have been substituted by a large-scale society based on formal organizational structures and physical distance. Similarly, French sociologist Emile Durkheim (1893) described a shift from organic to mechanic solidarity. The social contract is no longer bound to local practices based on family, tribe or tradition but is regulated by abstract legal and technical procedures administered by bureaucracies or big industry. Both Tönnies and Durkheim share a notion of decline, that something original, ideal and natural has vanished or disappeared. Such pessimistic accounts are not unusual among classical sociological theorists. Also Marx and Weber developed their ideas in a time characterized by the decline of traditional communities and the upcoming of larger societies and a new, unknown social reality.

The regret on behalf of traditional community is even more profound among normative thinkers. Conservative, republican and Marxist thinkers show a rarely seen agreement in mourning the decline of traditional community. They share the view that community is larger than the sum of individuals. Republican thinkers like Jean-Jacques Rousseau would even claim that human beings are not to be considered as humans outside the community.

Such ideas were put aside for a century; modern Western democracies are largely built on liberal notions that community is no more than the sum of individuals and that communities exist to serve the needs of the individuals, not the opposite. In recent decades, there has been a renewed focus on community, not at least in American political philosophy, where the so-called communitarian school of thinking builds upon republican philosophical ideas. Alisdair Macintyre (1981) and Michael Walzer (1983) have called for a renewal of community, a recognition of identity, sense and belonging and an establishment of smaller, communitarian political units. Community has also been brought to the political agenda by the new American Right, for instance in Sarah Palin's Tea Party Movement.

This accentuated focus on community and traditional republican ideals on citizenship and civic virtue coincides with the rise of the Internet. Therefore it might be no surprise that much thinking on social relationships online has centered on the metaphor and ideas of community. As I will argue later, even though this is natural, it might be somehow mistaken in order to grasp the true scope of online social interactions.

A SHORT HISTORY OF ONLINE SOCIAL FORMATIONS

Among the first internet based social formations we find the so-called MUDs, text-based role plays inspired by popular board games like Dungeons & Dragons. Although only remotely similar to today's high-resolution graphics game environments like World of Warcraft or EverQuest, they had cult-like status among early generation of dedicated Internet users, not at least adolescent males. A more general example of early social activity online is found in the so-called USENET groups, a kind of electronic bulletin boards where every possible topic could be discussed among the subscribers, from politics to porcelain painting. USENET was basically a separate Internet technology, just like the e-mail protocol and the World Wide Web. In the late nineties, however, it merged with the World Wide Web and today's remain of USENET is integrated into Google Groups. USENET was the first example that the Internet could be used forming communities across borders, based on shared interests rather than physical proximity.

Another early Internet "community" was the WELL in the San Fransciso Bay Area. It was initiated by a private software company as early as 1985 and based on fee-paying members. With 8000 users and 300 discussion groups it is often defined as an early success story, supporting ideas that the internet could be a forum for strong civil interaction (Rheingold, 1993). Even though the debates were characterized by respect and dialogue it is part of the stories that the users mainly belonged to the ICT elite abundant in the bay area. Minority groups or other disenfranchised were not mobilized, a tendency which has characterized other political discussion groups as well (see for instance Wilhelm, 2000; Linaa Jensen, 2006).

The early MUDs were soon followed by an abundance of online games based on improved graphics and slowly coming closer to simulations of physical reality. Connected by the Internet, gaming became a social activity where you played with others via the Internet or together in front of the screen. Thus, early scholarly expectations of gaming as making people asocial and narcissistic gave way to an understanding of gaming as a part of adolescents' social life (Turkle, 1995). In the latter half of the 90's online interaction became a part of many people's wider social life. E-mail lists prospered and although basically a de-central technology where people could not "see" each other, they created environments of shared information and knowledge. Some of those environments explicitly employed the metaphor of community; free web hosting communities GeoCities and Tripod allowed the users to build virtual "houses" and interact in 3D graphical environments.

The real big turn for online social interaction, however, remained to be seen. From the beginning of the third millennium online social network sites (boyd & Ellison, 2007: 211) based on profiles and mutual connections to "friends" became a dominant form of online social interaction. Basically they differ from online discussion groups and forums like "The WELL" where everybody can see everybody and all social interaction is visible to the members. Rather, they are based on personal profiles and connections to a limited number of "friends" within the network.

Some of the first online social networks were Swedish Lunarstorm (2000), Friendster (2002) and Orkut (2003). For some time, Friendster was the most popular whereas Orkut undertook a strange path to fame. It suddenly became very popular in Brazil and as most interactions on Orkut turned into Portuguese language, the non- Portuguese speakers left (Wikipedia, 2010). Orkut remains an example of the changing fashions of online networks and how fast audiences might appear and disappear.

MySpace was among the phenomena really kick-starting the media attention to online social network sites. It took off in 2003 designed as an online place where upcoming bands could present themselves and their music. Soon, however, almost everybody could enter, build their profile and form networks. MySpace is characterized by a colorful and somehow disorganized interface, urging people to be creative while building their personal profile.

In 2004, Mark Zuckerberg and two friends initiated a network for undergraduates at Harvard University. It was based on the logics of the face books, popular at American universities and high schools. Facebook became an instant success and soon dispersed to the whole campus, then to other universities and high schools and ultimately, within two years time, to the entire world. It has demonstrated phenomenal growth rates and in late 2009 it overtook MySpace as the world's largest online social network. MySpace remain extremely popular in the US however (Owyang, 2010).

Finally, LinkedIn, a business-like network for sharing work-related information is another example that networking rather than community building might attract the biggest audiences. Unlike Facebook, users can not automatically "friend" people. Instead they have to be related to the users' networks within one or two degrees of separation or they can be "friended" through recommendations from relatives in common.

This has been only a very limited discussion of social phenomena online. Today, users face an abundance of social possibilities online. The first e-mail lists and text-based role plays have been supplemented by all kinds of discussion boards, online games, metaverses, chat rooms, file sharing services and social networking sites. Earlier dominated by the English-speaking world, social formations online are now truly global phenomena. In populous countries like India and China, the Internet experience impressive growth rates, and the biggest Chinese online social network QQ might be a serious competitor to Facebook' status as the world's largest social network (Peng, 2010).

Social formations online are based on a variety of Internet technologies. Where file sharing services like Bit Torrent and Gnutella are based on different computers linked together by a minimum of software installed on each machine, discussion forums and most online social networks are based on huge, central servers. However, it is not the topic of this chapter to define different online social services based on their technological features. Rather I want to discuss the interfaces and the social reality of those services as they are experienced by the users, who ultimately shape and redefine them as social technologies.

We have come beyond early understandings that computers and the Internet were part of a virtual realm and fundamentally disconnected to the real world. Rather, there are close correspondence between online and offline actions as the Internet becomes integrated in everyday life practices. The big question is, however, whether and to which extent all these online social formations rightfully can be described in terms of "communities"?

DISCUSSING AND DEFINING ONLINE COMMUNITY

Although the characteristics of social interaction online have now been discussed for around twenty years and a lot of empirical evidence has been added to the theoretical speculations, conclusions on the state of community, social interaction and solidarity online remain unclear. To understand the possibilities and prospects of online communities it is necessary to address how the Internet changes and challenges traditional patterns of social formation.

There is no shortage of theoretical literature on the perspectives for social interaction and community online. Early works were mostly based on theoretical speculations where as recent works often build on a more empirical foundation.

Some of the early works were wildly optimistic on the behalf of the Internet's capacity to rejuvenate community and social coherence. Howard Rheingold has claimed that the Internet facilitates communication across borders and distances, enabling communication and, ultimately, understanding based on common interests and values. Thereby, new communities and relations can be created (Rheingold, 1993: 4-5). Differently from traditional communities the interactions take place through computer screens, leaving the bodies behind (ibid: 58). Douglas Schuler (1996) argued that the Internet can facilitate new locally based community networks, strengthening community life and civil society on a local basis.

Critics like Sproul & Faraj (1995) and Kiesler (1997) have addressed the lack of genuine social interaction and claimed a fragmentation of community when taking place online. The virtual character of online social relationship means that there are easy entry and exit options, thus making users much less committed and obliged than in "real", physical communities (Kolko & Reid, 1998). In such works, online formations are regarded as second range communities where genuine social relationships are difficult to obtain. The fluid social situation and the absence of physical cues and patterns online hinder the emotional engagement and social involvement characteristic for communities in the traditional sense (Kiesler, 1997).

As the purpose of this chapter is to critically examine whether the community metaphor is useful for describing social formations online, it might be relevant to survey some existing definitions of online community. Such definitions have come from a variety of perspectives: psychology, sociologi, politics and business studies. Thus, the definitions presented here are not exhaustive but as they all come from a sociological perspective, they might be particularly relevant as criteria of examining social formations online.

Jenny Preece (2000: 10) defines an online community as a computer-mediated service which is related to a shared purpose, such as an interest, need, information exchange, or service that provides a reason for the community. Ideally it supports and mediates social interaction and facilitates a sense of togetherness. There should

be formal or informal policies based on protocols, rules, and laws or tacit assumptions and rituals that guide people's interactions.

Parks (2011: 108) discusses whether online social networks fulfill criteria for virtual communities. He recognizes that virtual communities differ from traditional communities in the sense that they neither share geographical space nor a self-sufficient. However, he establish five other criteria which might be fulfilled: the ability to engage in collective action, shared rituals and social regulation, patterned interaction among members, identification and sense of belonging to the community and self awareness of being a community.

We find a stricter definition in Whittaker, Isaacs & O'Day (1997: 137) who claim that online communities are centered on shared goals, needs, interests or activity among the members. There are shared resources and access defined by rules. Online community is also characterized by repeated active participation, shared activities and often strong emotional ties. Finally there should be reciprocity of information, support and service and a shared context of social conventions, language and protocols.

Both three definitions follow the idea of Rheingold on communities based on interests (and maybe values) rather than geography, kinship, or solidarity. Further, all definitions address the technical and formal-legal dimensions of community as they emphasize certain common rules, policies and protocols. Preece and Parks include the presence of social rituals in their definitions while Whittaker, Isaacs and O'Day demand shared conventions. The big difference relate to the level of involvement. Where Preece is mainly occupied by the affordance of the "community", particularly Whittaker, Isaacs and O'Day are specific about the obligations of the members: they emphasize repeated, committed interaction among the members where Parks only demand "patterned interaction". No doubt the level of involvement are among the decisive criteria for online formations to be true communities as large involvement and interaction often spur the sense of belonging and identity which is a fundamental criterion of an online as well as an offline community.

Nonnecke and Preece (2000) have demonstrated, the vast majority of community members are "lurkers" who just follow the information and interaction but do not participate actively. Thus, a so-called "power law" (Simon: 1955) that 10 percent of a population accounts for 90 percent of the (inter)action also applies to online communities. If the researcher follows the strong criterion of Whittaker, Isaacs and O'Day there will only be limited audiences to investigate and one can ask the question whether online social formations can be communities at all, except for a little core of heavy users?

Instead of sticking to strict and maybe unrealistic criteria for fulfilling community ideals, the character of online social formations ought to be discussed through a critical examination of various aspects of sociality online and offline, employing evidence from empirical research so far. By that, we can approach an answer to the question whether social formations resemble community.

First, I will discuss the conditions of membership and commitment which might be quite different online than offline. Then, I raise the question of space in online interactions. Next, I will discuss the concept of genuine, social interaction. This leads to a discussion of identity, ending in a discussion of whether the boundary between online and offline interactions is vanishing.

MEMBERSHIP AND COMMITMENT

Traditional communities were defined by location, belonging or kinship. Thus, some were defined for life whereas others were at least hard to enter or leave. In modern society, individuals participate in a number of more or less obliging communities: from family and neighborhood to work places, associations and sports clubs. Those are defined

with various levels of entrance conditions and mutual obligations. However, such communities are still based on regular face to face interaction. Further, there are social costs affiliated with entering and leaving. It takes some time to be an accepted member of a physical community, whether a neighborhood or a sports club, and once the relationships are established leaving it might impose certain social and maybe physical costs. Sproull & Faraj (1995: 66-67) have claimed that such costs of entering and leaving are very low or non-existing in online communities. If Rheingold is right, anybody can enter an online community and as the members often are totally unknown and thus unrelated to your wider social life, there are no real costs associated with leaving as quickly as you enter. Thereby, the involvement and commitment declines.

Today there are reasons to modify such simplistic views. Virtual communities differ almost as much as "physical" communities. Some are just almost random associations of loosely connected individuals. This is true for e-mail lists or file sharing services. Others are constituted by large groups of dedicated users who in some cases even know each other "IRL". This was true for an early community like the WELL as well as for a travel community like Virtual Tourist (Linaa Jensen, 2008). No matter whether we define Facebook or games like World of Warcraft as communities, networks, games or something different, dedicated users who have invested time and effort in building a profile and forming social relations might and they might be reluctant to leave and then loose possible status and networks.

In sum, while most online social formations might be just as loose, disconnected and non-obliging as the critics would claim, some are coming close to traditional communities in terms of membership conditions and commitment. As more closely connected and committed, the users are, as more the virtual communities are similar to traditional ones.

THE QUESTION OF SPACE

As many traditional accounts on communities have focused on families, villages and cities, they seem to take for granted that a community is linked to a certain space. But well before the rise of the Internet, sociologists emphasized that the ties of solidarity and affiliation associated with community can exist across space. Theorists like Benedict Andersson (1983) demonstrate that communities might be just as strong or even stronger if they live solely in the minds of the members, if they are "imagined communities".

Paradoxically, since William Gibson (1984) invented the word "cyberspace" to describe the virtual realm of the Internet, many discussions of online phenomena have been centered around a metaphor of space. Online services have often strived to create an imagination of space, perhaps in order to familiarize the users with the new online realm. The early MUDs, although text-based games, struggled creating an illusion of space through certain codes and rules. Later computer games like World of Warcraft and online worlds as Second Life are based on graphical 3D-simulations of cities and landscapes. Further, free website hosts like GeoCities have urged their users to "buy land" or "build a home online". Physical references are constantly present in online discussion groups and the space metaphor is dominant in daily talks and perceptions of the Internet when we say "I found it on the Internet" or "I went into a discussion group" (Linaa Jensen, 2006: 23-24).

This might be no surprise as humans are used to orient themselves within a geometrical, geographical space. Thus, the online world only becomes comprehensible by simulating an experience of space. Humans are, after all, not designed to decode HMTL!

Although the Internet is most often perceived in spatial terms, technologically as well as cognitively, it differs from traditional communal spaces by the fact that people need not to be physically proximate in order to interact and communicate.

Further, members can join an unlimited number of communities and move across them without having to change physical position. Contrary to traditional communities like the village or the tribe, internet communities do not constitute the entire horizon of meaning of its participants. However, this is not unique for the Internet as the world of today is much more fragmented than the traditional, archaic world described by classical sociologists. Modern individuals participate in a variety of communities and change roles and behavior accordingly. Further, the criticism of online communities that they are not linked to a certain shared space might be of less importance as the sense of imagined community can be emotionally even stronger than the feeling of physical reality and proximity. The real benchmark, however, might be the character of the social interaction taking place online.

GENUINE SOCIAL INTERACTION OR NOT?

One of the most heavily debated questions in the literature on the Internet is whether genuine social and emotional interactions are possible online. It has been claimed that that the low logistical and social costs of participating and leaving (discussed above) hinders a true emotional engagement as known from families, friendships and neighborhoods (Kiesler, 1997). When people feel less obliged towards fellow members, the interactions often become superficial and sometimes dominated by unsocial behavior like hate-speech and radicalized exchanges.

It is also claimed that the lack of bodily presence and the possibility of remaining anonymous are obstacles towards genuine interaction (Doheny-Farina: 1996:65). Online there is a lack of body language, tacit cues and phatic communication which is often as important as the spoken word. This generates genuine misunderstandings and leaves the online interaction a second-range kind of communication (Kolko & Reid, 1998; Graham, 1999).

Another problem is that online communities are voluntary or non-obliging, based on common interests of beliefs. Even though homogeneity in some settings is an advantage, the problem in certain online communities is the absence of heterogeneity and challenging of one's beliefs and opinions. Wilhelm (1998) has demonstrated that American political discussion groups were centered on steadfast party positions or attitudes. The members confirmed each others' beliefs and the dominant opinions were never challenged for real. Deliberative ideals of listening to other (and maybe better) arguments and developing a more balanced and informed opinion can't be fulfilled under such conditions. Instead discussion boards can be havens for fanatics who can confirm each other's absurd beliefs. If you believe in witches or poltergeists, somebody online can confirm to you that they exist.

But then, why use time and effort to form online social relationships at all? Are we driven by curiosity, practical needs or maybe altruism, the urge to help others with support and information? While curiosity might be the reason for people to join in the first instance it is not sufficient to making stem stay for a long time. For Peter Kollock (1999: 227-28) it is mainly egoistic rather than altruistic motives that drive people to form online social relations, even though for instance participation in support groups, user forums or online social networks often benefit the higher good as well. Most groups demand no reciprocity of information. Everybody is welcome to provide or use, depending on the eagerness to publish or the need for getting information. But However, the result might be genuine forums where the information benefits everybody. That is one of the paradoxes of the very low cost of digital information.

Other studies demonstrate that users do not only benefit information-wise but also get supportive and emotional benefits. Nancy Baym (2000) has studied fan culture and fan groups online and documented that many users engage strongly emo-

tionally in such groups, both towards the objects of fandom and towards their fellow fans. Some even become personal friends because of their shared interests in the stars. The same is true for the field of virtual tourism (Linaa Jensen, 2008) and for patient groups dedicated to certain handicaps or diseases. Kimby (2006) has investigated a support groups for breast cancer patients and found that besides being a factual, informational platform they also act as forums for mutual support and emotional exchanges, even though the patients do not know each other physically.

Of course such examples might be exceptions in a vast ocean of online groups and networks. It might be unfair to compare interaction online to the intimate and emotional interaction based on close-knit offline community. But it is worth remembering that also physical communities differ regarding the level of emotional engagement and interaction.

This discussion is related to a wider sociological debates whether the rise of online social interaction differ that radically from traditional interaction that it fundamentally alters the rules and conditions of social behavior. Sudweeks & Simoff (1999) have claimed that behavior online is an entire new social field to be learned and integrated in the social competence of the individuals.

A number of studies have demonstrated, however, that the Internet does not fundamentally alter social rules of behavior. Gotved (1999) has shown that offline social behavior and rules to a large extent are replicated online. Markham (1998) has found that patterns well known from the physical world prevail when the interaction is moved to an online forum. Studies of social networks like MySpace and Facebook show that people use them as a kind of extension of "physical" life and that offline dynamics prevail online (boyd, 2011; Parks, 2011). Even though the Internet facilitates new ways of meeting and interaction, basic inherited rules for social code and behavior seem to prevail. One reason is the unfulfilled dream of fluent, postmodern identities online.

IDENTITY AND ONLINE SOCIAL RELATIONS

Early optimists like Rheingold and Sherry Turkle (1995) claimed that the Internet's possibilities of interaction with strangers and options of anonymity facilitated social experiments and new and different forms of interaction. Users were able to play roles, change their gender or age and create a whole new "me". Thereby, the Internet might be the ultimate realization of a utopian postmodern dream of plasticity and liquid identity (Haraway, 1991). A New York Times cartoon from 1995 portrays a dog in front of a computer saying "On the Internet, nobody knows you are a dog".

Although the Internet has often been regarded as a new virtual realm where physicality does not matter, social interaction and community formation online are not independent of physical and bodily reality. Online communication constantly refers to physical experience and users of online communities often seek to extend the virtual gatherings into the physical sphere. Herring (1993, 1999) has demonstrated that offline affiliation and status matters in online discussion groups has shown that gender roles and patterns prevail in online forums matter, and Kolko, Nakamura & Rodman (2000) has punctuated the myth that online relationships automatically are independent of racial differences and statuses.

Further, most findings from studies of online social relations demonstrate that people wants to know with whom they share, date or discuss. Judith Donath (1999) has shown that participants in USENET groups prefer to identify with name and e-mail address and that they expect other users to do the same. Examples of such logics are online social networks sites like Facebook and MySpace where people have to identify by their real name and where the profile most often include a real picture. Facebook and MySpace have reached a popularity which was never matched by avatar- or nickname based communities like Second Life and Habbo Hotel. People want to know with whom they communicate.

Thus, the socio-demographic logics of the Internet mostly resemble what we know about social life in general. The early post-modern dreams by Turkle and Haraway about communities where race, gender and body had no importance seem to be wildly over-exaggerated. Dynamics, rituals, rules and emotions known from offline community are also present online, not at least when there are close interaction between online and offline realms.

THE RELATIONSHIP BETWEEN ONLINE AND OFFLINE

When early optimists like Howard Rheingold pointed out that virtual community opened new possibilities, he believed that the communities were going to be a new utopia, something different and better than the real world. Such a viewpoint might have been partly true for the MUDs and other game environments where the virtual offered another kind of space where you could live and interact, at least throughout the duration of the game. On the other hand, pessimists criticized it as an escape from the real world with real emotions, interactions and consequences. Among others, Kiesler (1997) claimed that intensive use of the virtual possibilities leads to a decline in social engagement in the outside world like the family, friendships and the civil society in general.

The technical and social development as well as empirical evidence has run contrary to such claims. Rather than creating a brand new world beyond the screen, many online social phenomena have close affiliations to the "outside" world. Baym (1995) demonstrated early that online users often used their offline identities and that there seem to be close connection between online life and the offline reality. As discussed by Kimby (2006) patient communities strengthens its participants to cope with their life in "the real world". Dating fora are other examples that online participants seek to extend the online contacts to the physical world.

The dualism between the virtual and the physical is perhaps most obvious among online social networks like MySpace, LinkedIn, Facebook and Twitter relationships are mostly based on affiliations in the physical world rather pure online acquaintances (Ellison et. al., 2011). Thereby, Haythornthwaite & Wellman (2002) might be right when they claim that online communities are most successful if they fit closely together with existing communities.

Further, "virtual" communities are often closely tied to locality areas. Douglas Schuler (1996) demonstrates how online communities can be helpful in supporting local community life and vice versa. Wellman & Gulia (1999: 172) found that online relationships become a part of the users' daily life in general, confirming a long term tendency where individuals tend to organize themselves online based on common interests and not at least, common geography. Studies of for instance MySpace users demonstrate that users mainly connect to people with whom they share geographical locations. Thus, virtual communities are not so virtual after all (Parks, 2011: 120)

DISCUSSING ONLINE SOCIAL INTERACTION: FROM COMMUNITIES TO NETWORKS

Discussions of online social interaction and its consequences have come some way since the first early, mostly optimistic prophecies. It is beyond doubt that community online will never come to resemble traditional communities of villages, families and religious groups, constituting a fundamental part of individuals' life world and range of actions. I will argue, however, that this is besides the point. We have come beyond expecting the Internet to become the new Utopia where postmodern ideals can be realized and where body, status and gender loose significance. The Internet is used for good or for worse, it is characterized by genuine social interaction as well

as hate-speech, it is used for performing identity experiments as well as forming relations with those you already know, and it is sometimes used in order to enhance and augment the experience of the "so-called" real world.

It has been shown that membership is a necessary but not sufficient condition for belonging to an online community, as most members are "mere" lurkers and feel no obligations or emotional attachments towards the group, a prerequisite agreed on in most definitions. However, there is no profound agreement on the exact requirements of commitment and involvement. Where Preece employs quite loose criteria, Whittaker, Isaacs & O'Day require continuous, emotional involvement from members in order to qualify an online phenomenon as a community. Such disagreements are not reserved for discussions of online community but remains a source of dissent in debates on the state of social formations and community in general. Too strict definitions of online community might not encompass the diversified nature of online social formations and the fact that genuine social interaction and personal benefits often occur unexpectedly, as demonstrated for instance in the studies of fan communities and patient groups.

There is no agreement, neither, whether the Internet is only a forum for the like-minded or it can bridge the gap across differences and disagreements. Douglas Schuler and Howard Rheingold clearly emphasized new possibilities of interaction among like-minded or those with common interests, deliberative theorists like Barber (1998) and Coleman & Blumler (2009) points out the Internet's capacity of building bridges across differences to avoid what Putnam (2000: 178) has called "cyber balkanization". Scholars like Kiesler (1997) and Wilhelm (1998) have emphasized that online debates are virtual sounding boards characterized by no real dialogue.

An answer to unanimities online has been to impose a certain hierarchy or stratification. For instance, many online communities have had certain groups of users from "wizards" to "newbies" (Reid, 1999). This stratification was an answer to the anarchy of the early Internet where trolls and spammers often dominated and destroyed genuine social interaction (Stone, 1991). As online social networks tend to replace online discussion groups and forums as the dominant social phenomenon online, the problem is solved by using the network structure itself as a regulatory device. Only certain parts of the network can do certain things and from a users' perspective you can select the information available to your different connections. That brings us towards a "filter culture" where un-wanted information and contacts are de-selected, ultimately resulting in exactly cyber-balkanization. Thus, conflict and dissent seem to be fundamental conditions for inclusive communities.

Further, the claim that online community is fundamentally independent of geographical space is dubious. In sum, we have come beyond early divisions between the virtual and the real as distinct domains. Rather, they supplement each other in rhizome like structures where the participants move between virtual and physical acquaintances and relations. Thus, online social interaction is not an entity but rather a process (Fernback, 1999).

The Internet does not replace or substitute the wider social world, in fact it supplements it. The users do not necessarily reflect upon concepts of community and solidarity as they move on incorporating the Internet in their daily lives and employ the possibilities of searching information, buying tickets and maintaining social relationships. They interact socially as they strive to satisfy their own needs or perform special roles (Preece, 1999). Mostly they prefer to use their own names and identities rather than using avatars or playing roles. They don't perceive the Internet as a space or a library but rather as a network where they discuss, share knowledge and make new contacts. In their lived experience the online realm is not separated from the rest of the world but a practical tool to maintain personal and professional relations. Contrary to early post-modern inspired beliefs, physical embodiment still matters! Rather than being a separate world, the online social relations facilitate what I have elsewhere called an augmentation of the physical world (Linaa Jensen, 2010).

REFERENCES

Andersson, B. (1983). *(1991). Imagined communities*. London, UK: Verso.

Barber, B. (1998). *A place for us. How to make society civil and democracy strong*. New York, NY: Hill & Wang.

Baym, N. K. (1995). In Jones, S. (Ed.), *The emergence of community in computer-mediated communication, CyberSociety* (pp. 138–163). Newbury Park, CA: Sage.

Baym, N. K. (2000). *Tune in, log on: Soaps, fandom, and online community*. Thousand Oaks, CA: Sage.

Boyd, D. (2011). Social network sites as networked publics: Affordances, dynamics and implications. In Papacharissi, Z. (Ed.), *The networked self - identity, community and culture on social network sites* (pp. 39–58). New York, NY: Routledge.

Boyd, D., & Ellison, N. (2007). Social network sites: Definition, history and scholarship. *Journal of Computer-Mediated Communication, 13*(1). doi:10.1111/j.1083-6101.2007.00393.x

Coleman, S., & Blumler, J. (2009). *The Internet and democratic citizenship. Theory, practice and politics*. Cambridge, UK: Cambridge University Press.

Connolly, W. E. (1974). Essentially contested concepts in politics. In Connolly, W. E. (Ed.), *The terms of political discourse* (pp. 10–44). Lexington, MA: Heath.

Doheny-Farina, S. (1996). *The wired neighbour-hood*. New Haven, CT: Yale University Press.

Donath, J. (1999). Identity and deception in the virtual community. In P. Kollock & M. Smith (red.), *Communities in cyberspace* (pp. 29–59). London, UK: Routledge.

Durkheim, E. (1893). *(1993). The division of labour in society*. New York, NY: The Free Press.

Ellison, N., Lampe, C., Steinfield, C., & Vitak, J. (2011). With a little help from my friends: How social network sites affect social capital processes. In Papacharissi, Z. (Ed.), *The networked self - identity, community and culture on social network sites* (pp. 124–145). New York, NY: Routledge.

Fernback, J. (1999). There is a there there. Notes towards a definition of Cyber community. In Jones, S. (Ed.), *Doing Internet research. Critical essues and methods for examining the Net*. London, UK: Sage.

Gibson, W. (1984). *Neuromancer*. New York, NY: Berkley Publishing Group.

Goffman, E. (1990). *(1959). The presentation of self in everyday life*. London, UK: Penguin Books.

Gotved, S. (1999). *Cybersociologi. Det samme på en anden måde. PhD-dissertation*. Denmark: University of Copenhagen.

Graham, G. (1999). *The Internet: A philosophical inquiry*. London, UK: Routledge.

Haraway, D. (1991). *Simians, cyborgs and women: The reinvention of nature*. New York, NY: Routledge.

Haythornthwaite, C., & Wellman, B. (2002). The Internet in everyday life: An introduction. In Haythornthwaite, Caroline, & Barry Wellman (Ed.). *The Internet in everyday life* (3-45). Oxford, UK: Blackwell.

Herring, Susan C. (1993). Gender and democracy in computer-mediated communication. *Electronic Journal of Communication, 3*(2).

Herring, S. C. (1999). The rhetorical dynamics of gender harassment online. *The Information Society, 15*(3), 151–167. doi:10.1080/019722499128466

Kiesler, S. (red.) (1997). Culture of the Internet. Mahwah, NJ: Erlbaum.

Kimby, C. K. (2006). Communicating the breast cancer experience on the Internet – the shaping of patient identity. In H. Krause Hansen & J. Hoff (red.), Digital Governance://networked Societies. *Creating authority, community, and identity in a globalized world* (pp. 201-228). Frederiksberg, Denmark: Nordicom.

Kolko, B., Nakamura, L., & Rodman, G. (2000). *Race in Cyberspace*. New York, NY: Routledge.

Kolko, B., & Reid, E. (1998). Dissolution and fragmentation: Problems in online communities. In *S. G. Jones (red.), Cybersociety 2.0: Revisiting Computer-Mediated Communication and Community*. Thousand Oaks, CA: Sage.

Kollock, P. (1999). The economies of Online coo-paeration. Gifts and public goods in Cyberspace". In M. Smith & P. Kollock (Ed.). *Communities in Cyberspace* (220-242). London, UK: Routledge.

Linaa Jensen, J. (2006). *Den virtuelle kaffestue – deliberation og demokratisk inklusion i politiske debatter på internettet*. Århus, Denmark: Politica.

Linaa Jensen, J. (2007). The Internet omonopti-con. In H. Bang & A. Esmark (red.), *New publics with/out democracy* (pp. 351-380). København, Denmark: Samfundslitteratur Press/Nordicom.

Linaa Jensen, J. (2008). Virtual tourist: Knowledge communication in an online travel community. *International Journal of Web-based Communities, 4*(4), 503–522. doi:10.1504/IJWBC.2008.019553

Linaa Jensen, J. (2010). Augmentation of space: Four dimensions of spatial experiences of Google Earth. *Space and Culture*, *13*(1), 121–133. doi:10.1177/1206331209353693

MacIntyre, A. (1981). *After Virtue*. Notre Dame, IN: University of Notre Dame Press.

Markham, A. (1998). *Life Online*. Walnut Creek, CA: AltaMira Press.

Nonnecke, B., & Preece, J. (2003). Silent participants: Getting to know lurkers better. In *C. Leug & D. Fisher (red.), From usenet to coWebs: Interacting with social enformation spaces*. Amsterdam, Netherlands: Springer-Verlag.

Owyang, J. (2010). A collection of Social Network stats for 2010. *Web strategy* (http://www.web-strategist.com/ blog/2010/01/19/ a-collection-of-social-network-stats- for-2010). Link checked November 4th 2010.

Parks, M. (2011). Social Network sites as virtual communities. In Zizi Papacharissi (Ed.). *The Networked self - identity, community and culture on Social Network sites* (105-123). New York, NY: Routledge.

Peng, X. (Michael) (2010, May 13). China's Social Networking scene: An inside update. *Internet evolution*. Link checked November 4th 2010. (http://www.internetevolution.com/ author.asp? section_id= 789&doc_id=191887&f _src=internetevolution_ gnews).

Preece, J. (2000). *Online communities: Designing usability, supporting sociability*. Chichester, UK: Wiley Books.

Putnam, R. (2000). *Bowling alone*. New York, NY: Simon & Schuster.

Reid, E. M. (1999). Hierarchy and power. Social control in Cyberspace. In *M. A. Smith & P. Kollock (red.), Communities in Cyberspace* (pp. 107–133). New York, NY: Routledge.

Rheingold, H. (1993). *Virtual communities*. Cambridge, UK: MIT Press.

Schuler, D. (1996). *New community Networks. Wired for change*. New York, NY: Alklison-Weslery. Available online at http://www.scn.org/ncn/. Link checked November 4th 2010.

Simon, H. A. (1955). On a class of skew distribution functions. *Biometrika, 42*(¾), 425–440.

Smith, M., & Kollock, P. (1999). "Communities in Cyberspace. In M. Smith & P. Kollock (ed.). Communities in Cyberspace (3-27). London, UK: Routledge.

Sproull, L., & Faraj, S. (1995). Atheism, sex, and databases: The Net as a social technology. In Brian Kahin & James Keller (Eds.). *Public Access to the Internet* (62-81). Cambridge, UK: The MIT Press

Stone, A. R. (1991). Will the real body please stand up?: Boundary stories about virtual cultures. In *M. Benedikt (red.), Cyberspace: First steps*. Cambridge, UK: MIT Press.

Sudweeks, F., & Simoff, S. (1999). Complementary explorative data analysis, the reconciliation of quantitative and qualitative principles. In Jones, S. (Ed.), *Doing Internet research: Critical issues and methods for examining the Net*. Thousand Oaks, CA: Sage Publications.

Sundén, J. (2003). *Material virtualities: Approaching Online textual embodiment*. New York, NY: Peter Lang Publishing.

TechCrunch. (2008). http://www.techcrunch.com/ 2008/12/31/ top-social-media-sites-of-2008 -facebook-still -rising/. Retrieved November 4th 2010

Tönnies. Ferdinand (1887). *Gemeinschaft und Gesellschaft*. Leipzig: Fues's Verlag (reprint 2005, Darmstadt: Wissenschaftliche Buchgesellschaft)

Turkle, S. (1995). *Life on the screen*. New York, NY: Simon & Schuster.

Virilio, P. (1998). *Cyberworld. Det værstes politik.* København, Denmark: Introíte Publishers.

Walzer, M. (1983). *Spheres of Justice.* New York: Basic Books.

Wellman, B., & Gulia, M. (1999). Net-surfers don't ride alone: Virtual communities as communities. In *Barry Wellman (red.), Networks in the global village.* Boulder, CO: Westview.

Whittaker, S., Isaacs, E., & O'Day, V. (1997). Widening the Net. In *SIGCHI Bulletin, 29.* New York, NY: ACM Press.

Wikipedia (2010). Entries on *"community"* and *"Orkut".*

Wilhelm, A. (2000). *Democracy in the digital age: Challenges to political life in Cyberspace.* New York, NY: Routledge.

Section 3
Stimulating Virtual Communities:
Participation and Awareness

The reader will find in this section three chapters related to the development of functionalities for domain-specific virtual communities. These chapters describe and generalize advanced frameworks in collaborative on line laboratories, collaborative cultural text translation and collaborative design and simulation.

Chapter 7

Functionalities and Facets of Group Awareness in Collaborative Online Laboratories

Christophe Gravier
Université de Lyon, France

Michael Callaghan
University of Ulster, UK

ABSTRACT

This chapter examines the rationale and motivations for using Computer-Supported Collaborative Learning (CSCL) for Online Laboratories. It explores different classifications, facets and features of virtual, remote and hybrid laboratories (Gomes2009, Gravier2009a) and subsequently introduces and discusses a range of metaphors, which can be used to understand each approach (Kreijins2002, Northrup2001). It also attempts to classify each of these platforms based on how students learn in these environments i.e. working as individuals or collaboratively in peer based groups (Gravier2009). It discusses and defines the concept of "Collaborative Online Laboratories" as Remote, Virtual or Hybrid Laboratories where groups of users work collaboratively in online virtual communities to support and facilitate learning. Two practical examples of Collaborative Online Laboratories, (the OCELOT project, a Collaborative Remote Laboratory from the University of Saint-Etienne and the Engineering Education Island project, a Collaborative Virtual Laboratory from the University of Ulster) will be presented in the context of existing literature, our individual experiences in implementation and the functionality included in each platform to facilitate collaboration between learners. The chapter will conclude with a discussion of the author's experiences of practical implementation of these projects and the opportunities/barriers to future directions in Collaborative Online Laboratories.

DOI: 10.4018/978-1-60960-869-9.ch007

GROUP AWARENESS IN COLLABORATIVE ONLINE LABORATORIES: A STACK OR TWO TOWERS?

Motivations

One of the first definitions of Group Awareness (GA) was proposed by (Dourish 1992): "Awareness is an understanding of the activities of others, which provides a context for your own activity". In other words, GA is the "group context", where the group is the set of individuals, but where the group context is more than the sum of the context of each individual in the group (Lee 2004). Additionally conflicts, group partitioning, recommendations, etc. are new issues brought by the notion of a "group context" in addition the individuals' contexts.

Until recently online remote and virtual laboratories differed from the student's campus based experience as they only facilitated single user connections at any given time. This approach has proven successful as a viable alternative to being physically present in the laboratory as clearly evidenced by the number of working remote and virtual laboratories in everyday use (Gustavsson 2007, Lowe 2009, Gravier 2008). However in campus-based laboratories a key element of the learning process is peer facilitated learning through student interaction and the sharing of results/experiences. The concept of "Collaborative Online Laboratories" as Remote, Virtual or Hybrid Laboratories, where groups of users work collaboratively in online virtual communities to support and facilitate learning is a necessary and important development in this area and must seek to replicate the group dynamics of a distributed engineering team (Muller2007). This multi-facetted element of collaboration is important to the development of successful engineers and is an essential pedagogical objective of laboratory-based teaching. In addition, learning to work together remotely as part of an efficient distributed group of workers is an increasingly necessary skill for the next generation of engineers.

Group Awareness and Open Issues for Collaborative Online Laboratories

Face-to-face interactions, and therefore GA, were taken for granted in traditional laboratories. These are however under-studied interactions in the context of online laboratories, as we only found two synchronous collaborative laboratories to date in the literature. In the meantime, GA studies had shown that GA enhances knowledge sharing and limits the impact of the free ride[1] issue in Computer-Supported Collaborative Learning (CSCL) environments (Kreijins2003). While it is true that GA is difficult to implement in distributed systems (Gutwin2004), the effectiveness of GA for online laboratories situation is therefore unknown due to the lack of empirical studies on this subject, though previous research on its effectiveness in CSCL environments points in this directions.

This raises several issues that we are trying to tackle in our research work which we will focus on in this chapter:

- Is GA possible in Collaborative online Laboratories?
- If so, how can it be built in terms of functionality? What are the possible facets of GA in collaborative online laboratories?
- Does it enhance the Quality of Experience (QoE) of the laboratory session, especially by accurately recreating the traditional laboratories atmosphere and limiting free rides?
- Does it improve the learning experience of the students to the same extent as in single user online laboratories?
- How far can we go to bring the metaphor of the traditional laboratories online in terms of Human-to-Machine Interactions?

Table 1. Group awareness features in collaborative remote and virtual laboratories

Features	Collaborative Remote Laboratories	Collaborative Virtual Laboratories
Feedback from instrumentation and circuits under test	Video streaming	Interactive and dynamic 3D representation of the remote laboratory
Communication	Chat room	Text/chat windows
Group interactions	Colour coded annotation of individual interactions	Visibility of user interactions
Collaboration management	Rule-based moderation unit for collaboration	Delegated to the physical rendering of avatar

Group Awareness Functionalities for Collaborative Online Laboratories

In this context, the design of effective Collaborative Online Laboratories must include tools to facilitate remote working and GA. Students should feel they are learning as a group and that they can rely on the support of their peers in the learning process. In the previous section we presented two distinct approaches to remote collaborative working in this context, a Collaborative Remote Laboratory and a Collaborative Virtual Laboratory and discussed the different features of each approach i.e. graphical user interface based interactions and avatar-based interactions in virtual worlds. Table 1 classifies the relative features of each of these approaches.

From this table it would initially appear that the virtual laboratory approach differs substantially from the remote laboratory approach where the columns appear as two distinct towers with little or no similarity or overlap ("two towers" effect). However on closer examination it would seem that the core purpose of each of these elements is very similar when examined from a GA perspective. The tele-presence element of the Collaborative Online Laboratory effectively serves the same purpose at the physical presence of avatars e.g. awareness of who is in your group and is currently online. The same is true of the text-based communications where both systems tag and record users conversations although these are not individually colour coded in the virtual laboratory at this current moment in time. The feedback from the circuits/instrumentation is of a similar nature, where users can see changes happening and recorded in the chat text box, although in the virtual laboratory this is not colour coded at the moment but could be in a future iteration.

A well-known approach for constructing GA requires splitting the GA into three different modules (Caroll 2003):

- Social awareness: conscious presence of others, which attempts to answer the question: "who's who?"
- Action awareness: tagging authors and their actions, which attempts to answer the question: "who made what?"
- Activity awareness: representing the level of overall completion of the global objective of the group when given a measurable and specific objective, this attempts to answer the question: "How are thing's going overall?"

While we do not question this approach, we extend this approach in our models by suggesting there are other facets to GA:

- **Self awareness:** conscious understanding of the projection of one's own actions and the image he/she projects in the group, which attempts to answer the question: "What do I look like to others?" (is it a mirror?).

- **Wisdom of the crowd:** communication awareness of textual or oral interactions between students that facilitate peer help and learning, which attempts to answer the question "who is saying what?". This is the communicational ground set up for the contemporary socio-constructivism learning theory that suggests that students can also build knowledge when they act as a group. This can be explained by the fact that we have "learnt to learn" that way from our earlier age: learning is not the cognitive construction of knowledge but the internalization of social activity (Tudge2008). As communicating is part of the social interactions it is therefore part of the required GA for Collaborative Online Laboratories.

- **Avatar interactions:** consistent representation of a student identity with which others interact helps each individual to build their own representation of other individuals. We believe that this helps to enhance social bounds between users, and helps them to fill the gap between traditional textual Computer-Mediated Communications (chat rooms), and Face-To-Face communications.

We integrate "Activity awareness" from (Caroll2003) in our model as it seems expand to provide an overview of the tasks achieved so far in an Collaborative Online Laboratories (is the lab nearly finished? Did we answer properly? Can this assist the tutor in objective assessment? etc.). We will not go into detail here as it out of the scope of this chapter, however activity awareness in Collaborative Online Laboratories is a very challenging and young research field, that goes beyond online laboratories, It aims to find pattern

recognition models for sequences of actions by users in the field of activity tracking in computing.

All the functionality of the Collaborative Online Laboratories depends on the successful implementation of the previous function in the stack e.g. colour coded communication, tracking of the user interface interactions and rule based moderation of group activities. From this understanding we can catalogue how GA is constructed in the Collaborative Online Laboratories approach under the following headings: Self-Awareness, Tele-Presence (aka Social Awareness in (Caroll2003)), Wisdom of the crowd, Focus & Nimbus (aka Action awareness in (Caroll2003)), Avatar interactions, and Activity awareness.

We think that these functionalities are stackable: to address the issue of tele-presence first requires the user to be aware of his/her own actions, to address the wisdom of the crowd requires the users to be aware of who is online, etc. The model of functionalities for GA in Collaborative Online Laboratories therefore follows a pyramid of needs (similar to the Maslow pyramids of human needs).

Group Awareness Facets for Collaborative Online Laboratories

In order to implement these functionalities, a collaborative online laboratory can present different variations (facets). The first been that it can be a remote laboratory or a virtual laboratory. This should not hide all the other facets. While they are certainly others, we have tried to present the major facets and possible values in Table 2.

Implementations of Collaborative Online Laboratories

One of a main issues for (C)OL is the integration time (and associated cost). Aside from studying creative models or well-grounded approaches, the primary problem is the amount of software development involved in the creation of a (C)OL. As COL mainly emerge from research, that

Table 2. Facets of collaborative online laboratories

Facets	Possible Values	Description
Type	**Remote**	**A remote laboratory involves a device operated at distance over the Internet (tele-operation).**
	Virtual	A virtual laboratory involves an algorithm that emulates an existing or non-existing device (simulation).
	Hybrid	A hybrid laboratory is made of parts from a remote laboratory and parts from a virtual one.
Synchronicity	Synchronous	All users are connected in different places at the same time.
	Asynchronous	All users are connected in different places at different time.
Representation	WIMP	Windows-Icons-Mice-Pointer. This denotes the traditional 2D GUI for interacting with a device.
	Spatial metaphor	These are laboratories that try to not only represent the device to control, but also to reproduce all the environment around it. It is usually the case for 3D-based Online Laboratories.
Fidelity	Straight	Laboratories that aim at producing the best fidelity in representation of the lab (e.g. Using webcams).
	Contextual	Laboratories that use trade-offs between fidelity, and contextualisation of the GUI. For instance, hiding widgets when they are not necessary for the task decreases fidelity (it is not hidden in the real local laboratory), but increases the degree of contextual awareness of the GUI.
Walkthrough	Scenarized	Task-oriented laboratory with predefined sequences of actions (e.g. Expected sequences of actions corresponding to a lab question).
	Cognitive	Cognitive walkthrough allow the user to experience the laboratory by themselves through curiosity, discovery, and multiple tries, and attempts to understand how it works by example.
Objectives assignments	None	No objective is set either per individual or for the global group.
	Individual-based	Objectives are given per individual.
	Group-based	Objectives are given for the entire group, but not per individual.
	Both	Objectives are assigned to both the group and for each individual. This usually aims at promoting peer support as the group objective is usually higher than the sum of the individual objectives. This tries to support the idea that group context is more than the sum of the context of each individual in the group (cf. 2.1).
Collaboration management	Free for all	Every user can use the widgets without access management. While this usually leads to "scroll wars", it also favours communication among users.
	Policy-based	A policy is set through rules allowing individuals to control at a given time or for a given time frame.

means that clusters were developed around the world, with partial answers to the global problems discussed above, facets of Online Laboratories versus facets of Online Laboratories (Grav2009a). In term of Information Systems, this means that COL were developed in silos (Figure 1).

As each COL only answers part of the global problem, they also develop their own architecture and terms for the same concepts involved in

functionalities provided by the Online Laboratories. Recent works therefore focused on how to create frameworks for Online Laboratories, so that common software (AAA, logging, messages exchanges, etc.) could be factorized into a middleware as an API. The primary objective is to make programming new Online Labs easier (Jud2008, Gustavsson2007). Very few however, proposed to factorize the software involved in making

Figure 1. From silos to framework, and from framework to standardization

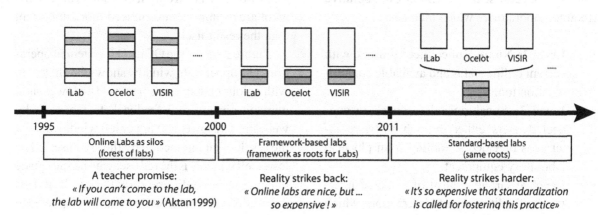

students collaborate (Gravier2008) - which means few frameworks in this regards are COL, most are Online Laboratories-. Meantime, at the moment collaborative 2D labs are slightly ahead in the curve with recording tools and feedback but virtual labs and hybrid virtual/online labs are starting to catch up.

TWO COLLABORATIVE ONLINE LABORATORIES CASE STUDIES

Experience in teaching engineering related subjects has shown that a complementary approach combining theoretical and practical exercises is vital for effective learning. Increasingly, teaching institutions offer remote access to virtual, remote and hybrid laboratories as part of an overall e-learning strategy. Recently, these highly functional and multi-facetted learning environments have started to facilitate collaborative group working, attempting to recreate the student's traditional campus based experience where peer support and interaction aid the learning process. Until relatively recently interface design to access remote/virtual laboratories have being typically two dimensional, based on a standard client server architecture, where the main focus has been functionality and the ability to configure and control remote campus based resources. Communications

and interaction between remotely based users has usually being facilitated by webcams, with video/audio and messaging/text based chat while elaborate, web based booking systems are used to schedule, plan and co-ordinate group sessions. The sense of presence and GA afforded to users of these systems has being limited to colour coded buttons/widgets or headshots on webcams. The growth and increasing common usage of 3D virtual worlds has dramatically changed the way users can interact online, allowing a sense of real physical presence through personalized avatars in immersive and highly interactive environments where remotely located instrumentation and test equipment is manifested as physically accessible objects. Two practical examples of these different approaches to Collaborative Online Laboratories are now presented and their relative features, functionality and approaches explored.

OCELOT Case Study (Collaborative Remote Laboratory)

The OCELOT project (Open Collaborative Environment for the Leveraging of Online instrumentation) from the University of Saint-Etienne examines and presents a framework for Computer-Supported Collaborative Learning (CSCL) in remote laboratories. OCELOT facilitates and classifies several scales of GA in Collaborative Remote Laboratories which includes;

- **Level 1:** Number of connected users, with current online status and available communication tools.
- **Level 2:** Synchronized feedback to connected users either through software interfaces or video streaming from physical laboratory equipment.
- **Level 3:** Group control of a shared interface to facilitate remote interactions which included tracking, recording and presentation of individual actions to connected users in the remote laboratory.
- **Level 4:** A facility/policy to moderate and co-ordinate group actions and decision-making.

Level 1 of GA is realized using the Publish/Subscribe paradigm. All connected users and their subsequent interactions with the remote physical devices through the Graphic User Interface (GUI) e.g. pushing a widget, is passed back to the server, recorded and subsequently displayed to all connected users in their group.

Level 2 of GA is facilitated by including a tele-presence indicator, built-in to the GUI of the OCELOT interface, which lists and individually colour codes all connected users. This allows users to see who is online and currently connected and ensures that all users are aware and notified of each other's presence and actions.

The colour coding of individual users enables the third level of group interaction, awareness. As each user interacts with individual elements of the GUI, the widget/button temporarily changes colour to match their allocated colour, clearly notifying the group that an interaction/change has taken place and identifying the user responsible for that change. This functionality and the ability to identify both the cause and sequence of interactions is important in the context of remote laboratories as in some instances the process or steps in achieving an output or result in the experiment are as important or indeed more important than the result itself.

Figure 2 shows the OCELOT system in operation. The upper right window shows the chatroom with colour coded user's names. The lower right window gives visual feedback to the users by webcam. The lower and upper left windows show the result of an interaction by the "red user". The lower left window is the red user who has just made a change to the configuration of the interface. This interaction is coloured coded red and displayed to the user in the "green" user in the upper left window. A video of the OCELOT project in operation is available here: http://diom.telecom-st-etienne. com/satin/einst/einst_demo.avi.

The fourth level of GA is focussed on administrating and establishing policies to structure the interactions for group sessions. This remote laboratory is a group activity and it is important that individual team members work together in a constructive manner to achieve a common goal (Gravier2008a). To do this fairly a rule based policy was implemented to ensure equal access and control of remote devices for each group member and while this approach cannot anticipate all eventualities in a dynamic group situation it can go some way to facilitating the smooth running of the process. Examples of rules in the OCELOT include simples rules e.g. "*Rule A*: If a user has both the Administrative role and also is the next user in the queue for system control, then and only then, the collaborative remote laboratory considers this user as the new operator of the remote laboratory". More complex rules are also used e.g. ; "*Rule B*: Allow a user to gain control of the system upon request, only if they had less accumulated operating time than the current user. Teachers and administrators are exempt from this rule and are allowed control/access on demand."

To technically implement the formal description of these rules, OCELOT uses Semantic Web technologies i.e. mainly ontologies serialized in W3C Ontology Web Language (OWL) and Se-

Figure 2. Group awareness (GA) provided in the OCELOT project

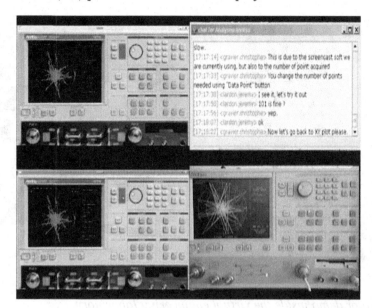

mantic Web Rule Language (SWRL) file formats. Some policies in this format are available online[2]. This approach and policy based user control of the remote laboratory can be changed dynamically if needed without restarting the application by the administrator.

This section introduced OCELOT, a Collaborative Remote Laboratory for Online Engineering applications and discussed examples of how user awareness and remote collaborative working/ group interactions can be formalised and facilitated in the remote laboratories. The next section examines another practical example of CSCL applied to online laboratory in the field of Virtual Laboratories.

The Engineering Education Island (Collaborative Online Laboratory)

In recent years there has been significant growth in the use of 3D virtual worlds for e-learning and distance education (Callaghan2008). These immersive environments offer the ability to create complex, highly interactive simulations using in-world modeling and scripting tools.

The Engineering Education Island project at the University of Ulster (Figure 3) is a virtual space dedicated to teaching engineering related subjects (Callaghan2009).

When residents first arrive on the Engineering Education Island they land at the welcome center (Figure 3), a large futuristic building which includes general information on the project. Each floor of the virtual laboratory contains a range of interactive engineering demonstrations and simulations including experiments related to AC and DC motors, electromagnets, magnetic flow in coils, half wave rectification, RC circuit analysis and Computer architectures (Figures 4 and 5).

Other facilities that are available on the Island include a virtual lecture theatre (Figure 6) where students can attend engineering-related classes and collaborative working facilities where students can work together remotely.

The virtual lecture theater includes the following functional components; a lectern for formal presentations, seating area for 50 students, interactive mini lecture slide show stand, main slideshow viewer, media centre for streaming video

Figure 3. Example simulations and collaborative group activities on engineering education

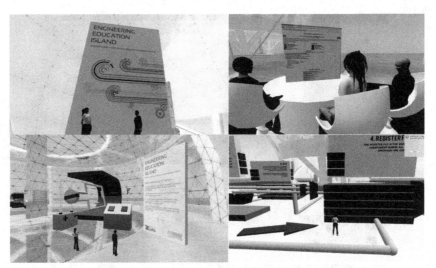

Figure 4. AC generator demo inside the virtual engineering laboratory

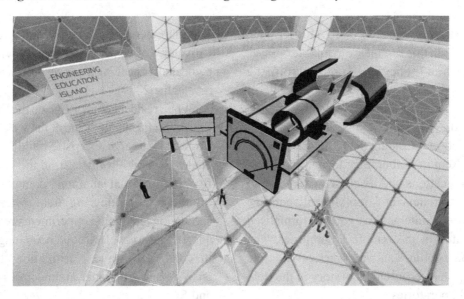

content and two message centers for student feedback. The collaborative working environment included learning booths with interactive quizzes, tables with pop-up boards and functionality to display a range of media including web pages and streaming video. Figure 7 shows students working collaboratively while interacting with a virtual display which imports interactive web pages into the virtual world.

Students can also use the quiz facility to assess their progress. To use this system the user reads the question and touches the texture (mouse right-hand click) and then enters the correct answer into the system using the text chat (Figure 8). The system then provides feedback to the student.

All of the buildings, interactive demos and content shown were built in-world using the Second Life modeling and scripting tools which

Figure 5. Direct current electric motor demo

Figure 6. Students attending a virtual lecture on VHDL

clearly shows the flexibility of the environment. Similar types of simulations are readily available elsewhere and are mostly web based and are usually created using Java or Adobe Flash. However creating the demonstrations in Second Life has a number of advantages. The virtual environment is immersive and allows residents to "walk around" and interact with the demonstrations in 3D space, viewing them from any conceivable angle. It also facilitates collaborative working and learning as groups of students and educators can occupy and interact in the same virtual space together. The in-world content creation and scripting tools also allow the creation of more complex and highly interactive simulations. Figure 9 shows the Giant PC project. The objective of this project was to teach students about computer architectures, components and hardware by recreating a large-scale Dell XPS 710 personal computer as a building. The scale of the building allowed users to

Figure 7. Remote collaborative working

Figure 8 Students using the quiz facility

browse around inside the PC, discovering how the PC works internally and the physical layout/ characteristics of the internal components.

Figure 10 shows a RC circuit simulator in Second Life which simulates the characteristics of a resistor/capacitance circuit.

This section of the chapter demonstrates how 3D immersive virtual worlds can be used to teach engineering related subject material in innovative and engaging ways. It will show how existing functionality and communication tools, readily available in virtual worlds, easily facilitate group and collaborative working experiences and foster the creation of supportive virtual communities in this area without the overheads and additional functionality required in traditional two dimensional client/server architectures. The virtual presence, facilitated by avatars allows the users

Figure 9. The Giant PC in Second Life

Figure 10. Virtual electronics engineering laboratory

to engage in more intuitive ways without complex booking or tracking systems.

CASE STUDIES COMPARISON

In the previous section, we have presented two real user cases that were:

- the Open Collaborative Environment for the Leverage of Online instrumentation (OCELOT), a J2EE online collaborative remote laboratories middleware and framework,
- the Engineering Education Island project (EEI), a Second Life Island which allows users to perform online collaborative virtual laboratories.

These two environments significantly differ from one another in term of facets they offer for making collaborative online laboratories. Table 3 is a synoptic view of the different choices made in each project.

While significantly different in term of facets, they are both collaborative online laboratories platforms, they are therefore governed by the 6 degrees of functionalities for group awareness that we proposed in the section "Group Awareness Facets for Collaborative Online Laboratories" (Self-Awareness, Tele-Presence, Wisdom of the crowd, Focus & Nimbus, Avatar interactions, and Activity awareness). It is interesting to see how these case studies perform in terms of GA functionalities.

- *Self-Awareness*: in the OCELOT approach users can immediately see the consequences of his/her actions through instant

Table 3. Synoptic view of group awareness (GA) facets proposed per case studies

Facets	Case studies	
	OCELOT	**EEI**
Type	Remote	Virtual
Synchronicity	Synchronous	Synchronous
Representation	WIMP	Spatial metaphor
Fidelity	Straight	Straight
Walkthrough	Cognitive	Cognitive
Objectives assignments	Group-based	Group-based
Collaboration management	Policy-based	Free for all

Table 4. Synoptic view of GA functionalities implemented per use cases

Degree of expected GA functionality	*OCELOT*	*EEI*
Self-Awareness	⊡	⊡
Tele-Presence	☑	☑
Wisdom of the crowd	☑	☑
Focus & Nimbus	☑	☐
Avatar interactions	☐	☑
Activity awareness	☐	☐

☐: the project do not address the functionality,
⊡: the project only address partially the functionality,
☑: the project fully match the expected GA functionality

feedback e.g. colour coding of the widget/button used, but they cannot see the image/presence of themselves that are send to others. At the opposite side of this, EEI let users perceive their avatar, yet it is not possible so far to have an acknowledgement/feedback of their actions (they are only notified of the result of their actions). In this, both projects partially address self-awareness.

- *Tele-Presence* (aka Social awareness in (Caroll2003)): the OCELOT approach makes it easier to determine who is in your group and currently online. EEI has an enhanced tele-presence indicator as part of the Second Life client.
- *Wisdom of the crowd*: both approaches allow communication with other students

and facilitate peer based support and learning through group interaction and discussions although the flexibility and rapid feedback in the OCELOT system allows for more flexibility in the configuration of the experiment.

- *Focus & Nimbus* (aka Action awareness in (Caroll2003)): the tracking facility in the OCELOT system allows each user to see and recall each other's action in the laboratory and to retrace their steps to the current state of the laboratory. This is useful for focussing the student's attention and recording laboratory processes.
- *Avatar interactions/communications*: Both provide interaction/communication tools in order to allow students to interact and exchange information freely.

Table 5. Research results

Issue	Result
Is GA possible in Collaborative online Laboratories?	Two cases studies illustrated that it is possible to different degrees. While these are good indications that complete GA may be possible, a full GA featured Collaborative Online Laboratory is not yet available.
If yes, how can it be built it in term of functionality?	We proposed six core functionalities: Self-Awareness, Tele-Presence, Wisdom of the crowd, Focus & Nimbus, Avatar interactions, and Activity awareness.
What are the possible facets of GA in collaborative online laboratories?	We proposed 7 facets: Type, Synchronicity, Representation, Fidelity, Walk-through, Objectives assignments, Collaboration management
Does it enhance the Quality of Experience (QoE) of the laboratory session, especially by better reproducing traditional laboratories and limiting the free ride problem?	Studies were conducted (Gravier2009) in the OCELOT project that tends to illustrate that the students had good experience overall, but also that they preferred Collaborative Online Laboratories over traditional single user Online Laboratories. The major benefit they saw was that it allows them to exchange results and offered peer support.
Does it improve the learning accuracy and completion rate of the students in a similar fashion to single user online laboratories?	Large-scale studies must be conducted to confirm this early result on an average set (43 users). Such tests must be conducted with group of students in the traditional distance curriculum, and with student in the same situation but who use their online laboratories in a collaborative manner. This question is left unanswered.
How far can we recreate the metaphor of the traditional laboratories online in term of Human-to-Machine Interactions?	The two projects illustrated that two facets can be explored in term of representation. On one hand, OCELOT provided a high fidelity GUI in a 2D environment, and on the other, EEI synthesized a complete collaborative online laboratories environment for the students around a hands-on approaches.

- *Activity* awareness: none of the presented use case implements it.

Table 4 sums this analysis.

CONCLUSION

Point to Point Answers to Question Raised in this Chapter

In the introduction of this chapter, we raised 5 major questions related to group awareness in collaborative online laboratories. In this section, we will highlight the results of our research in attempting to answer these questions.

For the reader's sake, we propose to sum up these answers in Table 5.

Open Issues for Collaborative Online Laboratories

We think that there are two major issues for Collaborative Online Laboratories in the future.

The first one is that to have full group awareness implemented in collaborative online laboratories is yet to be imagined and implemented. This is a crucial requirement in order to better evaluate the impact of each criterion of group awareness on the user's learning performance. In particular we suggest focusing on:

- Self awareness, with the objective of providing a mirror for each person on their actions, but also on the image/persona they send to others. For instance, is it possible to tell the user how the others perceive him, or how much help he needed, etc. And if yes, how does it benefit of the learning experience?
- Scenarization and contextual fidelity: is it possible to edit scenarios in order to bet-

ter evaluate what the users are doing? How could these scenarios enhance contextual fidelity, as we expect logical sequences of actions, and the user does not enter this sequence, would the next step be a widget suggesting the next step in the process to the user to reinforce and guide the learning process?

- Activity awareness: this is the major un-studied facet of group awareness in collaborative online laboratories. So far, we do not know the effects on the overall learning experience of giving precise information (true or false) on the overall achievement/progress of the group and the assigned objectives.

The second idea is to imagine collaborative online laboratories as a more flexible software platform. Today's Collaborative Online Laboratories are designed with predefined choices of values per facets (Type, Synchronicity, Representation, Fidelity, Walkthrough, Objectives assignments, Collaboration management). They therefore lack the ability to switch from one value of the facet to another inside the same session, given the context, group awareness, assignments, etc. For instance, part of the session can consist of playing a scenario, while another part of it can consist of a cognitive walkthrough of the user in the GUI. Another example is synchronicity: learners could start a laboratory altogether in a synchronous way, but they could also finish or redo it in an asynchronous way. This introduces the paradigm of adaptive collaborative online laboratories.

Final Thoughts

In this chapter, we have tried to build a common ground for researchers in the field of Virtual Communities in Collaborative Online Laboratories. There are a sizable quantity of Online Laboratories that are being developed every year on an *ad hoc* basis for particular local needs. Pressed by the students' demands, more and more Online Laboratories will evolve into Collaborative Online Laboratories, and while each one developed its own specificity given the context of usage, they all share some common architecture paradigms (n-tiers architecture, publish/subscribe paradigm for the message-oriented middleware, etc.). Those architectures are actually guided by a number of needs. These needs, actually, may be seen as a stack and not a two towers structure with, on one hand, Online Labs, and on the other, Virtual Labs. This stack is currently lacking a global frameworks implementation. We think that COL are not only "Second Best to Being There" (SBBT) (Aktan1999), but it also offers the perspectives of shaping teaching scenarios which are close to real distributed engineering team work (Muller2007). We may offer in this conclusion COL as "Next Best to Being Elsewhere" (NBBE), as a complementary to SBBT when the learning objective is to learn to be an engineer in a distributed team, instead of learning to be an engineer in a collocated room. This is of course of primary interest for distance online engineering education. There is no denying that working at distance is a very important facet of students future life as engineers in the modern pervasive society.

REFERENCES

Aktan B., Bohus, C. A., Crowl, L. A., & Shor, M. H. (1999). Distance learning applied to control engineering laboratories, IEEE Transactions on Education, 39(3), 320–326. 1996.

Callaghan, M. J., Harkin, J., McGinnity, T. M., & Maguire, L. P. (Jun 2008). Intelligent user support in autonomous remote experimentation environments, IEEE Transactions on Industrial Electronics, 55(6), 2355-2367. IEEE, ISSN 0278-0046.

Callaghan, M. J., McCusker, K., Losada, J., Harkin J. G, & Wilson, S. (November 2009). Engineering education island: Teaching engineering in virtual worlds. ITALICS (Innovation in Teaching And Learning in Information and Computer Sciences).

Carroll, J. M., Neale, D. C., Isenhour, P. L., Rossen, M. B., & McCrickard, D. S. (2003). Notification and awareness: Synchronizing task-oriented collaborative activity. *International Journal of Human-Computer Studies*, *58*, 605–632. doi:10.1016/S1071-5819(03)00024-7

Dillenbourg, P. (1999). What do you mean by collaborative learning? Amsterdam, NL: Pergamon, Elsevier Science, 1–16, 1999.

Dongman, L., Han, S., Park, I., Kang, S., Lee, K., Hyun, S. J., & Lee, G. (2004). A group-aware middleware for ubiquitous computing environments, Proc. of ICAT 2004, 2004.

Dourish, P., & Bellotti, V. (1992). Awareness and coordination in shared workspaces. In proceedings of the ACM Conference on Computer Supported Cooperative Work (CSCW'92), Toronto, Ontario, Canada: ACM Press.

Genci, J. (2009). The "Zero Cost" remote lab, icns, Fifth International Conference on Networking and Services, pp.572-575, 2009.

Gomes, L., & Bogosyan, S. (2009). Current trends in remote laboratories, Industrial Electronics, IEEE Transactions, 56(12), 4744 – 4756. ISSN: 0278-0046, 10.1109/TIE.2009.2033293, Dec. 2009.

Gravier, C., & Auer, M. E. (2009, Oct.-Dec.). Guest editorial: The many facets of remote laboratories in online engineering education. *IEEE Transactions on Learning Technologies*, *2*(4), 260–262. doi:10.1109/TLT.2009.53

Gravier, C., & Fayolle, J. (2009, June). Quality of learning: Using a semantic Web approach to enhance learner-control during collaborative remote laboratories [IJIL]. *International Journal of Innovation and Learning*, *6*(6), 606–624. doi:10.1504/IJIL.2009.026647

Gravier, C., Fayolle, J., & Bayard, B. (2008). Coping with collaborative and competitive episodes within collaborative remote laboratories, International Conference REV 2008, June 24th, Duesseldorf, Germany.

Gravier, C., Fayolle, J., Bayard, B., Lardon, J., Dusser, G., & Vérot, R. (2008). Putting reusability first: A paradigm switch in remote laboratories engineering, International Journal of Online Engineering, 5(1),16-22), February 2009.

Gustavsson, I., Zackrisson, J., Håkansson, L., Claesson, L., & Lagö, T. (2007). The VISIR project — an open source software initiative for distributed online laboratories, Proc. of Annual Int. Conf. on Remote Engineering and Virtual Instrumentation.

Gutwin, C., Penner, R., & Schneider, K. (2004). Group awareness in distributed software development", CHI letters, 6(3), 72-81, 2004. Harward, J., Del Alamo, J. A., Lerman, S. R., Bailey, P. H., Carpenter, J., DeLong, K., Zych, D. (2008, June). The iLab shared architecture: A web services infrastructure to build Communities of internet accessible laboratories. *Proceedings of the IEEE*, *96*(6), 931–950.

Kreijns, K., Kirschner, P. A., & Jochems, W. (2002). The sociability of computer supported collaborative learning environments. *Journal of Educational Technology & Society*, *5*(1), 822–837.

Kreijns, K., Kirschner, P. A., & Jochems, W. (2003). Identifying the pitfalls for social interaction in computer-supported collaborative learning environments: A review of the research. *Computers in Human Behavior, 19*, 335–353. doi:10.1016/S0747-5632(02)00057-2

Lowe, D., Murray, S., Weber, L., & De la Ville-fromoy, M. (2009). LabShare: Towards a national approach to laboratory sharing, 20th Australian Association for Engineering Education Conference, University of Adelaide, 6-9 December 2009, pp. 458--463, 2009

Muller, D., & Erbe, H. H. (2007). Collaborative remote laboratories in engineering education: Challenges and visions. In Gomes, L., & Garcia-Zubia, J. (Eds.), *Advances on remote laboratories and e-learning experiences* (pp. 35–59). University of Desto.

Northrup, P. (2001). A framework for designing interactivity into Web based instruction. *Educational Technology, 41*(2), 31–39.

Surowiecki, J. (2005). *The wisdom of crowds* (Books, A., Ed.). Reprinted 2005

Tudge, J. R. H. (1992). Processes and consequences of peer collaboration: A Vygotskian analysis. *Child Development, 63*(6), 1364–1379. doi:10.2307/1131562

ENDNOTES

[1] A free ride is basically where an individual in the CSCW session undermines group learning and peer support by not sharing his knowledge with his/her peers.

[2] http://dev.telecom-st-etienne.fr/satin/rlab/policies/studentminusoptime.swrl.owl

Chapter 8
Towards a Participative Platform for Cultural Texts Translators

Aurélien Bénel
ICD/Tech-CICO Lab UTT, France

Philippe Lacour
ENS, France & Marc Bloch Center, Germany

ABSTRACT

Although machine translation and translation memories are frequently used in business, they are inadequate to translate a text from a culture to another one. When faced with philosophy, literature or ancient texts, professional translators have to cope with the fact that the most important things to 'translate' are often in the style, in details, or even unwritten.

We advocate for changing the user interfaces and use patterns of a few computer-assisted translation techniques so that they could fit the interpretative tradition of cultural sciences. In particular, we will focus on what could foster intertextuality and enable the confrontation of different points of view on the same opus (several translators in several languages).

Provided as a participative Web platform, our software is designed as a collaboration and debate place for scholars around the world working on the same opus, author, time or genre. At the end of the chapter, this design is confronted with the observation of a face-to-face working session.

DOI: 10.4018/978-1-60960-869-9.ch008

INTRODUCTION

To scholars in social sciences or humanities, the so-called 'Web 2.0' (O'Reilly, 2005) means both new possibilities of cooperation and very surprising incarnations of rather familiar theoretical ideas. Indeed, it embodies – though in a very 'pop culture' way – some key aspects of *hermeneutics*, the theory and methods of interpretation (Lacour, 2010a; Bénel & Lejeune, 2009).

In these disciplines, translation has a singular status. Even if their discourses might include 'formal moments', the areas of human knowledge related to *culture* (as opposed to *nature*) are intrinsically bounded to the properties and possibilities of natural languages (Passeron, 2006). This assumption entails quite important consequences. In particular, these disciplines' key concepts are formulated in idioms characterized by their irreducible diversity. Translation difficulties arise when semantic fields do not exactly match in different languages. For instance 'citizenship' can mean either 'citoyenneté' or 'nationalité'. An accurate translation tries to preserve most of these existing ambiguities without adding any[1]. However, no translation can be perfect, and it is usually necessary to compare different translations to reveal all the original possible meanings.

Translation takes such a part in the interpretative tradition of *cultural sciences* embodied by 'Web 2.0' that one should be surprised that cultural texts platforms provide *either* interpretative translation features (e.g. *Perseus digital library*[2]) *or* participation features (e.g. *Wikisource*[3]). In our process to integrate both kind of features, we will first highlight several translation theory principles[4] and how they match (or not) typical *computer-assisted translation* tools. Then we will present the mockups of our platform together with their design rationale. To finish with, we will confront this design (based on translation theory) with a practical example as observed during a face-to-face working session.

BACKGROUND

Although computer-aided translation tools are widely used in business, they are carefully avoided in cultural sciences. In fact both machine translation and translation memories implicitly embed very questionable hypotheses concerning language.

From Machine Translation to Human Translation

Machine translation (see Figure 1) embeds a language theory in which translating could be reduced to applying a set of rules from a source language to a target language. First, this would require that a form could be replaced by another while preserving the meaning. On the contrary, both language theory and practice show that form-to-form translation (e.g. 'London' to 'Londres') is rare at any level (term to sentence). For example, when a translator cannot express a connotation in a translated form, she can move it on a neighbour form. Second, this would require the existence of language rules. For current theories, rules exist for genre but not for a whole language. In other words, they are not universal rules, but practical norms in use (Rastier, 2007). This last objection to rule-based machine translation could explain the renewed interest in computer-aided translation based on human translation. Among them, statistical machine translation is still not accurate enough to be used by professional, but, on the contrary, translation memories are widely used in translation agencies.

From Translation Memory to Concordance

A translation memory is a kind of database where translators store translated 'segments' so that they can be reused later. These segments are supposed to be large enough to be independent from their

Figure 1. Machine translation of a poem (screenshot)

Figure 2. Translation memory used on similar sentences (screenshot)

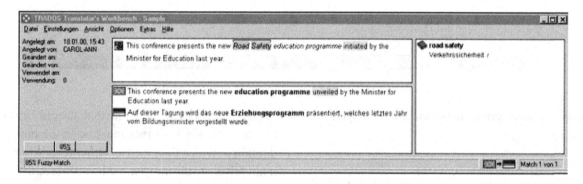

context, but small enough to be reusable as such or with a slight edit (see Figure 2).

The language theory embedded here may be less naive but is still questionable. First, getting context-independent segments is quite unrealistic. The context is indeed the whole text (Rastier, 1998). Second, large translation parts can only be reused on quotes or in very normative texts (laws, business letters, user manuals...). Third, translation memories sometimes mention a 'domain' on the segment but neither the author, nor the date and genre of the original text[5]. While their impact on translations can be low on mundane texts, they are known to be critical on cultural texts. Fourth, the name of the translator is usually neither store nor displayed, as if translations were 'data'

rather than the result of a creative and interpretative activity.

These objections could explain why cultural texts translators do not use translation memories while they have used *concordances* and bilingual dictionaries for centuries. Contrary to translation memories, these traditional tools for classical studies mention precise references to the context, as well as the author, and sometimes his trend (e.g. 'neoplatonicians', 'presocratics'...). Moreover, concordances are usually built from an homogeneous corpus (most of the time from texts by a single author). To finish with, it is worth noting that a comparative approach is embodied in some bilingual editions (especially for exegesis), in

Figure 3. A `texts-base' rather than a `data-base' (mock-up)

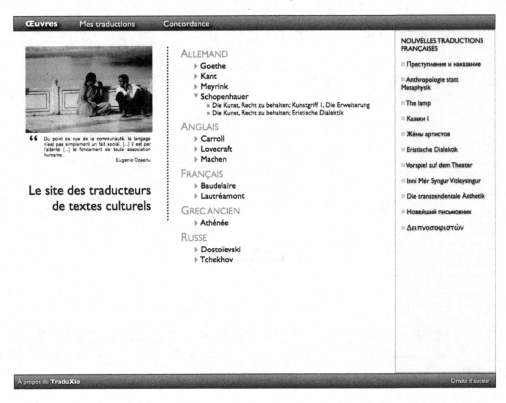

which concurrent translations are displayed on the same page.

TOWARD INTERSUBJECTIVE TRANSLATION

These theoretical objections led us to design a participative platform for human translation featuring a concordance.

As the main page reminds the guests (see Figure 3), the platform we designed is not a translation service but a service for translators, and not a 'database' but a 'texts-base'. The texts list at the middle of the page is primarily intended for translators. It aims at fostering the building of communities around a language and, if possible, around an author. The other list at the right side is intended for guests so that they can discover and read foreign texts recently translated into his/

her language. One should note that, the only texts that are listed in both lists must be in the public domain or with a free license. Other texts will remain private to the translator who uploaded them.

In prior works (Bénel & Lejeune, 2009), we offered a glimpse into 'Humanities 2.0' and how it could be brought by a digital workbench where documents would be interpreted by researchers from all over the world, and where their *viewpoints* could be compared. Contrary to our first experimentations where viewpoints were annotation structures, the viewpoints in this project are translations. More precisely, they are composed of translations of text fragments (see Figure 4). Even if our software could be used as *Wikisource*, our focus is not on getting an authoritative translation from different contributors, but to let the meaning of the text 'pop' from its confrontation with translations by different people in different languages.

Figure 4. A different translation for every translator (mock-up)

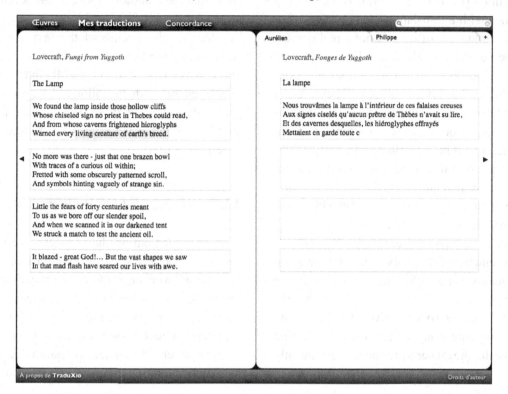

Provided that translations are stored fragment by fragment, it is possible to compute a multilingual concordance for every given expression (see Figure 5). For example, a French translator of *The Lamp* (see Figure 4) could search for other translated fragments containing "living creature of earth's breed". The concordance would be made from every translation done on the software (see Figure 5). Even copyrighted texts could be displayed provided that the extract respects 'fair use': in particular, the short quotations would link to online stores where to buy the complete work. In contrast, public domain texts (or texts with a free license) would be opened by such a link.

Figure 5. In-context translations search (mock-up)

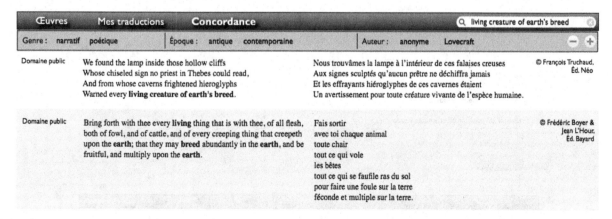

The link to the original context is not the only difference with a translation memory. First, because a random set of texts is not a real corpus, the concordance could be filtered on genre, time or author. Second, our software does not store short phrases but long fragments. They are not intended to be reused but only to give the translator insights. In our example, the sentence from *the Genesis* does not contain a translation of "living creature of earth's breed" that could be copied, but it suggests that the phrase connotes a creation story, and therefore could be translated by "toute créature vivante engendrée par la terre".

To store fragments of texts rather than out-of-context sentences is not only important for translation quality but also for authors' rights. In the platform we designed, there are neither derivative data that would be so `objective' that they would not have any author anymore, nor anthologies that would be the site owner's property. There are only texts that have authors. Once a text is removed, every fragment is removed too.

Because the license of the text affects the handling of the text on both the main page and the concordance, and because the attribution is displayed on both the bilingual pages and the concordance, all of these pages would allow a guest to report a licensing or attribution error (see Figure 6).

FUTURE RESEARCH DIRECTIONS

Before implementing the platform, we tried to test our hypotheses by observing a face-to-face translators' working session. The attendants were from a lab specialized in antique theater, sports and shows. They started to collectively translate an ancient Greek book about those topics.

The observed practices (illustrated here with verbatim quotations) corroborated the need for

Figure 6. Copyright compliance management (mock-up)

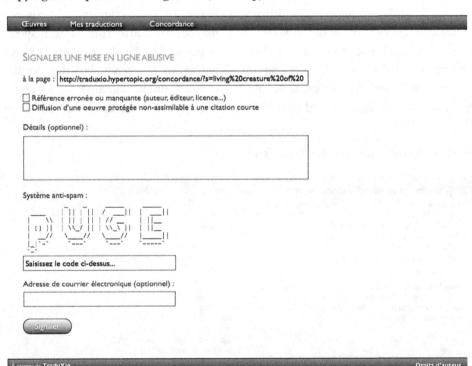

comparing translations of the same text, especially ancient and modern translations because criteria of what is a good translation changed. But they emphasized that the translations to study are not necessarily in the `target' language. Concordances will have to be designed like that as well.

The 18th [century] guy, he translates anyhow but he knew Greek well![6]

I look at the Italian translation.[7]

The need for a concordance was corroborated, but, what was more surprising was the value of a concordance *on the translation being made* to ensure coherence. Therefore the concordance could even be used on a platform with a single text. Because our main challenge for the next year will be the adoption of the platform by translators, this could be a critical advantage for us as a 'bootstrap' use.

'Poïeticos' is that there elsewhere?[8]

'Kinesis', we already met it and we already translated it by 'motion'.[9]

What was quite unexpected in a discipline where expertise is considered as the attribute of single scholars, was the team work being performed. For each session, one attendant had to prepare a rough translation, which had to be refined and augmented by the group. To handle such a cooperation, it is still unclear if it should be modeled as a single translation by a group (maybe with revisions history) or as a "patchwork" of translations done by single authors.

It is Valérie who translated [it]. I filled in what was missing.[10]

The type of the text being translated highlighted a few specific needs. First, as a text from the antiquity, the text has not an original typographi-

cal structure. Instead, punctuations, standard numbering, and section headings (called `rubrics' because they were written in red) were added by the philologists who 'established' the text. Section headings and numbering could be handled as `tags' on fragments. However editing the inner structure of the original text while preserving references is still a research challenge (Nelson, 1999). Second, because the 'original' text is in fact the result of the manuscripts transcriptions, our platform would probably need to be integrated with existing digital philology tools for transcribing a digital facsimile into plain text and preserving the variants from different manuscripts (Bozzi, 1993; Calabretto & Bozzi, 1998). Here again, referencing parts of such a composite document will be quite challenging.

Last but not least, what we observed on a physical session of an existing group cannot be directly extrapolated to distant communities that the platform aims at creating. In particular, we will have to foster the progressive building of trust between members (e.g. through new members sponsorship, participative promotion of translations, etc.).

CONCLUSION

We tried to understand why computer-assisted translation tools are avoided in cultural sciences. It appeared that machine translation embeds a very naive language theory, ignoring that there are usually no equivalent forms in two languages, mainly because of connotations and different available corpora. Translation memories would be more interesting since they are based on practical norms in use by humans rather than on formal and universal rules. However, because they are thought as a 'database', with the 'objective data' being the translated segments, they miss contexts, genres, authors, translators... everything a translator needs when he studies a concordance, prior translations, or a dictionary for classical studies.

By taking these objections into account, we designed a 'texts-base' rather than a 'database', a digital concordance rather than a translation memory. The software was designed in a 'Web 2.0' way, which means that all the content would be brought by the users themselves. We paid a lot of attention at the human interface so that it would allow the users to give access to useful published and unpublished content while not harming the potential value of it (as stated by the 'fair use' doctrine).

We tested our design by observing a face-to-face translators' working session. While it corroborated most of our hypotheses, it forced us to refine some of them and to list future research directions, such as computer-supported cooperative work models for cooperative translation and community trust building, as well as hypermedia models for digital philology.

REFERENCES

Bénel, A., & Lejeune, C. (2009). Humanities 2.0: Documents, interpretation and intersubjectivity in the digital age. *International Journal of Web Based Communities, 5*(4), 562–576. Retrieved November 15, 2010, from http://publi.tech-cico. fr/paper_details.php?paperid=106

Bozzi, A. (1993). Towards a philological worksta-tion. *Revue Informatique et Statistique dans les Sciences Humaines, 29*(1-4). Retrieved November 15, 2010, from http://promethee.philo.ulg.ac.be/ RISSHpdf/Annee1993/Articles/ABozzi.pdf

Calabretto, S., & Bozzi, A. (1998) The philo-logical workstation BAMBI (Better Access to Manuscripts and Browsing of Images). *Journal of Digital Information, 1*(3). Retrieved November 15, 2010, from https://journals.tdl.org/jodi/article/ viewArticle/10/20

Lacour, P. (2010). Portrait of the intellectual as a DJ: Wikipedia and the question of scientific exper-tise, *La Vie des Idées*, March 12, 2010. Retrieved November 15, 2010, from http://www.laviedesid-ees.fr/Portrait-of-the-intellectual-as-a.html

Nelson, Th. H. (1999). Xanalogical structure needed now more than ever. *ACM Computing Surveys, 31(*4). ACM Press. Retrieved November 15, 2010, from http://www.cs.brown.edu/memex/ ACM_HypertextTestbed/papers/60.html

O'Reilly, T. (2005). What is Web 2.0: *Design Pat-terns and Business Models for the Next Genera-tion of Software*. September 30, 2005. Retrieved November 15, 2010, from http://oreilly.com/web2/ archive/what-is-web-20.html

Passeron, J.-C. (2006). *Le raisonnement so-ciologique. L'espace non-poppérien du rai-sonnement naturel*. Albin Michel.

Rastier, F. (1998). *Sens et signification*. Protée, printemps 1998, 7–18.

Rastier, F. (2007). La traduction: *Interprétation et genèse du sens. Revue Texto!* Retrieved November 15, 2010, from http://www.revue-texto.net/index. php?id=2202

Savourel, Y. (2005, April 26). TMX 1.4b speci-fication. OSCAR recommendation. *Localisa-tion industry standards association*. Retrieved November 15, 2010, from http:// www.lisa.org/ fileadmin/ standards/ tmx1.4/ tmx.htm

ADDITIONAL READING

Bénel, A., Zhou, C., & Cahier, J.-P. (2010). Be-yond Web 2.0... And beyond the Semantic Web. In D. Randall & P. Salembier (Eds.), From CSCW to Web 2.0: *European Developments in Collab-orative Design*. London, UK: Springer Verlag. 155–171. Retrieved November 15, 2010, from

D'Iorio, P. (2007). Nietzsche on new paths: The *HyperNietzsche Project and Open Scholarship on the Web*. In M. C. Fornari & S. Franzese (Eds.), Friedrich Nietzsche. Edizioni e interpretazioni. Pisa: ETS. Retrieved November 15, 2010, from http://www.hypernietzsche.org/ doc/ files/ new-paths.pdf

Duteil-Mougel, C. (2004). Introduction à la sémantique interprétative. *Texto!* Retrieved November 15, 2010, from http:// www.revue-texto.net/ 1996-2007/ Reperes/ Themes/ Duteil/ Duteil_Intro.html

Granger, G.-G. (1994). *Les conditions protologiques des langues naturelles. Formes, operations, objets*. Paris, France: Vrin.

http:// benel.tech-cico.fr/ publi/ benel_SPRINGER_2010.pdf

http://www.uni-tuebingen.de/ uni/ nrk/ coseriu/ energeia/ zeitschrift/ 2009/ diskursivitaet.html

Lacour, P. (2009). Diskursivität. Zur logischen Erklärung der Hermeneutik Ricoeurs. *Energeia – Online Zeitschrift für Sprachwissenschaft und Sprachphilosophie*. Retrieved November 15, 2010, from

Lacour, P. (2010). *La nostalgie de l'individuel. Essai sur le rationalisme pratique de Gilles-Gaston Granger. Collection "Mathèsis"*. Paris, France: Vrin.

Tasman, P. (1957). Literary data processing. *IBM Journal of Research and Development, 1*(3), 249–256. doi:10.1147/rd.13.0249

Virbel, J. (1994). Annotation dynamique et lecture expérimentale: Vers une nouvelle glose ? *Littérature*, No 96. 91–105.

Zhou, C., & Bénel, A. (2008). From the crowd to communities: New interfaces for social tagging. *Paper presented at the international conference on the design of cooperative systems*, Carry-le-Rouet, France. Retrieved November 15, 2010, from http:// benel.tech-cico.fr/ publi/ zhou_COOP_08.pdf

KEY TERMS AND DEFINITIONS

Concordance: Alphabetical list of the principal words used in a corpus with their immediate contexts. Depending on their purpose, the extracts can be displayed in different ways (as a whole sentence, centered on the word, with a translation, etc.). The first known concordance was established by Dominicans on the 13th century. They are now computed automatically (Tasman, 1957).

Hermeneutics: The theory and practice of texts interpretation, historically created to decipher sacred texts, and generalized by philosophers (Schleiermacher, Dilthey, Gadamer...) as a foundation for the epistemology and methodology of humanities and social sciences. It constitutes the reflexive answer to the challenge of the polysemy expressed by a discourse under the complex (transphrastic) form of a text (Lacour, 2009). An interpretation stresses one – and only one – meaning. The polysemy of the text therefore logically unfolds into a variety of conflicting interpretations that constitute a polemic space of competing viewpoints. It also gave credit and legitimacy to an alternative approach of language, focusing not so much on rules and generalities as on creativity and singularity (Berner et Thouard, 2010).

Humanities 2.0: A provocative term to prompt thinking about the links that could exist between 'Web 2.0' and the social and human sciences. By focusing on documents (as opposed to data), on interpretation (as opposed to deduction), and on intersubjectivity (as opposed to consensus), Web 2.0 has surprising analogies with hermeneutics, and thus might better meet the needs of social and human sciences than traditional information technologies that are historically bound with logical positivism (Bénel et Lejeune, 2009).

Viewpoint: More than an opinion (anything goes) and less than a rigid and fixed semantics (Bénel et al., 2010; Zhou et Bénel, 2008).

Web 2.0: Contrary to a common misconception, the term does not refer to a technical innovation but to a change in Web use (O'Reilly, 2005).

A few years after the bursting of the dot-com bubble, Tim O'Reilly noted that the most popular Web sites shared several characteristics. One in particular was to "harness collective intelligence". Indeed, from books commentaries on *Amazon*, to 'tagged' pages on *Del.icio.us* or articles on *Wikipedia*, these contents are generated by the users rather than by the service provider. Internet participation, formerly reserved to a few specialized communities (open-source software, open directory project, open archives...) has become the major use model.

ENDNOTES

[1] For this reason, François Rastier (2007) notes that great translations often witness to a deeper comprehension of the original text than commentaries.

[2] http://www.perseus.tufts.edu/

[3] http://wikisource.org/

[4] Even in less erudite domains, we think that software designers should never consider an area of practice as if it were 'atheoretical'. Discovering users' conceptualizations is, in our opinion, one of the most important parts of the analysis.

[5] An in-house software has been reported to refute this as a general statement. However, it is significant that such clues about the original text are ignored by the format designed to "exchange translation memory data between tools and/or translation vendors with little or no loss of critical data during the process" (Savourel, 2005).

[6] Verbatim quotation: "Le type du XVIII°, il traduit n'importe comment mais il connaissait bien le grec !"

[7] Verbatim quotation: "Moi, je regarde la traduction italienne."

[8] Verbatim quotation: "'*Poïeticos*' est-ce que ça y est ailleurs ?"

[9] Verbatim quotation: "'*Kinesis*', on l'a déjà rencontré et on l'avait déjà traduit par 'mouvement'."

[10] Verbatim quotation: "C'est Valérie qui a traduit. J'ai complété ce qui manquait."

Chapter 9
Virtual Communities in a Services Innovation Context:
A Service Science and Mereotopology Based Method and Tool

Florie Bugeaud
University of Technology of Troyes, France

Eddie Soulier
University of Technology of Troyes, France

ABSTRACT

This chapter focuses on both the activities of the telecoms' innovators (i.e. actors of the innovation) and the emergence of some "service communities" which are interesting facets of virtual communities. These innovators are part of a remote and inter-professional network which forms a "design community". They are involved in the telecom operators' design process (opportunities research, service design, development, deployment and market launch). During the first stage, this community has to describe customers' services situations, discover lacks and opportunities and find some ideas of adapted solutions. Theoretical and professional difficulties have been noted during this key step. The main problem is related to the concept of service which is a multidimensional and still poorly understood object. Based on the service literature and the emergent field of Service Science, we propose a theoretical framework and a semi-formal semantic method to describe, co-model (through a mereotopological ontology of assembled and interconnected scenes) and simulate (through an animation of each scenario) the targeted Services Systems. These Services Systems are configurations of dynamic/processual entities that reveal not only the service field of experiences but also the actors' performances within different spatiotemporal situations.

DOI: 10.4018/978-1-60960-869-9.ch009

1. INTRODUCTION

This chapter is based on a real life project of research in the domain of services innovation. Although it has been more specifically experienced within the organization of a French telecommunication operator, it is applicable for most services providers. Several socio-economic and technologic evolutions have brought some important challenges for services providers. They now have to prove their capacity of innovation in order to support their corporate customers' value creation, to improve the final customers' experiences and to ensure their own strategic position within the market.

The emergence of new technologies enables and continuously improves the constitution of distributed projects teams. It implies the emergence of virtual interpersonal relations and the distribution of knowledge and competencies among teams' members. Virtual communities have a strategic role in the domain of services innovation. Services providers rely on such distributed teams of actors of the innovation (called "innovators"): designers, engineers, etc. These innovators form a virtual community of knowledge which is essential during all the steps of the design process. For example, Delalonde & Soulier (2007) were interested in the "knowledge management practices in a distributed research and development laboratory" of such a services provider (a telecom operator to be more precise). This laboratory deployed a knowledge database and some communities of practice sharing a virtual collaborative workplace. But the database was usually obsolete and employees were reluctant to ask and share knowledge with others. Delalonde & Soulier (2007) proposed a four steps model called RESONER: Information Retrieval, Caring, Negotiation, and Reification. This model specified a groupware dedicated to collaborative information retrieval and relying on "transparent profile construction based on user's activity, community's participation and shared documents" (Delalonde & Soulier, 2007). These model and

tool encouraged the emergence of informal knowledge networks and competencies awareness in a distributed context. Another example concerns the creation of a repository of the customers' business processes of a French telecom operator. The project team gathered several members of the R&D department (ergonomists, engineers, etc.). They made the hypothesis that knowledge and access to customers' internal information would be easier thanks to the provision of a repository of these customers' business processes. They thus created a web-based environment based on the Tibco platform (i.e. business integration and process management software) and invite all the actors of the R&D department (and most specifically the usages experts) to model every business process they know from a customer (or customers' segment). This tool encouraged the information sharing in a distributed context. But it had some limits that will be presented in the next section.

In this chapter we will focus more specifically on the remote and inter-professional work and network of innovators who have to detect new ideas of services/solutions during the opportunities research stage upstream of the design process (Bugeaud & Soulier, 2009). Theoretical and professional difficulties have been noted within this community. The basic problems are linked to the remote and inter-professional nature of the innovators' network. They form a "design community" that constrains the actors' work and interactions because they come from several disciplines (i.e. different professions and thus different vocabularies and understandings of the studied services) and they are localized in many different places. There are important misunderstandings and difficulties to collaborate within the design community. Innovators are currently working together with difficulties. These problems have been the object of a specific publication within an international workshop on "Virtual Environments and Collaboration" (Bugeaud & Soulier, 2009). One objective of our works is to propose a method and a tool that can finally promote the innovators' collaboration across distance and professions.

But the core problem is related to the concept of service which is a multidimensional object that is poorly understood by both the innovators and the literature (that rarely integrates its various dimensions and levels of analysis). We do not try to articulate the innovators' points of view. But, based on the service literature and the emergent field of the Service Science, we propose a common theoretical framework and a semi-formal semantic method to describe, co-model and then simulate/ animate services at an abstract and business level: the Service System. It corresponds to the spatio-temporal service situation of a customer (or a customers' segment) that the innovators have to describe. Based on a Service System description, they will be able to identify the assembled and interconnected scenes, to imagine the conceivable scenarios, to calculate the overall field of possible experiences and to imagine some adapted services/solutions. The Service System's entities are not some pre-existent or pre-determined elements but the result of a confrontation between the individual/an agent who observes (at least his consciousness) and the object he is observing. These entities are a kind of semantic processes (and not operational, we do not work on "business processes" and their modeling) or moments that intervene and interact with each other in some spatio-temporal spaces. These spaces look like micro-scenes which form a complete phenomenon (i.e. a set of dynamic entities) indicating a specific field of experiences. This last notion is essential given the fact that services are not bought and consumed products, but fully lived experiences by the customers who are involved since the service coproduction. In order to formalize Services Systems, we use some Mereological and General Process Theory (Seibt, 2009; Bugeaud & Soulier, 2010) based principles. The Service System is then a mereotopological hierarchy of interacting dynamic/processual entities. This mereotopological model gives the possibility to identify and

show the possible scenarios/pathways through the interconnected processual entities. These scenes and scenarios can be the object of animations that could help innovators which are not familiar with the modeling approach. It brings them a quite realistic view of the service system they study (i.e. a kind of movie or cartoon). Based on the model or the associated animations, they can deduct the associated service experiences and identify some lacks or opportunities for new solutions.

Moreover, as a Service System is based on a set of social acts (i.e. service = social relation, interactions), it can be interesting to discover the actors' performance. Here is another interesting facet of virtual communities in this project. Indeed, the emergence of processual and experiential configurations of entities (in other words, some interactions) reveals the emergence of some "service communities" which are so many possible configurations of "acting elements" (i.e. humans, artifacts, systems, etc.) at different moments and situations. This chapter thus addresses the work of the telecom's (or more generally services providers') "design community" (i.e. all the actors of the innovation process who are part of a remote and inter-professional network, who co-imagine and co-design some IT or telecom solutions and who are the users of our method and proposed tool) by the modeling and simulation of complex Services Systems, and the emergence of "service communities"(i.e. different groups of acting entities which are involved in the studied service situation at each main stage and / or in each possible scenarios). Here we found a social dimension at both the innovators' network level, and the service relation/interactions level. Even if we try to support the first one by providing an adapted tool to the design community, we especially focus on the second one by finding a way to represent the concept of service as a configuration / an arrangement of heterogeneous and interacting entities. We reuse the work of Bruno Latour (Actor Network Theory) who speaks about "social arrangements" (Latour, 2005).

The objective of this chapter is to promote a Services Systems modeling and simulation approach both for the improvement of the Service Science engineering perspective and the knowledge sharing and services co-modeling within a design community upstream of the design process of services providers.

This first section has introduced the fundamental notions and dimensions (social, dynamic, experience) that our works take into account. The next section quickly presents the context of this project aiming at supporting the work of the innovators' design community (i.e. describe some targeted services situations and find ideas of adapted or new IT/telecom services). Then section 3 describes the Service System concept and formalization as a configuration of dynamic and heterogeneous entities based on processual and mereotopological principles. Section 4 describes the proposed approach based on mereotopological ontologies for the knowledge sharing, the service animation, the service communities' emergence and the service/product design. It also gives some elements about the future platform's mechanisms. Finally, section 5 presents an experiment example within the e-health domain. Sections 6 and 7 give some future research directions and conclusions.

2. THE SERVICE DESIGN CONTEXT

2.1 The Design Process of Services Providers

The economic, organizational and sociologic evolutions and the global "service orientation" (growth of the tertiary sector and evolution of companies' business) have brought new issues for services providers. Moreover, the evolution of Information and Communication Technologies (ICT) has brought new ways to design and to deliver services. But it has also change the way of working within the organization of such services providers. To answer these challenges and to remain competitive, they try to propose more and more innovative and adapted services to their customers (Bugeaud & Soulier, 2009).

We base our work on the example of the telecommunication sector but it remains applicable to most services providers. Indeed, they all implement a similar innovation cycle which is generally shared between three main departments: the marketing department, the research department and the technological department (Figure 1).

The innovation cycle also presents four key "moments" or stages: the "opportunities research", the "service design", the "service development",

Figure 1. The innovation cycle

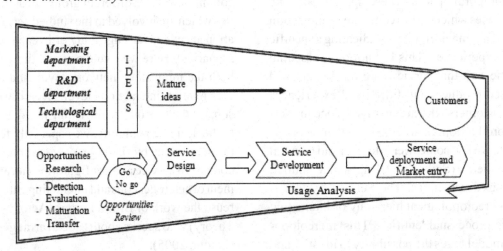

and the "service deployment and market entry". A more or less parallel and continuous step concerns the "usage analysis". Each phase is overseen by a Decision Committee. A Reading Committee makes a first selection of concepts upstream of the innovation cycle. Then it determines an "actions plan". At the end of the "opportunities research" step, an Anticipation Committee selects the major enriched and more pertinent concepts during an "opportunities review". Finally it validates (go/no go) their transfer towards the design and development steps.

2.2 The Innovators' Design Community and Design Reasoning

The "opportunities research" phase aims at identifying ideas of new services/solutions in order to anticipate or meet the customers' expectations (note that in this chapter we are more specifically interested in the corporate customers) and to ensure the operator market position. It is a key step gathering a lot of data, documents and actors. The sharing of information and arguments gives rise to a collaborative, analytical and cognitive practice in a specific community. Indeed, the remote (many locations) and inter-professional (many disciplines) network of the involved innovators forms a virtual community of knowledge: the "design community". It works as a social network of people coming from different locations and different professions, and interacting through specific media (phone, Internet, teleconferences, etc.) in order to co-describe a service situation and find some ideas of new solutions.

Their design reasoning (Bugeaud & Soulier, 2009) is based on two spaces: the concepts and the knowledge (C-K theory: Hatchuel & Weil, 2003). It needs and develops their individual and collective knowledge. They usually analyze the targeted corporate customer's sector, practices and business processes, and try to detect some opportunities. Their ideas go through four phases: "detection of not mature concepts/ideas", "evalu-

ation of these ideas regarding the global strategy and the potential created value", "maturation/enrichment" and "transfer to the anticipation committee". Nevertheless, their actual collaboration is insufficient to reach the necessary sharing and co-creation of knowledge. They are currently working together with difficulties given their different geographical locations and different professions. These innovators don't meet in real life. Some of them work on the same geographical location but the innovation's teams are distributed over the country. It is common to have two projects on the same subject in two different areas, or to have an old project or experts on an area that might interest/bring key information to a new project on another area, etc. There is no structured method (they often work independently of each other) and the existing modeling environments are not adapted (e.g. Mega or Tibco business process modeling platforms are too technical, operational and internal trade oriented and do not answer the question of "service" at this level of abstraction (but at a technical or, at best, functional level)). That is why it seems interesting to provide them a shared representation and an adapted tool.

Moreover, today the enrichment of the pipe of new ideas is essentially linked to a "bottom-up" approach starting from the work of the engineers/developers. They often realize a list of technical functionalities and propose them to the marketing experts who select the potential better ones. Some focus groups and retroactive descriptions of scenarios (or use cases) can help the designers and developers to finalize a concept and estimate the real desire of the users. But this interest for the customers' expectations and "real life" seems to arrive very late regarding the innovation cycle (Figure 1). They often test the usability of the service when they already have the prototype. Moreover the imagined use cases are sometimes quite taken away from the real life of customers. This is all the more paradoxical that supplied services must be adapted to real situations and must propose a rich and personalized experience.

Figure 2. Location of the main existing models according to the phases of the service lifecycle and the level of granularity

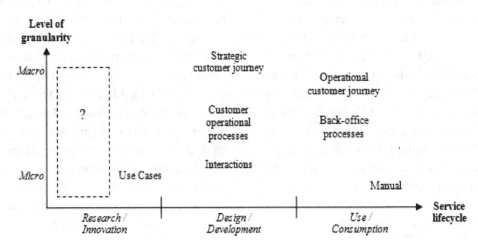

Indeed, the experience is a more and more key notion in the design of services. The customers do not any more buy and consume a product but they live a unique experience.

The Figure 2 presents the main tools and models that are currently used by the innovators at each stage of the service lifecycle (including the customer's perspective). For example, during the design phase, the innovators model some key operational processes of the targeted customer through BPMN or UML notations. They also realize some strategic "customers journeys" through the description of personae, the identification of a general scenario's steps, the detection of the underlying technologies and the realization of some sketch sheets to draw some propositions. But Figure 2 also clearly shows the lack of appropriate tools in the upstream phase (although this phase is a key phase for the overall cycle). To assure a better efficiency of the design process, it could be interesting to (it is important to!) introduce a "top-down" approach since the opportunities research step. Then the upstream innovators will be able to study the real service situation of the targeted customer and find some adapted ideas.

However, they meet some difficulties (in addition to the difficulties related to the nature of their network - see the beginning of the paragraph) that currently limit their design reasoning and make the introduction of an upstream experiential analysis of the service quite difficult. The fundamental problem is linked to the concept of "service" which is a multidimensional object disrupting their work. They have to co-design services but they do not define and use the word "service" in the same manner. A first step towards the description of the targeted services situations has recently consisted in the adoption of a more or less upstream method of processes description. This method has given rise to a repository of business processes (see the introduction) based on the Tibco platform. The objective of this repository was very close to our business objective since it aimed at the modeling of the customers' services and the availability of these models for all the innovators. The final objective was to help them discovering and understanding the studied services situations, but it was insufficient. This deficiency can be explained by three main facts:

- it does not solve the theoretical problem of defining the service concept although the innovators come from several disciplines ;

- it was based on the assumption that innovators would be familiar with modeling techniques and able to do the models themselves and understand these models ;
- it was based on a very internal view of the customers (i.e. corporate customers) through their business processes which cannot be considered as the overall services situations of the customers (i.e. their processes but also their interactions with their own customers and partners, the participation of their customers, their experiences, etc.).

The repository was thus far from the experiential, social, and even emotional dimensions of the notion of service. It obscured many aspects and views of the customers' services situations, and thus reduced the chances to discover or invent new solutions. Moreover it has been tested within a specific usages analysis team and not the overall innovation actors as it was originally planned. We therefore have made the hypothesis that they need for a shared definition of the service, a share representation of the targeted service situation and more generally a kind of collective mind to unify members and practices.

3. THE SERVICE FORMALIZATION AS A DYNAMIC SYSTEM

3.1 From Service to Service System: The Service Science

Several authors (e.g. Eiglier, 2004; Gadrey, 2000; Gallouj & Weinstein, 1997; Lenfle, 2005) have studied the notion of "service" in economic, sociologic or management perspectives. But it is still a hazy concept because of its numerous levels of analysis, characteristics and uses. There are four main areas: the service relationship, the flow and process of the service realization / delivery, the result, and the structuring of the offers system (Tannery, 2001). But neither the concept of experience nor the dynamic dimension (which are important service features) have been well identified and formalized. The concept of service is generally defined as an interactive and experiential phenomenon. The "dynamic dimension" means that services rely on a dynamic mechanism of interacting entities which creates and also explains the forming and evolution of the phenomenon through time and space in a value co-creation objective. The "experiential dimension" means that services not only provide a physical or moral or emotional (etc.) response to a specific customer's expectation but also a complete and unique experience. Each customer "lives" the service because he is totally involved in the simultaneous production, consumption and evaluation of that service (and his relationship with the provider). Each service can potentially offer a wide range of experiences. This ability to offer a special and rich experience to customers is a key differentiator for services providers.

The Service Science Management and Engineering (SSME) is an emergent field of research which has been initiated by IBM and several Universities. SSME has its origins in the service literature and has begun to emerge in the early 2000s. But it has actually won recognition since 2007 with a series of dedicated publications (IfM and IBM, 2007 ; Spohrer, 2007 ; etc.) and a symposium at the University of Cambridge ("Cambridge Service Science, Management and Engineering Symposium", July 2007, UK). Today, it is a more and more recognized discipline that is the object of numerous books, papers and conferences. It tries to gather all the synergies around "one" concept of service at a more abstract level than the one we usually find in the literature (especially in computer science, i.e. technical and reusable functionality). They conceive it as a complex system and not a merchandize. Services Systems are "dynamic value co-creation configurations of people, technology, shared information (such as language, laws, measures), internal and external service systems connected by value propositions" (Spohrer, 2007). Here we can recover the idea of the "dynamic dimension" of a service because a Service System is a dynamic configuration of heterogeneous and interacting entities. SSME is also very interested in the customer's view and the way of integrating the "experiencial dimension" within a Service System's description (Blomberg, 2007).

Moreover, the Service System's definition as a "dynamic configuration of heterogeneous entities" takes into account the "social dimension" of the concept of service. As Bruno Latour says in his Actor Network Theory (ANT), the "social" is "a trail of associations between heterogeneous elements". He speaks about "social arrangements" and wrote: "In the alternative view, 'social' is not some glue that could fix everything including what the other glues cannot fix; it is what is glued together by many other types of connectors" […] "specific associations provided by economics, linguistics, psychology, law, management, etc." […] "In this meaning of the adjective, social does not designate a thing among other things, like a black sheep among other white sheep, but a type of connection between things that are not themselves social" (Latour, 2005). Then, the social is an association / a progressive and provisional unification of heterogeneous entities / a human and non-human blend for connections. This is a fundamental point for our works which is totally in line with the definition of the service in the literature (i.e. a social relation (Gadrey, 2000)) and the definition of a Service System in the SSME field (i.e. a configuration of heterogeneous and interacting entities).

But, the SSME works do not go much further than this definition, yet. The system's borders, heart, elements and perspective are still not well identified.

3.2 A Collection of Heterogeneous and Processual Entities

Based on the SSME discussions, we conceive the service as a Service System (Bugeaud & Soulier, 2009) and we propose a definition of its structure and borders. The Service System is an artifact, the object of a co-production between a client and a supplier. But it is also a dynamic configuration or combination of heterogeneous and processual entities expressing a particular phenomenon and giving an access to the service field of experiences. In other words, these entities form "a service" at a given moment and in a given situation. We created a Service System framework (Figure 3) showing the service coproduction spaces (back-stage and on-stage spaces), the service elements (service object, service delivery system and service experience), the service interactions (underlying the service coproduction), its outputs (immediate and long term results and associated experience), etc.

Indeed in the field of innovation, it is necessary to conceive at the same time the concept of service, the targeted customers' segment and the system for its functioning (Lenfle, 2005). We therefore distinguish the "Service Object" (SO) and the "Service Delivery System" (SDS). The former corresponds to the idea or object of the innovation for a targeted customer or activity sector (e.g. in the telecom industry: service of mobility, con-

Figure 3. The Service System structure

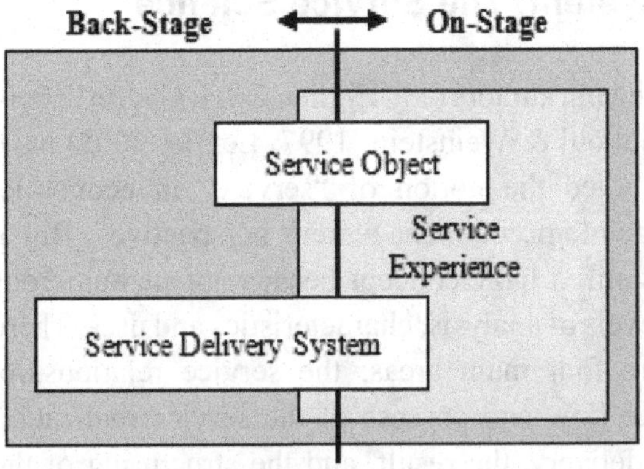

nectivity, security, cooperation or geolocalization). The initial SO can be broken down into sub-concepts which can be themselves broken down in an iterative way. Its structure must help the innovator to discover the service universe and to progress in the exploration of the relevant concepts that may become designed and sold objects. The latter is the hypothetic functioning of the Service Object. The SDS is linked to the notion of "servuction" which has been proposed by Eiglier and Langeard in 1987. It includes the customer, the physical support, the providers' employees (which are in front of the customer), its internal system of organization and the service as the result of interactions. Our works add to these elements the nature of the service target or medium (material, knowledge, information, relation) (Gallouj & Weinstein, 1997), the other customers and partners of the services provider. The initial servuction model considered the back-office of the services providers as a black box. This back-office is linked to their internal system of organization and it is a key element for the service furniture and support.

Nevertheless, the usual distinction between back-office and front-office is insufficient in the case of services because of the involvement of the customer within the provider's organization and processes. The back and front-office distinguishes two internal parts of an organization: the manufacturing and supporting departments (administration, finance, IT, infrastructure, etc.) and the customers-facing department(s) (sales, etc.). Given the fact that the involvement of the customers is more and more important (they are coproducers and sometimes codesigners of the service), their access and implication within the provider's organization increase. Now the "customers-facing" departments are not only sales or after sales services but also some internal and productive departments. That is why the "back-stage" and "on-stage" spaces have been introduced (note that they answer the metaphor of the theatre - see the end of the paragraph 4.1). The

former consists of the internal support processes and organization of the provider which are not visible to the customer (Lenfle & Midler, 2009). The latter consists of the interactions between the provider and the customer and all the activities and elements that are visible to the customer. The line between the back-stage and the on-stage depends on the visibility and the implication of the customer who access a part of the provider's internal organization. It also depends on the freedom of access that the provider allows to him.

Finally, since the consumption of the service is experiential (we "live" a service and not just buy and consume it), we introduce a third key element in the service system framework: the "Service Experience" (SE). The SO is associated to a specific SE within a particular context. The SDS is part of and at the same time increment the SE. The service coproduction gives rise to two results: the "output" and the "outcome". The former is the immediate effect of the service (e.g. the result of a training after one day is the things you have just memorized / the immediate result of your visit to the hairdresser is a new haircut) and the later is a more long term effect (e.g. the result of a training after one year is the knowledge you still have in mind and the practices you use / the longer term result of your visit to the hairdresser is your well-being in everyday life).

The elements of each view of the service (object, delivery system and experience) participate in the service system that we will try to represent in the next paragraphs. These are dynamic and heterogeneous elements that coalesce and interact to form a particular configuration at a given space-time. They will be integral but underlying parts of the proposed model.

3.3 An Intermediary and Operational Object for Co-Innovation

We make the hypothesis that the Service System can be used as an intermediary object (Vinck et al., 1996), in a metaphorical sense, for the innovators' coordination upstream of the innovation cycle. It can help them to work together despite their respective disciplines and the distributed nature of their work. It provides a unique and facilitating view for the cooperation and exchanges between innovators: a shared representation.

This shared representation could have two formalisms: a model and an animation. The second one is a kind of simulation or movie of the overall service system interacting elements. It aims at supporting the work of the innovators who are not familiar with the modeling approach. It brings them a quite realistic view of the service system they study (i.e. a kind of cartoon) and helps them to detect the potential lacks or opportunities (see the paragraph 4.3).

Moreover, the Service System is also a real operational object from a design perspective (e.g. a building plan is a useful intermediary object to insure the coordination between the client, the entrepreneur and the architect, but it is also a plan! It guides the building construction). It is an interesting operational tool for the design and the implementation of e-services based on the identification of transactions (i.e. it helps to make a bridge between the business and IT layers). Therefore, the Service System seems to be a potential useful tool to help the innovators to co-describe the targeted services situation and find some ideas. It also seems useful to build and bring a "collective mind" to these innovators.

3.4 Towards a Process-Oriented Knowledge Paradigm

The Service System is a configuration of heterogeneous and processual entities expressing a particular phenomenon. Then the question is: how to represent these kinds of informational collections of processes or procedural entities and characterize the provided experience? There are some existing models of the concept of service in the literature: for example the service offer (Eiglier & Langeard, 1987, 2004), the molecular model

(Shostack, 1977), etc. But even if their perspectives are different, these models and their authors always define the service through its content / its substance and neglect its performative and experiential nature. The Service System presents a hierarchical structure of elementary entities (related to the distinction between the main or central service and the peripheral services). It can thus be formalized through a hierarchical tree or an ontology given. But, as most of the representations we can found in the service literature and in collaborative systems, the traditional ontologies are object-oriented representations. They are based on the paradigm of the substance which often considers the processes/actions only as properties or secondary classes of things: "the particular performance of a human activity, such as a particular running or reading, or, the particular occurrence of a 'subject-less', 'absolute', or 'pure process': a snowing or thundering in a particular spatiotemporal region" (Seibt, 2009). This substantial principle does not fit the dynamic nature of the Service System (i.e. a collection of processes / dynamic entities). The documents, that are used by telecom innovators (i.e. available upstream of the design process) to describe the services situations they address, are structured with the service situation's episodes and interactions through a verbal and dynamic way. Moreover, we make the hypothesis that the reasoning of people is rather based on processes/transitions/movements than abstract concepts and their classification.

The representation of the "acting" service or the experience is therefore linked to the computation of the dimensions which impact its conceptualization as a process or a combination of parts in a given moment. Its elements can be considered as episodes or service tracks. We make the hypothesis that the reality is a continuous flow where "things" are processes. Their mode of existence is their dynamicity or "activity mode" and not their supposed universal substance. We therefore propose a third knowledge paradigm about "process-oriented knowledge" to represent each Service System. Unlike the paradigm of the substance which usually disconnects the conceptual representations from the field of experiences, our approach effectively takes into account the dynamic dimension and spacetime-related service experience.

In this vein, a new generation of ontologies has emerged: the processes ontology (Whitehead, 1929; Soulier, 2009). The conceptualization of dynamic categories is becoming possible thanks to a process-oriented metaphysics. It can be realized in a conventional way through aspectualities or in a less traditional way through an alternative theory to the paradigm of the substance (Seibt, 2009). According to our previous hypothesis, it is necessary to identify dynamic entities based on their activity mode and associated control (nature of the participants in the process/activity) rather than on objects (properties, identity, information structure, etc.). It does not disprove the need for a knowledge theory of the area. But this knowledge will be expressed as dynamic categories rather than static categories. This implies to reverse the usually adopted perspective: from static entities to "development"/"progress" whose spatio-temporal structure and arrangement are complex.

We propose an ontological alternative based on the Mereology and the General Process Theory principles (Bugeaud & Soulier, 2010) to formalize dynamic categories and their associated situations.

3.5 The Mereological and GPT Principles

As introduced before, the concept of service is more and more perceived as something that emerges from its elements' interactions. It is thus necessary to go from a semantic description and modeling (=concepts space) to a dynamic description and modeling (=geometric space). The existence of a specific service scenario depends more on the interaction of its elements than on its conceptual definition. We work on a spatio-temporal form and not a semantic concept. That

is why we base our method on the mereotopology principles. In the context of interactions, one track is to bring to together the graph theory, the relationship of composition (mereology) and the topology.

The Mereology comes from philosophy. It is based on the formal ontological study of the "part-whole" relationship (Varzi, 2003-2009 ; Husserl, 1970). The semantic relation "part_of" (called "meronymy") represents a hierarchical and partitive relationship (e.g. the roof of a house). The main principles of the Mereology are the transitivity, non-reflexivity and antisymmetry. The main kinds of meronymic relations can be established by the combination of three basic properties:

- **Configuration:** the parts support, or not, a structural or functional relationship with another individual or with the whole,
- **Homeomery:** the parts are, or are not, the same as the whole (same nature, same properties, etc.),
- **Separability:** the parts can, or cannot, be separated from the whole (without denaturing the whole's identity).

Winston et al. (1987) have identified six kinds of meronymic relationships (some of them are challenged by other authors): component-object, member-collection, portion-mass, material-object, phase-activity, area-zone. Some of them are more suited than others for the modeling of Services Systems: phase-activity ("script") and element-object (a service is an artifact and it is the object of a co-production). Some predicates have also been defined to describe these meronymic relationships: proper part, direct part, overlap, underlap, etc. Moreover, these relationships give rise to operations between entities such as sum, product or extension that can affect the parts of a whole.

Seibt uses such a mereological framework to investigate for an ontological theory of emergence (i.e. conceptual claim based on empirical phenomena) (Seibt, 2009). She proposes an extension where the meronymic relationships are non-standard and non-transitive. She has created an ontological framework for processes called the "General Process Theory" (GPT). This framework uses a new ontological category which is dynamic, concrete, non-particular (i.e. located in multiple and uncountable ways) and non-universal. An interesting point is linked to her interest for the interferences/interactions between processes. Indeed, when processes interact, they modify the representation of the complex process they form.

The GPT is based on:

- The mereological signature: homeomery and anhomeomery,
- A non-transitive "part-whole" relationship and some levels of partition (corresponding to the levels in the hierarchical tree and useful to identify and refer to entities / processes according to their position in a given partition),
- The principles of interference, mereological sum and product, spatio-temporal location.
- However, the non-transitivity principle choice changes the way of connecting some parts into a whole. The GPT reduces the number of possible relationships to the non-overlap and overlap. Another consequence is related to the operations of sum and product that can only be extended to the first partition level. Then any arbitrary amount of general processes can be created and any amount of general processes is itself a general process. Moreover, the "part_of" relationship does not necessarily involve a spatial or temporal inclusion. Processes can be arbitrarily dispersed in space and time.

3.6 A Mereotopological Formalization

In general, every verbal predication can be conceived as an activity and may play a different inferential role depending on the context. The GPT uses the definition of mereological properties, the analysis of mode of occurrence, the pattern classification of homeomery and the analysis of dynamic parameters in order to characterize each entity (as an event or an activity). It can thus answer the need of identifying the dynamic entities, the nature of participants, etc. This framework helps us to capture the systemic and the dynamic dimensions of a targeted Service System thanks to the definition and the representation of the "part-whole" relations and the interference/interactions between the processual entities of this Service System. We therefore used this framework to propose a mereo(whole and parts)-topo(parts interactions)logical formalization. It helps the innovators to discover the Service System universe (i.e. the service as it is experienced/lived and not its conceptual representation) and its possible configurations and then imagine adapted solutions.

The service, in an experiential perspective, appears as an "object" in a phenomenal sense, without any predetermined element or inference. It is based on space-time (moments) and causality relations. We gather some moments which forms the "essence" of the situation. The parts do not join into a collection by their qualities but by their functional relations. The mereology in a processual paradigm aims at modeling the moments which underlie the relation of the agent to the object (through psychic acts, etc.). It allows the co-determination between the consciousness and an object to reach at the idea of "objects experiences" which characterize their usages. These usages correspond to the relation between the product and the not prescribed but co-built use between the agent and what is proposed to him. Using the Mereology is a strong hypothesis to characterize the "social objects" in a holistic and structuralist perspective. Thus the objects of the experience can be modeled by a new theory of abstraction based on the "whole-parts" relation. It is thus a theory of the relation and not the object/category as the Aristotle and the Kant perspective. Objects are not only processual but also "intentional" because they arise from the coupling between an aim and something given. They are neither the reality such as it would be nor a representation of an object in the categorial sense: they are pure intuitions.

We therefore propose a formal model, a construction method and a tool to explain and implement the information and knowledge surrounding the Service System that the innovators are studying. The mereotopological model and its construction method allow the innovators to formalize and analyze each studied service situation as an association/configuration of processual entities. These processual entities look like assembled and interconnected micro-scenes within a spatio-temporal layout. Then, innovators can consider the progressive crystallization of the overall phenomenon where some tracks of new services can be identified.

4. THE SERVICE CO-MODELING AND SIMULATION METHOD AND TOOL

As introduced in the paragraph 2.2, the telecom operators' innovation cycle is based on the ability of the innovators (Figure 4) to find and develop new ideas of solutions. But the interest for the customers' expectations and "real life" occurs very late in the innovation cycle. That is why there is an important risk of irrelevance or non-appropriation of the designed solutions. The innovators have to represent and understand the service field of experiences in order to detect real lacks or opportunities. We therefore propose the inclusion of a new method to describe, model and simulate the targeted services systems (identification, configuration and reconfigurations of heterogeneous and dynamic elements) during the

opportunities research phase. This method is based on the previous mereotopological principles applied to the service system's processual entities. These entities will be extracted from the existing material, i.e. existing documents and knowledge which are available to the innovators (e.g. past projects, descriptions of usages scenarios by internal experts, press releases, online competitors' documentation, etc.). Customers will not be users of the model but only part of the service system's ingredients (such as all the elements of the Service Object, Service Delivery System and Service Experience – Figure 3). It answers the innovators' need for an adapted approach to catch the experiential and phenomenological nature of the service (it is experienced/lived by the customer and it is a dynamic and complex phenomenon) which are not well addressed by the currently used tools (class or activity diagrams, poorly described personae regarding the reality, etc.).

Figure 4. A shared representation for the innovators' design community

Figure 5. Schematic representation of a mereological ontology (Seibt, 2009)

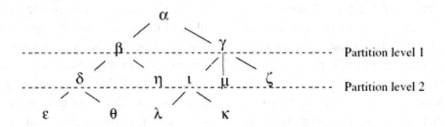

4.1 A Semi-Formal Method to Build Mereotopological Ontologies and Leverage the Design Community Knowledge

We created a semi-formal method to describe dynamic categories implementing information and knowledge related to the studied Service System. It requires the import of key documents, the extraction of candidate-terms, the generation of an actions network (Galois lattice) and the construction of a mereotopological ontology.

The first step (*Doc2Term*) concerns the constitution of a corpus and the extraction of key terms from this corpus. Indeed, the method requires relying on existing material describing the targeted service situation in different ways (i.e. through different dimensions). One of the first tasks the innovators have to do (before beginning a service's description) is to make an inventory of all the documentation they have (or can find) about this specific situation. It could be working documents of past projects, internal descriptions

of usages scenarios (following a focus group for example), press releases, online competitors' documentation, etc. These documents contain stabilized knowledge which is recognized by all the innovators. It is important to note that, as our purpose is to help in the design, these inputs (documents/texts) are not meaningful or inferencial but they contain the elements of a real object: the service. We use the speeches (in the broad sense) as means to feed our model by taking out processes or "eventualities". These processes are not only semantic and syntactic but dynamic elements of the object which is conceived in a spatiotemporal situation. The constitution of this corpus of documents about the studied Service System is an important step. The extraction of key terms helps formalizing the elements that were previously informal. Innovators can select some parts of the imported documentation and tags key entities. Moreover, they can modify the resulting structure (list of key entities) by deleting some of the candidate terms or adding some entities from their own knowledge of the targeted

Figure 6. The proposed method

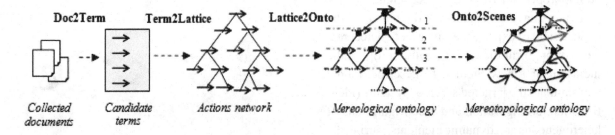

service situation (e.g. I am an innovator involved in a service description project about the management of animal health. As I worked on a close service situation a few years ago (it was about the veterinarians' work), I can detect on the list resulting from the *Doc2Term* step that an important processual entity is missing (the vaccine management). Thus I add it on the list).

The second step (*Term2Lattice*) is linked to the hypothesis that we all are accustomed to the paradigm of the substance. Therefore, we need to move from the conceptual space to a dynamic space (Seibt, 2009). In their works, Saillot et al. (2002) use the Galois Lattice in a logic of structuralization of the activities (on-line activities) that offers a more important hold/influence to the user (during his navigation on a website). They are thus more interested in a semantics of actions than in a semantics of objects. But they still start their study with the declarative and go towards the procedural world. They use the native link between objects and actions to reach their objective. Although we do not have the same objective (we aim at structuralizing the Service System and not improving an access mode), this can be used to go beyond the mental habituation we introduced and obtain a direct access to the processes world and therefore to the pragmatic. The benefit of such a network, for us, is to structure the key terms from *Doc2Term*, and then to consider a processual perspective. A further objective could be the simulation of the tasks as scenarios in the lattice. The Galois lattice is based on the following rules:

- **The triplet (O, A, I):** a set of objects O, a set of attributes A (i.e. actions which are applicable to the objects) and the binary relations I between O and A (Rule 1: I $\subseteq$ OxA).
- **Two "Galois connections":** An intension of Oz (Rule 2.1: f(Oz)=An, i.e. all the subsets of A with which the objects of Oz have a common binary relation) and Oj extension of As (Rule 2.2: f(As)=Oj, i.e. all the

subsets of O with which the actions of As have a common binary relationship).
- **The reciprocity of the Galois connections:** Oi is the extension of Ai and Ai is the intention of Oi (Rule 3: g(Ai)=Oi and f(Oi)=Ai). Then (Oi, Ai) is a "concept".
- **The order relation:** the set of concepts is ordered thanks to the inferiority (denoted $\leq$) and the inclusion (denoted $\subseteq$) relations (Rule 4: (Oi,Ai)$\leq$(On,An) if Oi $\subseteq$ An or Ai $\subseteq$ An).

We have created four algorithms based on these rules in order to transform the entities extracted from the upstream documents into an actions network. The resulting actions network helps us to identify "candidate processes". We thus obtain a network of the transformations/alterations of the studied service situation. This network characterizes a spatiotemporal situation and makes some sense emerge.

Once these dynamic/processual entities have been identified, the next step (*Lattice2Onto*) determines the ontological links between them and builds a complete representation. Here we use some mereological conditions and criteria which have been proposed by the General Process Theory (see 2.5). It helps us to distinguish the entities profiles and the kinds of interferences between them. The process typology is based on the:

- **Classical criteria:** dynamicity, unboundedness, distributivity, homeomerity,
- **Mode of occurrence criteria:** completeness, resumability, recurrence,
- **Mereological criteria:** homomerity and automerity pattern (according to spatial and temporal occurrence),
- **GPT Classification criteria:**
  - Participant structure (according to number and type of causal agents and patients),

○ Dynamic constitution (according to process architecture, e.g. sequences, forks, joints, cycles, etc.),

○ Dynamic shape (according to their trajectories, verbal aspects),

○ Dynamic context (according to its influence on the generative environment of the process).

Thanks to these criteria, we obtain several kinds of occurrence: activity, event, thing, substance and quality. In the case of Services Systems, the activity and event profiles seem relevant. We then look at the relationships between these entities (*Onto2Scenes*), the number of partition levels (i.e. levels in the tree) and the kinds of involved dynamics. Three main characteristics have to be taken into account:

• Profile of each process / entity and homeomy ("like-partedness") and automery ("self-partedness") degrees,

• Type of relationship: non-overlap or overlap,

• Type of operations: sum, product, cause.

The discovery of part-whole and parts' interactions relationships leads to build a mereotopological ontology. This framework allows the emergence of various types of dynamics (sequential, co-occurring, causal, etc.) when it is applied to a particular field. The final ontology is thus very useful to represent and imagine the possible dynamic configurations of a Service System expressing particular experiences. The modification or the introduction of a new input or information in the description of the Service System will automatically modify the ontology by restructuring the wholes, the parts and their relationships.

The mereotopological ontology is a good basis to extract a particular scenario/pathway in a particular spacetime and analyze its behavioral dimension (actors, tools, interactions, etc.). It is interesting to study each dynamic entity with regard to the overall network/ontology and not as an atomic element (e.g. "Paul mows the lawn" vs "Paul has spent a bad day at the office, he mows the lawn to relax himself and then he will go to dine in family"). It is thus possible to characterize each entity's context, previous and next processes (*Onto2Scene*). Based on the resulting diagram, it is possible to execute and simulate the selected scene (the whole and its parts) or scenario (the sequence of entities) trough an animation. Indeed, to go further, we propose to simulate the studied Service System (Bugeaud & Soulier, 2010) (see the paragraph 4.3). Animations are useful to understand, memorize and replay the studied service situation and experience. Innovators will be able to replay the simulation with multiple users' profiles: *"scenario-based techniques account for multiple user roles as well as a range of contextual influence"* (Haynes et al., 2009). This step is generally expensive but this kind of simulation approach reduces the required cost and time. They can thus simulate almost all the service interactions that could happen in the real service situation. Here the metaphor of the theatre is well suited: *"The metaphor that behavior is drama and the various principles that it engenders provide a framework for describing, understanding, and communicating about services experiences"* (Grove & Fisk, 1992). It is based on the universe (scenery, costumes, environment, atmosphere, characters, etc.), proceeding / process (actions, rebounds, etc.) and experience (roles, public profiles, knowledge and expectations, perception of the room, etc.). Automatic systems or video games are also a good metaphor. The latter are based on the creation of a universe and its objects, the development of possible scenarios, barriers, assistance, rules, etc. And it takes into account all the possible profiles of players, and presents them the rules.

4.2 A Way to Detect the Service Communities Involved Into the Service System

We have noted a difficulty to think of the service communities and the social perspective within the service experience. Nevertheless, the service is a set of transformations, developments, events in an experiential and interactional perspective. The design usually cuts out this set in several facts: the actors, the topics, the sequences, the problems, the tools, etc. It is then necessary to have an engine (in a logic of emergence) that allows to gather these elements. Our ontology allows exactly keeping the information which is associated to every dynamic entity after their extraction from the corpus of documents and their analysis through mereological and GPT criteria. So, through the mereotopological ontology, we can discover the actors of each moment or each part of the service situation, their roles and evolutions in the space and time. It allows us to envisage the clusterization of actors on a process, a particular scene or the overall situation.

In a more abstract way, we can say that the mereology gives the context of the intention (see 2.6) which gives an access to the social. It indicates artifactual, natural and social objects. These last ones are "social acts" or "structures of coordination" in which the human actors and the systems interact. Let us note however, that the clusterization of these actors is not made to the detriment of, or without link to, an organization. There are indeed social frameworks in which the service actors and their interactions join or not (among others, the customer / supplier relation). The actor is not an individual actor, he is "taken" in the social (e.g. he is in an act of purchase so he is a buyer).

To be more precise, based on the ontology we define the actors by their relations (and not by their pre-determined roles). The actors of the process inherit from the distribution of the whole in its parts: they inherit the relations between the processes in which they are involved in a different way according to the level of partition of the Service System. The actor is thus a result and there is no durability of the being as in the paradigm of the substance. He inherits from his participation/implication in the processes and some communities of the service arise from these participations.

Then, the discovery of the actors in a scene allows to consider the calculation of their implication in relation to each other, or their implication in a given space-time, the calculation of the gap between the role imagined by the designers and the real postures of the actors (e.g. "Paul is a child" because he goes to the school vs "Paul is a mother" because he takes care of his small brother) or the calculation of the services communities that would appear in a given situation.

Figure 7. Schematic representation of the service's actors' identification

Figure 8. The Onto Storia² global architecture (Bugeaud & Soulier, 2010)

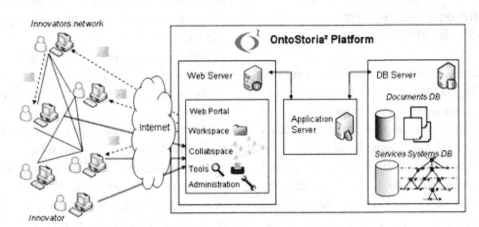

4.3 The OntoStoria² Platform and Main Mechanisms

To amplify the benefits of the Service System modeling and simulation, we proposed the creation of a Services Systems Design Studio (Figure 8). It aims at facilitating the exchanges between innovators and stimulating their work. We have decided to represent the distributed telecoms innovators thanks to a social network. The proposed tool uses the traditional mechanisms of social networks for the asynchronous access: profiles, tags, etc. The Service System models have been brokendown into several forms (to avoid the modeling activity rejection) that can be sent as electronic forms. The main steps are:

- proposition of a theme / a service situation to study by an innovator or a group,
- search for experts or interested innovators within the social network,
- sending of an invitation to participate and dissemination of the e-forms,
- enrichment and saving of the e-forms,
- extraction of the information and key documents,
- enrichment of the Services Systems repository,

- generation of the ontology and the animation,
- submission to innovators's group who then share their opinions/reactions,
- iterative re-generation of the model and animation,
- collective validation and generation of a final deliverable.

The models generation is based on the previous (see 3.1) semi-formal method to build a Service System representation. It is also possible to make some requests into the Services Systems repository. Finally, this tool can also be used in a direct access by an innovator or a working group (e.g. during a brainstorming) to model the Service System.

Moreover, the existing expertise and knowledge (K) and the existing telecoms services are already tagged. Here, it makes sense to imagine a way to look for common elements between the studied service system and this existing information into the operator's databases. This could help make suggestions of reuse or adaptation of existing services or tools / artifacts for a new situation. The addition of tags on the designed new Service System during its description seems therefore essential. These tags could be key elements for the connection between the existing telecoms

Figure 9. Generation of an animation

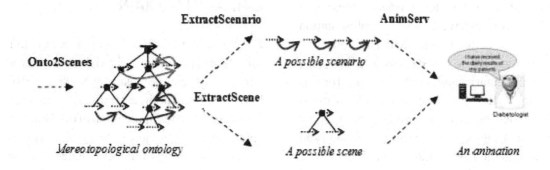

supply system, services and know-how, and the current concept (C) (C-K theory: Hatchuel & Weil, 2003) of Service System. This mechanism is currently under study in order to improve the proposed tool with such an automatic connection. Indeed we are working on a mechanism that will support the emergence of ideas by the detection of possible adaptations of existing services to a new requirement. It will propose some suggestions to the innovators which will be able to decide if such adaptations could be pertinent for such situation or customer.

Finally, some existing solutions allow the generation of an ergonomic expression of processes (e.g. the software suite OnMap, from the software publishing company Nomia, which enables the complete production of educational/training contents including animations based on business processes models). They model and simulate these processes and their associated micro-world. This kind of tool is useful for the communication, the usages illustration and the validation of a hypothetic functioning (especially in the case of a group of innovators who are not familiar with the modeling approach). Furthermore, our analysis of the opportunities research process within the organization of a telecom operators led us discover the regular use of "sketch sheets" or "drawing" of by the innovators (e.g. during brainstorming sessions) to illustrate either steps or technical elements of the described scenario. Designers are thus familiar with this type of pictorial/animated

representation. That is why it seems interesting to propose the simulation of a studied service system thanks to the generation of an animation (after the consolidation of the Services Systems repository) (Figure 9).

To do so, we have to imagine a mechanism for transforming a scenario or a scene (*ExtractScenario* or *ExtractScene* – Figure 9) into an animation (*AnimServ*). Today some examples of behavioral models' transformation (e.g. a UML activity diagram) into animations exist (e.g. Ermel & Bardohl, 2004). This mechanism requires the definition of an endogenous link between the possible elements of a business process and the elements of an animation in order to allow the passage from one to another. The technical engine identifies the semantics of all the objects of the process model by annotating them (action, role, event, etc.) and then combines them (according to the allowed links) to the animation's objects (figure, bubble action, etc.). By analogy, the characterization of the entities of the extracted scenario/scene (from the mereotopological model) allows us to associate them with some animation's objects. Indeed, each element of the Service System's scenario/scene (event, activity, interaction, participant, etc.) has to be translated into the programming language (e.g. Action Script) in order to be executed into a design and programming software (e.g. Flash). Although this kind of mechanism is still semi-automatic to date, we can consider it to support the innovators' work. The result is a pretty realistic animated scene. This virtualized Service System (and its context) can help innovators to have a common representation stemming from their individual and collective contributions. They can discuss and exchange some commentaries and annotations based on this animation. After some hypothetic modifications of the models or forms (and consequently of the animations), they validate the Service System and transfer it to the Anticipation Committee.

From a practical point of view, the main functionalities of the proposed tool (creation of a new project, search for and invitation of experts or potentially interested innovators, collection of some relevant documents, addition of relevant information within e-forms, importation of the documents and information within the project, selection and extraction of key terms, enrichment of the Services Systems repository, generation of the model, generation of the animations for the selected scenes or scenarios, possible modifications, individual and collective researches for new ideas according to the model or animations, generation of a final deliverable for the anticipation committee) aim at supporting the opportunities research step upstream of the innovation cycle (see paragraph 2). The objective is not to replace the current work and tools of the innovators (focus groups, on-site meetings, etc.) but to offer them an additional tool supporting their tasks of:

- discovery and description of the targeted services situations,
- detection of gaps or opportunities that an IT or telecom solution could fill.

It provides them an additional and different view of the services situations they must study. And it also provides them the ability to share resources and knowledge and to work together despite the distance and their respective professions.

5. EXPERIMENT IN THE E-HEALTH DOMAIN

Finally, as the e-health domain is a key domain for services providers and a rich field in terms of Services Systems (Bugeaud & Soulier, 2010) we have led a first experiment through two main steps. The former was the application of our OntoStoria[2] approach to a sample of the Service System of remote monitoring of diabetic patient. The latter was an experiment with a group of telecom innovators (sociologists, marketers and engineers).

5.1 First Step: The Remote Monitoring of Diabetics Modeling

This Service System has been the object of numerous studies but it has not been represented in a consensual way. The result of this first experiment was a mereotopological model presenting the processual universe of the remote monitoring of diabetics. Actually, this first test has been "hand-made" because the proposed web-based tool (see paragraph 4.3) was under development and because it was nevertheless fundamental to test our hypotheses and approach before intending to pursue the development. But tagging and encoding a set of documents in a manual way require significant work. It was thus difficult to test a large corpus of documents. That is why we have chosen (at first) to reduce the corpus of document concerning the remote monitoring of diabetes. We used different kinds of documents as inputs (*Doc2Term* – constitution of the corpus): sales brochures of the telecom operator we worked for, press articles about the diabetics monitoring and conferences presentations of the CERITD (i.e. a specialized center on the study and research on diabetes which is part of a French hospital). The key objects and actions of the remote monitoring of diabetic patients have been extracted from this corpus (*Doc2Term* – extraction of the key terms):

Figure 10. The remote monitoring of diabetics: Galois lattice on the sample (Bugeaud & Soulier, 2010)

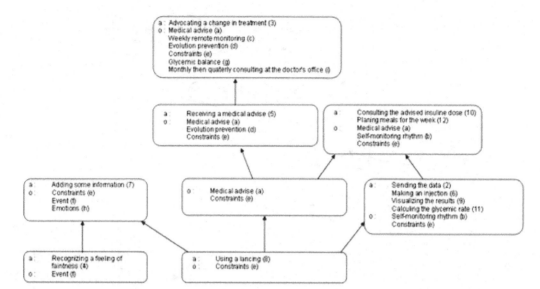

- **Objects:** medical advice, consultation, evolution prevention, constraints, events, emotions, weekly remote monitoring, blood sugar level balance, consulting at the doctor's office, self-monitoring rhythm, etc.

- **Actions:** sending the data, advocating a change in treatment, recognizing a feeling of faintness, receiving a medical advice, adding some information, using lancing, visualizing the results, calculating the blood glucose rate, planning the meals for the week, making an injection, etc.

The four "Galois-lattice-based" algorithms have been applied to the sample triplets (*Term2Lattice*) in order to build the Service System's Lattice (Figure 10).

Then the mereological ontology construction steps have been applied to our case (*Lattice2Onto*). The profile of each process of the sample has been identified thanks to the process typology and the part-whole relations have been detected. For example:

- "visualizing the results" meets the criteria of the activity profile,
- "adding some information" meets the criteria of the activity profile,
- "sending the data" meets the criteria of the event profile,
- the interference between "visualizing the results" and "sending the data" is a part-whole relationship,
- the interference between "adding some information" and "sending the data" is a part-whole relationship, etc.

Note that each whole within a part-whole relation can be analyzed as a micro or macro scene according to the partition level. Then, each entity's context, previous and next processes have been identified. The resulting interferences helped us to discover the possible scenarios/pathways within the ontology (*Onto2Scene*). For example:

- "visualizing the results" follows "using a lancing",
- "visualizing the results" precedes "adding some information",

Figure 11. The remote monitoring of diabetics: ontology on the sample

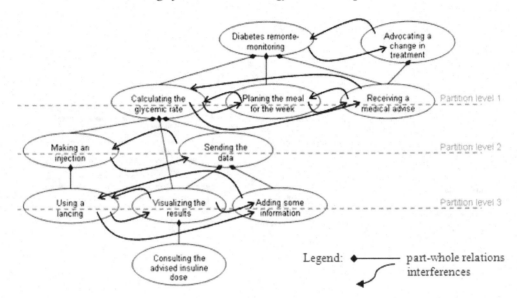

- "planning the meal of the week" is the consequence of "receiving a medical advice", etc.

Once all processes and interferences have been qualified, their dependencies help us to generate the ontological model (Figure 11).

Finally, we identified the constitutive ingredients (heterogeneous elements which take part in the configuration) of each scene. For example:

- "Making an injection":
  - Actors: the patient,
  - Tools: the lancing, the glycemic reader, the insulin syringe,
  - Substance: blood, insulin,
  - Metrics: blood sugar level, insulin dose,
- "Receiving a medical advice": o Actors: the diabetologist, the patient,
  - Tools: the doctor's computer, the Internet, the patient's phone, the sms,
  - Economic elements: the Internet connection price, the SMS price,
  - Information: the SMS message (medical advice), etc.

These elements are latent under the dynamic/processual entities. They correspond to the associated "object" entities.

5.2 Second Step: Experiment with a Group of Telecoms Innovators

During the second step, we made an experiment with a group of telecom innovators (sociologists, marketers and engineers). The objective was not to conduct an innovation but to simulate an opportunities research step (description of a specific service situation, discussion and detection of lacks and opportunities). We searched for six innovators within the organization of the studied telecom operator. We chose two people who already worked on a project concerning the field of the remote monitoring of diabetics, three who knew some things about the e-health domain and one who was totally unaware of this domain. The objective was to evaluate the contribution of our propositions and more exactly:

- the impact of the Service System model and modeling process...

- the impact and adequacy of the processual and mereological principles…
- the impact of the Service System animation…

…on the collective and individual representations of such a performative and experiential phenomenon. The question was thus: is our proposition (concept, model and method) adapted to support the design community's work? Does it provide interesting elements and new dimensions that could help the innovators to understand and analyze a service situation?

During a first sub-step, the group of innovators made an opportunities research session by phone (to recreate the remote and inter-professional nature of the activity). We gave us no information and told them to just try to co-describe the service and find new ideas of solutions. During a second sub-step, we gave us the documents we used for our first test (the diabetics' remote monitoring modelling according to our method). We then presented them the Service System concept and our ontological model. We invited them to annotate these propositions and to discuss it. At the end of each session, we asked them a set of questions such as: do you think you have reached an unanimous definition and description of this service? Have you shared and/or learned something? Did ideas appear? We also tried to know which differences they had noted between the two brainstorming.

Although this little experiment was not exhaustive, it allowed us to raise first results. The result showed interesting consequences of the use of the Service System and its models such as the reduction of the disagreement between the innovators and the improvement of the individual and collective representations of the remote monitoring of diabetics patients. Indeed, the innovators used the same level of abstraction (the overall service system and not only a technical or financial or sociological view) and were aware about the economic, social, technical dimensions, etc. of the studied service. Indeed, as the Service System's model relies on its definition as a configuration of heterogeneous entities, it is possible to identify the constitutive ingredients of the Service System (heterogeneous elements which take part in the configuration) (see the example in the previous paragraph). The comparison of the exchanged information, the perceptions of the users regarding the process and the quality of the representation, but also the number of ideas (e.g. a classical vocal server may be more relevant for old diabetics who are not familiar with PDAs and the Internet) encouraged the pursuit of our works.

6. FUTURE RESEARCH DIRECTIONS

Some questions could be interesting future research directions:

The size of the corpus of upstream documents can be problematic: how can we take into account the possibility of having too many documents or any document in entry?

This question is linked to the limitation we have encountered during our first "hand-made" test. This limitation could also be a forward problem within the tool. The more the number of input documents will be important, the more the number of extracted keys entities will be important, and the more the resulting model will be complex and potentially difficult to be read and understood by the innovators. The issue of the impact and the management of this limitation have to be analyzed.

The agreement on the resulting ontology is also an interesting point: how can the innovators come to an agreement about the contents and\or the nature of the reality so coded?

This question addresses the problem of the innovators' collaboration around the same concept and model. Even if the web-based studio provides them a collaborative space to share their respective knowledge and opinion, we can wonder how they would be able to agree on the model's entities and the model validation, and how they would be able to propose some ideas to the anticipation committee. One possible solution is to give the project leader (the innovator who has created the project in the studio and start work) the responsibility of validating and consolidating the project when he considers that it has been accomplished.

The emergence of some clusters of services communities has to be bounded: at what moment or size can we consider that it is effectively a "community"?

A study about the principles that could characterize a service community should be conducted. We have to define what kinds of interacting entities can be part of a service community, what kinds of media can be used by these interacting entities, or even from how many entities we can consider having an emerging community.

Moreover, it will be fundamental and interesting to realize another larger-scale experiment of the overall approach and the collaborative tool. To do so, we wanted to simulate a phase of research opportunities through the web-based studio. Then, for a given service situation (still in the e-health field or in a different field such as tourism or education), we can involve a larger number of innovators (from various professions) and try show other contributions of our proposition. For example, we would like to verify if:

- the number of exchanges within the design community (instant messaging, emails, phone calls, …) has increased,
- the number and quality of services ideas have increased,
- the processing time for an opportunities research step on a specific Service System has decreased (and thus the all cycle of innovation has decreased),

- the time to reach a decision (validation and transfer to the service design and development stage or not) has decreased (the Decision Committee has everything it needs to make a quick decision),
- the reuse of the existing and past projects and the reuse of the innovators' knowledge and experiences has increased.

7. CONCLUSION

In this chapter, we discuss the question of the knowledge sharing and co-modeling within a design community of innovators upstream of the design process of a services provider. We present the context and limits of their remote and inter-professional activity and propose a Service System design approach to answer these difficulties and support their cooperation and creativity. To go further, we were interested in the question of the conceptualization of the knowledge in a Service System. To be more precise, we were interested in the service as a dynamic phenomenon driven by its modes of apparition. This phenomenon is a whole and its parts are interacting moments or social acts involving several actors and a rich context. Then Services Systems are dynamic configurations/arrangements of heterogeneous and interacting entities (see SSME, see ANT). We thus go from a semantic description and modeling (=concepts space) to a dynamic description and modeling (=geometric space). That is why we base our method on the mereotopology principles. Moreover, we added a notion of service community deduced from the actors' participations in one or more processes of the Service System. This notion allows recovering the ideas of organization, social, actors and roles (the actor being identified according to its real participation within the process).

The proposed methodology helps to discover and to model the processes, their parts, their common parts and their interactions. Then, it helps to identify the actors, their participation in the process and the emergent service communities. In other words, it makes the users (the innovators) discovering a chain of "functions" in a kind of "history" of the studied service situation and also a chain of associated actors. Finally, the introduction of a new process or a new variable in the description of a Service System will change the ontology and consequently its animation. It means that the method and the associated tool handle all the iterations on the project. Thus, it will be possible to go back to and modify the list of imported documents, the list of selected entities, the identified scenarios, etc. And therefore regenerate the model and animations (without forgetting to update the services systems repository).

These works meet the needs of the innovators' design community by offering them, very early in the design process, a shared representation of the service situation as an experiential phenomenon and thus some dimensions of the service they did not know. Having been modeled and simulated, the service situation or its parts can be put compared to the technical environment and solutions of the services providers to consider the possible adaptations of existing solutions or the creation of news solutions.

Our proposition seems to be richer than the usual schema of Kant where everyone thinks through an abstracted structure of knowledge while we cannot describe the reality by predetermined categories but through what we are currently living. We do not describe what exists but what happens.

It is important for services providers' managers to understand the distinction between:

- an existing macro-level method: the services design process within the organization of a telecom operator,
- a new micro-level: the services systems modeling and simulation method within a group of innovators.

The first one corresponds to the managerial, economical and technical approach in which we include/position our proposition. The second one corresponds to our proposition. It is a technical view that includes the proposed design technique / Services Systems description approach. This is a direct contribution to SSME's perspective of Services Systems engineering. The chapter gives some methodological elements. We implemented a 4-step method aiming at helping services providers to reuse our approach:

- Analysis of the existing services design process: the associated approaches are in-house formalized methodologies (e.g. roadmap, time to market process, etc.),
- Analysis of the upstream stage of the design process: it is always a key phase where a lot of information, documents, actors, etc. are gathered and produced,
- Enrolment of the modeling and simulation method within this phase: it requires the innovators' training: definition of a project theme, identification of potential participants/innovators, addition of documents and information, fusion of the information, generation of the model and animations, detection of some ideas, generation of a deliverable, go/no go of the Anticipation Committee (see the different tasks in the paragraph 4.3 page 16),
- Evaluation of the results.

To conclude, in this chapter we discussed five ways to apprehend the concept of "virtual communities": the inter-professional and remote nature of the innovators' network, the use of the CK theory and social networks, the experiential and intentional nature of the service, the proposal of a collaborative tool, and the detection of the service communities.

REFERENCES

Blomberg, J. (2007). *Practice-oriented design of products, services and experiences. Service Science Lecture Series.* Berkeley, CA: University of California.

Bugeaud, F., & Soulier, E. (2009). Services systems to leverage innovators' knowledge: The Telecoms Industry case. In L.-M. Camarinha-Matos, I. Paraskakis, & H. Afsarmanesh (Eds.), *IFIP Advances in Information and Communication Technology: Vol. 307, Leveraging Knowledge for Innovation in Collaborative Networks, 10th IFIP WG 5.5 Working Conference on Virtual Enterprises (PROVE'09)* (pp. 563-570). Thessaloniki, Greece. October 07th-09th, Springer.

Bugeaud, F., & Soulier, E. (2010). Conception assistée de Systèmes de Services (SdS) à l'aide d'Ontologies Méréologiques. *Proceedings of the 21ème Journées Francophones d'Ingénierie des Connaissances (IC'10).* Nîmes, June 08-11.

Delalonde, C., & Soulier, E. (2007). Collaborative information retrieval in R&D distributed teams. *Proceedings of the 13th International Conference on Concurrent Engineering.* Sophia-Antipolis, September 18-22.

Eiglier, P. (2004). *Marketing et stratégie des services.* Paris, France: Economica.

Ermel, C., & Bardohl, R. (2004). Scenario animation for visual behavior models: A generic approach. Software and system modeling. *Special Section on Graph Transformations and Visual Modeling Techniques, 3*(2), 164–177.

Gadrey, J. (2000). The characterization of goods and services: An alternative approach. *Review of Income and Wealth, 46*(3), 369–387. doi:10.1111/j.1475-4991.2000.tb00848.x

Gallouj, F., & Weinstein, O. (1997). Innovation in services. *Research Policy, 26,* 537–556. doi:10.1016/S0048-7333(97)00030-9

Grove, S. J., & Fisk, R. P. (1992). The service experience as theatre. In Sherry, J. F., & Sternthal, B. (Eds.), *Advances in Consumer Research (Vol. 19,* pp. 455–461). Association for Consumer Research.

Hatchuel, A., & Weil, B. (2003). A new approach of innovative design: an introduction to C-K theory. *Proceedings of ICED,* Stockholm, Sweden.

Haynes, S. R., Purao, S., & Skattebo, A. L. (2009). Scenario-based methods for evaluating collaborative systems. *Computer Supported Cooperative Work, 18*(4), 331–356. doi:10.1007/s10606-009-9095-x

Husserl, E. (1970*). Logical Investigations, Vol. 2.* Findlay, J.N., trans. Routledge.

IfM & IBM. (2007). *Succeeding through service innovation: A discussion paper.* Cambridge, United Kingdom: University of Cambridge Institute for Manufacturing.

Latour, B. (2005). *Reassembling the social: An iIntroduction to actor-network theory.* Oxford, UK: Oxford UP.

Lenfle, S. (2005). Innovation in services: The contributions of design theory. *Proceedings of the 11th International Product Development Management Conference,* Dublin, Ireland.

Lenfle, S., & Midler, C. (2009). The launch of innovative product-related services: Lessons from automotive telematics. *Research Policy, 38,* 156–169. doi:10.1016/j.respol.2008.10.020

Saillot, I., Patou-Mathis, M., Richard, J. F., Sander, E., & Poitrenaud, S. (2002). Modéliser les activités cognitives des Hommes au Paléolithique. *Mathematiques et Sciences Humaines,* 159.

Seibt, J. (2009). Forms of emergent interaction in general process theory. *Synthese, 166,* 479–512. doi:10.1007/s11229-008-9373-z

Soulier, E. (2009). Storytelling, plateformes sociales et ontologies de processus pour la simulation du mouvement. *Habilitation à diriger des recherches.*

Spohrer, J., Maglio, P., Bailey, J., & Gruhl, D. (2007). Steps toward a science of service systems. *IEEE Computer, 40*(1), 71–77.

Tannery, F. (2001). Le management stratégique des services: Synthèse bibliographique et repérage des questions génériques. *Finance Contrôle Stratégie, 4*(2), 215–259.

Varzi, A.C. (2003-2009). *Standford Encyclopedia of Philosophy Mereology.*

Vinck, D., Jeantet, A., & Laureillard, P. (1996). Objects and other intermediaries in the sociotechnical process of product design: An exploratory approach. In J. Perrin & D. Vinck (Eds.), *The Role of Design in the Shaping of Technology: Vol.5* (pp.297-320*), COST A4 Social Sciences.* Bruxelles: EC Directorate General Science R&D.

Whitehead, A. N. (1929). *Process and Reality.* New York, NY: Macmillan.

Winston, M. E., Chaffin, R., & Herrmann, D. (1987). A Taxonomy of Part-Whole Relations. *Cognitive Science, 11*(4). doi:10.1207/s15516709cog1104_2

ADDITIONAL READING

Bugeaud, F., & Soulier, E. (2009). A collaborative environment to support and stimulate telecoms innovations through co-created models and virtual animation. *Proceedings of ICICKM – Mini-track Virtual Environments and Collaboration*, Montreal, Canada, October 1-2.

Chesbrough, H. (2005). Toward a science of services. *Harvard Business Review, 83*, 16–17.

Djellal, F., & Gallouj, F. (2005). Mapping innovation dynamics in hospitals. *Research Policy, 34*, 817–835. doi:10.1016/j.respol.2005.04.007

Girju, R., Badulescu, A., & Moldovan, D. (2006). Automatic discovery of part-whole relations. *Computational Linguistics, 32*(1), 83–135.

Glushko, R. J. (2008). Designing a service science discipline with discipline. *IBM Systems Journal, 47*(1), 15–26. doi:10.1147/sj.471.0015

Keet, C.M., & Artale, A. (2008). Representing and reasoning over a taxonomy of part-whole relations. *Applied Ontology Archive, 3*(1-2).

Le Priol, F., Blais, A., Desclés, J.-P., Djioua, B., Garcia-Flores, J., & Guibert, G. …Sauzay, B. (2006). Automatic annotation of localization and identification relations in platform EXCOM. *Proceedings of the 19th International Florida Artificial Intelligence Research Society Conference (FLAIRS'06)* (pp. 307-312), Melbourne, Australia, May 11-13.

Pinhanez, C. (2008). Service systems as customer-intensive systems and its implications for service science and engineering. *Proceedings of the 41st Hawaii International Conference on System Science (HICSS'08)* (p. 117), Hawaii, USA, January 10-14.

Precup, L., Mulligan, D., & O'Sullivan, D. (2003). Collaborative tool to support knowledge sharing and innovation in an R&D Project. *Proceedings of the International Conference of Concurrent Engineering (ICE'03)*, Espoo, Finland, June 16-18.

Rescher, N. (1996). *Process Metaphysics.* SUNY Press.

Seibt, J. (2004). Free process theory: Towards a typology of occurrings. *Axiomathes, 14*, 23–55. doi:10.1023/B:AXIO.0000006787.28366.d7

Soulier, E., & Bugeaud, F. (forthcoming). Méthodes et modèles pour les Systèmes d'Information. In Thévenot, J. (Ed.), *Master Système d'Information.* Paris: Eska, Collection Master.

Tabas, L. (2007). Designing for service systems. *Proceedings of the ISD Symposium and UCB iSchool Report.*

KEY TERMS AND DEFINITIONS

Design Community: It gathers all the actors of the innovation (the "innovators") who are part of a remote and inter-professional network, and who interact through specific medias in order to co-imagine and co-design some IT or telecom solutions. They are the users of our method and proposed tool. Service communities: It corresponds to the groups of actors and other acting elements which are involved in each main scene and/or in each possible scenario of a studied service situation. Opportunities research: It is the upstream stage of the innovation lifecycle of most services providers (the next stages are the service design, development, deployment and market launch). It requires the description of customers' services situations in order to detect some lacks and opportunities and to find some ideas of adapted solutions.

Service Science: The Service Science Management and Engineering (SSME) is an emergent field of research which has been initiated by IBM and several Universities in the early 2000s. It has won recognition since 2007 with a symposium at the University of Cambridge and a series of dedicated publications. It gathers all the synergies around "one" concept of service at a more abstract level than the one we usually find in the literature (especially in computer science, i.e. technical and reusable functionality): the Service System.

Service System: It is a dynamic value co-creation configuration of heterogeneous entities (activites/actions/operations, people, artifacts, information, etc.). It corresponds to the spatio-temporal service situation of a customer (or a customers' segment) that the innovators have to describe during the opportunities research step. Mereotopology: The mereology comes from philosophy. It is based on the formal ontological study of the "part-whole" relationship. The semantic relation "part_of" (called "meronymy") represents a hierarchical and partitive relationship (e.g. the roof of a house). The topology is based on the mathematical study of the spatial properties (e.g. connectivity) of geometric objets that are unchanged after deformations/distortions. The mereotopology is thus the combination of mereological and topological concepts and principles. It mixes part-whole relations, interactions relations, boundaries between parts, etc. Modeling: Here it corresponds to the graphic representation of a studied service situation. It represents the assembled and interconnected scenes of a service situation though a mereotopological model.

Simulation: Here it corresponds to the animation of a studied service situation. It brings to the innovators a quite realistic view of the service system they study (i.e. a kind of movie or cartoon). e-Health: It corresponds to the use of the ICT to meet the needs of citizens, patients, healthcare establishments and professionals, services providers, etc. It is link to key trends (e.g. people are living to a much older age; the number of people suffering from chronic illness is rapidly growing ; there are huge inequalities in the healthcare systems of different countries ; there are strong budgetary and regulatory constraints ; etc) and interesting opportunities (e.g. a patient-centered evolution (well-being and autonomy) ; a current technological "mutation" (high speed Internet, network organization, etc.) ; the most important market growth (between 15 and 20% in coming 5 years) ; etc.).

Section 4
Responsive Communities:
Semantics, Identity and Governance

Collaboration in virtual communities requires an environment where a semantic is clarified, a definition of identity is shared, and governance is well understood. These topics are discussed in the next chapters: semantic models are used to link virtual communities; identification and self-verification are deeply discussed and impact the design of virtual communities; and governance aspects are depicted, showing the tension between freedom and control in communities.

Chapter 10
Semantically Linking Virtual Communities

Rajendra Akerkar
Western Norway Research Institute, Norway

Terje Aaberge
Western Norway Research Institute, Norway

ABSTRACT

A Virtual Community can be defined as a group of people sharing interests and making use of electronic forms of communication for exchanges. The shared interests might be with respect to a topic or a domain of knowledge, but it might also be related to a task. With the advent of virtual communities, there is a growing need for providing methods to link these communities together in a meaningful way. In this chapter, we shall describe the usage of semantic technologies for enhancing community portals and connecting heterogeneous virtual community sites. We propose a framework for semantically interlinked virtual communities called SIVC that can be used for information structuring, export and information dissemination. We present the SIVC ontology which combines terms from vocabularies that already exist with new terms needed to describe the relationships between concepts in the domain of virtual community.

INTRODUCTION

A Virtual Community can be a virtual enterprise, a virtual team or a social virtual community. A virtual enterprise is usually defined as a temporary or permanent alliance of organizations for the accomplishment of a task by way of information and communication technology, a virtual team

is a group of people that rely primarily or exclusively on electronic forms of communication to work together in accomplishing goals (Palmer et al.,1997)] and a social virtual community is a community of interest on the Internet. Rheingold (1993) deals with the emergence of social virtual communities. He describes Virtual Communities as "social aggregations that emerge from the Net when enough people carry on those public discussions long enough, with sufficient human

DOI: 10.4018/978-1-60960-869-9.ch010

feeling, to form webs of personal relationships in cyberspace". Hagel and Armstrong (1997) look at virtual communities as "Virtual Enterprises". Many social communities on the Internet are opposed to the idea of commercialization but the authors argue that once these communities realize their full market potential they will be willing to engage in purchasing transactions.

Following Schubert (1999) we define Virtual Communities by:

Virtual Communities describe the union between individuals or organizations who share common values and interests using electronic media to communicate within a shared semantical space on a regular basis.

We propose a framework for semantically interlinked virtual communities (SIVC) that aims to interconnect virtual communities. SIVC will thus provide a way to overcome the limitations of current sites in making related pieces of information more accessible to users; by searching on one forum, the ontology and interface will allow users to find similar information on other sites that use a SIVC based system architecture.

A possible SIVC based search is illustrated by the following use case. A person is searching for information in view of the installation of a home automation system in his house. There is a post A discussing local system vendors on site 1, a forum dedicated to home automation, that references both a Usenet post B comparing various functions of a system controlling the physical environment and a mailing list post C explaining how to install home automation system. Presently the user will have to traverse at least three sites in order to find the relevant information. However, by making use of the SIVC ontology and remote RDF (Resource Description Framework) querying, he will access the necessary information through one search for the system installation on the home automation forum that also will yield the relevant text from the interlinked Usenet and mailing list posts B and C.

In this chapter, we shall describe the usage of semantic technologies for enhancing community portals and connecting heterogeneous virtual community sites. We shall overview ongoing standardization activities as well as research challenges and present an ontology for the domain of virtual communities. We shall also discuss how to combine different ontologies in architectures for community site interoperablity. Finally, we will describe some efforts towards implementing semantic technologies in virtual communities that focus on scientific collaborations.

RELATED WORK

The Harvest (Bowman, 1995) is an early system that can be used to gather information from diverse repositories to build, search, and replicate indexes, and to cache objects as they are retrieved across the Internet. Harvest uses the Summary Object Interchange Format (SOIF) to exchange metadata about resources. In contrast, Semantically Interlinked Open Communities (SIOC) uses RDF as the exchange format and allows mappings between different vocabularies, which is not envisioned in SOIF. Issue based information systems (IBIS) model (Rittel, 1970) uses discussions in the process of solving design issues and provides a detailed model for links between conversations. SIVC uses metadata and reply links to connect conversations on online community sites and can be extended to describe discussions. Various approaches for data integration on the Web, such as data representation languages, structural information retrieval, and query processing, are surveyed in (Florescu,, 1998). However, advanced database techniques have failed so far to surface on the Web. SIVC is providing a common vocabulary for data representation across virtual communities.

RDF Site Summary (RSS 1.0) is widely used in weblog systems and news sites. RSS 1.0 defines a lightweight vocabulary for syndicating news items, but is used for all sorts of data exchange.

Although RSS works well in practice, there are several issues: firstly, only the last "n" news items are typically exported in RSS. Secondly, most of the systems use non-RDF versions of RSS, which limit its use with other vocabularies.

SEMANTIC WEB AND ONTOLOGIES

The Semantic Web idea emerged from the confluence of several communities - artificial intelligence, hypertext, Web developers - and so there are a number of ways to appreciate its motivation and goals. Perhaps the easiest for one who does not belong to any of those communities is to consider that much of what we want to know is available on the Web. Thus the Web is, potentially, a great resource for software agents, which can be programmed to extract and fuse information from multiple, heterogeneous sources in response to a query (Berners-Lee, 2001). However, extracting meaning from text is a very challenging task for computer programs. While progress is being made, a robust solution is decades, if not generations away. So the Semantic Web is an approach to encoding and publishing information in ways that makes it easier for computers to understand, thus making the Web agent-friendly.

Ontology is the branch of philosophy that seeks to answer the question "what is there?". In computer science, an ontology represents a formal conceptualization of a domain. Typically, it specifies the nature of objects of the domain that organises them in classes of similar objects. The ontology thus implicitly or explicitly defines the terms denoting these classes and relationships. Current web ontology languages, designed to encode information on and for the Web, use the eXtensible Markup Language or XML both for specifying ontologies, and also for making assertions about the world using terms of the ontologies. A Semantic Web page begins by listing (as URLs) the locations of the ontologies to be used, then goes on to use those ontologies to make assertions about datasets, human beings, items for sale, etc. An agent, on coming to such a page, can import the specified ontologies and use that information to understand the semantics of the ensuing assertions. The World Wide Web Consortium (W3C) has developed standards to enable ontologies to be published on the Web as well as data and other assertions to be encoded using terms drawn from any published ontologies. These standards make it possible for programs and software agents to understand information published on the Web without the ambiguity and complex processing inherent in traditional unstructured forms (e.g., natural language) or rigidity and lack of flexibility inherent in structured representations (e.g., relational databases) (Akerkar, 2009).

The Resource Description Framework or RDF is a simple XML-based language to define computer-understandable vocabularies that people and programs can use to describe things of interest, such as Web sites, newspaper articles, email messages, people, books, events, or Web services. RDF mimics human languages in that it allows one to introduce new terms (individuals, classes and properties) that are defined (partially, at least) in terms of existing terms. RDF Schema extends RDF by providing vocabulary to build logical object-oriented schema, including a simple typing system, sub-classes, sup-properties, inheritance, etc. The Web Ontology Language OWL supports advanced capabilities, such as logical inference and translating descriptions using different ontologies (e.g., mapping a location specified as a ZIP code to one using latitude and longitude.)

A problem in the effort to construct an ontology for a domain is that there are typically many different ways of doing so. This is true whether the domain is in a science, is business-related or has to do with people and their relationships. Within a single discipline there can be disagreement about how to describe the world. Moreover, disciplines overlap and the overlapping area is often looked at from different points of view. One approach to the ontology heterogeneity problem

Figure 1. SIVC ontology

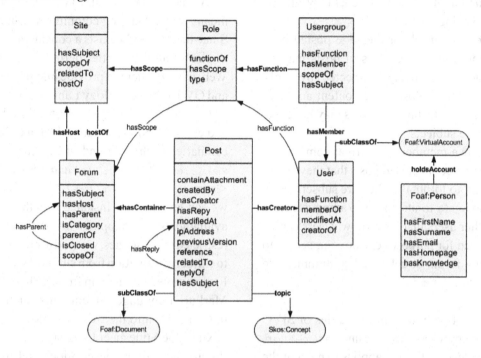

is to create a global schema to serve as an Inter-lingua for human and software agents. However, one of the principles of the Semantic Web is that it should be based on the same open, decentralized and distributed approach that has made the World Wide Web successful; anyone should be able to create, publish and use their own ontologies. In the open and dynamic environment of the Web, it is expected that the natural influences and forces of the market and "networking effect" will encourage coalescing to a smaller number of interoperable ontologies for a given domain. So the construction of a few global schemata is not the goal. Rather, we envision and are encouraging the development of a number of relatively small ontologies, some of which may overlap and some of which may be in conflict.

SEMANTIC LINKING

The SIVC ontology consists of two key parts: classes and properties that describe the informa-tion in online community sites and mappings that relate SIVC to existing vocabularies. The overview of classes and properties is given in the Figure 1.

Following are some key classes in the ontol-ogy:

1. **Site** is the location of a virtual community or set of communities, with users in groups creating posts on a set of forums. While an individual group of forums are simply hosted on a centralised site, in the future the concept of a 'site' may be extended. For instance, a subject thread could be formed by posts in a distributed group on a peer-to-peer environment.

2. **Forum** is a discussion area on which posts are made. Forum will usually discuss a cer-tain subject or set of related subjects. The hierarchy of forum can be defined in terms of parents and children, allowing the creation of structures conforming to subject categories. Examples of forum include mailing lists,

online bulletin boards, Usenet newsgroups and weblogs.

3. **Post** is an article or message posted by a user to a group. A series of posts may be threaded, *i.e.* being connected by reply relationships. Posts have content and may also have attachments. Posts may have one or more subjects.

4. **User** is a member of a virtual community. They are connected to posts that they create or edit, to forum that they are subscribed to or moderate, to sites that they administer, and to other users that they know. Users can be grouped for purposes of allowing access to certain forum or enhanced community site features.

There are two important properties of SIVC concepts, namely `hasSubject` and `hasCreator`.

A *hasSubject* definition applies to most of the concepts defined above, and subject metadata can be a useful way to match users and posts to each other. A user or a group of users can define subjects of interest when their profiles are created or modified. Regarding posts, it may be more difficult to require a user to assign a subject to a post at creation time. It is more likely that a group will have an associated subject or set of subjects that can be propagated to the posts it contains, but subjects can also be assigned to posts via a predefined taxonomy or by free-text keywords using 'folksonomy' tagging. In order to enable the location of related information across sites, the SKOS framework (Miles et al, 2004) can be used to relate the concepts represented by the subjects or tags, and to link subjects between community sites.

The `hasCreator` property links a post to the user profile of its author. Thus, we can follow the link from the post to the creator and locate the other posts by the same person. The community can be seen as a network of posts with users linked to each post, and there is also a network of other posts created by a given user originating from there.

A main function of SIVC is to provide a means for exchanging community instance data. Since there already exists a considerable number of classes and properties defined in RDF on the Web, it is sufficient to provide mappings in RDFs and OWL (Web Ontology Language), `<http://rdfs.org/sioc/mappings>`, to allow the import and export of SIVC instance data in different vocabularies, such as (Friend Of A Friend, `<http://xmlns.com/foaf/0.1/>`) and RSS 1.0 / Atom, `<http://purl.org/rss/1.0/>`. Therefore, we can leverage the instance data that is already available. Since mappings in SIVC are not only restricted to ontologies, we need to provide a means to extract information from simple data structures. For example, we can map from XML (eXtensible Markup Language) documents such as RSS 0.9x and 2.0 into the SIVC ontology using XSL (eXtensible Stylesheet Language) stylesheets. In this method, titles, descriptions and hyperlinks are extracted from XML documents, somewhat similar to how GRDDL (Gleaning Resource Descriptions from Dialects of Languages, `<http://www.w3.org/2004/01/rdxh/spec>`) is used to extract information from XHTML (eXtensible HyperText Markup Language) documents.

SEMANTIC VIRTUAL COMMUNITIES

Metadata

Information about resources on the Web is known as metadata, which stands for 'data about data'. The metadata for an object or resource can be any descriptive information about the object, including information that is useful to interpret and use the object, such as descriptions of the purpose or utility of the object and representations of the content of the object. For instance, object metadata can include the creation date of the object, what the object contains, where and how it is stored etc. Metadata associated with files and documents typically comprises the title, the subject, author, publication or modification date, size, format etc.

On the Web, metadata is used to provide information about documents and content items that is typically not displayed on-screen. This information can then be used by software such as search engines, aggregation and presentation applications. For example, search engines on the Web typically weight the keywords in the metadata of a Web page higher than the actual content of Web pages. Metadata can also be used for presentation purposes. A common example is the Cascading Style Sheets (CSS) standard, which uses simple metadata for describing the presentation of Web page elements. Metadata is therefore becoming particularly important in XML-based Web applications. Metadata is typically structured, especially in the context of managing electronic data, as on the Web. Structured metadata is typically in the form of labelled fields. For example, metadata about books in a library catalogue is usually stored in fields such as 'author', 'title', 'ISBN' and 'publisher'. On the Web, structured data is stored in metadata annotation tags. For example, in an HTML document, the document title is marked up as

```
<title>WNRI Homepage</title>
```

where the tags <title> and </title> are the start and end tags respectively, marking the start and end of the document title. In the Semantic Web, not all the information with metadata is expressed as text on Web pages. Thus, we require a more generalized way of specifying metadata. Expressing metadata about information requires the ability to refer to things in the World and the ability to make statements about them. Things in the World are represented by a URI (Uniform Resource Identifier) (URI). A URI is essentially a simple text string, similar to URLs, which specify the location of a Web resource. The second requirement for expressing metadata about Web information is a way to make statements about Web resources. This

is the functionality provided by RDF (Resource Description Format). RDF enables people to make statements about things in the world and relate them to Web resources using the simple language of URI triples.

Let us illustrate this with the help of the following two example RDF links (Bizer, 2009).

```
Subject: http://www.w3.org/People/
Berners-Lee/card#i
Predicate: http://xmlns.com/foaf/0.1/
member
Object: http://dig.csail.mit.edu/
data#DIG

Subject: http://data.linkedmdb.org/
resource/film/77
Predicate: http://www.w3.org/2002/07/
owl#sameAs
Object: http://dbpedia.org/resource/
Pulp_Fiction_%28film%29
```

The first link states that a resource identified by the URI `http://www.w3.org/People/Berners-Lee/card#i` is member of another resource called `http://dig.csail.mit.edu/data#DIG`. When the subject URI is dereferenced over the HTTP protocol, the dig.csail.mit.edu server answers with a RDF description of the identified resource, in this case the MIT Decentralized Information Group. When the object URI is dereferenced the W3C server provides an RDF graph describing Tim Berners-Lee. Dereferencing the predicate URI `http://xmlns.com/foaf/0.1/member` yields a definition of the link type *member*, described in RDF using the RDF Vocabulary Definition Language (RDFS). The second RDF link connects the description of the film Pulp Fiction in the Linked Movie Database with the description of the film provided by DBpedia, by stating that the URI `http://data.linkedmdb.org/resource/film/77` and the URI `http://dbpedia.org/resource/`

`Pulp_Fiction_%28film%29` refer to the same real-world entity - the film Pulp Fiction.

The Dublin Core is a metadata standard for describing digital objects (including web pages), usually expressed in XML. For example, the tag `dc:title` and `dc:creator` identifies the title of the Web resource and the person who authored it. Semantic Web tags are usually of the format `[namespace]:[tagname]` and we shall follow this convention throughout this document. Annotation tags such as these are already common within the Web community; witness the numerous news and weblogging sites offering RSS (RDF Site Summary) feeds. RSS is an RDF-based format for syndicating news-like content, such as new items from news sites and posts on personal weblogs. RSS-aware programs, such as news aggregators, check the RSS feed for changes and can react to the changes appropriately, for example by displaying new items or alerting the user to a new post at a particular site. This enables people to monitor a large number of web sites with minimal overhead. RSS-aggregators are becoming particularly widespread in the weblogging community. Webloggers often keep track of new postings to other people's weblogs. When the posts are infrequently made though, it is quite tiresome for people to continually check the weblog. With RSS, the news aggregators can poll the weblog and notify when any changes are made.

Most of the information on the Web is, however, unstructured. Automatic metadata generation is much more difficult for unstructured information. Research therefore typically focuses on providing semi-automatic annotation, in other words, providing intelligent annotation support to the user. The KIM platform (Popov et al. 2004), for example, uses information extraction techniques to extract certain types of information, such as people, places, dates etc. and annotate them automatically. A closely related problem to metadata generation is that of metadata use. Unless there are compelling uses of metadata, interest in generating annotations remains low and existing annotations and annotation tools are limited. However, much of the proposed use of metadata and tools to process metadata rely on the existence of lots of annotations. So, we face a chicken-and-egg problem.

ONTOLOGY CONSTRUCTION

There are various ontologies around created for social software, like Friend-of-a-Friend (foaf), Description-of-a-Project (doap), Semantically Interlinked Open Communities (SIOC) etc. and also different scientific communities have created more or less suitable ontologies which can be used to describe data. In order to define the metadata of a virtual community; we rely on two widely used ontologies on the Social Semantic Web: FOAF and SIOC.

FOAF is used to describe community members by their properties (name, email etc.). It allows reuse of an existing URI for a person that starts a virtual community instead of creating a new identity URI for the purpose. Moreover, since some Web 2.0 services already offer FOAF export, either directly as LiveJournal or thanks to external services as Flickr, people can reuse their existing URI from these services without having to dig in RDF modelling. Yet in case a person needs to create a new instance of foaf:Person, Linked Data principles allow them to identify uniquely with an already existing profile via a owl:sameAs link.

The FOAF ontology includes classes and properties found useful to describe people online. Consider the following example, drawn from the FOAF Vocabulary Specification and encoded using the XML serialization for RDF.

```
<foaf:Person>
<foaf:name>Jim Levine</foaf:name>
<foaf:mbox_sha1sum>231221fb0e3256f92
815fc201f9e9137262c282e</foaf:mbox_
sha1sum>
```

```
<foaf:homepage rdf:resource="http://
nfr.org/people/jlevine/" />
<foaf:img rdf:resource="http://nfr.
org/people/jlevine/db/jim.jpeg"/>
</foaf:Person>
```

This example encodes the information that "there is a `foaf:Person` with a `foaf:name` property of 'Jim Levine' and a `foaf:mbox_sha-1sum` property of 23...82e; this person stands in a foaf:homepage relationship to a thing called `http://nfr.org/people/jlevine/` and a foaf:img relationship to a thing called `http://nfr.org/people/jlevine/db/jim.jpeg`." FOAF defines 12 classes and 51 properties. The `foaf:knows` property is used to construct basic social networks, linking to instances of `foaf:Person`. The FOAF vocabulary is simple, which has encouraged its adoption and use, and extensible, making it suitable to a wide range of uses. As shown in (Ding, 2005), more than 150 different properties have been defined for the foaf:Person class and nearly 500 have actually been used with instances of foaf:Person. One way to view this situation is that it represents undisciplined chaos and that the lack of any centralized authority or standard for terms suggests that nothing useful will come out of it. An alternate view is that communities will be able to select and use terms that are useful and those which are widely used be integrated into consensus ontologies. In this view, the eventual result will be a relatively small number of widely used ontologies with mappings, as appropriate, between them. Less widely used terms, whether they are deprecated or newly introduced will remain on the edges.

While FOAF aims to model the people aspect, SIOC is used to define related user contexts thus providing a way to identify user accounts on a given virtual community service (Breslin, 2009). SIOC makes it possible for a person to subscribe to various services, i.e. a single `foaf:Person` can be connected to various `sioc:User`. It employs the distributed architecture of the Semantic Web to enable people to consolidate their identity across a network of services. In addition to the account aspect, SIOC can be used to model the virtual community service itself and the updates of any user by extending the SIOC types module with two new types: `sioct:CommunityPost` and `sioct:Community`, as respective subclasses of `sioc:Item` and `sioc:Container`, thus allowing a virtual community to contain (using sioc:container of) instances of CommunityPost. This also makes possible the modelling of a community post with the same SIOC and FOAF properties as blog posts and wiki pages. Moreover, the resulting taxonomi of SIOC types will allow people to access a dataset containing a set of `sioct:Community`, `sioct:WikiArticle` and `sioct:CommunityPost` with a single SPARQL query for all the data while leaving open the option to refine their search by restricting the type of the items to be retrieved. Thus, representing metadata in a machine-readable format is the first step in getting rid of proprietary data silos for virtual community content as it becomes possible to merge it with other Web 2.0 content that has been described in RDF. We also can rely on the connection between `sioc:User` and `foaf:Person` to find relevant content, e.g. answer queries like "List all my posts on the community during the last month of 2009", something that could not be done with non-semantic Web 2.0 data. To a large extent, this combination of FOAF and SIOC can be used as a solution to the data portability issues which depend on machine readable and interlinked data models to represent people, user accounts and data.

INFORMATION ANNOTATION

Virtual community posts are by nature relatively light in content. To identify the information they contain is however, one of the problematic areas for current systems. While hash tags can be useful, there is a need to describe some content more formally because of the problems of plain text-only descriptions. Instead of plain text or tags, using URIs and RDF to tag this information is preferable for two reasons: firstly, we rely on existing, unambiguous resource definitions to tag the content and secondly, we open community entries to the Linked Data Web in the case these URIs are available on the Web and in the better case, already linked to other content and thereby providing a path to the Global Graph.

There is therefore a need to extract URIs or concepts from plain text semi-automatically or to let users annotate it similarly to what they can already do on Twitter with hash tags, but with more efficient processing that can define URIs based on the annotated tags. The processor will then be able to extract the two hash tags and thanks to a predefined prefix mapping process, query DBpedia and GeoNames to retrieve URIs of the related concepts. The updates will automatically be linked to existing URIs rather than to simple and meaningless (from a software agent point of view) text strings. Such a way to extract information and to interlink with existing URIs makes content more easily retrievable on the Semantic Web.

DISTRIBUTED CONTENT

The virtual community system should be open and distributed, following the spirit of the Web architecture allowing a multitude of publishing services and aggregation servers to interact with each others. A publishing service makes the formulation of posts in RDF by one or more authors available on the Web. When a new post is published the service pings one or more aggregation servers, defined by the user, with the URI of the post that is then retrieved by the servers. As is presently the case with blogs we expect some people to deploy their own publishing services while others use public ones, as well as aggregation servers that can be public or dedicated to private communities of interest.

An aggregation server receives pings from publishers and retrieves posts it deems relevant for further use. The relevancy depends on the nature of the aggregation function of each server. Some servers may have a strict list of sources they aggregate while others try to provide inclusive views on the global activity on the Web. In any case, the community is open for new aggregators to provide new views. An open question is how publishers decide which aggregators to ping and whether publishers should let aggregators subscribe to them.

USER DATA

As a consequence of the distributed nature of the system, one feature of the SIVC architecture is that people can really own their data. By self-hosting a publishing service and then publishing to a virtual community aggregator server, they keep all their updates even if one service closes. Moreover, by hosting their data, people can reuse it in other applications, including future virtual community servers to which they want to publish and any Semantic Web applications. They can also mash it up with other RDF data they own or that is publicly available on the Web, or in case of corporate virtual community, in their organisation. We think that this feature, combining the distributed architecture and the data ownership and reuse aspect, is important, especially from a user rights and data portability point of view.

SECURITY AND PRIVACY ISSUES

The open and distributed nature of the architecture complicates the authentication requirements in some use cases. It is easy to publish posts in someone else's name or to fill a public aggregator with spam. Moreover, aggregators may need to authenticate to publishers if the posts are for a restricted audience only. One solution is to require publishers to register using OpenID on an aggregator server. The server delivers each registrant an API key (a password) for publishing their content on that server. Relying on OpenID allows servers to automatically discover the FOAF profile and the URI of a user as long as the OpenID provider can offer FOAF autodiscovery. Combined with the use of the foaf:openid property that was recently introduced in the FOAF specifications, it provides a lightweight authentication and security layer, making it possible for the server to partially ensure that someone publishing on it is really the person identified by the FOAF URI. Since one can deliver false information in a fake FOAF profile, additional strategies such as a network of trust between community members or graph signing[1] with public-key cryptography (PGP) should be needed.

DATA PORTABILITY

Data portability is the ability for people to reuse their data across interoperable applications, *i.e.* people can port the data they own from one place to another. It is crucial for a number of reasons. Firstly, people do not have to duplicate their personal profile definitions across a range of social websites. Secondly, keep your contacts (colleagues or friends) updated is becoming increasingly difficult as new sites appear. Thirdly, if you decide you want to change services from one platform to another, there are very few easy-to-use mechanisms for bringing your content items with you (photos, posts, etc.). But most importantly, users like to think that they have full control over their own data. That means having the freedom to bring their data with them if they choose to migrate to another virtual community. There is a growing feeling that companies need to support the wishes of their users in this direction. However, companies should also realise that providing mechanisms for data portability does not necessarily mean that users will leave their

sites en masse. The big players (e.g. Facebook's FQL, the Twitter API and the Flickr API) will, by providing open methods to access data on sites via APIs or query mechanisms or embedded markup, allow others to build new and interesting applications on top of their sites thus encouraging users to stay on board. Also, the users then feel happy in knowing that they have access to their data if they need it, building loyalty as opposed to anger against restrictive user data agreements. Lastly, these companies can open up avenues for an influx of new users who can easily bring their data over via data portability mechanisms.

RDFa FOR LINKING VIRTUAL COMMUNITIES

Virtual community expressed in RDFa can also be used to help create closer interlinks between the objects that make up virtual communities, i.e. posts, knowledge communities and user profiles. RDFa was created to help machines understand what humans intuitively get while browsing around the Web. RDFa is useful for embedding SIVC data directly in HTML documents such as blog. Recent approach to embed RDFa in Drupal[2] was a huge success and future work is leading in that direction. RDFa[3] is a set of XHTML attributes meant specifically to augment visual data with machine readable hints.

RDFa is based on the principles of Resource Description Framework (RDF). It is a specification strictly connected with XHTML, supported by the XHTML1.1 doctype. Let us consider a simple example of Web links. Humans understand what a link is pointing to usually by reading the linked text. Machines, however, have no idea. They just know that it's a link. RDFa provides the *"rel"* attribute to help bridge this gap. You add this attribute like you would any other. Instead of using the following to point to the W3C's RDFa primer:

```
<a href="http://www.w3.org/TR/xhtml-
rdfa-primer/"
    >The W3C's RDFa Primer</a>
```

You might use:

```
<a href="http://www.w3.org/TR/xhtml-
rdfa-primer/"
    rel="cite"
    >The W3C's RDFa Primer</a>
```

This will illustrate that we are citing the standard's official primer page.

In an article at ldap.com[4] Mark Wahl described how to embed SIOC RDFa in XHTML. Digital Bazaar CEO Manu Sporny has also written a three-part guide about how more semantic information could be incorporated into the Digg community pages using SIOC RDFa.

ISSUES

One of the main functions of SIVC is to provide a means for exchanging community instance data. Since there are already a considerable number of classes and properties defined in RDF on the Web, we provide mappings in RDFs and OWL (Web Ontology Language), <http://rdfs.org/sioc/mappings>, to allow the import and export of SIOC instance data in different vocabularies, such as (Friend Of A Friend, <http://xmlns.com/foaf/0.1/>) and RSS 1.0/Atom, <http://purl.org/rss/1.0/>. Therefore, we can leverage the instance data that is already available.

Since mappings in SIVC are not only restricted to ontologies, we need to provide a means to extract information from simple data structures. For example, we can map from XML (eXtensible Markup Language) documents such as RSS 0.9x and 2.0 into the SIVC ontology using XSL (eXtensible Stylesheet Language) stylesheets.

A general review of ontology-mapping methods was well-described by Kalfoglou and Schorlemmer (2003). Because ontologies are developed and managed independently the semantic mismatches between two or more ontologies are unavoidable. In essence, fully shared vocabularies are rather exceptional—a number of possible different semantic conflicts were identified by Shaw and Gaines (1989); other classifications were proposed by Hameed et al. (2001). Most of the ambiguities were related to the mismatch between concepts and terms,

- the same term (homonym) was used for different concepts
- distinct terms (synonyms) were used for the same concept
- different ontology representation languages were used
- a given concept was represented in different ontologies at different levels of detail
- a given domain was modelled in different ways

The vision of Semantic Web allowing agents to publish and exchange ontologies requires strong mechanisms supporting ontology merging and alignment (Hendler, 2001). Without them, it may be almost impossible to achieve the semantic interoperability in societies of autonomous Web agents.

Already developed methods for ontology alignment do not guarantee success. In particular, most of the methods used offer semiautomatic approaches which require human assistance (Noy & Musen, 2000; Silva & Rocha, 2003), but in real-live situations an automatic cooperation between autonomous agents is expected. Moreover, it is hardly possible that all of the agents will use the same method for aligning their ontologies, and this has remarkable consequences on knowledge sharing on the Semantic Web. General approach to the ontology alignment problem assumes the use of so-called similarity measures which relate concepts from different ontologies. A similarity measure is a function or procedure that analyzes the structure of ontologies to evaluate the level of correspondence between two given concepts (Andrea & Egenhofer, 2003; Lin, 1998; Maedche & Zacharias, 2002; Stuckenschmidt & Timm, 2002). The similarity functions developed use syntactical, lexical, or structural analysis. Other techniques have also been proposed, for example, Lin (1998) presents an information-theoretic definition of similarity and proposes a measure for computing string and taxonomical similarities. He compares it with several other approaches and shows that for different similarity measures applied to a chosen taxonomy similarity between certain concepts varies significantly, the same concerns string similarity between chosen pairs of words. Similarity measures may give different results for the same input data.

Many alignment methods require human-controlled tuning of parameters (Noy & Musen, 2000) or additional information (Andrea & Egenhofer, 2003), such as noun frequencies in language corpus or synonyms sets (Resnik, 1999) — in this case one can never guarantee that such information will always be available. The issues described create the possibility of new types of mismatch because it is not given that two agents aligning their ontologies will obtain the same result. The results depend on the method used. There is a need for a framework that allows the use of different methods and deals with the uncertainty resulting from differences between similarity measures exploited by the agents. Proposed solutions tend to enforce negotiations between the agents until they reach agreement (or not) over given concepts (Bailin & Truszkowski, 2001) or use a formal mathematical framework to evaluate the uncertainty resulting from the difference in the similarity measures used (Juszczyszyn, 2004). Although many successful experiments have been carried out, the problem of automated ontology alignment is still a research challenge and no ultimate solution has been presented.

Many virtual community services act as closed worlds like most of Web 2.0 services; only a few

of them allow interlinking with other services. For example, merging your latest blog posts or your Flickr pictures with your Twitter updates cannot be done except by HTML links or RSS. RSS provides syndication, i.e. real-time export of latest updates for a given user, but cannot be used to retrieve the complete update history at any later time. Moreover, those services do not expose their metadata for reuse. Twitter has adopted microformats for describing follower (subscriber) lists, but there is no simple way to retrieve metadata about the complete updates of any user (e.g. who did the update and when). One solution would be to combine the RSS feed of latest updates with the XML export of each update. Some scripts could then map them to Semantic Web vocabularies and URIs with potential use of external data, as SWAML does to find people URIs. Yet, the process can be quite complex and since it is based on RSS, only the latest updates would be available.

Apart from the metadata, the content of the updates does not carry any semantic information, thus making it difficult to reuse. Twitter users have adopted certain short-hand conventions in their writing called hash tags, but their semantics are not readily machine-processable thus raising the same ambiguity and heterogeneity problems that tagging causes. For example, the hash tag #apple could mean various things (fruit, computer etc.) depending on the context and can therefore not be automatically processed by computers. This lack of data formalism also makes finding relevant content difficult. While some services provide plain-text search engines, there is no way to answer queries like "What are the latest review updates on a movie" or "What is going on now near Banjara Hills".

Finally, one issue with services is their centralised architecture. Most services do not act in a client-server way, but require users to post their updates on a given platform, which is the same for publishing and reading data. This means that most of the time, published data belongs to the publishing site, and cannot be automatically re-used on multiple virtual community sites, or even re-used locally for other purposes. It can also be a problem to private communities, since users need to rely on an external service where they cannot completely control privacy and security. We believe that the Semantic Web is an elegant solution to opening these data from proprietary silos and to providing machine-processable data and metadata to virtual community as well as to delivering an open and distributed environment for virtual community.

SCIENTIFIC COLLABORATION FRAMEWORK

The Science Collaboration Framework (SCF) (Das et al. 2008) is a reusable, open-source software toolkit to establish structured virtual organisations for researchers in biomedicine that leverages existing biomedical ontologies and RDF resources on the Semantic Web. To create interoperable communities, the SCF community knowledge is structured in a machine interpretable format as well as reuse existing, available knowledge bases. SCF supports structured virtual community discourse amongst biomedical researchers that is centred on a variety of interlinked heterogeneous data resources such as research articles, news items, interviews, and other viewpoint.

The SCF GPL software[5] consists of the Drupal core content management system and customised modules. Drupal is a very flexible and modular system and allows the implementation of custom content and functionality by developing a new module, in PHP code, that implements Drupal interfaces. Any community that wants to use SCF and has an existing Drupal site can install a SCF module easily through a forms-based administrative interface. A community administrator has the option of installing selections of these modules if there is an existing Drupal site or of installing the entire framework, with configuration being per-formed through the normal Drupal administrative control panel. At the other end of the spectrum, a developer can extend SCF functionality and create new custom content. Another advantage of choosing Drupal is that we can leverage a large active community of over 2000 developers.

The SCF framework provides the ability to publish articles, interviews and news; annotate these with biological resources such as genes, animal models and antibodies; and create informal discourse of community members around these resources as well as the current scientific articles. The information of a content type (e.g. gene, article) is contained in a unit called 'node' in Drupal; a site can create instances of gene nodes, article nodes, etc. using these modules. Bioinformatics data tends to be heterogeneous; hence there was a need to instantiate nodes from heterogeneous data sources such as XML and RDF.

The knowledge representation of biological resources is based on the SWAN ontology. Gene information is imparted into the Drupal system from a remote existing RDF repository using the RDF query language (SPARQL) interface. SCF use 'foaf:Person' class to represent the member and 'foaf:topic interest' to capture his or her research interest. The architecture makes it possible to define common schemas in OWL for a set of Web communities and to enable interoperability across biological resources, SWAN research statements or other objects of interest defined in the shared schemas. It is planned to make these graphs available via RDFa embedded within the HTML, and this work is being carried out in parallel with efforts to integrate RDFa into Drupal core[6].

CHALLENGES

There are some challenges for SIVC. The main challenge is adoption by community sites, *i.e.* how can the users be enticed to make use of the SIVC ontology. By using concepts that can be easily understood by site administrators and by providing properties that are automatically created by an end-user, the SIVC ontology can be adopted in a useful way. A second challenge is how best to use SIVC with existing ontologies. This can be partially solved by mappings and interfaces to commonly-used ontologies. Another challenge is how SIVC will scale. We will keep the scaling challenge in mind when creating a future architecture for an interconnected system of community sites.

Making community semantics more explicit would enable new community members to make use of it without having to acquire it gradually. This could make their interactions with the community more meaningful and less wasteful. Moreover, explicit semantics would lend itself to machine processing. Making user's semantics accessible to machines allows them to process the community archive, mine it and present information to the community in an intelligent and context-suitable way than is presently taking place.

CONCLUSION

We have presented the SIVC ontology in this chapter. We have seen how instance data in SIVC can be exchanged among virtual community sites. Our initial SIVC ontology can also be used to enable more complex scenarios. In the future, we intend to exploit the characteristics of intra and inter-community links to guide query routing in a P2P-like environment.

REFERENCES

Akerkar, R. (2009). *The foundations of semantic Web: XML, RDF & ontology*. London, UK: Alpha Science Intl Ltd.

Andrea, M., & Egenhofer, M. (2003). Determining semantic similarity among entity classes from different ontologies. *IEEE Transactions on Knowledge and Data Engineering, 15*, 442–456. doi:10.1109/TKDE.2003.1185844

Berners-Lee, T., Hendler, J., & Lassila, O. (2001). The Semantic Web. *Scientific American, 284*(5), 34–43. doi:10.1038/scientificamerican0501-34

Bizer, C., Heath, T., & Berners-Lee, T. (2009). Linked data- the story so far. In Heath, T., Hepp, M., and Bizer, C. (Eds.). Special issue on linked data, *International Journal on Semantic Web and Information Systems (IJSWIS)*. http:// linkeddata. org/ docs/ ijswis-special-issue.

Bowman, C., Danzig, P., Hardy, D., Manber, U., & Schwartz, M. (1995). The Harvest information discovery and access system. *Computer Networks and ISDN Systems, 28*(1–2), 119–125. doi:10.1016/0169-7552(95)00098-5

Breslin, J., Passant, A., & Decker, S. (2009). *The social Semantic Web*. Berlin, Germany: Springer Verlag. doi:10.1007/978-3-642-01172-6

Das, S., Girard, T., Weitzman, L., Lewis-Bowen, A., & Clark, T. (2008). Building bio-medical Web communities using a semantically aware content management system, *Briefings in Bioinformatics*.

Ding, L., Zhou, L., Finin, T., & Joshi, A. (2005, January). How the Semantic Web is being used: An analysis of FOAF, *Proceedings of the 38th International Conference on System Sciences*, Hawaii, USA.

Florescu, D., Levy, A., & Mendelzon, A. (1998). Database techniques for the World-Wide Web: A Survey. *SIGMOD Record, 27*(3), 59–74. doi:10.1145/290593.290605

Gomez-Perez, A., & Corcho, O. (2002). Ontology languages for the Semantic Web. *IEEE Intelligent Systems, 17*(1), 54–60. doi:10.1109/5254.988453

Hagel, J., & Armstrong, A. (1997). *Net gain: Expanding markets through virtual communities*. Boston, MA: Harvard Business School Press.

Hameed, A., Sleeman, D., & Preece, A. (2001). Detecting mismatches among experts' ontologies acquired through knowledge elicitation. *21st International Conference on Knowledge Based Systems and Applied Artificial Intelligence ES2001*, Cambridge, UK.

Hendler, J. (2001). Agents and the Semantic Web. *IEEE Intelligent Systems*, *16*(2), 30–37. doi:10.1109/5254.920597

Juszczyszyn, K. (2004). Knowledge sharing in agent's society with multiple ontologies. In (Ed.), International Series on Advanced Intelligence, Vol. 10, *Intelligent Technologies for Inconsistent Information Processing* (pp. 129-144). Australia: Advanced Knowledge International Ltd.

Kalfoglou, Y., & Schorlemmer, M. (2003). Ontology mapping: The state of the art. *The Knowledge Engineering Review*, *18*(1), 1–31. doi:10.1017/S0269888903000651

Lin, D. (1998). An information-theoretic definition of similarity. *International Conference on Machine Learning, ICML'98*, Madison, WI.

Maedche, A., & Zacharias, V. (2002). *Clustering ontology-based metadata in the Semantic Web*. Berlin, Germany: Springer-Verlag.

Miles, A., Rogers, N., & Beckett, D. (2004) *SKOS Core RDF Vocabulary*. <http:// www.w3.org/ 2004/ 02/ skos/core/>

Noy, N. F., & Musen, M. A. (2000). PROMPT: Algorithm and tool for automated ontology merging and alignment. *17th National Conference. On Artificial Intelligence*, Austin, TX, USA.

Palmer, J. W., & Speier, C. (1997) A typology of virtual organizations: An empirical study. In J. Gupta (Ed.), *Proceedings of the Association for Information Systems, America conference*, Indianapolis, IN, USA.

Popov, B., Kiryakov, A., Ognyano, D., Manov, D., & Kirilov, A. (2004). KIM: A semantic platform for information extraction and retrieval. *Natural Language Engineering, 10,* 375–392. doi:10.1017/S135132490400347X

Resnik, P. (1999). Semantic similarity in a taxonomy: An information-based measure and its application to problems of ambiguity in natural language. *Journal of Artificial Intelligence Research, 1*, 95–130.

Rheingold, H. (1993). *The virtual community: Homesteading on the electronic frontier*. Reading, Massachusetts: Addison-Wesley Publishing Company.

Rittel, H. & Kunz. W. (1970) *Issues as elements of information systems. Working Paper* 131. Berkeley Ca, USA: University of California Center for Planning and Development Research.

Schubert, P. (1999). *Aufbau und management virtueller Geschäftsgemeinschaften in electronic commerce Umgebungen*. St. Gallen: Dissertation.

Shaw, M., & Gaines, B. R. (1989). Comparing conceptual structures: Consensus, conflict, correspondence and contrast. *Knowledge Acquisition, 1*(4), 341–363. doi:10.1016/S1042-8143(89)80010-X

Silva, N., & Rocha, J. (2003). Semantic Web complex ontology mapping. Proceedings of the *IEEE/WIC International Conference on Web Intelligence*. Porto, Portugal.

Staab, S. (2002). Emergent semantics. *IEEE Intelligent Systems*, 78–86. doi:10.1109/5254.988491

Stuckenschmidt, H., & Timm, I. (2002). Adaptation of communication vocabularies using shared ontologies. Proceedings of the *Second International Workshop on Ontologies in Agent Systems (OAS)*. Bologna, Italy.

KEY TERMS AND DEFINITIONS

FOAF: Friend of a friend is a machine-readable ontology describing persons, their activities and their relations to other people and objects.

Metadata: Metadata describes other data. It provides information about a certain item's content. Vocabulary: it is a list of terms that have been enumerated explicitly.

Ontology: An ontology is a specification of a conceptualization.

RDF: RDF is a standard model for data interchange on the Web. RDF has features that facilitate data merging even if the underlying schemas differ, and it specifically supports the evolution of schemas over time without requiring all the data consumers to be changed. RDF extends the linking structure of the Web to use URIs to name the relationship between things as well as the two ends of the link.

RDFa: A Resource Description Framework – in – attributes (RDFa) is a W3C Recommendation that adds a set of attribute level extensions to XHTML for embedding rich metadata within Web documents.

Semantic Link: Semantic links are links with semantic properties (factors or tags), closely related to the links in the semantic network.

ENDNOTES

[1] http://usefulinc.com/foaf/signingFoafFiles
[2] http://groups.drupal.org/node/16597
[3] http://www.w3.org/TR/xhtml-rdfa-primer/
[4] http://www.ldap.com/1/commentary/wahl/20070725_01.shtml
[5] http://sciencecollaboration.org/
[6] http://groups.drupal.org/node/16597

Chapter 11
Identification vs. Self-Verification in Virtual Communities (VC):
Theoretical Gaps and Design Implications

Kathy Ning Shen
University of Wollongong in Dubai, UAE

ABSTRACT

Identity-related processes have been identified as important in explaining virtual community (VC) member behavior as well as informing system design of VCs. In particular, the two distinct identity processes of self-verification and identification have been identified and investigated separately, portrayed as two distinctive or contradictory identity processes with different practical implications. This chapter compares and reconciles these two theoretical perspectives in explaining VC participation. Based on a critical and comprehensive review of prior literature, the author identifies three major theoretical gaps that suggest how VC research and management can be advanced through an identity perspective. Finally, the chapter is concluded by discussing key implications of applying identity perspectives in VC research and future research agenda.

INTRODUCTION

Virtual communities (VCs), sometimes called online communities, describe the mediated social spaces in the digital environment that allow groups to form and be sustained primarily through ongo-

ing virtual communication processes (Bagozzi & Dholakia, 2002). Much evidence has shown their potent influence in bringing together far-flung, like-minded individuals (Hagel & Armstrong, 1997) and their commercial and/or social values (Gupta & Kim, 2004). A growing number of companies are building VCs to facilitate peer-

DOI: 10.4018/978-1-60960-869-9.ch011

to-peer help, foster new ideas and innovation, and build knowledge competencies. VCs are also used to reap the knowledge located in customers. Many firms are hosting online user communities to collect feedback and ideas and to strengthen their innovation process. Additionally, VCs have emerged to leverage the knowledge embedded in professionals, e.g., open-source communities and communities of practice. Such communities are sustained by their members' voluntary participation to generate content (Lee, Vogel, & Limayem, 2003). Thus, a key challenge for most VCs is to ensure on-going participation.

Prior research in information systems has demonstrated Identity-related processes to be important in explaining VC member behavior as well as informing system VC design. Particularly, two distinct identity processes have been discussed, e.g., identification and self-verification. Identification means that the individual defines him/herself in terms of the membership in the group. The resulting perceptions of oneness with or belonging to the group provide a more autonomous motivation resulting not only in a higher quality of engagement (e.g., greater persistence, effort) but also in more positive experiences such as enjoyment, sense of purpose, and well-being (Ryan & Deci, 2001). In contrast, self-verification assumes that stable self-views provide people with a crucial source of coherence, an invaluable means of defining their existence, and guiding social interaction (cf. Swann Jr., Rentfrow, & Guinn, 2003). Thus, people are motivated to validate and confirm their self-concepts, even when those self-concepts are negative (McNulty & Swann Jr., 1994), which also drives member participation and active social exchange in VCs (Chan, Bhandar, Oh, & Chan, 2004; Ma & Agarwal, 2007). Different from identification that reflects influences exerted from the collective; self-verification focuses on the communication of self-concepts defined by individuals.

In most IS research, identification and self-verification have been investigated separately and portrayed as two distinctive or contradictory identity processes with different practical implications. Research on identification usually emphasizes the collective influences and anonymity of individuals and agrees that the salient personal identity would undermine the identification with the collective (Postmes, Spears, & Lea, 1998). But research on self-verification argues for making personal/role identity salient and recognized (Ma & Agarwal, 2007). While identity confirmation emphasizes an individual's self-concept; most prior studies on identification assume antagonism of individuality in the formation of identification, and agree that the salient personal identity would undermine the identification with the collective (Postmes et al. 2000).

Since VCs usually integrate various IT features which may incur complicated community dynamics with diversified social psychological consequences, it is likely that both identity processes co-exist to influence VC members' interaction within VCs. Thus, it is necessary to examine these competing identity processes simultaneously in driving community participation and informing system VC design. Moreover, integrating these identity processes will offer a more holistic understanding about group dynamics in VCs, which entails important managerial implications.

In this chapter, the author will compare and reconcile these two theoretical perspectives in explaining VC participation. The main objective of this chapter is to inform how VC research and management can be advanced from identity perspectives. This chapter is organized as follows. The following two sections provide a thorough review of two research streams: identification and self-verification. Theoretical models and empirical work in organizational, community, and general group contexts are identified and discussed. Although limited research has been conducted in the context of computer-mediated communication (CMC), prior research from multiple disciplines in different physical settings may provide insights in understanding identity processes in VCs. The following section summarizes and analyzes prior literature, and three theoretical gaps are identified and discussed. Finally, the chapter concludes by discussing the key implications of applying identity perspectives in VC research and a future research agenda.

IDENTIFICATION: SOCIAL INFLUENCE FROM THE COLLECTIVE

Traditionally, research on identification has been dominated by the perspective of social identity theory and self-categorization theory (Bergami & Bagozzi, 2000). According to these theories, identification means that a person comes to view him- or herself as a member of a particular social entity (e.g., ethnic groups, gender groups, organizations or artificial groups) through cognitive processes of social comparison and categorization. It is necessary to note that some studies consider identification as a cognitive state of self-categorization while others define it as the process of comparison of personal attributes with organization attributes. However, it is important to differentiate identification as a cognitive state from its antecedents and effects as the comparison processes may not be the only antecedents for the development of self-categorization (Bergami & Bagozzi, 2000). Hence, in this chapter, *identification is used to refer to the cognitive state while the term "identification process" will be used for the related identity processes.*

A similar term used in prior studies is social identity salience. Although some researchers consider it exchangeable with identification, the literature on identification formation tends to differentiate social identity salience and strength of identification (Forehand, Deshpande, & Reed II, 2002). Strength of identification is an enduring association between an individual's sense of self and his or her identity, whereas identity salience is the momentary activation of a particular social

identity. Since the main purpose of VC design and management is to obtain the long-term commitment from individual members, a strong and enduring association is preferred. In this chapter therefore, identification refers to the enduring cognitive state of self-categorization.

Social Identity Theory and Self-Categorization Theory

The notion of identification with a social category (e.g., gender, occupation, organizations, more short-lived and transient groups) is most often discussed by those who draw on social identity theory and self-categorization theory (M.A. Hogg & Abrams, 1988; Turner, 1991). The next section reviews these two theories.

Social Identity Theory

Social identity was first proposed by Tajfel (1972) and refers to "the individual's knowledge that he belongs to certain social groups together with some emotional and value significance to him of this group membership" (p292). Assuming that a system of social categorizations can create and define an individual's own place in society, social identity is used to explain how self is conceptualized, based on intergroup comparisons. Further, social identity theory also posits that each individual strives to achieve a positive social identity. This implies that social comparison between in-group and salient out-group(s) aims at the establishment of a positive distinctiveness of the in-group compared to the other out-groups.

Following social identity theory, self-concept or "the totality of self-descriptions and self-evaluations subjectively available to an individual" (Hogg & Abrams, 1988) p24) encompasses two conceptual distinctive parts: 1) personal identities based on idiosyncratic characteristics, e.g., personality traits, and 2) social identities derived from salient group classifications (Tajfel & Turner, 1986). It should be noted that the conceptual distinction between individual-based and group-based aspects of the self is not accompanied by the consistent position on vocabulary. Terms for group-based aspects of the self also include collective, and allocentric; while the individual-based aspects of the self are also termed as individualistic, private, and idiocentric.

Self-Categorization Theory

Self-categorization theory was proposed by Turner (1985) and his colleagues (Turner, Hogg, Oakes, Reicher, & Wetherell, 1987) as an extension of social identity theory. In this theory they specify in detail how social categorization produces prototype-based depersonalization of self and others and thus generates social identity phenomena. Self-categorization or social categorization of self is a cognitive process whereby self is assimilated to the in-group prototype and depersonalizes self-conception, i.e., self is no longer represented as 'unique individual' but as an embodiment of the relevant prototype. Once identified with a social category, the individual tends to define him- or herself in terms of the defining features of the social category which renders the self stereotypically "interchangeable" with other group members, and stereotypically distinct from outsiders (Hogg & Abrams, 1988). Accordingly, Ashforth and Mael (1989) define identification as the "perception of oneness with or belongingness" to the social category; Dutton et al. (1994) consider identification as "a cognitive connection between the definition of an organization and the definition a person applies to him- or herself." Later Ellemers et al. (1999) proposed that one's social identification comprises three components: 1) a cognitive component or self-categorization, referring to a cognitive awareness of one's membership in a social group; 2) an evaluative component or group self-esteem, referring to a positive and negative value connotation attached to this group membership; and 3) an emotional component or affective commitment, referring to a sense of emo-tional involvement with the group. Prior research has demonstrated the construct validity for this three-dimensional conceptualization (Bergami & Bagozzi, 2000).

According to self-categorization theory, one crucial determinant of social identification is the fit between a social categorization and reality in both its comparative and normative aspects (S. Alexander Haslam, Oakes, Reynolds, & Turner, 1999; P. J. Oakes, 1987). Comparative fit means a set of stimuli is more likely to be categorized as a single entity when the intraclass differences between those items are seen to be smaller than the interclass differences between those items and others that are included in a given comparative contexts. Normative fit refers to the content-related aspects of the match between category specification and the instances being represented. In addition, both types of fit determine social identification in interaction with perceiver readiness or cognitive accessibility (P. J. Oakes, 1987). Accessibility is the readiness of a given category to become activated in the person. It is a function of the person's current tasks and goals and of the likelihood that certain objects or events will occur in the situation (P. J. Oakes, Haslam, & Turner, 1994). This means that people are more likely to define themselves in terms of a particular identity to the extent that it has prior meaning for them and it matches subjectively relevant comparative and normative features of reality. Thus, this theory means that context plays an important role in making certain aspects of the self salient, leading to a dynamic and fluctuating self-definition.

Identification in Physical Settings

Traditionally, social identity theories have been applied in 1) artificial groups where people are assigned randomly to treatments (e.g., (N Ellemers, et al., 1999); 2) categories where people are grouped according to social or demographic attributes, e.g., gender, race, ethnicity, religion, occupation, (e.g., (Ethier & Deaux, 1994); 3) naturally occurring small groups such as sororities (e.g., (E. R. Smith & Henry, 1996); and 4) working organizations (e.g., (Ashforth & Mael, 1989; Bergami & Bagozzi, 2000). However, the amount of research on how people develop identification with a collective or antecedents of identification is far less than that examining the effect of identification. As the objective of this chapter is to understand identification as an identity process in VCs, the literature review is focused on identification formation in different physical settings, which is believed to provide valuable insight on understanding the similar phenomenon in VCs.

It should be noted that in some prior studies, identity salience and strength of identification are used interchangeably. As the focus of this research is the strength of identification, the studies using identity salience will be included in the review only when the construct definition and measures indicate the synonymy with the concept of identification in this research. In the following section, the major theoretical development and related empirical studies in organizational, community and general group settings are reviewed.

ORGANIZATIONAL IDENTIFICATION: COMPARISON MODELS

As suggested by the self-categorization theory, identification stems from a member's assessments of the fit between his or her categorizations of the organization and his or her self-categorization (Foreman & Whetten, 2002). A comparison approach is therefore employed and four types of comparison identified in prior studies, i.e., perceived organizational identity vs. self-definition (Dutton, et al., 1994), organizational identity elements vs. member expectations (Whetten, Lewis, & Mischel, 1992), social identity vs. self-identity (Ashforth & Mael, 1989), and current organizational identity vs. ideal organizational identity (Reger, Gustafson, DeMarie, & Mullane, 1994).

Of the four types of comparison, the theory proposed by Dutton et al. (1994) has been empirically tested and recently also extended to investigate the customer-company identification (Bhattacharya & Sen, 2003). Dutton et al. (1994) argue that two key organizational images influence the strength of individuals' identification with their organization, i.e., their perceptions of the organizational identity and their beliefs about how outsiders view their organization. The strength of a members' organizational identification reflects the degree to which the content of the member's self-concept is tied to his or her organizational membership. When organizational identification is strong, a member's self-concept has incorporated a large part of what he or she believes is distinctive, central, and enduring about the organization into what he or she believes is distinctive, central and enduring about him- or herself.

Organizational identity is shaped by the organization's goals, missions, structure, practices, values and action that are central to the organization, distinctive from other organizations, and relatively enduring over time (Scott & Lane, 2000). The perception of organizational identity helps individuals understand the question: "What does this organization stands for?" An organizational identity is perceived as attractive when it satisfies one or more self-definitional needs, i.e., self-continuity, self-distinctiveness, and self-enhancement (Dutton, et al., 1994). Then the attractiveness of the perceived identity leads to stronger organizational identification.

Moreover, Dutton et al. (1994) suggest that the attractiveness of a construed organizational image also influences the strength of organizational identification. Construed external image refers to a member's (insider's) beliefs about outsiders' perceptions of the organization, which is different from organizational reputation defined as the "outsider's" beliefs about what distinguishes an organization. A construed external image tells the member how outsiders think of him/her if this person associates with this organization (Dutto et al 1994). As a powerful reflection of public opinion, a construed external image strengthens members' organizational identification when perceived as attractive, i.e., members believe the image contains attributes that distinguish an organization in positive, socially valued terms.

This theory was empirically tested by Dukerich et al. (2002) in investigating the cooperative behavior in the context of health care systems. They surveyed 1,504 physicians and collected follow-up data from 285 physicians a year later. The results provided the robust support for the Dutton et al.'s theory (1994) but also suggested that the mediating effect of identification vary for different target behaviors.

This model has also been extended to informal membership contexts to examine customer-company (C-C) identification (Bhattacharya & Sen, 2003). In their extension, two moderators were identified for the link between perceived identity attractiveness and C-C identification, i.e., embeddedness and salience. Embeddedness places consumers closer to the center of the social network embodied by the company, making them feel more integrated in the network (O'Hara, Beehr, & Colarelli, 1994). It also makes it easy and important for customers to categorize themselves socially in terms of the company's identity. Another moderator is identity salience, or the extent to which specific identity information dominates a person's working memory. Identity salience could be heightened by factors such as the intensity of the company's efforts on corporate image communication. Specifically, initiatives such as corporate advertising and public relations not only educate consumers about the company's identity but also make it more salient relative to other competing social identities. Identity salience is incorporated into the C-C identification model because the variation among consumers in the extent to which the company identity is accessible is much greater than that in the employee-employer context.

Later Ahearne et al. (2005) operationalized the C-C identification model and identified an external image of the company, perceived salesperson characteristics and perceived company characteristics as the antecedents for customer-company identification. They argued that the favorable perceptions of the customer would lead to a strong identification with the company. They surveyed 178 physicians for their perception of and identification with a pharmaceutical manufacturer. The study showed that the surveyed physicians did identify with the company and that identification had strong and positive consequences both in terms of in-role (e.g., product utilization) and extra-role (e.g., word-of-mouth) behaviors. The authors also demonstrated that identification was influenced by the customers' perception of both the company as well as the boundary-spanning agent.

Different from Dutton et al.'s (1994) model, the model proposed by Reger et al. (1994) argues for the comparison between current organizational identity and the ideal organizational identity, from which organizational identification is developed. The "preferred", "expected" or "ideal" organizational identity essentially acts as an extension of the members' self-identity. The greater gap between these two identities will lead to a low identification with the organization. Later, Foreman et al. (2002) applied this model to understand the identification in multiple-identity organizations. Two organizational identities were conceptualized, i.e., normative and utilitarian, with respect to two different value systems. A normative system emphasizes traditions, symbols, internalization of an ideology and altruism; a utilitarian system is characterized by economic rationality, maximization of profits and self-interest. Reger et al.'s empirical study was conducted with 2,000 members of rural co-ops and the main argument in their model was supported.

Community Identification

Apart from organizations, communities represent another arena to investigate identification and its associated phenomena. Since VCs can be viewed as the online version of physical communities, research on community identification is also an important input for understanding VC identification.

Broadly speaking, a community can be described as a set of people with some kind of shared element, which can vary widely from a situation, such as living in a particular place, to some kind of interest, belief or value. However, defining a community has proven to be more of a challenge. Until now, there remains an essential division between territorial/locality based conceptions of community and those concerned with social/ network relationships (Puddifoot, 1995). Lack of a consistent and precise definition of community leads to further confusion regarding community identity and social identification with a community. "Can there be such a thing as identity when applied to community?" and "how might community identity be distinguished from other forms of identity, e.g., personal identity, organizational identity?" (Puddifoot, 1995). Hence, research on community identification has focused mainly on clarifying the construct per se and its relationship with a psychological sense of community (PSOC), another important concept in community research.

PSOC was first proposed by (Chavis, Hogge, McMillan, & Wandersman, 1986) and remains an important construct in community research. It is proposed that PSOC consists of four elements that work dynamically together to create and maintain an overall sense of community (McMillan & Chavis, 1986): 1) Membership which creates feelings of emotional safety with a sense of belonging to, and identification with, the larger collective, 2) Influence which characterizes the reciprocal relationship of the individual and the community in terms of their ability to affect each other, 3) Fulfillment of Needs, which enables individuals to get their needs met through cooperative behavior

within the community, thereby reinforcing the individuals' appropriate community behavior, and 4) Emotional Connection which is the emotional support stemming from the struggles and successes of community living. This PSOC model accommodates "community" conceptualized as a geographical territory (neighborhood) and as a relational network (work, political, or recreational interests) (Chipuer & Pretty, 1999).

Although the importance of PSOC is widely acknowledged, little consensus has been reached in theoretical and methodological developments of this construct. Conceptually, researchers still have a lively debate regarding the psychological dimensions underlying PSOC, e.g., a cognition, a behavior, or an individual affective state. Operationally, the ongoing search for a definitive "psychological" construction of sense of community, and for links between it and well-being, has generated several different scales. Moreover, dimensions expressed "theoretically" are not smoothly related to what has been discovered at the operational level. Finally, it has been proposed that "sense of community" or PSOC could actually be "setting-specific" (Hill, 1996; Hughey, Speer, & Peterson, 1999). Thus, some researchers turn to the conceptualization which establishes in detail the locus (e.g., boundaries, physical, and social identifying features) of the community in question or community identity.

Puddifoot (1995) was one of the pioneers to investigate community identity. Inspired by a series of surveys about residents' opinions regarding the preferred form of future local government as well as prior research on PSOC, social cohesion, and community satisfaction; Puddifoot (1995) developed a taxonomy for community identity. In this taxonomy, dimensions referring to the first of six elements, locus, pertain to the perception by community members of the boundaries of their community, its key physical, environmental, and built features, and patterns of social-cultural relations. The dimensions of the second element, distinctiveness, refer to the perceived relative distinctiveness of one's community, and the third, identification, denote a sense of affiliation, belongingness, and emotional connectedness. Dimensions pertaining to the fourth element, orientation, express the personal orientation of the individual to his/her community, that is, the individual's degree of personal investment in the community, attraction to the community, perceived future in it, sense of emotional safety, personal involvement, or sense of alienation from the community. The last two elements are concerned with evaluation of the quality of community life and evaluation of community functioning, e.g., the provision of community services.

In a recent empirical study, Puddifoot (2003) extended this conceptualization to incorporate community features shared by the general others. It is reasoned that only when a common ground is established, does it become reasonable to suppose that the aggregation of many individual responses might lead to a meaningful characterization of the identity of that community. In this study, six factors were identified for sense of community identity: sense of personal support, sense of personal contentedness, sense of personal involvement, perceived community engagement, perceived neighborliness, and perceived settledness. Empirical evidence also demonstrated that sense of community identity should be treated as distinct from PSOC. Moreover, sense of community identity was shown to have a better psychometrical quality than the scales for PSOC.

Only recently, community researchers started to explore the utility of using a social identity theory framework to understand the relationship of community identification to PSOC. It is suggested that differences in levels of PSOC may be understood in terms of the degree to which members identify with their community. Smith et al. (1999) examined PSOC and in-group identification with one's neighborhood, incorporating social identity theory measures of identification as well as traditional PSOC measures. Identification emerged as distinct from other PSOC dimensions

and was also a significant predictor of overall sense of community. Cameron (2004) further developed a three-dimensional model of social identification with a community: centrality, which is the cognitive prominence of a given group membership; in-group affect, the emotional evaluation of that group membership; and in-group ties, the perception of similarity and bonds with other group members. Obst and her colleagues conducted several empirical studies to explore the interplay between PSOC and identification and reported that identification emerged as a separate dimension of PSOC in both geographical and relational communities (Obst, Zinkiewicz, & Smith, 2002; P. L. Obst & K. M. White, 2005). In one recent study, Obst and White (2005) examined separate dimensions of social identification as predictors of PSOC and accounted for the factor of context salience. The results indicated that In-group tie was consistently the strongest predictor of PSOC and that the strength of In-group Affect and Centrality varied for the group or community context. The authors implied that identification and PSOC, although strongly related, may examine different aspects of community processes.

DETERMINANTS FOR IDENTIFICATION

Most studies on social identity theories have been conducted in general group settings, where various factors that may influence the development of identification with the referent group are explored. Some are related to the nature of groups, e.g., status, stability, permeability, and legitimacy (see Mullen, Brown, & Smith, 1992), for an overview); while others are individual motivational factors, e.g., individual distinctiveness (Brewer, 1991) and uncertainty reduction (Hogg & Abrams, 1993). This section will review the factors that affect the development of social identification.

Group distinctiveness in the form of relative status has been cited as one of the most important factors driving social identification because "positively valued distinctiveness" is usually regarded as the goal of social comparison (Tajfel 1972). High status groups serve to enhance individuals' self-esteem and therefore are favored in social comparison and categorization. Ellemers et al. (1992) demonstrated empirically that individuals assigned to high-status groups identified more strongly with the groups than did people in low-status groups.

Prior research suggests that the structural variable --- relative group size --- is another important factor for developing identification with the group. More specifically, it is assumed that being a member of minority group poses a threat to a person's self-esteem. Since social identity theory posits that each individual strives for a positive self-esteem, one way to enhance the minority group members' self-esteem is to perceive more in-group homogeneity and to identify more strongly with their group (Bernd Simon & Brown, 1987). But sometimes the numerical distinctiveness can also serve to enhance self-esteem. According to optimal distinctiveness theory (Brewer, 1991), people are driven by two basic needs, i.e., the need to belong and the need to be different. While providing assimilation to a collective, small groups offer a higher level of distinctiveness than do larger groups. Brewer and Weber (1994) found evidence that minority in-group members display more intergroup comparisons, whereas majority in-group members display interpersonal comparison.

Associated with group distinctiveness, boundary salience has been demonstrated as a main factor to influence self-categorization. Brewer's (1979) review of the experimental research on intergroup bias reveals that one major consequence of social identification, is that intergroup bias (e.g., reward allocation or evaluation) increases as the salience of the boundary between the in-group and out-group increases. In some extreme cases (e.g., gender group, ethnic/racial background) the boundary is ascribed and usually impermeable.

Such groups are typically homogeneous and their members tend to develop a strong subjective identification with the groups (Deaux & Martin, 2003). In another study, Gaertner et al. (1993) found that intergroup bias can be reduced by transforming group members' cognitive representations of the aggregate of in-group and out-group members from a "two groups" representation to a more inclusive "one group" representation.

Oakes et al. (1995) have discussed another factor related to the development of identification with a group, i.e., familiarity. They argue that when individuals become more familiar with a group, they are more likely to categorize themselves as the members of the group, which creates a high homogeneity within the group. This is related to the argument of "subjective uncertainty reduction" (Hogg & Abrams, 1993) which assumes that people will feel uncomfortable with uncertainty arising from understanding the world. The need to reduce such uncertainty can be fulfilled by achieving perceived agreement and consensus with others, or identifying with certain social categories. This analysis does not involve intergroup comparison but only emphasizes processes at the individual level.

To sum up, the research reviewed above reveals several group and individual factors that may affect identification development (see Table 1). In order to strengthen the member's identification, the group/collective should have a clearly defined boundary to separate it from the other groups. A distinctive group, in forms of either relative number or status, will have more chances to have highly identified members. Finally, identification may also result from the need to reduce uncertainty. People tend to identify with whom they are familiar with.

Table 1. Identification in physical settings

	Formal Organization	**Communities**	**General Social Groups**
Characteristics	Legitimate and visible organizational boundaries; Existence of organizational identity	Physical boundaries may exist and visible; Existence of community identity may be debatable.	Based on existing social categories (e.g., gender, ethics)
Constructs/ Theories	Comparison approaches based on social identity theories: 1. perceived organizational identity vs. self-definition 2. organizational identity elements vs. member expectations 3. social identity vs. self-identity 4. current organizational identity vs. ideal organizational identity Only the first one was empirically validated.	Psychological sense of community; Community identification	Social identity theories
How People develop identification/ Determinants for identification	An attractive organizational identity that satisfies one or more self-definitional needs, i.e., self-continuity, self-distinctiveness, and self-enhancement, will lead to high identification.		Determinants of identification: nature of groups, e.g., status, stability, permeability, and legitimacy Individual characteristics e.g., individual distinctiveness and uncertainty reduction.

IDENTIFICATION IN COMPUTER-MEDIATED COMMUNICATION (CMC)

While most identification research has been done in physical settings, some researchers have started examining this phenomenon in the context of CMC. As is known, CMC is different from face-to-face communication in many ways, e.g., limited synchronicity of interaction, free from space and time dependencies. Most explanations of media effects in CMC, however, focus on the reduced capacity of CMC to convey social information about communication partners, e.g., reduction in "social cues" (Tanis & Postmes, 2003), anonymity (Douglas & McGarty, 2001), and deindividuation (Postmes, et al., 1998), which is expected to affect individual behaviors and social influences. This idea also inspires the study of identification in the context of CMC.

Traditionally, CMC is known for giving people strategic freedom to express themselves due to anonymity and unaccountability. In extreme cases, the communicator is deindividuated or being deprived of awareness of the individual identity of

the self and of the others (Hiltz, Turoff, & Johnson, 1989). The resulting effects of deindividuation in CMC are identical to disruptive effects suggested by theories of deindividuation in social psychology (Postmes & Spears, 1998): decreased awareness of the social environment and of the self leads to decreased adherence to social norms. In contrast, an account of the consequences of varying identifiability (which may be termed as "deindividuation manipulations") has been offered from the social identity perspective, i.e., Social Identity Model of Deindividuation Effect (SIDE; Postmes, et al., 1998; Spears, Lea, Corneliussen, Postmes, & Haar, 2002). According to this theory, deindividuation manipulations have consequences for the relative salience of personal and social identities. Factors that have traditionally been identified as causing deindividuation, such as the combination of anonymity and group immersion (Zimbardo, 1969) or interaction via a computer network (Jessup, Connolly, & Tansik, 1990), do not lead to the loss of identity but rather to enhance salience of social identity. Correspondingly, the observation that there is a loss of internal control over action under deindividuation manipulations is actually due to the strengthened control from those standards inherent with the relevant social identification. This is because the relative lack of individuation in CMC smoothes the difference among the group members. Motivated to reduce the uncertainty in social interaction, members tend to be more sensitive to any salient social identity cues and over-attribute them to group members, leading to an extenuated similarity and unity of the group and causing people to be perceived as group members rather than idiosyncratic individuals (Lea, Spears, & de Groot, 2001). In short, the deindividuation gives rise to a strong social identification in the context of CMC. Foil and O'Conner (2005), based on SIDE, even advocate the usage of lean media with high role clarity and team legitimacy in order to develop identification in virtual teams.

SUMMARY

This section has presented the concept of identification and the related research on identification formation. Prior research on identification following social identity theory and self-identification theory emphasizes the influences from social identities. People develop identification with a social entity via depersonalization. Although identification formation has been discussed in both physical and virtual settings, research on this topic is still in its infancy. Research on organizational identification has proposed several theoretical models but lacks empirical validation. The understanding of community identification is still at the elementary stage, and the conceptualization needs further clarification. In the virtual setting, only one technological factor, identifiability, was examined from the social identity perspective. Although prior research in various settings has provided insight on VC identification, further theoretical and empirical development is of more imperative. In the following section, prior research

that emphasizes the influences from personal identities or individuality will be reviewed.

THE ROLE OF INDIVIDUALS IN GROUPS

Readings of social identity theory and self-categorization theory have led researchers to draw the conclusion that identification will necessarily lead to depersonalization and interchangeability of individual group members and ultimately lead to increased perceptions of cohesion. This idea is implicit in the interpersonal-intergroup continuum, which treats personal identity and social identity as polar opposites (Tajfel, 1978). As reviewed in the previous sections, most prior research on identification typically considers individuals and groups as representatives of antagonistic forces, that is, the expression of personal identity as being mutually exclusive with developing strong social identification, e.g., SIDE model.

Such a social deterministic view neglects the fact that the collective typically benefits from heterogeneity and individual creativity, as illustrated by the classic community where solidarity co-exists with a successful division of labor (Postmes, Haslam, & Swaab, 2005). Actually, individuality and personal identity expression have been recognized as an important component in many collective actions. For instance, the explicit expression of personal identities of employees is argued to counteract the negative consequences of superordinate identities (Haslam, Eggins, & Reynolds, 2003). Another example is the dual concern model (Pruitt & Carnevale, 1993; Pruitt & Rubin, 1986) in which the success of any negotiation process is seen to depend on an ability to take the perspective of, and show concern for, both self and others. Rich evidence has been documented to support the positive roles of recognition for individuality as an important mechanism to elevate desired behaviors (e.g., participation) and create favorable social consequences for the contributor (e.g., high self-esteem) (Blau, 1964; Fisher & Ackerman, 1998).

Self-Verification Theory and Identity Confirmation

In the tradition of the symbolic interactionists (e.g., Cooley, 1902; Mead, 1934), people are assumed to have a fundamental desire to know what to expect from their worlds (cf. Swann Jr., 1983). This need is associated with a strong tendency to seek self-confirmatory evidence for the self-concepts (Swann Jr. & Read, 1981). Self-verification theory (Swann Jr., 1983) assumes that stable self-views provide people with a crucial source of coherence, an invaluable means of defining their existence and guiding social interaction (cf. Swann Jr., et al., 2003). Thus, people are motivated to validate and confirm their self-concepts, even when those self-concepts are negative (McNulty & Swann Jr., 1994). In doing so, people allow others or encourage others to see them as they see themselves, a process which helps to obtain coherence in mental and social life and ensures the social interaction unfolding smoothly. Identity confirmation, then, refers to a state that exists when an individual's social environment is consistent with his or her "self-identities" and is conceptualized in terms of congruence between how a group member defines him- or herself and how other group members define that person (Milton & Westphal, 2005). In contrast with the social identity approach where the group shapes individuals' self-views, self-verification theory argues for the active role of individuals in shaping their actual and perceived experiences within groups.

Two classes of self-verification activities have been proposed in the search for self-verifying evaluations. Behaviorally, people systematically communicate self-views to fellow members in order to ensure that the evaluations they receive will confirm their self-views. Such activities include displaying identity cues (e.g., clothes and postures), selective interaction and/or resisting discrepant feedback. In the second class of activities, cognitively people use their self-views to guide the selection, retention, and interpretation of their experiences in groups (Swann Jr., et al., 2003). Prior research has shown that identity confirmation via interpersonal congruence leads to positive outcomes in intimate and social relations (Broxton, 1963; Swann Jr., De La Ronde, & Hixon, 1994) and in MBA study groups (Polzer, Milton, & Swann, 2002). Recently, Milton and Westphal (2005) demonstrated that a social network embedded with identity confirmation ties can enhance cooperation in work groups.

Identity Confirmation in CMC

CMC provides individuals with another space for exploring new identities and/or extending existing identities (Donath, 1999). Although direct application of self-verification theory is still rare, the notion of identity confirmation has been widely applied in prior research on individual behavior in CMC, e.g., virtual team or VCs. For instance, Hars and Ou (2002) demonstrated peer recognition for the focal person's contribution as a form of extrinsic reward for participating in VCs, leading to a high dedication to open source programming. Chan et al. (2004) further identified different forms of recognition, i.e., identity, expertise and tangible recognition, and reported the positive linkages between recognition and VC participation.

Another construct of respect, reflecting peers' judgments about their status within the group, has also been demonstrated to influence the aspects of behavior that flow from concerns at the individual level (Tyler & Smith, 1999). In particular, those who feel respected work harder and display more voluntary behavior that is considered to be helpful for the group (Doosje, Ellemers, & Spears, 1999). A similar term, reputation, is also used to mean an individual's recognition as a valuable member among the members of the expertise-sharing network (Franke & Shah, 2003; Tiwana

& Bush, 2005). As building reputation takes time and effort and reputation is also valuable for individuals, people tend to exhibit reputation-preserving behavior, a tendency to safeguard and preserve developed reputation. Supporting evidence has been reported among Ebay users (Arkes & Blumer, 1985), as well as members of e-mail groups (Owens, Neale, & Sutton, 2000).

Recently, Ma & Agarwal (2007), relying on self-verification theory, proposed that consonance between the focal person's self-concept and the others' perception of the focal person would enhance the focal person's knowledge contribution to, and satisfaction with a VC.

Individuality in Identification

Given the value of individuality in collective action, researchers following social identity theories have begun to question the traditional antagonistic view towards personal and social identities and thus are beginning to understand the role of individuality or personal identities in identification formation. Three theories will be reviewed below.

Actualizing Social and Personal Identity Resources (ASPIRe model)

Proposed by Haslam et al. (2003), this model represents an initial attempt to demonstrate how social and personal identity resources might be assessed and utilized by organizations in an attempt to measure and make the most of their social capital. Key features of this theory are 1) identities must be accepted as self-relevant and self-defining by employees rather than being imposed upon them, 2) where they make an important contribution to employees' self concept, organizations must allow subgroup identities to be voiced and to have an impact on higher-level decisions, and 3) a range of positive organizational outcomes are contingent upon an ability to develop shared goals and a shared identity that is premised upon lower-level goals relevant to the personal and subgroup identities of employees.

Based on the assumptions above, Haslam et al. (2003) postulate four temporal stages. The first is "Ascertaining Identity Resources" (AIRing). In this stage, organizations need to identify those self-categorizations that are seen by employees as most relevant to their ability to do their work and to distinguish these from identities that are not perceived to be self-relevant. Relevant identities would differ dramatically not just between organizations whose core business is quite different, but also between different organizations with the same core business and even the same business at different times.

The second stage is called "Subgroup Caucusing" (Sub-Casing). This stage is used to allow each of the subgroups identified at the end of the AIRing phase to engage in internal discussion and debate so that members can not only identify and agree upon shared goals, understand structural and other barriers in achieving those goals, but also identify and internalize the shared identity that is relevant to these goals. Within subgroups that participate in Sub-Casing, there would be evidence of more trust, superior communication, more enthusiasm and more creativity than within subgroups that do not go through this process.

The third phase is "Superordinate Consensualizing" (Super-Casing). As the goals identified in the previous stage may be quite diversified or polarized, the main task of this phase is to provide a common organizational forum that brings together the different subgroups to engage in further discussion and debate. The resulting social identity is different from that which is informed in the initial AIRing phase in so far as it builds upon the explicitly recognized subgroup identities that emerged during Sub-Casing. While the social identity that underpinned the AIRing phase may be relatively mechanical, the organizational identity that emerges in Super-Casing is more organic, i.e., its content defines the superordinate group in a way that allows for and incorporates subgroup difference.

The final phase is "Organic Goal-Setting" (OR-Ganizing), where organizations need to capitalize on the outcomes of the previous three phases. This process focuses on evaluating the appropriateness for the organization of the superordinate goals that emerged from Super-Casing. Members' participation is expected as they will be more likely to have a sense of ownership of the organization's decisions, goals, and plans and to perceive them to be fair and appropriate.

A Model of Individuality in Social Identity

To reconcile the expression of individuality with the formation of social identification, Postmes et al. (2005) proposed a model of individuality in social identity. This model is built upon the notion of organic solidarity (Durkheim, 1984). In his original work, Durkheim suggested that solidarity can arise out of differentiation within the group, between individuals (and sub-groups), and out of the roles, attributes, and skills that those individuals bring to the collective. In other words, both individualism and collectivism may serve as a means to achieve solidarity. By extension, Postmes et al. (2005) argue that identification with a social entity can be deduced not only from the superordinate identity but also from the expression of individuality. In this sense, identification formation is conceptualized along the continuum. On the one end, members recognize and share a certain common attribute that is given meaning at a supraindividual level and within an intergroup context. Such groups can be characterized as having a more or less deductive social identity (cf. Turner, 1982). Along a second continuum, identification can be formed from the bottom up through communication and also be inferred from expressions of individuality (cf. Sassenberg & Postmes, 2002). Such groups can be characterized as being formed more or less inductively (cf. Turner, 1982). Both paths can generate equally strong social identification, but individuality plays a more central role in the

inductive identification and a more peripheral role in the deductive identification.

Postmes et al. (2005) also point out that inductive identification does not occur in all groups; rather, its significance in identification development is contingent upon the group characteristics. In this study, they compared the two types of groups, i.e., common-bond group vs. common identity group. Common-bond groups are formed based on interpersonal relationships with mutual bonds among the members who are identifiable to each other, e.g., friendship groups. Common identity groups, on the other hand, are formed based on the shared superordinate identities. Examples of such groups can be found in those contexts where a group is part of a clearly defined larger (inter)group context, and where the overarching identity or intergroup context is obvious and pertinent. In the experiment, they demonstrated that equally important social identification was generated through either the inductive path in a common-bond group or the deductive path in a common-identity group.

Optimal Distinctiveness Theory

This theory was first proposed by Brewer (1991, 1993) in order to reconcile individuality in social identity. According to this theory, people are driven by countervailing drives for distinctiveness and inclusiveness, such that in large, overly inclusive groups, individuals will be motivated to achieve greater distinctiveness. Similarly, if people's needs for distinctiveness are overly indulged, then they will be driven to seek inclusiveness in a social group. People's strongest group identities, then, should be with those groups that provide an optimal balance between inclusiveness and distinctiveness. Hornsey and Jetten (2004) further elaborated on several strategies that can be used to balance the need to belong and to be different. For instance, identification with numerically distinct groups or groups that are strongly differentiated from the mainstream will bring a sense of belonging and distinctiveness at the same time. But in a large scale group, people tend to differentiate themselves from the others within the group and still remain loyal.

Suggestive empirical evidence of the compatibility of group formation and individualization processes has been found in minority-majority intergroup contexts. For instance, Simon, Aufderheide, & Hastedt (2000) showed that for majority members, group-level information processing, a common indicator of group formation, increased when individuation was made possible by way of preceding self-description tasks. Kempmeier and Simon (2001) further proposed two components of individuality, i.e., differentiation (or distinctiveness) and independence (or self-determination). Their empirical study revealed two moderators for such compatibility. The first one is group size. Minority group formation is more compatible with individuation in terms of differentiation than with individuation in terms of independence. But they failed to find the opposite effect for majority group formation. The second moderator is members' comparison orientation, either intergroup or intragroup. Group formation was generally more compatible with individuation in terms of differentiation (as opposed to independence) when an intergroup orientation was affected, whereas the opposite was found when an intragroup orientation was affected.

SUMMARY

In addition to social identities, personal identity or individuality also serves as an important influence on individual behavior. This section reviewed self-verification theory and associated research on identity confirmation in CMC. This theory was presented as opposing social identity theories because of its emphasis on individuality. However, recent development in research from social identity perspectives shows a converging trend to reconcile the tension between personal identities and social identities, suggesting both identity processes need to be considered in understanding individual behavior within a collective. In the next section, a critical analysis of literature will be offered based on the literature review in section 2 and section 3. Theoretical voids will be identified for further theoretical development and empirical investigation.

CRITICAL ANALYSIS OF LITERATURE

The last two sections have reviewed the main theories and studies on two identity processes. Most prior research following social identity theory and self-categorization theory emphasizes the role of social identity in shaping self-concept and explaining individual behavior while self-verification theory focuses on the active role of individuality/personal identity, suggesting a bottom-up influence on individual behavior. Of more relevance, both identification and identity confirmation have been applied in virtual settings to explain individual behavior. Based on the review, the following theoretical gaps leading to further theoretical development will be discussed in this section.

IDENTIFICATION VS. SELF-VERIFICATION

Most prior research follows either social identity theories or self-verification theory and examines identification and identity confirmation in isolation. Although put as two distinct perspectives in understanding individual behavior in a group, identification and self-verification are not exclusive. They reflect identity processes operated at two different levels. While identification emphasizes the comparison between self-views and the collective identity, the self-verification perspective focuses on the negotiation between an individual's identities and the others' perception of the focal person, operating at the relational level. Any individual in a group is inevitably subject to influences from both the collective and the others. Moreover, they imply that there are two different motivations related to self-view. While identity confirmation emphasizes the demand for stability of self-view, identification suggests motivation for self-enhancement, self-esteem and uncertainty reduction. These motivations, although different, are not necessarily in conflict. Thus, as research in both fields has provided much evidence to support identification/identity confirmation as a significant factor for individual participation in a group, it is natural to question which identity process is more dominant in determining community participation or whether they are equally important.

Berger, Cunningham, & Drumwright (2006) have identified two routes for identity changes in social alliances, a type of corporate social marketing initiative, whereby individuals develop more aligned personal identities and identification with their organizations. Recent development in social identity theories also tries to reconcile the tension between individuality (personal identity) and social identity, e.g., (Haslam, et al., 2003; Postmes, et al., 2005). Researchers suggest more research be needed to understand multiple routes to identity change.

Further, prior research has shown that these two perspectives have distinct implications for community design and management which may undermine each other. For instance, research from self-verification perspective favors the personal identity and encourages self-expression and individuality, which may undermine the process of depersonalization and lead to a low level of identification (e.g., SIDE). On the other hand, reducing identifiability to enhance identification, as suggested in social identity research, may prevent an individual's self-view from getting recognized and confirmed. Therefore, it is important to take a comprehensive view towards identity processes, i.e., examine identification and identity confirmation simultaneously, to fully understand the effects of design factors.

ORGANIZATIONAL IDENTIFICATION VS. COMMUNITY IDENTIFICATION

Both organizations and communities are facing the collective action problem, which motivates researchers on both sides to develop similar conceptualization, i.e., identification for organization and PSOC for community, in parallel with little interdisciplinary research. The isolation mainly results from the assumptions about the fundamental differences between the organization and community. Traditionally, communities are considered as naturally "bounded" by chance of birth, proximity of residence, the happenstance of geographic relocation (Bagozzi & Dholakia, 2002) or the spontaneous interests. The informal, organic, and self-organizing nature of communities makes them resistant to supervision and interference, which are very common in formal organizations (Wenger & Snyder, 2000). Another reason for the lack of interdisciplinary research may come from the fact that the term "community" has not entered the business vernacular and become an alternative to formal organizations until recently (Wenger & Snyder, 2000). However, such differences are vanishing with contemporary organizational designs and strategies. For instance, communities of practice are found inside organizations and demonstrated to be a valuable source for cooperation and innovation (Ferran-Urdaneta, 1999; Wenger & Snyder, 2000). Some leading companies also take the leap to cultivate or nurture communities within the organization. As internal and external organizational boundaries are blurring with expanding social alliances and/or cooperative networks (Bartel, 2001), communities are also thriving across organizational boundaries, e.g., customer communities (Hagel & Armstrong, 1997; Williams & Cothrel, 2000).

Thus, there are points at which the organization and community literatures tend to converge and may benefit from interdisciplinary research. First, both identification and PSOC refer to a psychological connection between members and the associated collective. Both literatures assume that membership in an organization/community is not necessary for identification/PSOC to occur. Overlaps exist in the conceptualization of PSOC where identification is considered as one dimension. Despite its narrower scope than that of PSOC, the construct of identification appears to be more rigorous and has received more empirical support than PSOC. Second, recent developments in community research also support the application of social identity theories in understanding community processes. Community identification is demonstrated to be conceptually distinct from PSOC, and shown to have better psychometrical characteristics as well as explanatory power. Thus, community identification represents a promising direction to converge two literatures.

However, compared to organizational identification research, research in community identification is still in its infancy. First, the conceptualization itself is less developed. Although the distinction between organization and community is reduced, most identification research is conducted in the context of formal organizations or social categories. In such contexts, group boundaries are often demarcated clearly by the organization itself, e.g., administrative titles or functional departments, and a preexisting collective identity can be assumed. However, for the collectives characterized with fluid boundaries and/or relying on the negotiation of members, e.g., communities, will it be possible for members to develop strong identification? And how different will it be from identification in a formal organization context? Second, what has been understudied in both disciplines is how identification can be managed. We still lack the knowledge of the antecedents of identification in general.

IDENTIFICATION FORMATION: OFFLINE VS. ONLINE

As reviewed in prior sections, both identification and identity confirmation have been applied in virtual settings. What make virtual settings different from their offline counterparts are the influences of IT artifacts on identity management. The design of IT artifacts determines social processes and what individuals can do in presenting and communicating their identities. However, according to the literature review, the influence of IT artifacts has been overlooked in most prior research except for one exception (Ma & Agarwal, 2007). In this study, Ma identified IT artifacts of VC that have impacts on identity confirmation. Although insightful, these conceptualizations favor self-verification over identification. Given the reduced physical contact among members, the cohesion-building consequences of identification with virtual collectives may be especially important for sustaining VC (Wiesenfeld, Raghuram, & Garud, 2001). However, most prior research takes identification as given without investigating its formation. Even though some studies based on SIDE investigate the effect of anonymity, one of CMC characteristics, on identification. What is identified in those studies is usually an existing social category rather than the virtual group or the VC itself. As VCs are increasingly used for commercial purposes, managers need to understand the effective interventions to cultivate identification in virtual settings. More particularly, system design needs to be considered as a major part of such interventions in the future research.

FUTURE RESEARCH AGENDA AND IMPLICATIONS FOR VC DESIGN

To seek a sense of belonging and/or to confirm self-concepts are important social activities in VCs. These identity communication activities are both the means for and one of ends of social

Figure 1. Understanding VC design and consequences from identity perspectives

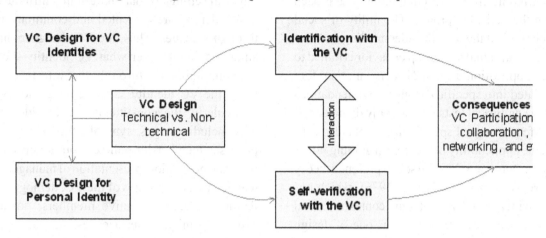

interaction. Particularly developing identification is the key to forge a VC. While to support social interaction and to sustain VCs have been considered as one of design objectives, it is indispensable to understand the implications of various IT artifacts on these identity processes.

Furthermore, VC design goes beyond the technical sides and includes institutional design. VC moderators or administrators need to be involved constantly in managing and maintaining online social exchange among members. While most of them practice based on trial & error, it is necessary to make such management activities more informed with explicit objectives. Existing evidence has shown the importance of identification in forging a community. Perhaps shaping the VC identities, encouraging identification with the VC, and understanding identity dynamics among members should be on the list of VC moderators/administrators' agenda.

Compared to the other concepts, such as, social presence and awareness, identity processes have not attracted enough attention from design point of view. While most prior studies have focused on understanding the role of identity processes in various user behaviors, our knowledge about identity processes per se, and particularly how they may inform VC design remains limited.

Based on the critical review, the authors would like to discuss the following research directors and the associated implications for VC design as summarized in Figure 1.

IDENTITY PROCESSES AND VC DESIGN

Currently, we have witnessed an obvious trend of integration in many kinds of information system design. Especially VC has become a platform integrating various IT features and supporting different human activities. There are two approaches for VC design. One is ethnographic (and ethnomethodological) approaches, as many studies conducted in the fields like Computer Supported Cooperative Work (CSCW). Researchers provide numerous rich descriptions of tasks, problems, people, and work and social settings, which have led to design suggestions and system requirements for new CSCW technology. Prototypes are evaluated empirically but not theoretically (because there was no generalizable theory to test). The result has been perhaps excellent designs but, typically, little sustained work to develop first principles that can be applied elsewhere.

Different from the ethnographic approach is the theoretical approach. The utility of social psychological theories in understanding and predicting individual and group behavior is mined to guide application design. Theories are therefore translated into specific design recommendations and the empirical tests will not only demonstrate the effectiveness of specific design but also confirm the applicability of theories in guiding future design. One example is the social presence theory (Short, Williams, & Christie, 1976), which has been widely used in different contexts. Social presence has been considered as one of design guidelines, which advocates that the design of CMC should be as proximate to face-to-face communication as possible.

Following the theoretical approach, identification and self-verification could be also considered as important theoretical underpinning to inform existing design and to guide future design. This is because a great part of social interaction in VCs involves identification communication either as means or ends. On the one hand, the sense of belonging (identification) or to confirm "who I am" (self-verification) is one of goals of members participating in a VC; on the other hand, existing research has demonstrated that identification and/or confirmed self-concepts are also solutions to problem of under contribution in VCs. Thus, how to design for identity processes should be an inherent in VC design. Specifically, the following research questions should be investigated:

- How should VCs be designed for identification?
- How should VCs be designed for self-verification?

Existing research on how to develop identification in physical setting has provided some useful insight. In order to develop identification with a VC, the VC should have an enduring identity that is attractive to members. What makes a VC identity different from a collective identity in physical settings is that all defining attributes of a VC identity are presented and communicated through websites. Thus, the VC designers have an active control over what VC identity should be communicated through the interface and make the VC identity salient among members. Particularly, the constituents of VC identities may including logos, symbols, the statement of purposes, membership policies, community initiatives and promotion, presentation of management teams, interaction states of the VC, demographic features (e.g., size, active members, postings and etc.), unique interface design, and unique functionality design. All these features make VC boundaries visible and help members answer the question, "What does this VC stand for?" To the extent that more constituents of VC identities are conferred on the VC, the VC is likely to become a more salient target for identification, and this is especially relevant in VCs that are purely online where perceived legitimacy is often lowest.

If the above approach describe the effort from VC designers or top-down approach, identification in VCs may be also developed bottom-up, resulting from the interaction and exchange among members. In other words, VC identity could be negotiated among members rather than defined by VC designers. The resulting VC identity is considered as relevant and attractive to members. This is particularly necessary for those general VCs without a specific theme. Then it is necessary to trigger some VC activities to engage members in such identity negotiation/discussion.

As for supporting self-verification, Ma and Argwal (2007) identified four categories of existing VC features, i.e., virtual co-presence, persistent labeling, self-presentation, and deep profiling, which can facilitate members to verify their self-concepts in VCs. Virtual co-presence refers to artifacts that provide a sense of being together with other people in a shared virtual environment (e.g., the 'who is online' feature). Persistent labeling refers to the artifacts that guarantee a consistent identification (e.g., user ID) for

Table 2. Identity processes and VC design

	Supporting Identification	**Supporting Self-Verification**
VC Design	• Logos & symbols; • Statement of purposes; Membership policies; • Community initiatives and promotion, • Presentation of management teams; • Interaction states of the VC, Demographic features (e.g., size, active members, postings and etc.); • Unique interface • Unique functionality	• Virtual co-presence: the 'who is online' feature. • Persistent labeling: consistent user ID • Self-presentation: visual presentations, unique IDs, personal profiles, avatars, signature files and weblogs. • Deep profiling: search functions for retrieving the historical activity records and feedback systems.
Identity Communication	VC Identity	Personal Identity

VC members. Self-presentation includes features used to convey personal identities. Features in this category include visual presentations, unique IDs, personal profiles, avatars, signature files and weblogs. Deep profiling designates features that help to infer profiles of specific members from historical records. Member profiles can be built through both referential and inferential techniques. Some online communities provide search functions for retrieving the historical activity records of a particular member or of a particular discussion subject. More sophisticated designs incorporate content hit counters, ratings of contributions and participants (usually done by administrators) and peer evaluations, as well as displaying the value of contribution, and oversight or review of the contribution.

As Table 2 indicated, the conceptualization of VC artifacts can be extended using "personal vs. VC identities" as a framework. The perspective of identity communication provides additional insight. For instance, if the intended objective is to encourage identification with a VC and reduce the in-group/out-group separation within the community, then in creating user profile or registering for a VC, what should be the compulsory fields? What should be the default setting for the user information visible to the others? Is it always necessary to indicate the location, sex, or tenure/hierarchy? Demographic profile may produce a profound impact on social interaction. Especially when the information about the social categories

is visible to the other members, the person may automatically apply certain social norms, which may lead to a more salient identification with the respective social categories than with the VC.

Although a few studies have attempted to conceptualize IT artifacts from identity perspectives (e.g., (Ma & Agarwal, 2007; Shen & Khalifa, 2010) more empirical research is necessary to accumulate evidence and to refine our understanding. The features in Table 2 are based on existing VC design. Nevertheless, such a framework will help not only understand the effects of existing design features on VC participation as mediated through various identity processes but also guide the future development

INTERACTION BETWEEN IDENTIFICATION AND SELF-VERIFICATION

As VCs become an integrated platform with various IT features, multiple psychological/social psychological mechanisms need to be examined simultaneously to gain the complete insight on the complexity induced by technological settings. Identification and self-verification are two identity processes working in parallel, representing two distinctive needs of human beings. In the past, researchers have examined their roles in VC participation separately and suggest distinctive design implications, as discussed in section 2. Thus, rather than focusing on a single mechanism, future research should account for dual-identity processes in explaining member/group behavior and the effects of system design. It is important to reveal whether these identity processes are competing and exclusive to each other or actually complementary to each other. Answers to this question will have implications for VC management as well as VC design. For instance, if these two processes are exclusive in driving VC participation, e.g., highlighting self-identity or individuality expression dampens development of identification or vice versa, efforts need to be invested in facilitating the desired identity process and controlling the other one. Otherwise, if these two identity processes operate simultaneously without contradicting each other, then the understanding of their relative importance in driving VC participation will also be helpful in guiding the resource allocation within a VC. Furthermore, these two identity processes may not be completely independent. Social identities acquired by VC members may influence their strategies and behavior in communicating and verifying their self-identities. Meanwhile, members' individuality expression may also play an important role in negotiating and shaping the collective identity. How these two identity processes influence each other in a VC is a challenging question to answer. Future research should take a dynamic and longitudinal approach and aim to develop process models to explicate the transformation between these two identity processes. To summarize, the following research questions can be formulated to guide future endeavors in uncovering the dual-identity processes in VCs:

- Are identification and self-verification exclusive or complementary to one another in affecting VC participation?

Particularly, identification has been studied in many contexts, e.g., groups, organizations, communities, and more particularly VCs. However, most prior research on organizational identification has focused on theoretical development, which has received limited empirical testing (Foreman & Whetten, 2002, pp. 618). In the context of communities, studies on identification have just started and many controversies still remain in several fundamental areas, such as the existence of community identities. In the IS field where VCs have received much interest, most prior studies take identification or theories developed in organizational contexts as given without exploring the specificity brought by IT artifacts. Future research should advance the theoretical work on identification to develop the conceptualization of VC identities and develop a research model to explain identification formation in VCs. To summarize, the following research questions can be formulated:

- What are the effective constituents of VC identity? How do members negotiate a VC identity? How does the management team shape the VC identity?
- How is a VC identity communicated within and across the VC?
- How do members develop identification with a VC?

Contextualizing Identity Processes

Finally, the demand for investigating the dual-identity processes in VCs also gives rise to better appreciating the dynamics and diversity in VCs. In most prior studies, researchers usually adopt existing typologies, e.g., communities of interest, fantasy, transaction, relation, and focus on one category of VCs, assuming homogeneity within the category. However, such an assumption may not hold. Our knowledge of VC characteristics and their interaction with individual behavior and group dynamics is limited. Thus, future research may aim to develop a more sophisticated and comprehensive typology for VC categorization. And a contingency approach to incorporate community characteristics into VC research might be useful to contextualize identity processes and their interaction with IT artifacts and consequences.

Prior research on identification reveals that group characteristics should be considered as important contingences influencing different routes to develop identification. For instance, Postmes et al. (2005) argue that the context where intergroup dynamics is not obvious or given from the start will be more likely to induce members to actively construct a norm or shared viewpoint. In another study, Postmes et al. (2005) demonstrate that the nature of group formation, i.e., common-bond vs. common-identity, also influences the formation of identification. However, research in this field is still in its infantry. Existing studies only provide limited and sparse evidence. In this researcher's experience, there is no evidence for group effects in the real setting. More exploratory work is needed in this regard to understand the role of community characteristics. To summarize, the following research questions can be formulated:

- What are the community factors that influence the relative importance of these two identity processes in driving VC participation?
- What are the community factors that shape the interaction between these two identity processes?

CONCLUSION

In conclusion, identity processes in the context of VCs are interesting phenomena to explore, which will also offer rich and insightful understanding about members' behavior in VCs and provide important implications for VC management intervention and system design. This chapter compares and reconciles the two theoretical perspectives of identification and self-verification in understanding VC participation. Based on a critical review of prior literature, the author identifies theoretical

gaps, and discusses areas for future research as well as its implications for VC design.

REFERENCES

Ahearne, M., Bhattacharya, C. B., & Thomas, G. (2005). Antecedents and consequences of customer-company identification: Expanding the role of relationship marketing. *The Journal of Applied Psychology*, *90*(3), 574–585. doi:10.1037/0021-9010.90.3.574

Arkes, H. R., & Blumer, C. (1985). The psychology of sunk cost. *Organizational Behavior and Human Decision Processes*, *35*, 124–140. doi:10.1016/0749-5978(85)90049-4

Ashforth, B. E., & Mael, F. (1989). Social identity theory and the organization. *Academy of Management Review*, *14*(1), 20–39.

Bagozzi, R. P., & Dholakia, U. M. (2002). Intentional social action in virtual communities. *Journal of Interactive Marketing*, *16*(2), 2–21. doi:10.1002/dir.10006

Bartel, C. A. (2001). Social comparisons in boundary-spanning work: Effects of community outreach on members' organizational identity and identification. *Administrative Science Quarterly*, *46*(3), 379–413. doi:10.2307/3094869

Bergami, M., & Bagozzi, R. P. (2000). Self-categorization, affective commitment and group self-esteem as distinct aspects of social identity in the organization. *The British Journal of Social Psychology*, *39*(4), 555–577. doi:10.1348/014466600164633

Berger, I. E., Cunningham, P. H., & Drumwright, M. E. (2006). Identity, identification, and relationship through social alliances. *Journal of the Academy of Marketing Science*, *34*(2), 128–137. doi:10.1177/0092070305284973

Bhattacharya, C. B., & Sen, S. (2003). Consumer-company identification: A framework for understanding consumers' relationships with companies. *Journal of Marketing, 67*(2), 76–88. doi:10.1509/jmkg.67.2.76.18609

Blau, P. M. (1964). *Exchange and Power in Social Life*. New York, NY: Wiley.

Brewer, M. B. (1979). In-group bias in the minimal intergroup situation: A cognitive-motivational analysis. *Psychological Bulletin, 86*, 307–324. doi:10.1037/0033-2909.86.2.307

Brewer, M. B. (1991). The social self: On being the same and different at the same time. *Personality and Social Psychology Bulletin, 17*, 475–482. doi:10.1177/01461672291175001

Brewer, M. B. (1993). The role of distinctiveness in social identity and group behaviour. In Hogg, M., & Abrams, D. (Eds.), *Group motivation: Social psychological perspectives* (pp. 1–16). New York, NY: Harvester-Wheatsheaf.

Brewer, M. B., & Weber, J. G. (1994). Self-evaluation effects of interpersonal versus intergroup social comparison. *Journal of Personality and Social Psychology, 66*, 268–275. doi:10.1037/0022-3514.66.2.268

Broxton, J. A. (1963). A test of interpersonal attraction predictions derived from balance theory. *Journal of Abnormal and Social Psychology, 66*, 394–397. doi:10.1037/h0047657

Cameron, J. (2004). A three factor model of social identity. *Self and Identity, 3*, 239–262. doi:10.1080/13576500444000047

Chan, C. M. L., Bhandar, M., Oh, L.-B., & Chan, H.-C. (2004). *Recognition and Participation in a Virtual Community*. Paper presented at the Proceedings of the 37th Hawaii International Conference on System Sciences, Hawaii, USA.

Chavis, D., Hogge, J., McMillan, D., & Wandersman, A. (1986). Sense of community through Brunswick's lens: A first look. *Journal of Community Psychology, 14*, 24–40. doi:10.1002/1520-6629(198601)14:1<24::AID-JCOP2290140104>3.0.CO;2-P

Chipuer, M., & Pretty, M. H. (1999). A review of the sense of community index: Current uses, factor structure, reliability. *Journal of Community Psychology, 27*(6), 643–658. doi:10.1002/(SICI)1520-6629(199911)27:6<643::AID-JCOP2>3.0.CO;2-B

Cooley, C. H. (1902). *Human nature and the social order*. New York, NY: Scribner.

Deaux, K., & Martin, D. (2003). Interpersonal networks and social categories: Specifying levels of context in identity processes. *Social Psychology Quarterly, 66*(2), 101–117. doi:10.2307/1519842

Donath, J. (1999). Identity and deception in the virtual community. In Smith, M., & Kollock, P. (Eds.), *Communities in Cyberspace* (pp. 29–59). London, UK; New York, NY: Routledge.

Doosje, B., Ellemers, N., & Spears, R. (1999). Commitment and intergroup behaviour. In Ellemers, N., Spears, R., & Doosje, B. (Eds.), *Social Identity*. London, UK: Blackwell.

Douglas, K. M., & McGarty, C. (2001). Identifiability and self-presentation: Computer-mediated communication and intergroup interaction. *The British Journal of Social Psychology, 40*, 399–416. doi:10.1348/014466601164894

Dukerich, J. M., Golden, B. R., & Shortell, S. M. (2002). Beauty is in the eye of the beholder: The impact of organizational identification, identity, and image on the cooperative behaviors of physicians. *Administrative Science Quarterly, 47*(3), 507–533. doi:10.2307/3094849

Durkheim, E. (1984). *The division of labour in society*. London, UK: MacMillan.

Dutton, J. E., Dukerich, J. M., & Harquail, C. V. (1994). Organizational images and member identification. *Administrative Science Quarterly, 39*(2), 239–263. doi:10.2307/2393235

Ellemers, N., Doosje, B., van Knippenberg, A., & Wilke, H. (1992). Status protection in high status minority groups. *European Journal of Social Psychology, 22*, 123–140. doi:10.1002/ejsp.2420220203

Ellemers, N., Kortekaas, P., & Ouwerkerk, J. W. (1999). Self-categorisation, commitment to the group and group self-esteem as related but distinct aspects of social identity. *European Journal of Social Psychology, 29*(2-3), 371–389. doi:10.1002/(SICI)1099-0992(199903/05)29:2/3<371::AID-EJSP932>3.0.CO;2-U

Ethier, K. A., & Deaux, K. (1994). Negotiating social identiy when contexts change: Maintaining identification and responding to threat. *Journal of Personality and Social Psychology, 67*(2), 243–251. doi:10.1037/0022-3514.67.2.243

Ferran-Urdaneta, C. (1999). *Terms or communities? Organizational structures for knowledge management.* Paper presented at the SIGCPR'99, New Orleans, LA. USA.

Fiol, C. M., & O'Connor, E. J. (2005). Identification in face-to-face, hybrid, and pure virtual teams: untangling the contradictions. *Organization Science, 16*(1), 19–32. doi:10.1287/orsc.1040.0101

Fisher, R. J., & Ackerman, D. (1998). The effects of recognition and group need on volunteerism: A social norm perspective. *The Journal of Consumer Research, 25*, 262–275. doi:10.1086/209538

Forehand, M. R., Deshpande, R., & Reed, A. II. (2002). Identity salience and the influence of differential activation of the social self-schema on advertising response. *The Journal of Applied Psychology, 87*(6), 1086–1099. doi:10.1037/0021-9010.87.6.1086

Foreman, P., & Whetten, D. A. (2002). Members' identification with multiple-identity organizations. *Organization Science, 13*(6), 618–635. doi:10.1287/orsc.13.6.618.493

Franke, N., & Shah, S. (2003). How communities support innovative activities: An exploration of assistance and sharing among end-users. *Research Policy, 32*(1), 157–178. doi:10.1016/S0048-7333(02)00006-9

Gaertner, S. L., Dovidio, J. F., Anastasio, P. A., Bachman, B. A., & Rust, M. C. (1993). The common ingroup identity model: Recategorization and the reduction of intergroup bias. In W. Stroebe & M. Hewstone (Eds.), *European Review of Social Psychology, 4*, (1-26). Chichester, UK: Wiley.

Gupta, S., & Kim, H. W. (2004). *Enhancing the commitment to virtual community: A belief and feeling based approach.* Paper presented at the Twenty-Fifth International Conference on Information Systems.

Hagel, J., & Armstrong, A. (1997). *Net gain: Expanding markets through virtual communities.* Mass, USA: Harvard Business School Press.

Hars, A., & Ou, S. (2002). Working for free? Motivations of participating in open source projects. *International Journal of Electronic Commerce, 6*(3), 25–39.

Haslam, S. A., Eggins, R. A., & Reynolds, K. J. (2003). The ASPIRe model: Actualizing social and personal identity resources to enhance organizational outcomes. *Journal of Occupational and Organizational Psychology, 76*, 83–113. doi:10.1348/096317903321208907

Haslam, S. A., Oakes, P. J., Reynolds, K. J., & Turner, J. C. (1999). Social identity salience and the emergence of stereotype consensus. *Personality and Social Psychology Bulletin, 25*(7), 809–818. doi:10.1177/0146167299025007004

Hill, J. L. (1996). Psychological sense of community: Suggestions for future research. *Journal of Community Psychology, 24,* 431–438. doi:10.1002/(SICI)1520-6629(199610)24:4<431::AID-JCOP10>3.0.CO;2-T

Hiltz, S. R., Turoff, M., & Johnson, K. (1989). Experiments in group decision making, 3: Disinhibition, deindividuation, and group processes in pen name and real name computer conferences. *Decision Support Systems, 5,* 217–232. doi:10.1016/0167-9236(89)90008-0

Hogg, M., & Abrams, D. (1993). Towards a single-process Uncertainty-reduction model of social motivation in groups. In Hogg, M., & Abrams, D. (Eds.), *Group motivation: Social psychological perspectives* (pp. 173–190). New York, NY: Harvester Wheatsheaf.

Hogg, M. A., & Abrams, D. (1988). *Social identifications: A social psychology of intergroup relations and group processes.* London, UK: Routledge.

Hornsey, M. J., & Jetten, J. (2004). The individual within the group: Balancing the need to belong with the need to be different. *Personality and Social Psychology Review, 8*(3), 248–264. doi:10.1207/s15327957pspr0803_2

Hughey, J., Speer, W., & Peterson, N. A. (1999). Sense of community in community organisations: Structure and evidence of validity. *Journal of Community Psychology, 27*(1), 97–13. doi:10.1002/(SICI)1520-6629(199901)27:1<97::AID-JCOP7>3.0.CO;2-K

Jessup, L. M., Connolly, T., & Tansik, D. A. (1990). Toward a theory of automated group work: The deindividuating effects of anonymity. *Small Group Research, 21,* 333–348. doi:10.1177/1046496490213003

Kampmeier, C., & Simon, B. (2001). Individuality and group formation: The role of independence and differentiation. *Journal of Personality and Social Psychology, 81*(3), 448–462. doi:10.1037/0022-3514.81.3.448

Lea, M., Spears, R., & de Groot, D. (2001). Knowing me, knowing you: Anonymity effects on social identity processes within groups. *Personality and Social Psychology Bulletin, 27,* 526–537. doi:10.1177/0146167201275002

Lee, F. S. L., Vogel, D., & Limayem, M. (2003). Virtual community informatics: A review and research agenda. *Journal of Information Technology and Application, 5*(1), 47–61.

Ma, M., & Agarwal, R. (2007). Through a glass darkly: Information Technology design, identity verification, and knowledge contribution in online communities. *Information Systems Research, 18*(1), 42–67. doi:10.1287/isre.1070.0113

McMillan, D. W., & Chavis, D. M. (1986). Sense of community: A definition and a theory. *Journal of Community Psychology, 14,* 6–23. doi:10.1002/1520-6629(198601)14:1<6::AID-JCOP2290140103>3.0.CO;2-I

McNulty, S. E., & Swann, W. B. Jr. (1994). Identity negotiation in roommate relationships: The self as architext and consequence of social reality. *Journal of Personality and Social Psychology, 67*(6), 1012–1023. doi:10.1037/0022-3514.67.6.1012

Mead, G. H. (1934). *Mind, self, and society.* Chicago, IL: University of Chicago Press.

Milton, L. P., & Westphal, J. D. (2005). Identity confirmation networks and cooperation in work groups. *Academy of Management Journal, 48*(2), 191–212. doi:10.5465/AMJ.2005.16928393

Mullen, B., Brown, R. J., & Smith, C. (1992). Ingroup bias as a function of salience, relevance, and status: An integration. *European Journal of Social Psychology*, *22*, 103–122. doi:10.1002/ejsp.2420220202

O'Hara, K. B., Beehr, T. A., & Colarelli, S. M. (1994). Organizational centrality: A third dimension of intraorganizational career movement. *The Journal of Applied Behavioral Science*, *30*(2), 198–216. doi:10.1177/0021886394302004

Oakes, P. J. (1987). The salience of social categories. In Turner, J. C., Hogg, M. A., Oakes, P. J., Reicher, S. D., & Wetherell, M. S. (Eds.), *Rediscovering the social group: A self-categorization theory* (pp. 117–141). Oxford, UK: Blackwell.

Oakes, P. J., Haslam, S. A., Morrison, B., & Grace, D. (1995). Becoming an in-group: Reexamining the impact of familiarity on perceptions of group homogeneity. *Social Psychology Quarterly*, *58*(1), 52–61. doi:10.2307/2787143

Oakes, P. J., Haslam, S. A., & Turner, J. C. (1994). *Stereotyping and social reality*. Oxford, UK: Blackwell.

Obst, P., & White, K. (2005). Three-dimensional strength of identification across group memberships: A confirmatory factor analysis. *Self and Identity*, *4*, 69–80. doi:10.1080/13576500444000182

Obst, P., Zinkiewicz, L., & Smith, S. (2002). An exploration of sense of community, part 3: Dimensions and predictors of psychological sense of community in geographical communities. *Journal of Community Psychology*, *30*(1), 119–133. doi:10.1002/jcop.1054

Obst, P. L., & White, K. M. (2005). An exploration of the interplay between psychological sense of community, social identification and salience. *Journal of Community & Applied Social Psychology*, *15*, 127–135. doi:10.1002/casp.813

Owens, D., Neale, M., & Sutton, R. (2000). Technologies of status management: Status dynamics In email communications. In Neale, M. A., Mannix, E. A., & Griffith, T. L. (Eds.), *Research on Groups and Teams* (*Vol. 3*, pp. 205–230). Greenwich, CT: JAI Press. doi:10.1016/S1534-0856(00)03011-5

Polzer, J. T., Milton, L. P., & Swann, W. B. Jr. (2002). Capitalizing on diversity: Interpersonal congruence in small work groups. *Administrative Science Quarterly*, *47*, 296–324. doi:10.2307/3094807

Postmes, T., Haslam, S. A., & Swaab, R. I. (2005). Social influence in small groups: An interactive model of social identity formation. *European Review of Social Psychology*, *16*, 1–42. doi:10.1080/10463280440000062

Postmes, T., & Spears, R. (1998). Deindividuation and antinormative behavior: A meta-analysis. *Psychological Bulletin*, *123*(3), 238–259. doi:10.1037/0033-2909.123.3.238

Postmes, T., Spears, R., & Lea, M. (1998). Breaching or building social boundaries? SIDE-effects of computer-mediated communication. *Communication Research*, *25*(6), 689–715. doi:10.1177/009365098025006006

Pruitt, D. G., & Carnevale, P. J. (1993). *Negotiation in social conflict*. Milton Keynes, UK: Open University Press.

Pruitt, D. G., & Rubin, J. Z. (1986). *Social conflict: Escalation, stalemate and settlement*. New York, NY: McGraw-Hill.

Puddifoot, J. (1995). Dimensions of community identity. *Journal of Community & Applied Social Psychology*, *5*, 357–370. doi:10.1002/casp.2450050507

Puddifoot, J. E. (2003). Exploring personal and shared sense of community identity in Durham city, England. *Journal of Community Psychology*, *31*(1), 87–106. doi:10.1002/jcop.10039

Reger, R. K., Gustafson, L. T., DeMarie, S. M., & Mullane, J. V. (1994). Reframing the organization: Why implementing total quality is easier said than done. *Academy of Management Review, 19*, 565–584.

Ryan, R. M., & Deci, E. L. (2001). To be happy or to be self-fulfilled: A review of research on hedonic and eudaimonic well-being. *Annual Review of Psychology, 52*, 141–166. doi:10.1146/annurev.psych.52.1.141

Sassenberg, K., & Postmes, T. (2002). Cognitive and strategic processes in small groups: Effects of anonymity of the self and anonymity of the group on social influence. *The British Journal of Social Psychology, 41*, 463–480. doi:10.1348/014466602760344313

Scott, S. G., & Lane, V. R. (2000). A stakeholder approach to organizational identity. *Academy of Management Review, 25*(1), 43–62.

Shen, K. N., & Khalifa, M. (2010, June 6-9th). *Explaining virtual community participation: Accounting for the IT artifacts through identification and identity confirmation.* Paper presented at the The 18th European Conference on Information Systems, Pretoria, South Africa.

Short, J., Williams, E., & Christie, B. (1976). *The Social Psychology of Telecommunications.* London, UK: Wiley.

Simon, B., Aufderheide, B., & Hastedt, C. (2000). The double negative effect: The (almost) paradoxical role of the indiviudal self in minority and majority members' information processing. *The British Journal of Social Psychology, 39*, 73–93. doi:10.1348/014466600164345

Simon, B., & Brown, R. (1987). Perceived intra-group homogeneity in minority-majority contexts. *Journal of Personality and Social Psychology, 53*(4), 703–711. doi:10.1037/0022-3514.53.4.703

Smith, E. R., & Henry, S. (1996). An ingroup becomes part of the self: Response time evidence. *Personality and Social Psychology Bulletin, 22*, 635–642. doi:10.1177/0146167296226008

Smith, S. G., Zinkiewicz, L., & Ryall, C. T. (1999). Sense of community: Yet another group identification? *Australian Journal of Psychology, 51*, 18.

Spears, R., Lea, M., Corneliussen, R. A., Postmes, T., & Haar, W. T. (2002). Computer-mediated communication as a channel for social resistance: The strategic side of SIDE. *Small Group Research, 33*(5), 555–574. doi:10.1177/104649602237170

Swann, W. B. Jr. (1987). Identity negotiation: Where two roads meet. *Journal of Personality and Social Psychology, 53*(6), 1038–1051. doi:10.1037/0022-3514.53.6.1038

Swann, W. B. Jr, De La Ronde, C., & Hixon, J. G. (1994). Authenticity and positivity strivings in marriage and courtship. *Journal of Personality and Social Psychology, 66*, 857–869. doi:10.1037/0022-3514.66.5.857

Swann, W. B. Jr, & Read, S. J. (1981). Acquiring self-knowledge: The search for feedback that fits. *Journal of Personality and Social Psychology, 41*, 1119–1128. doi:10.1037/0022-3514.41.6.1119

Swann, W. B. Jr, Rentfrow, P. J., & Guinn, J. S. (2003). Self-verification: The search for coherence. In Leary, M. R., & Tangney, J. P. (Eds.), *Handbook of Self and Identity* (pp. 367–383). New York, NY: Guilford Press.

Tajfel, H. (1972). La categorisation sociale (Social categorization). In Moscovici, S. (Ed.), *Introduction a la Psychologie Sociale* (pp. 272–302). Paris, France: Larouse.

Tajfel, H. (1978). *Differentiation between social groups: Studies in the social psychology of intergroup relations.* London, UK: Academic Press.

Tajfel, H., & Turner, J. C. (1986). The social identity theory of intergroup behavior. In Worchel, S., & Austin, L. W. (Eds.), *Psychology of intergroup relations* (2nd ed., pp. 7–24). Chicago, IL: Nelson-Hall.

Tanis, M., & Postmes, T. (2003). Social cues and impression formation in CMC. *The Journal of Communication, 53*(4), 676–693. doi:10.1111/j.1460-2466.2003.tb02917.x

Tiwana, A., & Bush, A. A. (2005). Continuance in expertise-sharing networks: A social perspective. *IEEE Transactions on Engineering Management, 52*(1), 85–101. doi:10.1109/TEM.2004.839956

Turner, J. C. (1982). Towards a cognitive redefinition of the social group. In Tajfel, H. (Ed.), *Social identity and intergroup relations* (pp. 15–40). Cambridge, UK: Cambridge University Press.

Turner, J. C. (1985). Social categorization and the self-concept: A social cognitive theory of group behavior. In Lawler, E. J. (Ed.), *Advances in Group Processes* (*Vol. 2*, pp. 77–122). Greenwich, CT: JAI Press.

Turner, J. C. (1991). *Social Influence*. Milton Keynes, UK: Open University Press.

Turner, J. C., Hogg, M. A., Oakes, P. J., Reicher, S. D., & Wetherell, M. S. (1987). *Rediscovering the social group: A self-categorization theory*. Oxford, UK: Blackwell.

Tyler, T. R., & Smith, H. J. (1999). Justice, social identity, and group processes. In Tyler, T. R., Kramer, R., & John, O. P. (Eds.), *The psychology of the social self*. Mahwah, NJ: Erlbaum.

Wenger, E., & Snyder, W. (2000). Communities of practice: The organizational frontier. *Harvard Business Review, 78*(1), 139–145.

Whetten, D. A., Lewis, D., & Mischel, L. J. (1992). *Towards an integrated model of organizational identity and member commitment*. Paper presented at the the Academy of Management, Las Vegas, NV.

Wiesenfeld, B. M., Raghuram, S., & Garud, R. (2001). Organizational identification among virtual workers: The role of need for affiliation and perceived work-based social support. *Journal of Management, 27*, 213–229.

Williams, R. L., & Cothrel, J. (2000). Four smart ways to run online communities. *Sloan Management Review, 41*(4), 81–91.

Zimbardo, P. G. (1969). The human choice: Individuation, reason, and order vs. deindividuation, impulse and chaos. In W. J. Arnold & D. Levine (Eds.), *Nebraska Symposium on Motivation* (Vol. 17, pp. 237-307). Lincoln, NE: University of Nebraska Press.

KEY TERMS AND DEFINITIONS

Deep Profiling: Deep profiling designates features that help to infer profiles of specific members from historical records.

Identification: A person comes to view him- or herself as a member of a particular social entity (e.g., ethnic groups, gender groups, organizations or artificial groups) through cognitive processes of social comparison and categorization.

Identity Confirmation: A state that exists when an individual's social environment is consistent with his or her "self-identities" and is conceptualized in terms of congruence between how a group member defines him- or herself and how other group members define that person.

Optimal Distinctiveness Theory: People are driven by countervailing drives for distinctiveness and inclusiveness.

Persistent Labeling: The artifacts that guarantee a consistent identification (e.g., user ID) for VC members.

Self-Categorization or Social Categorization of Self: A cognitive process whereby self is assimilated to the in-group prototype and depersonalizes self-conception, i.e., self is no longer represented as 'unique individual' but as an embodiment of the relevant prototype.

Self-Presentation: Self-presentation includes features used to convey personal identities. Features in this category include visual presentations, unique IDs, personal profiles, avatars, signature files and weblogs.

Self-Verification Theory: The assumption that stable self-views provide people with a crucial source of coherence, an invaluable means of defining their existence and guiding social interaction. Thus, people are motivated to validate and confirm their self-concepts, even when those self-concepts are negative.

Social Identity: The individual's knowledge that he belongs to certain social groups together with some emotional and value significance to him of this group membership.

Virtual Co-Resence: Artifacts that provide a sense of being together with other people in a shared virtual environment (e.g., the 'who is online' feature).

Virtual Communities: Sometimes called online communities, describe the mediated social spaces in the digital environment that allow groups to form and be sustained primarily through ongoing virtual communication processes.

Chapter 12
Freedom, Control, Security:
Current and Future Implications for Internet Governance

Martin Hans Knahl
University of Applied Sciences Furtwangen, Germany

Geoff Cox
Aarhus University, Denmark

ABSTRACT

Internet Governance is concerned with the organisation, control, and strategic development of the Internet. It is a prominent and widely debated topic Furthermore, from the operational perspective, administrative control and technical operation of the Internet are crucially relevant issues for the global dissemination of information, online virtual communities and the global economy. Therefore political and technological aspects and considerations are interconnected and cannot be separated. Key Internet operation and maintenance organisations such as the Internet Corporation for Assigned Names and Numbers (ICANN) are stakeholders in the process of defining the scope and agenda of future Internet governance with significant implications for virtual communities and online services. These developments have a major impact and are omnipresent in the operation of the Internet with additional implications regarding Internet security and control aspects inside Internet groups and communities. Governance and security are issues motivated by the need of protection - protection from from perceived chaos and instability, real physical or symbolic violence or even terrorism. However the question of who governs and secures the Internet against such threats remains an open issue. Furthermore it must be asked who will protect us from security. These issues are discussed from different perspectives at different scales. The Botnet case study further demonstrates how control is distributed both horizontally and vertically in keeping with contemporary forms of governance and security, reflected in the technical infrastructures of the Internet itself.

DOI: 10.4018/978-1-60960-869-9.ch012

INTRODUCTION

Then there is electricity — the demon, the angel, the mighty physical power, the all-pervading intelligence... Is that a humbug too? Is it a fact... that, by means of electricity, the world of matter has become a great nerve, vibrating thousands of miles in a breathless point of time? Rather, the round globe is a vast head, a brain instinct with intelligence! Or shall we say it is itself a thought, nothing but thought, and no longer the substance which we deemed it!

If you mean the telegraph... it is an excellent thing — that is, of course, if the speculators in cotton and politics don't get possession of it. A great thing... particularly as regards the detection of bank robbers and murderers. (Hawthorne, 1851)

The thoughts of the writer Nathaniel Hawthorne were inspired by the development of electricity and the telegraph in the mid 19th century. Much as Jules Verne envisioned extensive journeys and moon landings, Hawthorne tried to foresee the contradictory possibilities of electronic communication. Hawthorne speculates that global connectivity may lead to new horizons, a claim

that has been repeated with regards to the Internet by more contemporary commentators (Lessig, 2006; Mitchell, 1996). Given the widespread use and alleged pervasiveness, the questions of how to develop, operate and control the Internet involves the controversial and complex issue of governance.

The term *governance* derives from the Greek verb κυβερνάω (*kubernáo*) meaning *to steer* (and thus also making reference to cybernetics) and generally politics provides the means by which the governance process is operated (Wikipedia, 2010). Conceiving of Internet governance in this way, one can encounter the process in States and State organisations, profit and non-profit corporations, NGOs and other associations (e.g. social networks, project-teams) engaged in the general operation, management and control of Internet-related activities (Marsden, 2008). A number of regulators impact upon the process and define the role and limitation of Internet Governance; for instance compare the issues relating to Architecture, Market, Norms and Regulation in Figure 1 (Lessig, 2006: 123). These different aspects clearly impact upon governance and confirm it as a political issue, for example in the social costs of the Internet. Solum further identifies cybersquatting as a prime

Figure 1. Internet governance regulators

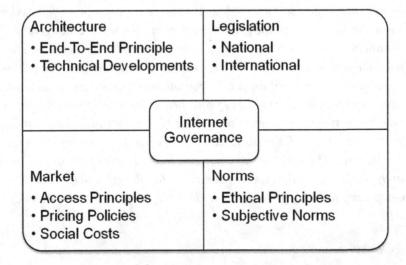

example of social costs: the "registration of a domain name that infringes a trademark for the sole purpose of extracting a payment for transfer of the domain name" (Bygrave, 2009). This lies in contrast to the Coase-Theorem (associated with the economist Ronald Coase) that states that the assignment of entitlements does not affect the efficiency of outcomes (i.e. that the distributional effect does not result in economic inefficiency), so that negotiations between cybersquatters and trademark owners generate positive transaction costs. Hence regulations (e.g. in the form of national and international trade laws, Domain Name policies) can facilitate and steer this process as part of Internet governance.

Trust in the governance process of the Internet and further between users is a key factor for users in any online community (such as those derived from social networks or those using online transaction services). Liu et. al. (2008) address the problem of predicting whether users trust each other and propose a classification approach to address what they refer to as the trust prediction problem. They develop a taxonomy to obtain an extensive set of key features derived from user attributes and user interactions in an online community and demonstrate that trust among users can be effectively predicted using pre-trained classifiers. Thus the aim is to recognise security requirements and to ultimately design and implement trust into any online experience. In a widely cited paper, Ben Shneiderman proposed two key principles associated with this: *"Invite participation by ensuring trust"* and *"Accelerate action by clarifying responsibility"*, together with guidelines such as *"disclose patterns of past performance"*, *"get certifications from third parties"*, *"clarify each participant's responsibilities"* or *"provide clear guarantees with compensation"* (Shneiderman, 2000). Governance in this sense is tied to the idea of encouraging users to largely govern themselves through their active participa-

tion (Foucault, 2010), and this is the case with Internet developments in general.

THE DEVELOPMENT CONTEXT

Saltzer, Reed and Clark (1984) define the End-to-End principle of the Internet. It manifests that the inherent implementation and features of the Internet services themselves are placed on the edge of the network rather than within the core of the network (Saltzer, 1984). The End-to-End principle has been the foundation of the ARPANET and the Internet. It still provides the fundamental, if somewhat compromised, characteristic of all communication services (Saltzer, 1984; Bygrave 2008; Lessig, 2006) and has proved crucial for the development of new services such as Messaging or E-Mail. Soon after the creation of the ARPANET, the service of sending messages from individual to individual on a one-to-one and one-to-many basis became widely used. Licklider, one of the early system administrators of the early ARPANET described the use of the messaging service:

It soon became obvious that the ARPANET was becoming a human-communication medium with very important advantages over normal U.S. mail and over telephone calls. One of the advantages of the message systems over letter mail was that, in an ARPANET message, one could write tersely and type imperfectly, even to an older person in a superior position and even to a person one did not know very well, and the recipient took no offense. The formality and perfection that most people expect in a typed letter did not become associated with network messages, probably because the network was so much faster, so much more like the telephone. (Licklider & Vezza, 1978)

Other forms of communication, associated with what Howard Rheingold coined "virtual communities" in 1994 (Rheingold, 1994) would become referred to as weblogs or blogs, further facilitating user-oriented content generation:

The liberating news about virtual communities is that you don't have to be a professional writer, artist, or television journalist in order to express yourself to others. Everyone can be a publisher or a broadcaster now. Many-to-many communications media have proved to be popular and democratic (Rheingold, 2002: 121)

In the meantime, E-Mail and ongoing service innovations such as the World Wide Web (WWW) have become widely used and essential tools of personal and business interaction. Its relative impact is comparable to the introduction of regular mail service and trade when introduced centuries ago albeit at a very short period of time. Mitchell argues that just as railroads have been a major influence on settlement patterns and economics of the 19th century, and as automobiles have further influenced settlement, commerce and recreation in the 20th century, computer networks will influence our daily life to a large extent in the 21st century (Mitchell, 2000). The relative openness, fastness and cheapness of communication services have wide ranging political and governance implications that have only recently begun to be explored (Hart, 2008). One challenge for Internet governance is how to preserve the overall positive effects of the lower cost of transactions and the pervasiveness of global communications, whilst making sure that values such as personal privacy, market transparency and even national security are also protected. E-mail for example is the primary vehicle for distributing spam, viruses, worms, phishing expeditions and denial of service attacks.

Furthermore, Cloud Computing, the trend of placing services and data onto the Internet itself (and not on the users' system or hard disc) has the potential to turn the Internet into an all encompassing utility, comparable to the electric utilities that changed how businesses operated and brought the modern world into existence (Carr, 2009). Similar to electricity, IT services have the potential to become mere utilities through the adoption of Web Services and Cloud Computing. A tension between freedom and control is further invoked in such developments as communications technologies and new forms of governance converge.

In his book "City of Bits", Mitchell reflects upon this tension inherent to the architecture of the Internet and the communities it serves:

Architecture, laws, and customs maintain and represent whatever balance has been struck. As we construct and inhabit cyberspace communities, we will have to make and maintain similar bargains - though they will be embodied in software structures and electronic access controls rather than in architectural arrangements ... since electronic data collection and digital collation techniques are so much more powerful than any that could be deployed in the past, they provide the means to create the ultimate Foucaultian dystopia. (Mitchell, 2000)

Hart (2008) comments that current research on "*Internet issues and governance forums tends to focus primarily on the domain name system and ICANN, including research on WSIS, even though many other crucial issues, and particularly those associated with e-commerce and trade in digital products in the WTO and the OECD are of equal importance.*" Hart (2008) further argues that "*North-South forums like ... WSIS are important more as a proving ground for the idea of a 'multi-stakeholder approach' to global governance than for describing and explaining the most important emerging international regimes for ICTs*" and that "*the G8 and the OECD, are considerably more important overall for ICT regime creation and maintenance*". So whilst it is obvious that governance issues are important at the level of legislation and policy, it is also evident that network forms of organization actually prescribe control structures. The ability of networked communication technologies to allow interconnections indicates their ideological power, and despite appearances how scale-free networks contain hubs and hierarchies. Barabási (2002) indicates how scale-free networks like the Internet can be seen to offer "directness".

Although the overall structure of the Internet is largely non-hierarchicaland it must conform to the way TCP/IP protocols connect one machine to others, it is also subject to the DNS (Domain Name System) information stored in decentralised databases, organised in hierarchical, inverted tree-structures. For example, in the current model the Internet's address structure (DNS), which enables communication between the world's computers, is managed by the California-based, not-for-profit Internet Corporation for Assigned Names and Numbers (ICANN) under contract to the US department of commerce (Wray 2005). In question is the centralisation of control and whether other countries should be allowed more control over their Internet domains. Barabási (2002) also outlines that the Internet is organized into four continents so is hardly the metaphor of global community it purports to be. That ICANN are currently in the process of formulating the scope and agenda of future Internet governance holds significant implications for online communities. Clearly more detail is required to understand how networks operate both technically and politically.

One of the key challenges for social trust in Virtual Communities is estimating how much users will trust each other (Globeck, 2008). Given the billions of users on the Web and hundreds of online social networks with more than a billion accounts among them, it is thus rather unlikely that any two users will know one another in the classical sense. This leads to challenges with regards to identity and authenticity. Privacy Enhanced Mail (PEM), is an early IETF proposal specified in RFC 1421 in February 1993 to provide secure email communication using public key cryptography. Given its dependency on prior deployment of a hierarchical public key infrastructure (PKI) with a single root, it lacked market acceptance and was not widely deployed or used. Deployment

of a PKI proved difficult due to high operational costs and legal implications (i.e. legal liability of the root and 'policy' Certificate Authorities). From a governance point of view, such an approach is controversial given the inherent imposition of a central authority. Thus opposition to this approach became widespread and alternative approaches were proposed, notably Phil Zimmermann's Web of Trust as the PKI infrastructure for Pretty Good Privacy (PGP). Web of trust is a concept used in PGP and other OpenPGP compatible systems to authenticate the binding between a user on one hand and a public key on the other hand. As with Virtual Communities, there are many independent webs of trust, and any user can belong to multiple webs through their identity certificate. Pretty Good Privacy (PGP) provides data encryption and decryption to ensure cryptographic privacy and authentication for data communication thus providing a basis service for Virtual Communities. PGP aims to provide a secure mechanism for signing, encrypting and decrypting e-mails.

SECURITY IMPLICATIONS: THE CASE OF BOTNETS

The global increase of Internet connectivity (e.g. based on "always-on" broadband connections) undoubtedly brings tremendous economic and social opportunities. However, software developers and *malware* authors have also discovered great potential facilitated through vulnerable Internet service, operating systems and inept Internet users (Grizzard, 2007). As security threats increase typical users remain ignorant of what an expert might call "common-sense" approaches to avoid being compromised (or to keep systems "clean" or "uninfected"). These are facilitated through virus propagation, spam, click fraud, phishing, and activities have boomed through collections of software robots, or bots, that run autonomously – collectively referred to as *Botnet*s. In this context the term Botnets refers to a network of computers using distributed computing software but are typically associated with malicious software. A Botnet usually constitutes a collection or network of compromised computers running software usually installed via worms, Trojan horses or backdoors under a common command-and-control infrastructure. These systems are sometimes also referred to as Zombie computers. A large portion of the affected run Microsoft Windows operating systems, however other operating systems can be affected. Numerous Botnets have been found on the Internet, and examples include a Botnet revealed by the Dutch police with 1.5 million nodes (Keitzer, 2005) and another Botnet with 10,000-nodes identified by the Norwegian ISP Telenor (Leyden, 2004). To further counteract Botnets international coordinated efforts to discover and remove Botnets have also been initiated (Leyden, 2005). It widely assumed that the vast majority of Botnets today are used to distribute spam mails. Thus systems can use captured to transmit huge numbers (i.e. millions) of messages simultaneously. Given the fact that messages are sent through "ordinary" users a higher level of resilience with regards to spam filters is achieved. The program installed by a Botnet may further violate a system's security or components (e.g. hard disc) and monitor its user's passwords or keystrokes to gather private data.

Botnets have been identified as one of the key threats to network security, especially the peer-to-peer (P2P) based Botnets. One way of countering botnets is by target-attacking the weaknesses of high degree nodes or edges of the botnets (Li et al, 2010). Security experts need to know the features of the topology of botnets. Inspired by the method of complex network, Li et al(2010) propose a growing model of botnets that focuses on the network metrics of Botnets.

Botnets provide us with a good example to reveal the inherent structures and topology of the Internet and how freedom and control – as in the case of Virtual Communities - are negotiated, if not compromised. In cases of security violation,

it can be demonstrated how networks are a manifestation of ideology. This is what Galloway and Thacker describe, in "The Exploit" (taking their title from a term used by hackers to identify and utilise vulnerabilities in networks), as the new "network-network symmetry" of power where control is distributed relatively autonomously in horizontal organisational units and at the same time into rigid vertical hierarchies or even directed commands (Galloway & Thacker, 2007). Their description is largely a socio-technical truism, and one that supports the arguments that networks and sovereignty are not incompatible. This is precisely what software developers and malware authors have discovered, as they *exploit* vulnerable operating systems, Internet service and security software. Tactics are propagated through various means such as Botnets.

In response the area of software security is a booming industry, and a number of security-industry recommendations and standards have been developed. A set of common characteristics to identify the nature of known vulnerabilities has further been mapped into taxonomies to provide a framework for the examination of known and potential future vulnerabilities. Work and recommendations on security related taxonomies dates from the 1970s with varying degree of effectiveness. These can provide a framework for the examination of known and potential future vulnerabilities. Igure et al (2008) suggest the following properties for an efficient taxonomy of attacks and vulnerabilities in Computer Systems:

- Application- or system-specific taxonomy
- Taxonomy must be layered or hierarchical
- **First level of classification:** attack impact
- **Second level of classification:** system-specific attack
- **Third level of classification:** system components (attack targets)
- **Fourth level of classification:** system features (source of vulnerability)
- Classes need not be mutually exclusive

Figure 2. Agobot commands, comp (Harford, 2006)

Agobot	Description	Category
bot.open	Open a specific file on a host	Command and control language
bot.die	Command that terminates the bot	Command and control language
si_chanpass	Variable for IRC server information - Channel Password	Command and control language
scan.addnetrange <IP Range> <Priority>	Scans & adds an IP address range to a bot	Propagation and scanning command
scan.startall	Directs all bots to start scanning their network ranges	Propagation and scanning command
scan.listnetranges	Returns all network ranges registered with a bot	Propagation and scanning command
ddos.httpflood <url> <number> <referrer> <delay> <recursive>	Starts an HTTP flood	Exploitation and attack machanisms
ddos.udpflood <target> <port> <0=rand> <time> <delay>	Starts a UDP flood	Exploitation and attack machanisms
ddos.stop	Stops floods	Exploitation and attack machanisms

Rogue software is usually installed via worms, Trojan horses or backdoors under a common command-and-control infrastructure. A program installed by a Botnet can violate a system's components (e.g. hard disc) and monitor its user's activities (e.g. passwords, keystrokes) to gather private data from services (such as security relevant data such as login IDs and passwords, credit card numbers). The retrieved data is then distributed over the Internet to its 'master' node.

A number of major Botnet source codebases such as Agobot (Figure 2), SDBot, SpyBot have been identified and discussed in literature (Cook, 2005; Harford, 2006). Harford (2006) suggests that Agobot, also commonly referred to as Phatbot, is based on the most sophisticated Botnet source code (e.g. when compared to SDBot and SpyBot) and consists of around 20.000 C/C++ lines of code.

A typical Botnet implementation contains of numerous components such as an Internet Relay Chat (IRC) command and control mechanism and services to compromise security (e.g. to collect Paypal passwords or search registry entries). Thus the Botnet command language is derived from standard IRC as defined by the Internet Engineering Task Force (Kalt, 2000) and includes directives to request a bot to perform specific functions such as bot.open to open a specific file on a compro-

mised host. Thus close monitoring of IRC related traffic can facilitate the detection of Botnets through the identification of anomalies. Propagation mechanisms enable the Botnet to scan for and detect new systems for the Botnet. One mechanism is to take advantage of the IP addressing structure that is based on network, subnet and host IDs to implement the scanning of entire IP address ranges. The exploitation and attack mechanisms are generally attempted in combination with propagation and scanning and provide various means to attack a system (e.g. Agobot provides a brute-force password scanner for SQL servers and different types of generic denial of service attacks such as HTTP floods in the DDoS module).

Botnets can undoubtedly cause severe disruption on targeted sites. A Botnet may control a large number of 'hijacked' systems predominantly to target systems (e.g. a web community or a website) with connection and data requests in a distributed denial of service (DDoS) attack. Ultimately systems may be unable to handle excessive requests and will subsequently crash. This may bring down an entire data centre with it. The American blog site Six Apart is an example for a company that suffered from a Distributed Denial of Service (DDOS) attack of a Botnet in

May 2006. Within a few minutes of the attack, the company's servers had become unavailable and the blogs of 10 million customers were no longer available (Berinato 2006). Six Apart further established that the attack was not aimed against itself but rather against one of its customers, an Israeli company named Blue Security, which had offered a spam-counter attack service (Berinato 2006). However the Botnet assault continued for weeks, causing harm to many other companies and sites. Ultimately Blue Security could not withstand the attack and went out of business.

There are a large number of similar cases that illustrate insecurity issues surrounding Botnets and the ways in which vulnerability in the system is exploited in communities. With the popularity of filesharing and the high volumes of computers connected to Peer-to-Peer (P2P) networks, systems have also become increasingly vulnerable to attack. An example Trojan horse is Trojan. Peacomm that provides the basis for building a P2P Botnet (Grizzard, 2007). The threat is typically "attached" to an an email with a somewhat relevant and catchy subject (e.g. 'U.S. Secretary of State Condoleezza Rice has kicked German Chancellor Angela Merkel'), and attachments (e.g. 'Full Story.exe') and often an empty message body. The executable is a Trojan Horse which modifies a system's process (e.g. services.exe process) and adds hidden threads. The 'infected' system then attempts to establish P2P communication via UDP using a set of given IP addresses to obtain additional malicious files. Using a firewall with egress filtering, it can be detected that the services.exe process attempts to connect to a remote address via a UDP port. Subsequently the system will receive additional IP addresses, in essence building up a distributed network. To facilitate the process, the Trojan further maintains a list of unsuitable peers. The strategy of using peer-to-peer communication spreads the load and further improves the robustness of the Botnet, particularly when compared to the traditional approach of using centralised command & control servers.

It is difficult, if not impossible, to determine the size of the problem and this in itself generates insecuritiy (e.g. of users or communities) of another type. Some computer security analysts believe that a minimum of 10% of home PCs have been included in Botnets (Carr, 2007). Other analysts, including Vint Cerf (one of the inventors of the Internet and now a top Google executive) was quoted at the World Economic Forum in February 2007 that Botnets have become "pandemic" and that up to one quarter of all systems connected to the Internet may become part of a Botnet (Carr, 2007; Weber, 2007). It would appear that the issue of security is reducible to the challenge of managing the inherent insecurities of networked relations. The many examples serve to demonstrate how control is distributed both horizontally and vertically and that online communities provide the territory for this activity. The ability of networked communications technologies to allow interconnections and participation indicates their power, and despite surface appearances how scale-free networks demonstrate directedness.

It can be concluded that botnet attacks impose serious threats to the modern Internet and Virtual Communities. Given that money is a determining force driving the growth in botnet attacks, Lie e. Al. (2009) propose an economic approach to take away the financial incentives by introducing the uncertainty level to make the optimal botnet size infeasible for the botnet operators. Thus as the chance of uncertainty increases, both botnet masters' and attackers' profits can fall dramatically.

CONCLUSION

The Case for a Better Understanding of Security and Networks

The loosely coupled, hierarchical and ultimately insecure networks of the internet, with their ever growing numbers of users and capacity, provide a challenging environment to ensure common policies and behaviour based on suggested principles. Rheingold (2000) and other authors agree that Virtual Communities that embed many of the nuances of public conferencing, private communication or hybrid entities will require changes in these principles. However, Rheingold (2000) further states that the identification of these issues provides a platform to focus societal debate about values, risks, and liberties. Thus if substantial financial benefits or control can be derived through "Net-snooping", and the inherent architectural principles of the Internet make it difficult to protect Virtual Communities on one side and to track perpetrators on the other, no regulation or law will ever be able to adequately protect Virtual Communities and individual users.

The tension between freedom and control is inherent to the Internet and the communities it serves reflecting its contradictory development. Lessig argues that the initial variant of the Internet rendered difficult for politics to control Internet usage and developments whilst "software was the product of hackers and individuals outside of any institution of effective control" (e.g. Universities or research institutes) (Lessig, 2006: 72). However, he further concludes that "as code has become the product of companies, the power of [politics] has increased" given the fact that "when commerce writes code, then code can be controlled, because commercial entities can be controlled" (Lessig, 2006: 72).

The security industry's nested interests of creating awareness or even fear regarding perceived insecurity is impacting upon the ability of users and online communities to assess the latest developments in security. This creates a power differential, where a number of companies, together with the media, exercise immense control over the notion of security (Cox & Knahl, 2009). Thus, in the style of a self-fulfilling prophecy, the industry intensifies the dependency of the users to get the latest security intensified by feelings of insecurity. According to different market surveys the size

of the IT security market is experiencing rapid growth (Thomson, 2008). Given that estimates of the size of the security market will vary depending on the source, the included elements of when, how and for whom the data was collected means the actual size is difficult to establish. According to figures from Gartner, sales of enterprise security products rose by nearly 20 per cent in 2007 and were worth $10.4bn. According to Gartner, Symantec is market leader (26%) followed by McAfee (11%) and the strongest growth is in the area of Email security (45%); from a geographical perspective, Latin America is the fastest growing region for Enterprise Security Products (over 40% sales growth) and North America (47.5%) and Western Europe (31.7%) have the biggest market share (Thomson 2008). Ruggero Contu from Gartner has been quoted that "compliance, data leakage and privacy issues, along with the need to tackle the fast evolving and sophisticated threat environment, are among the major drivers fuelling the growth of spending on security" (Thomson, 2008).

Furthermore Post and Kagan (2007) raise the pressing question whether IT security controls are a burden or benefit. According to the results of their study *"34% of the respondents perceived interference or delays caused by the computer security systems as a consequence of their current business environment... general employees perceive that increases (more onerous measures) in security policies and practices result in greater interference(s) with their job responsibilities."* They suggest that users should be part of creating a security policy and suggest the testing of security restrictions on users to minimize task interference. In this sense online communities might begin to take more control over their security needs and thus perhaps develop less paranoid responses based on a better understanding of the Internet's vulnerabilities.

The point is that the issue of security demonstrates some of the core principles that relate to governance more generally under neoliberal conditions. To add detail here, many commentators turn to Foucault's lectures on governmentality delivered between 1982-3 (Foucault, 2010). Foucault draws out a distinction between early liberalism and contemporary neoliberalism. Neoliberalism replaces the regulatory function of the state to the market with the market itself, and emphasizes the human subject in different terms reacting to the market rather than the limits of government. The goal of government becomes the constitution of certain types of subjectivity in line with competition within, and reducible to, the logic of free markets. Like the scale-free network, a certain exercise of power is demonstrated.

What we wish to argue in this chapter is for better understanding of the networks that communities occupy in recognition of the need to rethink the way that power in managed within them. It is clear that networks reflect contemporary political dynamics and a technical awareness of this is also required to fully understand what is at stake. The architecture of the Internet is distributed and fragmented but nevertheless imagined in terms of its totality, which remains a fantasy. As the example of botnets aimed to demonstrate, further discussion is required on the relations between the human and inhuman elements that constitute the network. Networks involve shifts of scale such that action can no longer be attributed to individuals or communities but also to distributed coded actions that operate throughout it. Control and freedom and the feelings of security associated with both are distributed in keeping with the technical infrastructures of the Internet itself.

REFERENCES

Barabási, A.-L. (2002). *Linked: The new science of networks*. Cambridge, MA: Perseus.

Barlow, J. P. (2000). *The debate over Internet Governance: A snapshot in the year 2000*. Harvard, MA. URL: http:// cyber.law.harvard.edu/ is99/ governance/ barlow.html [Last Accessed 2010-03-10]

Bygrave, L. A. (2009). *Internet governance: Infrastructure and institutions*. Oxford, UK: Oxford Univ. Press. Online im Internet: URL: http:// www. gbv.de/ dms/ spk/ sbb/ recht/ toc/ 581075692.pdf

Carr, N. (2007). Botnets - A hidden menace that threaten the future of the Internet. *The Guardian*. April 5, 2007.

Carr, N. G. (2008). *The big switch: Rewiring the world, from Edison to Google*. 1st ed. New York, NY: Norton. Online im Internet: URL: http:// www.gbv.de/ dms/ bsz/ toc/ bsz27866685xinh.pdf

Cox, G., & Knahl, M. (2009). Critique of software security. Book chapter in Wolfgang Sutzl (ed.): Creating insecurity: *Art and culture in the age of security* (pp. 27-43). New York, NY: Autonomedia.

Foucault, M. (2010). *The government of self and others: Lectures at the College de France 1982-1983*. Basingstoke, UK: Palgrave Macmillan.

Galloway, A. R., & Thacker, E. (2007). *The exploit: A theory of networks*. Minneapolis, MN: University of Minnesota Press.

Globeck, J. (2008). Weaving a web of trust. *Science, 321*, 1640–1641. doi:10.1126/science.1163357

Goth, G. (2007). Fast-moving zombies: Botnets stay a step ahead of the fixes. *IEEE Internet Computing, 11*(2), 7–9. doi:10.1109/MIC.2007.32

Grizzard, J., Sharma, V., Nummery, C., Kang, B. B., & Dagon, D. (2007). Peer-to-peer Botnets: Overview and case study. *HotBots '07 / 4th USENIX Symposium on Networked Systems Design & Implementation (NSDI '07)*. Cambridge, MA, April 11-13, 2007.

Hart, J. A. (2008). Global Internet Governance. *Conference of the International Public Affairs. Association of Indiana University, Bloomington, Indiana,* April 11, 2008.

Hawthorne, Nathaniel (1851). *House of the Seven Gables*

Kalt, C. (2000). Internet relay chat: Architecture. *Network Working Group / Internet Engineering Task Force Request for Comments: 2810.* April 2000.

Keizer, G. (2005). Dutch Botnet bigger than expected. *TechWeb Technology News.* October 21, 2005.

Lessig, L. (2006). *Code: Version 2.0* (2nd ed.). New York, NY: Basic Books.

Lessig, L. (2009). In defense of piracy. *The Wall Street Journal* 16. September. Online im Internet: URL: http:// online.wsj.com/ ar3cle/ SB122367645363324303.html [Last Accessed 2009-12-12]

Leyden, John (2004). Telenor takes down 'massive' Botnet. *Enterprise Security.* September 9, 2004.

Leyden, John (2005). ISPs urged to throttle spam zombies: International clean-up campaign. *The Register.* May 24, 2005.

Li, X., et al. (2010). The growing model of Botnets. *2010 International Conference on Green Circuits and Systems (ICGCS), pp.* 414-419.

Li, Z. (2009). Botnet Economics: Uncertainty Matters. In *Managing Information Risk and the Economics of Security* (pp. 245–267). Springer. doi:10.1007/978-0-387-09762-6_12

Licklider, J.C.R., & Vezza, Albert (1978). Applications of Information Networks. *Proceedings of the IEEE, 66.*

Liu, H., Lim, E., Lauw, H. W., Le, M., Sun, A., Srivastava, J., & Kim, Y. (2008). Predicting trusts among users of online communities: An epinions case study. In *Proceedings of the 9th ACM Conference on Electronic Commerce* (Chicago, Il, USA, July 08 - 12, 2008). EC '08. ACM, New York, NY, 310-319.

Marsden, C. (2008). Beyond europe: The Internet, regulation, and multistakeholder governance—Representing the consumer interest? [Springer.]. *Journal of Consumer Policy, 31*(1), 115–132. doi:10.1007/s10603-007-9056-z

Mitchell, W. J. (2000). *City of bits: Space, place, and the infobahn. 7. print.* Cambridge, MA: MIT Press.

Post, G.V., & Kagan, A. (2007). Evaluating information security tradeoffs: Restricting access can interfere with user tasks. *Elsevier / Computers & Security. No. 26,* 229-237, 2007.

Rheingold, H. (1994). *The virtual community: Homesteading on the electronic frontier.* New York, NY: HarperPerennial.

Rheingold, H. (2000). *The virtual community: Homesteading on the electronic frontier.* London, UK: MIT Press.

Rheingold, H. (2002). *Smart mobs: The next social revolution.* Cambridge, Mass.: Perseus.

Saltzer, Jerome H., & David P. (1984). End-to-end arguments in system design. *ACM transactions on computer science,* 277–278.

Shneiderman, B. (2000). Designing trust into online experiences. *Communications of the ACM, 43*(12), December 2000.

Thomson, I. (2008). *Enterprise security software market booms. vnunet.com.* June 18, 2008. http:// www.vnunet.com/ vnunet/ news/ 2219275/ enterprise-software-market

Vinay M. Igure, Ronald D. Williams (2008). Taxonomies of Attacks and Vulnerabilities in Computer Systems. *IEEE Communications Surveys & Tutorials.* 1st Quarter 2008.

Weber, T. (2007). Criminals 'may overwhelm the Web'. *BBC News website.* January 25, 2007. Wikipedia. *Governance.* URL: http://en.wikipedia.org/wiki/ Governance [Last Accessed 2010-03-11]

Wray, R. (2005). EU says Internet could fall apart. *The Guardian,* October 12, 2005. http://echnology.guardian.co.uk/news/story/0,16559,1589967,00.html

Compilation of References

Ahearne, M., Bhattacharya, C. B., & Thomas, G. (2005). Antecedents and consequences of customer-company identification: Expanding the role of relationship marketing. *The Journal of Applied Psychology*, *90*(3), 574–585. doi:10.1037/0021-9010.90.3.574

Akerkar, R. (2009). *The foundations of semantic Web: XML, RDF & ontology*. London, UK: Alpha Science Intl Ltd.

Aktan B., Bohus, C. A., Crowl, L. A., & Shor, M. H. (1999). Distance learning applied to control engineering laboratories, IEEE Transactions on Education, 39(3), 320–326. 1996.

Andersson, B. (1983). *(1991). Imagined communities*. London, UK: Verso.

Andrea, M., & Egenhofer, M. (2003). Determining semantic similarity among entity classes from different ontologies. *IEEE Transactions on Knowledge and Data Engineering*, *15*, 442–456. doi:10.1109/TKDE.2003.1185844

Aral, S., & Van Alstyne, M. (2007). *Network structure and information advantage*: Structural Determinants of Access to Novel Information and their Performance Implications, MIT, Retrieved June 28, 2010, from http://ssrn.com/abstract=958158

Arbaugh, J. B. (2004). Learning to learn online: A study of perceptual changes between multiple online course experiences. *The Internet and Higher Education*, *7*, 169–182. doi:10.1016/j.iheduc.2004.06.001

Argote, L. (1999). *Organizational learning: Creating, retaining c transferring knowledge*. Norwell, MA, USA: Kluwer Academic Publishers.

Arkes, H. R., & Blumer, C. (1985). The psychology of sunk cost. *Organizational Behavior and Human Decision Processes*, *35*, 124–140. doi:10.1016/0749-5978(85)90049-4

Ashforth, B. E., & Mael, F. (1989). Social identity theory and the organization. *Academy of Management Review*, *14*(1), 20–39.

Bagozzi, R. P., & Dholakia, U. M. (2002). Intentional social action in virtual communities. *Journal of Interactive Marketing*, *16*(2), 2–21. doi:10.1002/dir.10006

Barabási, A.-L. (2002). *Linked: The new science of networks*. Cambridge, MA: Perseus.

Baran, B., & Çağıltay, K. (2006). Knowledge management and online communities of practice in teacher education. *The Turkish Online Journal of Educational Technology – TOJE, V* (3), 12-19.

Barber, B. (1998). *A place for us. How to make society civil and democracy strong*. New York, NY: Hill & Wang.

Barlow, J. P. (2000). *The debate over Internet Governance: A snapshot in the year 2000*. Harvard, MA. URL: http://cyber.law.harvard.edu/ is99/ governance/ barlow.html [Last Accessed 2010-03-10]

Barnes, C., Mercer, G., & Shakespeare, T. (1999). *Exploring Disability: A Sociological Introduction*. Cambridge, UK: Blackwell Publishers.

Barros, B., & Verdejo, M. F. (2000). Analyzing student interaction processes in order to improve collaboration: The degree approach. *International Journal of Artificial Intelligence in Education, Vol, 11*, 221–241.

Bartel, C. A. (2001). Social comparisons in boundary-spanning work: Effects of community outreach on members' organizational identity and identification. *Administrative Science Quarterly, 46*(3), 379–413. doi:10.2307/3094869

Baym, N. K. (2000). *Tune in, log on: Soaps, fandom, and online community*. Thousand Oaks, CA: Sage.

Baym, N. K. (1995). In Jones, S. (Ed.), *The emergence of community in computer-mediated communication, CyberSociety* (pp. 138–163). Newbury Park, CA: Sage.

Beaugrande, R. D., & Dressler, W. U. (1981). *Einfuhrung in die textlinguistik*. Tubingen: Niemeyer.

Belk, Russell W., Wallendorf, M., Sherry, J., Holbrook, M., & Roberts, S. (1988). Collectors and collecting. [Ed. Michael J. Houston, TX.]. *Advances in Consumer Research. Association for Consumer Research (U. S.), 15*.

Bellotti, V., Ducheneaut, N., Howard, M. A., & Smith, I. E. (2002). Taskmaster: Recasting email as task management. *CSCW workshop on re-designing e-mail for the 21st century*. New Orleans, LA.

Bénel, A., & Lejeune, C. (2009). Humanities 2.0: Documents, interpretation and intersubjectivity in the digital age. *International Journal of Web Based Communities, 5*(4), 562–576. Retrieved November 15, 2010, from http://publi.tech-cico.fr/paper_details.php?paperid=106

Bergami, M., & Bagozzi, R. P. (2000). Self-categorization, affective commitment and group self-esteem as distinct aspects of social identity in the organization. *The British Journal of Social Psychology, 39*(4), 555–577. doi:10.1348/014466600164633

Berger, I. E., Cunningham, P. H., & Drumwright, M. E. (2006). Identity, identification, and relationship through social alliances. *Journal of the Academy of Marketing Science, 34*(2), 128–137. doi:10.1177/0092070305284973

Berners-Lee, T., Hendler, J., & Lassila, O. (2001). The Semantic Web. *Scientific American, 284*(5), 34–43. doi:10.1038/scientificamerican0501-34

Bhattacharya, C. B., & Sen, S. (2003). Consumer-company identification: A framework for understanding consumers' relationships with companies. *Journal of Marketing, 67*(2), 76–88. doi:10.1509/jmkg.67.2.76.18609

Bizer, C., Heath, T., & Berners-Lee, T. (2009). Linked data- the story so far. In Heath, T., Hepp, M., and Bizer, C. (Eds.). Special issue on linked data, *International Journal on Semantic Web and Information Systems (IJSWIS)*. http://linkeddata.org/ docs/ ijswis-special-issue.

Blau, P. M. (1964). *Exchange and Power in Social Life*. New York, NY: Wiley.

Blomberg, J. (2007). *Practice-oriented design of products, services and experiences. Service Science Lecture Series*. Berkeley, CA: University of California.

Boone, M. E. (2001). *Managing inter@ctivity*. New York, NY: McGraw-Hill.

Borgatti, S. P., & Everett, M. G. (1999). Models of core periphery structures. *Social Networks, 21*(4), 375–395. doi:10.1016/S0378-8733(99)00019-2

Bouckaert, R., Frank, E., Hall, M., Kirkby, R., Reutemann, P., Seewald, A., & Scuse, D. (2010). *WEKA Manual for Version 3-6-2*. Hamilton, New Zealand: University of Waikato.

Bourdieu, P. (1980). Le capital social: Notes provisoires. *Actes de la Recherche en Sciences Sociales, 3*(31), 2–3.

Bourdieu, P. (1993). *Sociology in question*. London, UK: Sage.

Bourdieu, P. (1986). The forms of capital. In Richardson, J. G. (Ed.), *Handbook of theory and research for the sociology of education* (pp. 241–258). Greenwood, New York.

Bowman, C., Danzig, P., Hardy, D., Manber, U., & Schwartz, M. (1995). The Harvest information discovery and access system. *Computer Networks and ISDN Systems, 28*(1–2), 119–125. doi:10.1016/0169-7552(95)00098-5

Boyd, D., & Ellison, N. (2007). Social network sites: Definition, history and scholarship. *Journal of Computer-Mediated Communication, 13*(1). doi:10.1111/j.1083-6101.2007.00393.x

Boyd, D. (2011). Social network sites as networked publics: Affordances, dynamics and implications. In Papacharissi, Z. (Ed.), *The networked self - identity, community and culture on social network sites* (pp. 39–58). New York, NY: Routledge.

Bozzi, A. (1993). Towards a philological workstation. *Revue Informatique et Statistique dans les Sciences Humaines, 29*(1-4). Retrieved November 15, 2010, from http://promethee.philo.ulg.ac.be/RISSHpdf/Annee1993/Articles/ABozzi.pdf

Brady, D. (2004, August 2). Cult brands, *Business Week.* New York, NY: Bloomberg L.P.

Breiger, R. L. (2004). The Analysis of Social Network. In Hardy, M., & Bryman, A. (Eds.), *Handbook of Data Analysis (505)*. London, UK: Sage.

Breslin, J., Passant, A., & Decker, S. (2009). *The social Semantic Web*. Berlin, Germany: Springer Verlag. doi:10.1007/978-3-642-01172-6

Brew, L. S. (2008). The role of student feedback in evaluating and revising a blended learning course. *The Internet and Higher Education, 11*, 98–105. doi:10.1016/j.iheduc.2008.06.002

Brewer, M. B. (1979). In-group bias in the minimal intergroup situation: A cognitive-motivational analysis. *Psychological Bulletin, 86*, 307–324. doi:10.1037/0033-2909.86.2.307

Brewer, M. B. (1991). The social self: On being the same and different at the same time. *Personality and Social Psychology Bulletin, 17*, 475–482. doi:10.1177/0146167291175001

Brewer, M. B., & Weber, J. G. (1994). Self-evaluation effects of interpersonal versus intergroup social comparison. *Journal of Personality and Social Psychology, 66*, 268–275. doi:10.1037/0022-3514.66.2.268

Brewer, M. B. (1993). The role of distinctiveness in social identity and group behaviour. In Hogg, M., & Abrams, D. (Eds.), *Group motivation: Social psychological perspectives* (pp. 1–16). New York, NY: Harvester-Wheatsheaf.

Brown, J. S., & Duguid, P. (1991). Organizational learning and communities-of-practice: Toward a unified view of working, learning, and innovation. *Organization Science, 2*(1), 40–57. doi:10.1287/orsc.2.1.40

Brown J. S., & Duguid, P. (1995, October 11). *The Social Life of Documents. EDventure Holdings,* (1-18). New York, NY.

Broxton, J. A. (1963). A test of interpersonal attraction predictions derived from balance theory. *Journal of Abnormal and Social Psychology, 66*, 394–397. doi:10.1037/h0047657

Bugeaud, F., & Soulier, E. (2009). Services systems to leverage innovators' knowledge: The Telecoms Industry case. In L.-M. Camarinha-Matos, I. Paraskakis, & H. Afsarmanesh (Eds.), *IFIP Advances in Information and Communication Technology: Vol. 307, Leveraging Knowledge for Innovation in Collaborative Networks, 10th IFIP WG 5.5 Working Conference on Virtual Enterprises (PROVE'09)* (pp. 563-570). Thessaloniki, Greece. October 07th-09th, Springer.

Bugeaud, F., & Soulier, E. (2010). Conception assistée de Systèmes de Services (SdS) à l'aide d'Ontologies Méréologiques. *Proceedings of the 21ème Journées Francophones d'Ingénierie des Connaissances (IC'10)*. Nîmes, June 08-11.

Bulu, S. T., & Yildirim, Z. (2008). Communication behaviors and trust in collaborative online teams. *Journal of Educational Technology & Society, 11*(1), 132–147.

Burt, R. S. (2000). The network structure of social capital. In R. I. Sutton & B. M. Staw (Eds.), *Research in Organizational Behavior (pp. 345-423)*. Greenwich, CT: Jai Press.

Bygrave, L. A. (2009). *Internet governance: Infrastructure and institutions.* Oxford, UK: Oxford Univ. Press. Online im Internet: URL: http:// www.gbv.de/ dms/ spk/ sbb/ recht/ toc/ 581075692.pdf

Calabretto, S., & Bozzi, A. (1998) The philological workstation BAMBI (Better Access to Manuscripts and Browsing of Images). *Journal of Digital Information, 1*(3). Retrieved November 15, 2010, from https://journals.tdl.org/jodi/article/viewArticle/10/20

Callaghan, M. J., Harkin, J., McGinnity, T. M., & Maguire, L. P. (Jun 2008). Intelligent user support in autonomous remote experimentation environments, IEEE Transactions on Industrial Electronics, 55(6), 2355-2367. IEEE, ISSN 0278-0046.

Callaghan, M. J., McCusker, K., Losada, J., Harkin J. G, & Wilson, S. (November 2009). Engineering education island: Teaching engineering in virtual worlds. ITALICS (Innovation in Teaching And Learning in Information and Computer Sciences).

Callamard, A. (1999a). *Documenting Human Rights Violations by State Agents*. Montreal, Canada: Amnesty International and Canadian Human Rights Foundation.

Callamard, A. (1999b). *A methodology for Gender-Sensitive Research*. Montreal, Canada: Amnesty International and Canadian Human Rights Foundation.

Cameron, J. (2004). A three factor model of social identity. *Self and Identity*, *3*, 239–262. doi:10.1080/13576500444000047

Carr, N. (2007). Botnets - A hidden menace that threaten the future of the Internet. *The Guardian*. April 5, 2007.

Carr, N. G. (2008). *The big switch: Rewiring the world, from Edison to Google*. 1st ed. New York, NY: Norton. Online im Internet: URL: http:// www.gbv.de/ dms/ bsz/ toc/ bsz27866685xinh.pdf

Carroll, J. M., Neale, D. C., Isenhour, P. L., Rossen, M. B., & McCrickard, D. S. (2003). Notification and awareness: Synchronizing task-oriented collaborative activity. *International Journal of Human-Computer Studies*, *58*, 605–632. doi:10.1016/S1071-5819(03)00024-7

Chan, C. M. L., Bhandar, M., Oh, L.-B., & Chan, H.-C. (2004). *Recognition and Participation in a Virtual Community*. Paper presented at the Proceedings of the 37th Hawaii International Conference on System Sciences, Hawaii, USA.

Chapman C., Clinton J., & Kerber R (2005). *CRISP-DM 1.0, Step-by-step data mining guide*.

Chavis, D., Hogge, J., McMillan, D., & Wandersman, A. (1986). Sense of community through Brunswick's lens: A first look. *Journal of Community Psychology*, *14*, 24–40. doi:10.1002/1520-6629(198601)14:1<24::AID-JCOP2290140104>3.0.CO;2-P

Chipuer, M., & Pretty, M. H. (1999). A review of the sense of community index: Current uses, factor structure, reliability. *Journal of Community Psychology*, *27*(6), 643–658. doi:10.1002/(SICI)1520-6629(199911)27:6<643::AID-JCOP2>3.0.CO;2-B

Coleman, J. S. (1988). Social capital in the creation of human capital. *American Journal of Sociology*, *94*, 95–121. doi:10.1086/228943

Coleman, S., & Blumler, J. (2009). *The Internet and democratic citizenship. Theory, practice and politics*. Cambridge, UK: Cambridge University Press.

Connolly, W. E. (1974). Essentially contested concepts in politics. In Connolly, W. E. (Ed.), *The terms of political discourse* (pp. 10–44). Lexington, MA: Heath.

Cooley, C. H. (1902). *Human nature and the social order*. New York, NY: Scribner.

Cothrel, J., & Williams, R. L. (1999). On-line communities: Helping them form and grow. *Journal of Knowledge Management*, *31*, 54–60. doi:10.1108/13673279910259394

Cova, B., & Cova, V. (2002). Tribal marketing: The tribalization of society and its impact on the conduct of marketing. *European Journal of Marketing*, *36*.

Cox, G., & Knahl, M. (2009). Critique of software security. Book chapter in Wolfgang Sutzl (ed.): Creating insecurity: *Art and culture in the age of security* (pp. 27-43). New York, NY: Autonomedia.

Cross, R., Borgatti, S. P., & Parker, A. (2002). Making Invisible work visible: Using social network analysis to support strategic collaboration. *California Management Review*, *44*(2), 25–46.

Cummings, J., & Cross, R. (2003). Structural properties of work groups and their consequences for performance. *Social Networks*, *25*(3), 197–210. doi:10.1016/S0378-8733(02)00049-7

Dall'Olmo Riley, F., & De Chernatony, L. (2000). The service brand as relationship builder. *British Journal of Management*, *11*(2), 137–150. doi:10.1111/1467-8551.t01-1-00156

Das, S., Girard, T., Weitzman, L., Lewis-Bowen, A., & Clark, T. (2008). Building bio-medical Web communities using a semantically aware content management system, *Briefings in Bioinformatics*.

Davenport, T., H., De Long, D., W., & Beers, M., C. (1998). Successful Knowledge Management Projects. *Sloan Management Review*, *39*(2), 43–57.

Davenport, T. H. (2005). *Thinking for a living: How to get better performance and results from knowledge workers*. Boston, MA: Harvard Business School Press.

Davenport, T. H. (2007). Information technologies for knowledge management. In Ichijo, K., & Nonaka, I. (Eds.), *Knowledge creation and management. New challenges for managers* (pp. 97–109). New York, NY: Oxford University Press.

Deaux, K., & Martin, D. (2003). Interpersonal networks and social categories: Specifying levels of context in identity processes. *Social Psychology Quarterly, 66*(2), 101–117. doi:10.2307/1519842

Delalonde, C., & Soulier, E. (2007). Collaborative information retrieval in R&D distributed teams. *Proceedings of the 13th International Conference on Concurrent Engineering.* Sophia-Antipolis, September 18-22.

Delavari, N., Beikzadeh, M. R., & Amnuaisuk, S. K. (2005). Application of enhanced analysis model for data mining processes in higher educational system, *Proceedings of ITHET 6th Annual International Conference.* Juan Dolio, Dominican Republic.

Delavari, N., Beikzadeh, M. R., & Shirazi, M. R. A. (2004). A new model for using data mining in higher educational system, *Proceedings of 5th International Conference on Information Technology based Higher Education and Training: ITEHT '04,* Istanbul, Turkey.

Dillenbourg, P. (1999). What do you mean by collaborative learning? Amsterdam, NL: Pergamon, Elsevier Science, 1–16, 1999.

Ding, L., Zhou, L., Finin, T., & Joshi, A. (2005, January). How the Semantic Web is being used:An analysis of FOAF, *Proceedings of the 38th International Conference on System Sciences,* Hawaii, USA.

Disability Rights Promotion International (DRPI). (2003). *Phase 1 report: Opportunities, methodologies, and training resources for disability rights monitoring.* Toronto, Canada: Disability Rights Promotion International.

Doheny-Farina, S. (1996). *The wired neighbourhood.* New Haven, CT: Yale University Press.

Donath, J. (1999). Identity and deception in the virtual community. In *P. Kollock & M. Smith (red.), Communities in cyberspace* (pp. 29–59). London, UK: Routledge.

Dongman, L., Han, S., Park, I., Kang, S., Lee, K., Hyun, S. J., & Lee, G. (2004). A group-aware middleware for ubiquitous computing environments, Proc. of ICAT 2004, 2004.

Doosje, B., Ellemers, N., & Spears, R. (1999). Commitment and intergroup behaviour. In Ellemers, N., Spears, R., & Doosje, B. (Eds.), *Social Identity.* London, UK: Blackwell.

Douglas, K. M., & McGarty, C. (2001). Identifiability and self-presentation: Computer-mediated communication and intergroup interaction. *The British Journal of Social Psychology, 40,* 399–416. doi:10.1348/014466601164894

Dourish, P., & Bellotti, V. (1992). Awareness and coordination in shared workspaces. In proceedings of the ACM Conference on Computer Supported Cooperative Work (CSCW'92), Toronto, Ontario, Canada: ACM Press.

Dukerich, J. M., Golden, B. R., & Shortell, S. M. (2002). Beauty is in the eye of the beholder: The impact of organizational identification, identity, and image on the cooperative behaviors of physicians. *Administrative Science Quarterly, 47*(3), 507–533. doi:10.2307/3094849

Durkheim, E. (1893). *(1993). The division of labour in society.* New York, NY: The Free Press.

Durkheim, E. (1984). *The division of labour in society.* London, UK: MacMillan.

Dutton, J. E., Dukerich, J. M., & Harquail, C. V. (1994). Organizational images and member identification. *Administrative Science Quarterly, 39*(2), 239–263. doi:10.2307/2393235

Dwyer, F. R., Schurr, P. H., & Oh, S. (1987). Developing buyer-seller relationships. *Journal of Marketing, 51*(2), 11–27. doi:10.2307/1251126

Dyer, H. J. (2000). *Collaborative advantage: Winning through extended enterprise supplier networks.* New York, NY: Oxford University Press.

Eiglier, P. (2004). *Marketing et stratégie des services.* Paris, France: Economica.

El Morr, C. (Ed.). (2007). *Encyclopedia in Mobile Computing & Commerce.* Hershey, PA: Information Science Reference.

El Morr, C., & Kawash, J. (2007). Mobile virtual communities research: A synthesis of current trends and a look at future perspectives. *International Journal of Web Based Communities, 3*(4), 386–403. doi:10.1504/IJWBC.2007.015865

Ellemers, N., Doosje, B., van Knippenberg, A., & Wilke, H. (1992). Status protection in high status minority groups. *European Journal of Social Psychology, 22,* 123–140. doi:10.1002/ejsp.2420220203

Ellemers, N., Kortekaas, P., & Ouwerkerk, J. W. (1999). Self-categorisation, commitment to the group and group self-esteem as related but distinct aspects of social identity. *European Journal of Social Psychology, 29*(2-3), 371–389. doi:10.1002/(SICI)1099-0992(199903/05)29:2/3<371::AID-EJSP932>3.0.CO;2-U

Ellison, N., Lampe, C., Steinfield, C., & Vitak, J. (2011). With a little help from my friends: How social network sites affect social capital processes. In Papacharissi, Z. (Ed.), *The networked self - identity, community and culture on social network sites* (pp. 124–145). New York, NY: Routledge.

Eom, S. B., & Arbaugh, J. B. (2011). *Student satisfaction and learning outcomes in e-learning: An introduction to empirical research.* Hershey, PA: Information Science Reference. doi:10.4018/978-1-60960-615-2

Erickson, T., & Kellogg, W. A. (2003). Knowledge Communities: Online Environments for Supporting Knowledge Management and its Social Context. In M. Ackerman, V. Pipek, & V Wulf (Eds.), *Beyond knowledge management: Sharing expertise* (299-325). Cambridge, MA.: MIT Press.

Ermel, C., & Bardohl, R. (2004). Scenario animation for visual behavior models: A generic approach. Software and system modeling. *Special Section on Graph Transformations and Visual Modeling Techniques, 3*(2), 164–177.

Eskenazi, M., Black, A. W., Raux, A., & Langner, B. (2008). *Let's go lab: A platform for evaluation of spoken dialogue systems with real world users.* Brisbane, Australia: Interspeech.

Ethier, K. A., & Deaux, K. (1994). Negotiating social identiy when contexts change: Maintaining identification and responding to threat. *Journal of Personality and Social Psychology, 67*(2), 243–251. doi:10.1037/0022-3514.67.2.243

Fernandez, V., & Rivard, S. (2007). KM: Knowledge networks. *Annals of Telecommunications, 62*(7/8: *Knowledge Management: Knowledge Networks*), 723-733.

Fernback, J. (1999). There is a there there. Notes towards a definition of Cyber community. In Jones, S. (Ed.), *Doing Internet research. Critical essues and methods for examining the Net.* London, UK: Sage.

Ferran-Urdaneta, C. (1999). *Terms or communities? Organizational structures for knowledge management.* Paper presented at the SIGCPR'99, New Orleans, LA. USA.

Fiol, C. M., & O'Connor, E. J. (2005). Identification in face-to-face, hybrid, and pure virtual teams: untangling the contradictions. *Organization Science, 16*(1), 19–32. doi:10.1287/orsc.1040.0101

Fischer, G. (2001). Communities of interest: Learning through the interaction of multiple knowledge systems. In *24th Annual Information Systems Research Seminar in Scandinavia* (IRIS'24). Ulvik, Norway.

Fisher, R. J., & Ackerman, D. (1998). The effects of recognition and group need on volunteerism: A social norm perspective. *The Journal of Consumer Research, 25,* 262–275. doi:10.1086/209538

Florescu, D., Levy, A., & Mendelzon, A. (1998). Database techniques for the World-Wide Web: A Survey. *SIGMOD Record, 27*(3), 59–74. doi:10.1145/290593.290605

Forehand, M. R., Deshpande, R., & Reed, A. II. (2002). Identity salience and the influence of differential activation of the social self-schema on advertising response. *The Journal of Applied Psychology, 87*(6), 1086–1099. doi:10.1037/0021-9010.87.6.1086

Foreman, P., & Whetten, D. A. (2002). Members' identification with multiple-identity organizations. *Organization Science, 13*(6), 618–635. doi:10.1287/orsc.13.6.618.493

Foster, F., & Falkowski, G. (1999). Organization network analysis: A tool for building a learning organization. *Knowledge and Process Management*, 6(1), 53–60. doi:10.1002/(SICI)1099-1441(199903)6:1<53::AID-KPM38>3.0.CO;2-Y

Foucault, M. (2010). *The government of self and others: Lectures at the College de France 1982-1983*. Basingstoke, UK: Palgrave Macmillan.

Fougeyrollas, P., Cloutier, R., Bergeron, H., Côté, J., & Michel, G. S. (1999). *The Quebec classification: Disability creation process*. Québec, Canada: International Network on the Disability Creation Process.

Fournier, S. (1998). Consumers and their brands: Developing relationship theory in consumer research. *The Journal of Consumer Research*, 24(March), 343–373. doi:10.1086/209515

Fournier, S., & Lee, L. (2009). Getting brand communities right. *Harvard Business Review*, 105–111.

Franke, N., & Shah, S. (2003). How communities support innovative activities: An exploration of assistance and sharing among end-users. *Research Policy*, 32(1), 157–178. doi:10.1016/S0048-7333(02)00006-9

Fredskild, T. U. (2008). Distance learning students in communities of practice, *International Journal of Media, Technology and Lifelong Learning*, 3(4). Available at: www.seminar.net

Gadrey, J. (2000). The characterization of goods and services: An alternative approach. *Review of Income and Wealth*, 46(3), 369–387. doi:10.1111/j.1475-4991.2000.tb00848.x

Gaertner, S. L., Dovidio, J. F., Anastasio, P. A., Bachman, B. A., & Rust, M. C. (1993). The common ingroup identity model: Recategorization and the reduction of intergroup bias. In W. Stroebe & M. Hewstone (Eds.), *European Review of Social Psychology*, 4, (1-26). Chichester, UK: Wiley.

Gallouj, F., & Weinstein, O. (1997). Innovation in services. *Research Policy*, 26, 537–556. doi:10.1016/S0048-7333(97)00030-9

Galloway, A. R., & Thacker, E. (2007). *The exploit: A theory of networks*. Minneapolis, MN: University of Minnesota Press.

Garrison, D. R., Anderson, T., & Archer, W. (2000). *Critical enquiry in a text-based environment*: Computer conferencing in higher education. *The Internet and Higher Education*, 2(2-3), 87–105. doi:10.1016/S1096-7516(00)00016-6

Gartner (2009). De La Vergne, H. J., Milanesi, C., Zimmermann, A., Cozza, R., Nguyen, T. H., Gupta, A., & CK Lu (in press). *Competitive Landscape: Mobile Devices, Worldwide, 4Q09 and 2009*.

Genci, J. (2009). The "Zero Cost" remote lab, icns, Fifth International Conference on Networking and Services, pp.572-575, 2009.

Ghoshal, S., & Bartlett, C. A. (1997). *The individualized corporation*. New York, NY: Harper Business.

Gibson, W. (1984). *Neuromancer*. New York, NY: Berkley Publishing Group.

Globeck, J. (2008). Weaving a web of trust. *Science*, 321, 1640–1641. doi:10.1126/science.1163357

Gloor, P. (2006). *Swarm creativity. Competitive advantage through collaborative innovation networks*. New York, NY: Oxford University Press.

Gloor, P., & Zhao, Y. (2006). Analyzing actors and their discussion topics by semantic social network analysis, *Proceedings of 10th IEEE International Conference on Information Visualization IV06*. London, UK.

Goffman, E. (1990). *(1959). The presentation of self in everyday life*. London, UK: Penguin Books.

Gomes, L., & Bogosyan, S. (2009). Current trends in remote laboratories, Industrial Electronics, IEEE Transactions, 56(12), 4744 – 4756. ISSN: 0278-0046, 10.1109/TIE.2009.2033293, Dec. 2009.

Gomez-Perez, A., & Corcho, O. (2002). Ontology languages for the Semantic Web. *IEEE Intelligent Systems*, 17(1), 54–60. doi:10.1109/5254.988453

Gongla, P., & Rizzuto, C.R. (2001). Evolving communities of practice: IBM global service experience, *IBM System Journals*, 40.

Goodwin, J., & Emirbayer, M. (1999). Network analysis, culture, and the problem of agency. *American Journal of Sociology*, 99(1), 1411–1454.

Goth, G. (2007). Fast-moving zombies: Botnets stay a step ahead of the fixes. *IEEE Internet Computing, 11*(2), 7–9. doi:10.1109/MIC.2007.32

Gotved, S. (1999). *Cybersociologi. Det samme på en anden måde. PhD-dissertation.* Denmark: University of Copenhagen.

Graham, G. (1999). *The Internet: A philosophical inquiry.* London, UK: Routledge.

Granovetter, M. (1973, May). The strength of weak ties. *American Journal of Sociology, 78*(6), 1360–1380. doi:10.1086/225469

Gravier, C., & Auer, M. E. (2009, Oct.-Dec.). Guest editorial: The many facets of remote laboratories in online engineering education. *IEEE Transactions on Learning Technologies, 2*(4), 260–262. doi:10.1109/TLT.2009.53

Gravier, C., & Fayolle, J. (2009, June). Quality of learning: Using a semantic Web approach to enhance learner-control during collaborative remote laboratories [IJIL]. *International Journal of Innovation and Learning, 6*(6), 606–624. doi:10.1504/IJIL.2009.026647

Gravier, C., Fayolle, J., & Bayard, B. (2008). Coping with collaborative and competitive episodes within collaborative remote laboratories, International Conference REV 2008, June 24th, Duesseldorf, Germany.

Gravier, C., Fayolle, J., Bayard, B., Lardon, J., Dusser, G., & Vérot, R. (2008). Putting reusability first: A paradigm switch in remote laboratories engineering, International Journal of Online Engineering, 5(1),16-22), February 2009.

Gretchko, S., Gloor, P., Taylor, A., & Kleinert, R. (2002). *Collaborative knowledge network.* Deloitte Research.

Grippa, F., Zilli, A., Laubacher, R., & Gloor, P. (2006). Email may not reflect the social network, *Proceedings Annual Conference of the North American Association for Computational Social and Organizational Sciences Conference,* Indiana, USA.

Grizzard, J., Sharma, V., Nummery, C., Kang, B. B., & Dagon, D. (2007). Peer-to-peer Botnets: Overview and case study. *HotBots '07 / 4th USENIX Symposium on Networked Systems Design & Implementation (NSDI '07).* Cambridge, MA, April 11-13, 2007.

Grove, S. J., & Fisk, R. P. (1992). The service experience as theatre. In Sherry, J. F., & Sternthal, B. (Eds.), *Advances in Consumer Research* (*Vol. 19*, pp. 455–461). Association for Consumer Research.

Grundstein, M. (2004). De la capitalisation des connaissances au management des connaissances dans l'entreprise. In Imed Boughzala and Jean-Louis Ermine (Eds.), *Management des connaissances en entreprise* (25-54). Paris, France: Lavoisier.

Guardado, M., & Shi, L. (2007). ESL students' experiences of online peer feedback. *Computers and Composition, 24,* 443–461. doi:10.1016/j.compcom.2007.03.002

Gupta, S., & Kim, H. W. (2004). *Enhancing the commitment to virtual community: A belief and feeling based approach.* Paper presented at the Twenty-Fifth International Conference on Information Systems.

Gustavsson, I., Zackrisson, J., Håkansson, L., Claesson, L., & Lagö, T. (2007). The VISIR project — an open source software initiative for distributed online laboratories, Proc. of Annual Int. Conf. on Remote Engineering and Virtual Instrumentation.

Gutwin, C., Penner, R., & Schneider, K. (2004). Group awareness in distributed software development", CHI letters, 6(3), 72-81, 2004. Harward, J., Del Alamo, J. A., Lerman, S. R., Bailey, P. H., Carpenter, J., DeLong, K., Zych, D. (2008, June). The iLab shared architecture: A web services infrastructure to build Communities of internet accessible laboratories. *Proceedings of the IEEE, 96*(6), 931–950.

Haas, P. M. (1992). Introduction: Epistemic communities and international policy coordination. *International Organization, 46*(1), 1–35. doi:10.1017/S0020818300001442

Hagel, J., & Armstrong, A. G. (1997). *Net gain: Expanding markets through virtual communities.* Boston, MA: Harvard Business School Press.

Hameed, A., Sleeman, D., & Preece, A. (2001). Detecting mismatches among experts' ontologies acquired through knowledge elicitation. *21st International Conference on Knowledge Based Systems and Applied Artificial Intelligence ES2001,* Cambridge, UK.

Hanewald, R. (2009). Sustainability in an online community of practice: The case study of a group of secondary school educators in Victoria. *Australian Journal of Teacher Education Group of Secondary School Educators in Victoria, 34*(5), 26–42.

Hara, N., & Kling, R. (2002). *IT supports for communities of practice: An empirically-based framework.* Bloomington, IN: Center for Social Informatics, Indiana University.

Haraway, D. (1991). *Simians, cyborgs and women: The reinvention of nature.* New York, NY: Routledge.

Hars, A., & Ou, S. (2002). Working for free? Motivations of participating in open source projects. *International Journal of Electronic Commerce, 6*(3), 25–39.

Hart, J. A. (2008). Global Internet Governance. *Conference of the International Public Affairs. Association of Indiana University, Bloomington, Indiana,* April 11, 2008.

Hartikainen, M., Salonen, E., & Turunen, M. (2004). Subjective evaluation of spoken dialogue systems using SERVQUAL method. In *Proceedings of the Eighth International Conference on Spoken Language Processing (INTERSPEECH 2004-ICSLP).* Jeju Island, Korea.

Haslam, S. A., Eggins, R. A., & Reynolds, K. J. (2003). The ASPIRe model: Actualizing social and personal identity resources to enhance organizational outcomes. *Journal of Occupational and Organizational Psychology, 76,* 83–113. doi:10.1348/096317903321208907

Haslam, S. A., Oakes, P. J., Reynolds, K. J., & Turner, J. C. (1999). Social identity salience and the emergence of stereotype consensus. *Personality and Social Psychology Bulletin, 25*(7), 809–818. doi:10.1177/0146167299025007004

Hatchuel, A., & Weil, B. (2003). A new approach of innovative design: an introduction to C-K theory. *Proceedings of ICED,* Stockholm, Sweden.

Hawthorne, Nathaniel (1851). *House of the Seven Gables*

Haynes, S. R., Purao, S., & Skattebo, A. L. (2009). Scenario-based methods for evaluating collaborative systems. *Computer Supported Cooperative Work, 18*(4), 331–356. doi:10.1007/s10606-009-9095-x

Haythornthwaite, C., & Wellman, B. (2002). The Internet in everyday life: An introduction. In Haythornthwaite, Caroline, & Barry Wellman (Ed.). *The Internet in everyday life* (3-45). Oxford, UK: Blackwell.

Hendler, J. (2001). Agents and the Semantic Web. *IEEE Intelligent Systems, 16*(2), 30–37. doi:10.1109/5254.920597

Herring, S. C. (1999). The rhetorical dynamics of gender harassment online. *The Information Society, 15*(3), 151–167. doi:10.1080/019722499128466

Herring, Susan C. (1993). Gender and democracy in computer-mediated communication. *Electronic Journal of Communication, 3*(2).

Hesselbein, F., & Johnston, R. (2002). *On leading change.* San Francisco: Jossey-Bass.

Hildreth, P. M., Kimble, C., & Wright, P. (1998). Computer mediated communications and international communities of practice [Erasmus University, The Netherlands]. *Proceedings of Ethicomp, 98,* 275–286.

Hildreth, P. M., & Kimble, C. (2002). The duality of knowledge. *Information Research, 8,*(1).

Hill, J. L. (1996). Psychological sense of community: Suggestions for future research. *Journal of Community Psychology, 24,* 431–438. doi:10.1002/(SICI)1520-6629(199610)24:4<431::AID-JCOP10>3.0.CO;2-T

Hiltz, S. R., Turoff, M., & Johnson, K. (1989). Experiments in group decision making, 3: Disinhibition, deindividuation, and group processes in pen name and real name computer conferences. *Decision Support Systems, 5,* 217–232. doi:10.1016/0167-9236(89)90008-0

Hiscock, J. (2001, March 1). Most trusted brands, *Marketing,* 32-3.

Hogg, M. A., & Abrams, D. (1988). *Social identifications: A social psychology of intergroup relations and group processes.* London, UK: Routledge.

Hogg, M., & Abrams, D. (1993). Towards a single-process Uncertainty-reduction model of social motivation in groups. In Hogg, M., & Abrams, D. (Eds.), *Group motivation: Social psychological perspectives* (pp. 173–190). New York, NY: Harvester Wheatsheaf.

Holsti, O. (1969). *Content analysis for the social sciences and humanities*. Reading, MA: Addison-Wesley.

Hornsey, M. J., & Jetten, J. (2004). The individual within the group: Balancing the need to belong with the need to be different. *Personality and Social Psychology Review*, *8*(3), 248–264. doi:10.1207/s15327957pspr0803_2

Hughey, J., Speer, W., & Peterson, N. A. (1999). Sense of community in community organisations: Structure and evidence of validity. *Journal of Community Psychology*, *27*(1), 97–13. doi:10.1002/(SICI)1520-6629(199901)27:1<97::AID-JCOP7>3.0.CO;2-K

Husserl, E. (1970*). Logical Investigations, Vol. 2*. Findlay, J.N., trans. Routledge.

Hutchins, E. (1995). *Cognition in the wild*. Cambridge, MA: The MIT Press.

IfM & IBM. (2007). *Succeeding through service innovation: A discussion paper*. Cambridge, United Kingdom: University of Cambridge Institute for Manufacturing.

International Disability Rights Monitor. (2004). *International disability rights monitor*. Chicago, IL: Center for International Rehabilitation.

International Disability Rights Monitor (IDRM). (2004). *International disability rights monitor*. Chicago, IL: Center for International Rehabilitation.

Jessup, L. M., Connolly, T., & Tansik, D. A. (1990). Toward a theory of automated group work: The deindividuating effects of anonymity. *Small Group Research*, *21*, 333–348. doi:10.1177/1046496490213003

Jokinen, K., & McTear, M. (2009). *Spoken dialogue systems*. San Rafael, CA: Morgan & Claypool Publishers.

Juszczyszyn, K. (2004). Knowledge sharing in agent's society with multiple ontologies. In (Ed.), International Series on Advanced Intelligence, Vol. 10, *Intelligent Technologies for Inconsistent Information Processing* (pp. 129-144). Australia: Advanced Knowledge International Ltd.

Kadushin, C. (2004). Basic network concepts: *Introduction to social network theory*. Retrieved on June 28, 2010, from http://home.earthlink.net/~ckadushin/.

Kalfoglou, Y., & Schorlemmer, M. (2003). Ontology mapping: The state of the art. *The Knowledge Engineering Review*, *18*(1), 1–31. doi:10.1017/S0269888903000651

Kalman, D. M. (2009). Brand communities, marketing, and media, *Terrella Media*. From http://www.terrella.com.

Kalt, C. (2000). Internet relay chat: Architecture. *Network Working Group / Internet Engineering Task Force Request for Comments: 2810*. April 2000.

Kampmeier, C., & Simon, B. (2001). Individuality and group formation: The role of independence and differentiation. *Journal of Personality and Social Psychology*, *81*(3), 448–462. doi:10.1037/0022-3514.81.3.448

Kapferer, J.-N. (1992). *Strategic brand management*. New York, NY: Free Press.

Keizer, G. (2005). Dutch Botnet bigger than expected. *TechWeb Technology News*. October 21, 2005.

Kiesler, S. (red.) (1997). Culture of the Internet. Mahwah, NJ: Erlbaum.

Kimble, C., Hildreth, P., & Wright, P. (2001). Communities of Practice: Going virtual. In Malhotra, Y. (Ed.), *Knowledge management and business model innovation* (pp. 220–234). Hershey, PA, USA: IGI Global.

Kimby, C. K. (2006). Communicating the breast cancer experience on the Internet – the shaping of patient identity. In H. Krause Hansen & J. Hoff (red.), Digital Governance://networked Societies. *Creating authority, community, and identity in a globalized world* (pp. 201-228). Frederiksberg, Denmark: Nordicom.

Kolko, B., Nakamura, L., & Rodman, G. (2000). *Race in Cyberspace*. New York, NY: Routledge.

Kolko, B., & Reid, E. (1998). Dissolution and fragmentation: Problems in online communities. In S. G. Jones (red.), *Cybersociety 2.0: Revisiting Computer-Mediated Communication and Community*. Thousand Oaks, CA: Sage.

Kollock, P. (1999). The economies of Online coopaeration. Gifts and public goods in Cyberspace". In M. Smith & P. Kollock (Ed.). *Communities in Cyberspace* (220-242). London, UK: Routledge.

Kozinets, R. (1999). E-tribalized marketing?: The strategic implications of virtual communities of consumption. *European Management Journal, 17*(3), 252–264. doi:10.1016/S0263-2373(99)00004-3

Krackhardt, D. (1994). Graph theoretical dimension of informal organizations. In Carley, K., & Prietula, M. (Eds.), *Computational organizational theories*. Hillsdale, NJ: Lawrence Erlbaum Associates, Inc.

Kreijns, K., Kirschner, P. A., & Jochems, W. (2002). The sociability of computer supported collaborative learning environments. *Journal of Educational Technology & Society, 5*(1), 822–837.

Kreijns, K., Kirschner, P. A., & Jochems, W. (2003). Identifying the pitfalls for social interaction in computer-supported collaborative learning environments: A review of the research. *Computers in Human Behavior, 19*, 335–353. doi:10.1016/S0747-5632(02)00057-2

Krippendorff, K. (2004). *Content analysis: An introduction to its methodology*. Thousand Oaks, CA: Sage.

Kumbasar, E., Romney, A. K., & Batchelder, W. H. (1994). Systematic biases in social perception. *American Journal of Sociology, 100*(2), 477–505. doi:10.1086/230544

Lacour, P. (2010). Portrait of the intellectual as a DJ: Wikipedia and the question of scientific expertise, *La Vie des Idées*, March 12, 2010. Retrieved November 15, 2010, from http://www.laviedesidees.fr/Portrait-of-the-intellectual-as-a.html

Latour, B. (2005). *Reassembling the social: An iIntroduction to actor-network theory*. Oxford, UK: Oxford UP.

Laurent, M., & Bretier, P. (2010). MPOWERS: A multi points of view evaluation refinement studio. In *SIGDIAL 2010, The 11th Annual SIGdial Meeting on Discourse and Dialogue*. Tokyo, Japan.

Laurent, M., Bretier, P., & Manquillet, C. (2010). Ad-hoc evaluations along the lifecycle of industrial spoken dialogue systems: Heading to harmonisation? In *LREC 2010: 7th International Conference on Language Resources and Evaluation*. Malta.

Laurent, M., Kanellos, I., & Bretier, P. (2010). Considering the subjectivity to rationalise evaluation approaches: The example of spoken dialogue systems. In *QoMEx '10, Second International Workshop on Quality of Multimedia Experience*. Trondheim, Norway.

Lave, J., & Wenger, E. (1991). *Situated learning: Legitimate peripheral participation*. Cambridge, MA: Cambridge University Press.

Lea, M., Spears, R., & de Groot, D. (2001). Knowing me, knowing you: Anonymity effects on social identity processes within groups. *Personality and Social Psychology Bulletin, 27*, 526–537. doi:10.1177/0146167201275002

Lee, F. S. L., Vogel, D., & Limayem, M. (2003). Virtual community informatics: A review and research agenda. *Journal of Information Technology and Application, 5*(1), 47–61.

Lenfle, S., & Midler, C. (2009). The launch of innovative product-related services: Lessons from automotive telematics. *Research Policy, 38*, 156–169. doi:10.1016/j.respol.2008.10.020

Lenfle, S. (2005). Innovation in services: The contributions of design theory. *Proceedings of the 11th International Product Development Management Conference*, Dublin, Ireland.

Lesser, E. L., & Storck, J. (2001). *Communities of practice and organizational performance*. Retrieved June 28, 2010, from http://research.ibm.com/journals/sj/404/lesser.html

Lessig, L. (2006). *Code: Version 2.0* (2nd ed.). New York, NY: Basic Books.

Lessig, L. (2009). In defense of piracy. *The Wall Street Journal* 16. September. Online im Internet: URL: http://online.wsj.com/ ar3cle/ SB122367645363324303.html [Last Accessed 2009-12-12]

Lévy, P. (2002). *Cyberdémocratie*. Paris, France: Odile Jacob.

Leyden, John (2004). Telenor takes down 'massive' Botnet. *Enterprise Security.* September 9, 2004.

Leyden, John (2005). ISPs urged to throttle spam zombies: International clean-up campaign. *The Register.* May 24, 2005.

Li, Z. (2009). Botnet Economics: Uncertainty Matters. In *Managing Information Risk and the Economics of Security* (pp. 245–267). Springer. doi:10.1007/978-0-387-09762-6_12

Li, X., et al. (2010). The growing model of Botnets. *2010 International Conference on Green Circuits and Systems (ICGCS), pp.* 414-419.

Licklider, J.C.R., & Vezza, Albert (1978). Applications of Information Networks. *Proceedings of the IEEE, 66.*

Lin, D. (1998). An information-theoretic definition of similarity. *International Conference on Machine Learning, ICML'98*, Madison, WI.

Linaa Jensen, J. (2006). *Den virtuelle kaffestue – deliberation og demokratisk inklusion i politiske debatter på internettet.* Århus, Denmark: Politica.

Linaa Jensen, J. (2008). Virtual tourist: Knowledge communication in an online travel community. *International Journal of Web-based Communities, 4*(4), 503–522. doi:10.1504/IJWBC.2008.019553

Linaa Jensen, J. (2010). Augmentation of space: Four dimensions of spatial experiences of Google Earth. *Space and Culture, 13*(1), 121–133. doi:10.1177/1206331209353693

Linaa Jensen, J. (2007). The Internet omonopticon. In H. Bang & A. Esmark (red.), *New publics with/out democracy* (pp. 351-380). København, Denmark: Samfundslitteratur Press/Nordicom.

Liu, H., Lim, E., Lauw, H. W., Le, M., Sun, A., Srivastava, J., & Kim, Y. (2008). Predicting trusts among users of online communities: An epinions case study. In *Proceedings of the 9th ACM Conference on Electronic Commerce* (Chicago, Il, USA, July 08 - 12, 2008). EC '08. ACM, New York, NY, 310-319.

LORINO, P. (2007). Communities of inquiry and knowledge creation in organizations: The process model in management. *Annals of Telecommunications, 62*(7/8: *Knowledge Management: Knowledge Networks)*, 753-771.

Lowe, D., Murray, S., Weber, L., & De la Villefromoy, M. (2009). LabShare: Towards a national approach to laboratory sharing, 20th Australian Association for Engineering Education Conference, University of Adelaide, 6-9 December 2009, pp. 458--463, 2009

Luan, J. (2002). Data mining and its applications in higher education. In Serban, A., & Luan, J. (Eds.), *Knowledge management: Building a competitive advantage for higher education. New Directions for Institutional Research, No. 113.* San Francisco, CA: Jossey Bass.

Ma, M., & Agarwal, R. (2007). Through a glass darkly: Information Technology design, identity verification, and knowledge contribution in online communities. *Information Systems Research, 18*(1), 42–67. doi:10.1287/isre.1070.0113

Ma, Y., Liu, B., Wong, C. K., Yu, P. S., & Lee, S. M. (2000). Targeting the right students using data mining, *Proceedings of the Sixth ACM SIGKDD International Conference on Knowledge Discovery and Data Mining (457-464)*, Boston, MA.

MacIntyre, A. (1981). *After Virtue.* Notre Dame, IN: University of Notre Dame Press.

Maedche, A., & Zacharias, V. (2002). *Clustering ontology-based metadata in the Semantic Web.* Berlin, Germany: Springer-Verlag.

Markham, A. (1998). *Life Online.* Walnut Creek, CA: AltaMira Press.

Marsden, C. (2008). Beyond europe: The Internet, regulation, and multistakeholder governance—Representing the consumer interest? [Springer.]. *Journal of Consumer Policy, 31*(1), 115–132. doi:10.1007/s10603-007-9056-z

Marsh, E. E., & White, M. D. (2006). Content analysis: A flexible methodology. *Library and Information Science, 55*(1), 22–45.

McDonald, M., Dorn, B., & McDonald, G. (2004). A statistical analysis of student performance in online computer science courses, Proceedings of the 35th SIGCSE Technical Symposium on Computer Science Education (71-74), Norfolk, Virginia.

McMillan, D. W., & Chavis, D. M. (1986). Sense of community: A definition and a theory. *Journal of Community Psychology, 14*, 6–23. doi:10.1002/1520-6629(198601)14:1<6::AID-JCOP2290140103>3.0.CO;2-I

McNulty, S. E., & Swann, W. B. Jr. (1994). Identity negotiation in roommate relationships: The self as architext and consequence of social reality. *Journal of Personality and Social Psychology, 67*(6), 1012–1023. doi:10.1037/0022-3514.67.6.1012

Mead, G. H. (1934). *Mind, self, and society*. Chicago, IL: University of Chicago Press.

Merali, Y., & Davies, J. (2001). *Knowledge capture and utilization in virtual communities*. Paper presented at the proceedings of the 1st International Conference on Knowledge Capture.

Midler, C. (1995). *L'auto qui n'existait pas, management des projets et transformation de l'entreprise*. Paris, France: InterEditions.

Miles, A., Rogers, N., & Beckett, D. (2004) *SKOS Core RDF Vocabulary*. <http:// www.w3.org/ 2004/ 02/ skos/ core/>

Milton, L. P., & Westphal, J. D. (2005). Identity confirmation networks and cooperation in work groups. *Academy of Management Journal, 48*(2), 191–212. doi:10.5465/AMJ.2005.16928393

Mitchell, J. (2002). *The potential for communities of practice to underpin the National Training Framework*. Melbourne, Australia: Australian National Training Authority.

Mitchell, W. J. (2000). *City of bits: Space, place, and the infobahn. 7. print*. Cambridge, MA: MIT Press.

Möller, S. (2005). *Quality of telephone-based spoken dialogue systems*. New York, NY: Springer-Verlag New York, Inc.

Morgan, R. M., & Hunt, S. D. (1994). The commitment trust theory of relationship marketing. *Journal of Marketing, 58*, 20–38. doi:10.2307/1252308

Morin, E. (1990). *Introduction à la pensée complexe, Communication et complexité*. Paris, France: ESF éditions.

Mullen, B., Brown, R. J., & Smith, C. (1992). Ingroup bias as a function of salience, relevance, and status: An integration. *European Journal of Social Psychology, 22*, 103–122. doi:10.1002/ejsp.2420220202

Muller, D., & Erbe, H. H. (2007). Collaborative remote laboratories in engineering education: Challenges and visions. In Gomes, L., & Garcia-Zubia, J. (Eds.), *Advances on remote laboratories and e-learning experiences* (pp. 35–59). University of Desto.

Muniz, A., & O'Guinn, T. (2001, March). Brand community. *The Journal of Consumer Research*, 412–432. doi:10.1086/319618

Muniz, A., & O'Guinn, T. (2005). Communal consumption and the brand. In Ratneshwar, S., & Mick, D. G. (Eds.), *Inside consumption. Consumer motives, goals, and desires*. New York, NY: Routledge.

Mykota, D., & Duncan, R. (2007). Learner characteristics ad predictors of online social presence. *Canadian Journal of Education, 30*(1), 157–170. doi:10.2307/20466630

Naphiet, J., & Ghoshal, S. (1998). Social capital, intellectual capital and the organizational advantage. *Academy of Management Review, 23*(2), 242–266.

Narbonne, Y. (2005). *Complexité et systémique*. London, UK; Paris, France: Hermès - Lavoisier.

Nelson, Th. H. (1999). Xanalogical structure needed now more than ever. *ACM Computing Surveys, 31*(4). ACM Press. Retrieved November 15, 2010, from http://www.cs.brown.edu/memex/ACM_HypertextTestbed/papers/60.html

Nonaka, I. (1991). The knowledge creating company. *Harvard Business Review, 69*, 96–104.

Nonaka, I., & Takeuchi, H. (1995). *The knowledge-creating company: How Japanese companies create the dynamics of Innovation*. New York, NY: Oxford University Press.

Nonnecke, B., & Preece, J. (2003). Silent participants: Getting to know lurkers better. In *C. Leug & D. Fisher (red.), From usenet to coWebs: Interacting with social enformation spaces*. Amsterdam, Netherlands: Springer-Verlag.

Northrup, P. (2001). A framework for designing interactivity into Web based instruction. *Educational Technology, 41*(2), 31–39.

Noy, N. F., & Musen, M. A. (2000). PROMPT: Algorithm and tool for automated ontology merging and alignment. *17th National Conference. On Artificial Intelligence*, Austin, TX, USA.

O'Hara, K. B., Beehr, T. A., & Colarelli, S. M. (1994). Organizational centrality: A third dimension of intraorganizational career movement. *The Journal of Applied Behavioral Science, 30*(2), 198–216. doi:10.1177/0021886394302004

Oakes, P. J., Haslam, S. A., Morrison, B., & Grace, D. (1995). Becoming an in-group: Reexamining the impact of familiarity on perceptions of group homogeneity. *Social Psychology Quarterly, 58*(1), 52–61. doi:10.2307/2787143

Oakes, P. J., Haslam, S. A., & Turner, J. C. (1994). *Stereotyping and social reality*. Oxford, UK: Blackwell.

Oakes, P. J. (1987). The salience of social categories. In Turner, J. C., Hogg, M. A., Oakes, P. J., Reicher, S. D., & Wetherell, M. S. (Eds.), *Rediscovering the social group: A self-categorization theory* (pp. 117–141). Oxford, UK: Blackwell.

Obst, P., & White, K. (2005). Three-dimensional strength of identification across group memberships: A confirmatory factor analysis. *Self and Identity, 4*, 69–80. doi:10.1080/13576500444000182

Obst, P., Zinkiewicz, L., & Smith, S. (2002). An exploration of sense of community, part 3: Dimensions and predictors of psychological sense of community in geographical communities. *Journal of Community Psychology, 30*(1), 119–133. doi:10.1002/jcop.1054

Obst, P. L., & White, K. M. (2005). An exploration of the interplay between psychological sense of community, social identification and salience. *Journal of Community & Applied Social Psychology, 15*, 127–135. doi:10.1002/casp.813

O'Reilly, T. (2005). What is Web 2.0: *Design Patterns and Business Models for the Next Generation of Software*. September 30, 2005. Retrieved November 15, 2010, from http://oreilly.com/web2/archive/what-is-web-20.html

Orr, J. E. (1991). *Talking about machines: An ethnography of a modern job*. Ithaca, NY: Cornell University Press.

Owens, D., Neale, M., & Sutton, R. (2000). Technologies of status management: Status dynamics In email communications. In Neale, M. A., Mannix, E. A., & Griffith, T. L. (Eds.), *Research on Groups and Teams* (*Vol. 3*, pp. 205–230). Greenwich, CT: JAI Press. doi:10.1016/S1534-0856(00)03011-5

Owyang, J. (2010). A collection of Social Network stats for 2010. *Web strategy* (http://www.web-strategist.com/blog/2010/01/19/ a-collection-of-social-network-stats-for-2010). Link checked November 4th 2010.

Paek, T. (2001). Empirical methods for evaluating dialog systems. In *Proceedings of the Second SIGdial Workshop on Discourse and Dialogue*. Aalborg, Denmark.

Palmer, J. W., & Speier, C. (1997) A typology of virtual organizations: An empirical study. In J. Gupta (Ed.), *Proceedings of the Association for Information Systems, America conference*, Indianapolis, IN, USA.

Parks, M. (2011). Social Network sites as virtual communities. In Zizi Papacharissi (Ed.). *The Networked self - identity, community and culture on Social Network sites* (105-123). New York, NY: Routledge.

Passeron, J.-C. (2006). *Le raisonnement sociologique. L'espace non-poppérien du raisonnement naturel*. Albin Michel.

Patterson, M., & O'Malley, L. (2006). Brands, consumers and relationships: A review. *Irish Marketing Review, 18*(1&2).

Patton, M. Q. (1987). *How to use qualitative methods in evaluation*. Newbury Park, CA: Sage.

Peng, X. (Michael) (2010, May 13). China's Social Networking scene: An inside update. *Internet evolution*. Link checked November 4th 2010. (http://www.internetevolution.com/ author.asp? section_id= 789&doc_id=191887&f _src=internetevolution_ gnews).

Pfeffer, J., & Hinds, P. J. (2003). Why organizations don't "know what they know": Cognitive and motivational factors affecting the transfer of expertise. In M. Ackerman, V. Pipek, & V Wulf (Eds.), *Sharing expertise: Beyond knowledge management* (3-26). Cambridge, MA: MIT Press.

Polanyi, M. (1966). *The tacit dimension*. London, UK: Routledge & Kegan.

Polzer, J. T., Milton, L. P., & Swann, W. B. Jr. (2002). Capitalizing on diversity: Interpersonal congruence in small work groups. *Administrative Science Quarterly*, *47*, 296–324. doi:10.2307/3094807

Popov, B., Kiryakov, A., Ognyano, D., Manov, D., & Kirilov, A. (2004). KIM: A semantic platform for information extraction and retrieval. *Natural Language Engineering*, *10*, 375–392. doi:10.1017/S135132490400347X

Post, G.V., & Kagan, A. (2007). Evaluating information security tradeoffs: Restricting access can interfere with user tasks. *Elsevier / Computers & Security. No. 26*, 229-237, 2007.

Postmes, T., Haslam, S. A., & Swaab, R. I. (2005). Social influence in small groups: An interactive model of social identity formation. *European Review of Social Psychology*, *16*, 1–42. doi:10.1080/10463280440000062

Postmes, T., & Spears, R. (1998). Deindividuation and antinormative behavior: A meta-analysis. *Psychological Bulletin*, *123*(3), 238–259. doi:10.1037/0033-2909.123.3.238

Postmes, T., Spears, R., & Lea, M. (1998). Breaching or building social boundaries? SIDE-effects of computer-mediated communication. *Communication Research*, *25*(6), 689–715. doi:10.1177/009365098025006006

Prax, J.-Y. (2003). *Le manuel du knowledge management: Une approche de 2e génération*. Dunod.

Preece, J. (2000). *Online communities. Designing usability, suporting sociability*. Chichester West Sussex, UK: John Wiley and Sons Ltd Baffins Lane.

Pruitt, D. G., & Carnevale, P. J. (1993). *Negotiation in social conflict*. Milton Keynes, UK: Open University Press.

Pruitt, D. G., & Rubin, J. Z. (1986). *Social conflict: Escalation, stalemate and settlement*. New York, NY: McGraw-Hill.

Prykop, C., & Heitman, M. (2006). Designing mobile brand communities: Concept and empirical illustration. *Journal of Organizational Computing and Electronic Commerce*, *16*(3/4), 301–323.

Puddifoot, J. (1995). Dimensions of community identity. *Journal of Community & Applied Social Psychology*, *5*, 357–370. doi:10.1002/casp.2450050507

Puddifoot, J. E. (2003). Exploring personal and shared sense of community identity in Durham city, England. *Journal of Community Psychology*, *31*(1), 87–106. doi:10.1002/jcop.10039

Putnam, R. D. (1995). Bowling alone: America's declining social capital. *Journal of Democracy*, *6*(1), 65–78. doi:10.1353/jod.1995.0002

Putnam, R. (2000). *Bowling alone*. New York, NY: Simon & Schuster.

Quinn, G., & Degener, T. (Eds.). (2002). *Human rights and disability: The current use and future potential of United Nations human rights instruments in the context of disability*. Geneva, Switzerland: United Nations, Office of the High Commissioner for Human Rights.

Ragan, C. L., & Tello, S. (2005, November 17). Building the learning community community: The power of online learning. Orlando, Florida, USA: Sloan-C International Conference.

Ramesh, B., & Tiwana, A. (1999). Supporting collaborative process knowledge management in new product development teams. *Decision Support Systems*, *27*(1-2), 213–235. doi:10.1016/S0167-9236(99)00045-7

Ranjan, J., & Malik, K. (2007). Effective educational process: A Data Mining Approach. *Vine*, *37*(4), 502–515. doi:10.1108/03055720710838551

Rapid-i.com. (2008). *Rapid-i*: Rapid Intelligence, Rapid Solutions. Retrieved on June 10, 2008

Rastier, F. (1998). *Sens et signification*. Protée, printemps 1998, 7–18.

Rastier, F. (2007). La traduction: *Interprétation et genèse du sens. Revue Texto!* Retrieved November 15, 2010, from http://www.revue-texto.net/index.php?id=2202

Reger, R. K., Gustafson, L. T., DeMarie, S. M., & Mullane, J. V. (1994). Reframing the organization: Why implementing total quality is easier said than done. *Academy of Management Review*, *19*, 565–584.

Reid, E. M. (1999). Hierarchy and power. Social control in Cyberspace. In *M. A. Smith & P. Kollock (red.), Communities in Cyberspace* (pp. 107–133). New York, NY: Routledge.

Resnik, P. (1999). Semantic similarity in a taxonomy: An information-based measure and its application to problems of ambiguity in natural language. *Journal of Artificial Intelligence Research, 1*, 95–130.

Rheingold, H. (1993). *The virtual community: Homesteading on the electronic frontier*. Reading, Massachusetts: MIT Press.

Rheingold, H. (2000). *The virtual community: Homesteading on the electronic frontier*. London, UK: MIT Press.

Rheingold, H. (2002). *Smart mobs: The next social revolution*. Cambridge, Mass.: Perseus.

Rioux, M. (1997). Disability: The place of judgment in a world of fact. *Journal of Intellectual Disability Research, 4*(1), 102–111. doi:10.1111/j.1365-2788.1997.tb00686.x

Rioux, M. (2001). Bending towards justice. In Barton, L. (Ed.), *Disability, politics and the struggle for change*. London, UK: David Fulton Publishers.

Rittel, H. & Kunz. W. (1970) *Issues as elements of information systems. Working Paper* 131. Berkeley Ca, USA: University of California Center for Planning and Development Research.

Roberts, K. (2006). *Lovemarks. The future beyond brands. Saatchi & Saatchi Designer Edition*. Brooklyn, NY: Powerhouse Books.

Rourke, L., Anderson, T., Garrison, D. R., & Archer, W. (2001). Methodological issues in the content analysis of computer conference transcripts. *International Journal of Artificial Intelligence in Education, 12*(1), 8–22.

Rourke, L., Anderson, T., Garrison, D. R., & Archer, W. (2001). Assessing social presence in screen text-based computer conferencing. *Journal of Distance Education, 14*. Available at http://auspace.athabascau.ca: 8080/ dspace/bitstream/2149/732/1/ Assessing%20Social%20 Presence%20In%20 Asynchronous%20Text-based%20 Computer%20 Conferencing.pdf.

Ryan, R. M., & Deci, E. L. (2001). To be happy or to be self-fulfilled: A review of research on hedonic and eudaimonic well-being. *Annual Review of Psychology, 52*, 141–166. doi:10.1146/annurev.psych.52.1.141

Saillot, I., Patou-Mathis, M., Richard, J. F., Sander, E., & Poitrenaud, S. (2002). Modéliser les activités cognitives des Hommes au Paléolithique. *Mathematiques et Sciences Humaines,* 159.

Saltzer, Jerome H., & David P. (1984). End-to-end arguments in system design. *ACM transactions on computer science*, 277–278.

Sassenberg, K., & Postmes, T. (2002). Cognitive and strategic processes in small groups: Effects of anonymity of the self and anonymity of the group on social influence. *The British Journal of Social Psychology, 41*, 463–480. doi:10.1348/014466602760344313

Savourel, Y. (2005, April 26). TMX 1.4b specification. OS-CAR recommendation. *Localisation industry standards association*. Retrieved November 15, 2010, from http:// www.lisa.org/ fileadmin/ standards/ tmx1.4/ tmx.htm

Sawhney, M., & Prandelli, E. (2000, Summer). Communities of creation: Managing distributed innovation in turbulent markets. *California Management Review, 42*(4).

Schau, H. J., Muniz, A. M. Jr, & Arnould, E. J. (2009). How brand community practices create value. *Journal of Marketing, 73*, 30–51. doi:10.1509/jmkg.73.5.30

Schubert, P. (1999). *Aufbau und management virtueller Geschäftsgemeinschaften in electronic commerce Umgebungen*. St. Gallen: Dissertation.

Schuler, D. (1996). *New community Networks. Wired for change*. New York, NY: Alklison-Weslery. Available online at http://www.scn.org/ncn/. Link checked November 4th 2010.

Schultz, F., & Pucher, H. F. (2003). Wissensmanagement bei Wolkswagen. *Industrie Management, 19*(3), 64–66.

Scott, S. G., & Lane, V. R. (2000). A stakeholder approach to organizational identity. *Academy of Management Review, 25*(1), 43–62.

Seibt, J. (2009). Forms of emergent interaction in general process theory. *Synthese, 166*, 479–512. doi:10.1007/ s11229-008-9373-z

Semprini, A. (1992). *Le marketing de la marque*. Parigi, Liaisons.

Serrano Núñez, Y. S. (2005). Assessing faculty's social presence indicators in online courses at the Inter American University of Puerto Rico, Bayamón Campus. *Focus (San Francisco, Calif.)*, *4*(1), 47–49.

Shakespeare, T. (1999). What is a Disabled Person? In Jones, M., & Marks, L. B. (Eds.), *Disabilty, diversAbility and legal change* (pp. 25–35). The Hague, Netherlands: Martinus Nijhoff Publishers.

Shaw, M., & Gaines, B. R. (1989). Comparing conceptual structures: Consensus, conflict, correspondence and contrast. *Knowledge Acquisition*, *1*(4), 341–363. doi:10.1016/S1042-8143(89)80010-X

Shen, K. N., & Khalifa, M. (2010, June 6-9th). *Explaining virtual community participation: Accounting for the IT artifacts through identification and identity confirmation.* Paper presented at the The 18th European Conference on Information Systems, Pretoria, South Africa.

Shneiderman, B. (2000). Designing trust into online experiences. *Communications of the ACM, 43*(12), December 2000.

Short, J., Williams, E., & Christie, B. (1976). *The Social Psychology of Telecommunications.* London, UK: Wiley.

Shyamala, K., & Rajagopalan, S. P. (2006). Data mining model for a better higher educational system. *Information Technology Journal*, *5*(3), 560–564. doi:10.3923/itj.2006.560.564

Silva, N., & Rocha, J. (2003). Semantic Web complex ontology mapping. Proceedings of the *IEEE/WIC International Conference on Web Intelligence.* Porto, Portugal.

Simon, B., Aufderheide, B., & Hastedt, C. (2000). The double negative effect: The (almost) paradoxical role of the indiviudal self in minority and majority members' information processing. *The British Journal of Social Psychology*, *39*, 73–93. doi:10.1348/014466600164345

Simon, B., & Brown, R. (1987). Perceived intragroup homogeneity in minority-majority contexts. *Journal of Personality and Social Psychology*, *53*(4), 703–711. doi:10.1037/0022-3514.53.4.703

Simon, H. A. (1955). On a class of skew distribution functions. *Biometrika, 42*(¾), 425–440.

Smith, E. R., & Henry, S. (1996). An ingroup becomes part of the self: Response time evidence. *Personality and Social Psychology Bulletin*, *22*, 635–642. doi:10.1177/0146167296226008

Smith, S. G., Zinkiewicz, L., & Ryall, C. T. (1999). Sense of community: Yet another group identification? *Australian Journal of Psychology*, *51*, 18.

Smith, M., & Kollock, P. (1999). "Communities in Cyberspace. In M. Smith & P. Kollock (ed.). Communities in Cyberspace (3-27). London, UK: Routledge.

Soulier, E. (2004). Les communautés de pratique pour la gestion des connaissances. In *Management des connaisances en entreprise*, 149-179. Paris, France: Lavoisier.

Soulier, E. (2009). Storytelling, plateformes sociales et ontologies de processus pour la simulation du mouvement. *Habilation à diriger des recherches.*

Spears, R., Lea, M., Corneliussen, R. A., Postmes, T., & Haar, W. T. (2002). Computer-mediated communication as a channel for social resistance: The strategic side of SIDE. *Small Group Research*, *33*(5), 555–574. doi:10.1177/104649602237170

Spohrer, J., Maglio, P., Bailey, J., & Gruhl, D. (2007). Steps toward a science of service systems. *IEEE Computer*, *40*(1), 71–77.

Sproull, L., & Faraj, S. (1995). Atheism, sex, and databases: The Net as a social technology. In Brian Kahin & James Keller (Eds.). *Public Access to the Internet* (62-81). Cambridge, UK: The MIT Press

Staab, S. (2002). Emergent semantics. *IEEE Intelligent Systems*, 78–86. doi:10.1109/5254.988491

Stein, A., Hawking, P., & Sharma, P. (2005). *A classification of u-commerce location based tourism applications.* Paper presented at the 11th Australasian World Wide Web Conference (AUSWeb05).

Stinchcombe, A. L. (1990). *Information and Organizations.* Berkley, CA: University of California Press.

Stone, A. R. (1991). Will the real body please stand up?: Boundary stories about virtual cultures. In *M. Benedikt (red.), Cyberspace: First steps.* Cambridge, UK: MIT Press).

Stuckenschmidt, H., & Timm, I. (2002). Adaptation of communication vocabularies using shared ontologies. Proceedings of the *Second International Workshop on Ontologies in Agent Systems (OAS)*. Bologna, Italy.

Stufflebeam, D. I. (1980). *L'évaluation en éducation et la prise de décision*. Ottawa, Canada: Edition NHP.

Sudweeks, F., & Simoff, S. (1999). Complementary explorative data analysis, the reconciliation of quantitative and qualitative principles. In Jones, S. (Ed.), *Doing Internet research: Critical issues and methods for examining the Net*. Thousand Oaks, CA: Sage Publications.

Sundén, J. (2003). *Material virtualities: Approaching Online textual embodiment*. New York, NY: Peter Lang Publishing.

Surowiecki, J. (2005). *The wisdom of crowds* (Books, A., Ed.). Reprinted 2005

Swann, W. B. Jr. (1987). Identity negotiation: Where two roads meet. *Journal of Personality and Social Psychology*, *53*(6), 1038–1051. doi:10.1037/0022-3514.53.6.1038

Swann, W. B. Jr, De La Ronde, C., & Hixon, J. G. (1994). Authenticity and positivity strivings in marriage and courtship. *Journal of Personality and Social Psychology*, *66*, 857–869. doi:10.1037/0022-3514.66.5.857

Swann, W. B. Jr, & Read, S. J. (1981). Acquiring self-knowledge: The search for feedback that fits. *Journal of Personality and Social Psychology*, *41*, 1119–1128. doi:10.1037/0022-3514.41.6.1119

Swann, W. B. Jr, Rentfrow, P. J., & Guinn, J. S. (2003). Self-verification: The search for coherence. In Leary, M. R., & Tangney, J. P. (Eds.), *Handbook of Self and Identity* (pp. 367–383). New York, NY: Guilford Press.

Tajfel, H. (1978). *Differentiation between social groups: Studies in the social psychology of intergroup relations*. London, UK: Academic Press.

Tajfel, H. (1972). La categorisation sociale (Social categorization). In Moscovici, S. (Ed.), *Introduction a la Psychologie Sociale* (pp. 272–302). Paris, France: Larouse.

Tajfel, H., & Turner, J. C. (1986). The social identity theory of intergroup behavior. In Worchel, S., & Austin, L. W. (Eds.), *Psychology of intergroup relations* (2nd ed., pp. 7–24). Chicago, IL: Nelson-Hall.

Talavera, L., & Gaudioso, E. (2004). Mining student data to characterize similar behavior groups in unstructured collaboration spaces, *presented at Workshop on Artificial Intelligence in Computer Supported Collaborative Learning at European Conference on Artificial Intelligence*, Valencia, Spain, pp *17-23*.

Tanis, M., & Postmes, T. (2003). Social cues and impression formation in CMC. *The Journal of Communication*, *53*(4), 676–693. doi:10.1111/j.1460-2466.2003.tb02917.x

Tannery, F. (2001). Le management stratégique des services: Synthèse bibliographique et repérage des questions génériques. *Finance Contrôle Stratégie*, *4*(2), 215–259.

TechCrunch. (2008). http://www.techcrunch.com/ 2008/12/31/ top-social-media-sites-of-2008 -facebook-still -rising/. Retrieved November 4th 2010

Thomas, C. (2002). Disability theory: Key ideas, issues and thinkers. In Barnes, C., Oliver, M., & Barton, L. (Eds.), *Disability studies today* (pp. 38–57). Cambridge, UK: Polity Press.

Thomson, I. (2008). *Enterprise security software market booms. vnunet.com*. June 18, 2008. http:// www.vnunet. com/ vnunet/ news/ 2219275/ enterprise-software-market

Tichy, N., Tushman, M., & Fombrun, L. (1979). Social network analysis for organizations. *Academy of Management Review*, *4*(4), 507–519.

Tiwana, A., & Bush, A. A. (2005). Continuance in expertise-sharing networks: A social perspective. *IEEE Transactions on Engineering Management*, *52*(1), 85–101. doi:10.1109/TEM.2004.839956

Tönnies. Ferdinand (1887). *Gemeinschaft und Gesellschaft*. Leipzig: Fues's Verlag (reprint 2005, Darmstadt: Wissenschaftliche Buchgesellschaft)

Tu, C.-H., & McIsaac, M. (2002). The relationship of social presence and interaction in online classes. *American Journal of Distance Education*, *16*(3), 131–150. doi:10.1207/S15389286AJDE1603_2

Tuckman, B. (1965). Developmental sequence in small groups. *Psychological Bulletin*, *63*(6), 384–399. doi:10.1037/h0022100

Tudge, J. R. H. (1992). Processes and consequences of peer collaboration: A Vygotskian analysis. *Child Development*, *63*(6), 1364–1379. doi:10.2307/1131562

Turkle, S. (1995). *Life on the screen*. New York, NY: Simon & Schuster.

Turner, J. C. (1991). *Social Influence*. Milton Keynes, UK: Open University Press.

Turner, J. C., Hogg, M. A., Oakes, P. J., Reicher, S. D., & Wetherell, M. S. (1987). *Rediscovering the social group: A self-categorization theory*. Oxford, UK: Blackwell.

Turner, J. C. (1985). Social categorization and the self-concept: A social cognitive theory of group behavior. In Lawler, E. J. (Ed.), *Advances in Group Processes* (*Vol. 2*, pp. 77–122). Greenwich, CT: JAI Press.

Turner, J. C. (1982). Towards a cognitive redefinition of the social group. In Tajfel, H. (Ed.), *Social identity and intergroup relations* (pp. 15–40). Cambridge, UK: Cambridge University Press.

Tyler, J., Wilkinson, D., & Huberman, B. (2003). *Email as spectroscopy: Automated discovery of community structure within organizations*. Palo Alto, CA: HP Laboratories.

Tyler, T. R., & Smith, H. J. (1999). Justice, social identity, and group processes. In Tyler, T. R., Kramer, R., & John, O. P. (Eds.), *The psychology of the social self*. Mahwah, NJ: Erlbaum.

U.S. Department of Health and Human Services. (2008). Research-based Web design & usability guidelines. Retrieved June 13, 2008, from http://www.usability.gov / pdfs/guidelines.html

Van Brakel, P. S. (2010). Mentoring doctoral students within a virtual community of practice - With special reference to their information recording behaviour. *Proceedings of Informing Science & IT Education Conference* (pp. 439-448). InSITE.

Varzi, A.C. (2003-2009). *Standford Encyclopedia of Philosophy Mereology*.

Vinay M. Igure, Ronald D. Williams (2008). Taxonomies of Attacks and Vulnerabilities in Computer Systems. *IEEE Communications Surveys & Tutorials*. 1st Quarter 2008.

Vinck, D., Jeantet, A., & Laureillard, P. (1996). Objects and other intermediaries in the sociotechnical process of product design: An exploratory approach. In J. Perrin & D. Vinck (Eds.), *The Role of Design in the Shaping of Technology: Vol.5* (pp.297-320*), COST A4 Social Sciences*. Bruxelles: EC Directorate General Science R&D.

Virilio, P. (1998). *Cyberworld. Det værstes politik*. København, Denmark: Introíte Publishers.

Waiyamai, K. (2004). Improving quality of graduate students by data mining, Faculty of Engineering, Kasetsart University, *Frontiers of ICT Research International Symposium*.

Walker, M. A., Litman, D. J., Kamm, C. A., & Abella, A. (1997). PARADISE: A framework for evaluating spoken dialogue agents. In *Proceedings of the 35th Annual Meeting of the Association for Computational Linguistics* (ACL-97), 271–280. Madrid, Spain.

Walzer, M. (1983). *Spheres of Justice*. New York: Basic Books.

Wassermann, S., & Faust, K. (1994). *Social network analysis: Methods and applications*. New York, NY: Cambridge University Press.

Weber, T. (2007). Criminals 'may overwhelm the Web'. *BBC News website*. January 25, 2007. Wikipedia. *Governance*. URL: http:// en.wikipedia.org/ wiki/ Governance [Last Accessed 2010-03-11]

Weissman, D. (2000). *A social ontology*. New Haven, CT: Yale University Press.

Wellman, B. (1996). Computer networks as social networks: Collaborative work, telework, and virtual community. *Annual Review of Sociology*, *22*(8), 213–238. doi:10.1146/annurev.soc.22.1.213

Wellman, B., & Gulia, M. (1999). Net-surfers don't ride alone: Virtual communities as communities. In *Barry Wellman (red.), Networks in the global village*. Boulder, CO: Westview.

Wenger, E. (1998). *Communities of practice: Learning, meaning, and identity*. New York, NY: Cambridge University Press.

Wenger, E., McDermott, R., & Snyder, W. M. (2002). *Cultivating communities of practice: A guide to managing knowledge, 1 edition.* Boston, MA: Harvard Business Press.

Wenger, E. C., & Snyder, W. M. (2000). Communities of practice: The organizational frontier. *Harvard Business Review, 78*(1), 139–145.

Wenger, E. (2006). *Communities of practice - A brief introduction.* Available at: http://www.ewenger.com/theory/ index.htm.

Whetten, D. A., Lewis, D., & Mischel, L. J. (1992). *Towards an integrated model of organizational identity and member commitment.* Paper presented at the the Academy of Management, Las Vegas, NV.

White, D. R., & Harary, F. (2001). The cohesiveness of blocks in social networks: Node connectivity and conditional density. *Sociological Methodology, 31*(1), 305–359. doi:10.1111/0081-1750.00098

Whitehead, A. N. (1929). *Process and Reality.* New York, NY: Macmillan.

Whittaker, S., Isaacs, E., & O'Day, V. (1997). Widening the Net. In *SIGCHI Bulletin, 29.* New York, NY: ACM Press.

Whittaker, S., & Sidner, C. (1996). Email overload: Exploring personal information management of email, *Proceedings of CHI* (276-283). ACM Press

Widyantoro, D. H., Loerger, T. R., & Yen, J. (2001). Learning user interest dynamics with a three-descriptor representation. *Journal of the American Society for Information Science and Technology, 52*(3), 212–225. doi:10.1002/1532-2890(2000)9999:9999<::AID-ASI1615>3.0.CO;2-O

Wiesenfeld, B. M., Raghuram, S., & Garud, R. (2001). Organizational identification among virtual workers: The role of need for affiliation and perceived work-based social support. *Journal of Management, 27,* 213–229.

Wikipedia (2010). Entries on *"community"* and *"Orkut".*

Wilhelm, A. (2000). *Democracy in the digital age: Challenges to political life in Cyberspace.* New York, NY: Routledge.

Williams, R. L., & Cothrel, J. (2000). Four smart ways to run online communities. *Sloan Management Review, 41*(4), 81–91.

Wilson, T., Wiebe, J., & Hoffmann, P. (2005). Recognizing contextual polarity in phrase-level sentiment analysis, *Proceedings of the 2005 Conference on Empirical Methods in Natural Language Processing (EMNLP),* (pp. 347–354).

Winston, M. E., Chaffin, R., & Herrmann, D. (1987). A Taxonomy of Part-Whole Relations. *Cognitive Science, 11*(4). doi:10.1207/s15516709cog1104_2

Witten, I., & Frank, E. (2005). *Data mining: practical machine learning tools and techniques.* Elsevier.

World Wide Web Consortium. (2008). Web content accessibility guidelines. Retrieved on June 13, 2008, from http://www.w3.org/TR/WCAG20/

Wray, R. (2005). EU says Internet could fall apart. *The Guardian,* October 12, 2005. http:// echnology.guardian.co.uk/ news/ story/ 0,16559,1589967,00.html

Xiaobin, F., Jay Budzik, H., & Kristian, J. (2000). *Mining navigation history for recommendation.* Paper presented at the International Conference on Intelligent User Interfaces.

Yu, S., Al-Jadir, L., & Spaccapietra, S. (May 9, 2005). *Matching user's semantics with data semantics in location-based services.* Paper presented at the 1st Workshop on Semantics in Mobile Environments (SME 05) in conjunction with MDM 2005, Ayia Napa, Cyprus.

Zimbardo, P. G. (1969). The human choice: Individuation, reason, and order vs. deindividuation, impulse and chaos. In W. J. Arnold & D. Levine (Eds.), *Nebraska Symposium on Motivation* (Vol. 17, pp. 237-307). Lincoln, NE: University of Nebraska Press.

Zimitat, C. (2007). Capturing community of practice knowledge for student learning. *Innovations in Education and Teaching International, 44*(3), 321–330. doi:10.1080/14703290701486753

About the Contributors

Christo El Morr received a PhD in Biomedical Engineering, Compiègne University of Technology-France, 1997). He is an adjunct Professor of Health Informatics at York University, Canada; and an Assistant Professor of information Systems at the American University of Kuwait, Kuwait. His research interests are cross-disciplinary in Virtual Communities, e-Health, e-Collaboration, PACS and Health Information Systems integration.

Pierre Maret received a Ph.D. in computer science in 1995. He is presently a professor at the University of Lyon in Saint Etienne, France. His research interests are in virtual communities, social networks, context awareness and knowledge modeling.

* * *

Terje Aaberge graduated from the University of Geneva in 1975 in mathematical physics. He was employed by Department of Theoretical Physics at this university from 1973 to 1982 and has since and until 2005 been visiting researcher at the department. During this time he has authored more than 20 research papers mainly on problems concerning the axiomatic of or the modelling in the theory of special relativity, quantum physics, continuum dynamics and thermodynamics. He was employed in the private sector from 1983 to 1992 and is at Western Norway Research Institute since 1992. He has worked on best practice methods of information retrieval and dissemination on the Internet. He is now primarily working in the domains of logic and semantic technologies.

Rajendra Akerkar is a senior researcher at Western Norway Research Institute, Norway. His research and teaching (Masters & PhD level) experience includes over 18 years in the Academia spanning different universities in Asia, Europe and North America. He has vast experience of coordinating large scale international research activities through Technomathematics Research Foundation, Kolhapur, India. He serves on the editorial board of over 6 international journals. He is the editor-in-chief of 'International Journal of Computer Science & Applications'. He is also an associate editor of "International Journal of Metadata, Semantics and Ontologies". He has been working on semantic technologies, knowledge representation and reasoning, Web intelligence, with applications to various real world problems. He has authored/co-authored 12 books and more than 90 research articles.

Aurélien Bénel is an associate professor of computer science at an interdisciplinary CSCW laboratory in Troyes (France). His research interests focus on 'digital hermeneutics'. He aims at providing knowledge and cooperation models, along with computer-human interfaces that could fit the methods, theories and practices of humanities and social sciences. This resulted in a set of hypermedia software applications that are used in archaeology, history of art, and sociology.

Constanța-Nicoleta Bodea is professor at the Academy of Economic Study Bucharest (ASE), Faculty of Cybernetics, Statistics and Economic Informatics, Economic Informatics Department. Currently, she teaches Artificial Intelligence, Data Mining and Project Management. She coordinates numerous research projects at national level and achieved a high expertise in managing projects with multiple consortia. She is author of 11 books and more than 50 papers on Project Management, Information Systems, and Artificial Intelligence, being honored by IPMA with the Outstanding Research Contributions in 2007.

Florie Bugeaud is a graduate of the University of Paris 5 (Descartes) in Computer Science Methods applied to Business Management (MIAGE). She is a PhD student in Computer Science at the University of Technology of Troyes (Tech-CICO laboratory - Cooperative Technologies for Innovation and Organizational Changes) and the Orange Labs (R&D center – Services for Enterprises). She is working on the modeling and the simulation of Services Systems. Her activities aim at the specification of the service concept, in the telecoms innovation field, and the support of the innovators' network during their research for innovative services ideas.

Michael Callaghan is a Senior Lecturer in the School of Computing and Intelligent Systems at the University of Ulster, Northern Ireland. He holds a Bachelor of Technology in Electronic Engineering and a Master's of Science in Computing and Design, and is a member of the IEEE and ACM. He is a distinguished fellow of the University of Ulster and currently leads the Serious Games and Virtual Worlds research team at the Intelligent Systems Research Centre (ISRC).

Geoff Cox is currently a Researcher in Digital Aesthetics as part of the Digital Urban Living Research Center, Aarhus University (DK). He is also an occasional artist, and Associate Curator of Online Projects, Arnolfini, Bristol (UK), adjunct faculty, Transart Institute, Berlin/New York (DE/US), Associate Professor (Reader), University of Plymouth (UK), where he is part of KURATOR/Art and Social Technologies Research group. He is an editor for the DATA Browser book series (published by Autonomedia, New York), and co-edited 'Economising Culture' (2004), 'Engineering Culture' (2005) and 'Creating Insecurity' (2009). He is working on a new book with the tentative title 'Coding Praxis'.

Maria-Iuliana Dascălu has a Master Degree in Project Management from the Academy of Economic Studies, Bucharest, Romania (2008) and a Bachelor Degree in Computer Science from the Alexandru-Ioan Cuza University, Iasi, Romania (2006). She is a PhD student in Economic Informatics at the Academy of Economic Studies, combining her work experience as a programmer with numerous research activities. Her research relates to computer-assisted testing with applications in e-learning environments for project management, competences development systems and their benefits to adult education. Maria Dascălu is a Certified Project Management Associate (2008). She also conducted a research stage at the University of Gothenburg, Sweden, from October 2009 to May 2010.

Marco De Maggio has a PhD in "e-business" at eBusiness Management Section of Scuola Superiore ISUFI - University of Salento, Italy. His research field concerns the development of Methodologies for the analysis and management of Organizational Learning Patterns inside Organizations and Communities of Practice. His focus is mainly on the development of tools and methodologies for the monitoring of the organizational behavior responsible for Social Capital creation. Visiting Scholar at MIT – Boston, MA, he experimented the application of Content and Social Network analysis supported by computer-aided systems for the improvement in the analysis of Virtual Communities

Mihaela Dinca is a statistical consultant and coordinator of the Disability Rights Promotion International Canada (DRPI-Canada) project. Over the last 12 years, she has conducted several research projects in biomedical field, population health, and environmental risk assessment and has been involved in WHO projects in community health. Throughout her involvement with these projects, she designed and implemented methodological frameworks and conducted complex statistical analyses on data from several population surveys and complex sample designs (e.g. Canadian Ethnic Diversity Survey (EDS); National Survey of Giving, Volunteering and Participating (NSGVP); Participation and Activity Limitation Survey (PALS); Canadian Community Health Survey (CCHS) and National Population Health Survey (NPHS)). Mihaela has published in the area of literacy and disability, social determinants of health, ecosystem modeling, and biomedical field. She received her B.Sc. from University of Bucharest, Romania and her M.A.Sc. from Ryerson University, Canada.

Paola Falcone received a Ph.D. in Marketing from the University of Rome "La Sapienza" and now is Lecturer of the Marketing Lab for public institutions and firms for the Faculty of Communication Sciences. She is also Lecturer of Research Methods and Communication for health Organizations for the Faculty of Medicine and Surgery in the same University. She is Marketing and Communication trainer for firms, public and not-for profit organizations. Her research interests include service marketing, internet marketing and communication through the new media (with specific focus on online communities), marketing networks for small organizations. A part of her research has been specifically focused on not-for-profit organizations. She is Director of the Research and Training Division of the CRC in Rome.

Christophe Gravier is a researcher (Chargé de Recherche) at University of Saint-Etienne, from which he received his PhD in Computer Science after a Master of Science in Telecommunications, Networks and Services from INSA de Lyon. His ongoing research focuses on adaptive systems and semantic technologies in Online Engineering and Next Generation Networks. Since 2009, he has been the Vice-President of Academic Relations and Research of the International Association of Online Engineering.

Francesca Grippa is a researcher in Knowledge Management at the eBusiness Management Section, Scuola Superiore ISUFI, University of Salento, Italy. Her current research interest is in applying Social Network Analysis to monitoring learning communities. She holds a PhD in e-Business, discussing a thesis on a methodology to measure social networks implied by different communication media. She got her Master's Degree in Business Management at eBMS-ISUFI, Italy. She is also interested in integrating Knowledge Management and e-Learning Strategies.

Jakob Linaa Jensen (M.A. politics, Ph.D.) is associate professor at the Department of Information and Media Studies, University of Aarhus, Denmark. He has published three books and numerous international articles on social formations online, specifically social media, political participation and the public sphere in the digital age and tourism practices online and offline. His most recent research project addresses mediatization and cultural citizenship, how digital media affects patterns of consumption, citizenry and political participation in the 21st century.

Martin Knahl is currently a Professor at the University of Applied Sciences Furtwangen, Germany. He is a Research Fellow at the Centre for Information Security and Control at the University of Plymouth, UK. His research interests are in the areas of IT Management and Internet Governance.

Philippe Lacour is a graduate from the Ecole Normale Supérieure in Paris. He holds the French National Teaching Degree ("agrégation"), a PhD in Philosophy and a Master's Degree in Legal Theory. He taught and studied in various universities abroad (USA, Italy, Germany, Belgium). He is currently an Assistant Professor at the Institut d'Etudes Politiques in Paris, a member of the International Center for the study of Contemporary French Philosophy (CIEPFC, ENS Paris) and the co-director of the Translation Studies section at the Centre Marc Bloch in Berlin. His main research topics include philosophy of language, epistemology of human sciences, social theory and normative philosophy (contemporary theories of Justice). He also has a genuine interest for Translation Studies, from a philosophical, legal and technological perspective. He runs an NGO which has been developping for four years a digital environment dedicated to the collaborative translation of cultural texts: Tradu Xio.

Marianne Laurent joined the Orange Labs in Lannion, France, as a Ph.D. student in 2008. After a Master in Management from Grenoble Ecole de Management, she graduated in 2007 with a Master of Engineering from Telecom Bretagne. Her studies, both technical and managerial, mainly focused on the Management of Enterprise Information Systems. She started her career in IS project management within Thales in the UK before she joined the dialog team of Orange. Her thesis, supervised by Philippe Bretier (Orange Labs) and Ioannis Kanellos (Telecom Bretagne), is an exploratory work on the evaluation of Spoken Dialogue Systems. She tends to understand heuristics guiding the design of evaluation with reference to decision-making situations.

Radu Ioan Mogos is a PhD student at the Faculty of Cybernetics, Statistics and Economic IT, Bucharest Academy of Economic Studies. He is working as IT analyst at the IT Department. He is a member of the Romania Project Management Association. Research domains include artificial intelligence and project management. He is author of one book and is project member in several projects.

Marcia Rioux At York University, Toronto, Marcia Rioux is a Professor in the School of Health Policy and Management; in the MA and PhD(Critical Disability Studies and in the M.A./PhD in Health Policy and Equity. She is as well the Director of the York UniversityInstitute of Health Research. She teaches a core course in the newly inaugurated PhD (Critical Disability Studies) at the University of Zagreb, Croatia. With Bengt Lindqvist, she is the co-Director of Disability Rights Promotion International, a multi-year project to monitor disability rights nationally and internationally. Professor Rioux's research includes health and human rights, universal education, international monitoring of disability rights, the impact of globalization on welfare policy, literacy policy, disability policy, and social inclusion. Dr. Rioux has lectured throughout the Americas, Europe, Africa and Asia. She has been an advisor to federal and provincial commissions, parliamentary committees, and international NGO's as well as United Nations agencies. She has edited a number of collected volumes and nearly 70 book chapters and articles on disability rights. She recently completed an appointment as a Distinguished Visiting Fellow at the Institute for Advanced Study at LaTrobe University in Melbourne, Australia. Her PhD is in Jurisprudence and Social Policy from Boalt Hall Law School at the University of California, Berkeley.

Kathy Ning Shen is currently an Assistant Professor in the Faculty of Business and Management at the University of Wollongong in Dubai. Her research interests include human-computer interaction; virtual communities, knowledge management, IT investment and enterprise applications. She has published over 40 refereed journal and conference articles. Her work has appeared in journals such as *Journal of the American Society for Information Science and Technology, Communications of the ACM, Journal of Computer Information Systems, Behaviour & Information Technology, International Journal of Human-Computer Interaction, AIS Transaction on Human-Computer Interaction*, and etc.

Eddie Soulier is a Professor in Computer Science and Management of Information System Science at the University of Technology of Troyes (Tech-CICO laboratory - Cooperative Technologies for Innovation and Organizational Changes). He has a PhD in Computer Science, a master on Political Science and another one on Economy. His interests are on story-telling, theory of communities, caring models for communities' infrastructures and social computing. He is scientific editor of a special thematic volume dedicated to communities of practice in the main Management of Information System review in France (SIM), and editor of book on story-telling (Hermes Science Publishing, 2005).

Julien Subercaze has obtained B.Sc in Computer Science from University of Rennes, M.Sc from the University Karlsruhe and Ph.D from the University of Lyon. He is since 2009 member in the LaHC (Saint-Etienne, France). His research interests are in the fields of Semantic Agent and Knowledge Management.

Robin Teigland is an Associate Professor at the Center for Strategy and Competitiveness at the Stockholm School of Economics (SSE) as well as the caretaker of SSE's island in Second Life. She is also the Director of SSE's PhD program in Business Administration and a member of the faculty of the International Management PhD program at the University of Agder in Norway. Robin's research interests revolve around the creation and diffusion of knowledge in social networks and the impact on competitive advantage. The focus of her current research is on investigating how virtual worlds and social media are enabling firms to create value outside the boundaries of the firm. Robin is currently leading NVWN <www.nordicworlds.net>, a two year international project investigating innovation and entrepreneurship through virtual worlds and the 3D internet financed by the Nordic Innovation Center. Robin has published numerous articles in international books and academic journals, and in 2008 she received the "Researcher of the Year" award at the Stockholm School of Economics. She has participated as PI in two EU projects: "Impact Assessment of the Participation of SMEs in the Thematic Programmes of FP5 and FP6 for Research and Technological Development (RTD)" and "Structuring Effects of Community Research – The Impact of the Framework Programme on Research and Technological Development (RTD) on Network Formation". In addition, she is a reviewer for numerous funding agencies and academic journals as well as a globally sought after speaker. Robin really enjoys teaching students at the Stockholm School of Economics and lecturing for executives. Robin is from the USA and grew up in Nashville, Tennessee (but she does not sing :-)). She holds a B.A. in Economics from Stanford University, an M.B.A. from The Wharton School, and an M.A. in International Studies from the University of Pennsylvania. In 1992 she moved to Sweden to work as a consultant for McKinsey & Company, Inc. before starting her PhD at the Stockholm School of Economics. She is married to a Norwegian and has five children, from whom she is constantly learning! More information on Robin is at www.knowledgenetworking.org.

Index

A

Academy of Economic Studies (AEC) 75, 78-79, 118

Actions 17, 53, 83, 124, 130, 138-139, 142, 147-150, 167, 172, 176-178, 182-183, 190, 218, 246

activity mode 172-173

Actor Network Theory (ANT) 165, 170, 186

actors of the innovation 163-165, 190

Actualizing Social and Personal Identity Resources (ASPIRe model) 220, 231

Agobot 243

anhomeomery 174

Anticipation Committee 167, 182, 186-187

API key 201

ARPANET 239

Ascertaining Identity Resources (AIRing) 220

aspectualities 173

association rule 92, 119

Automatic Speech Recognition (ACR) 32

B

Botnet 237, 242-244, 247

BPMN 168

brands 15-28, 129

Business Intelligence (BI) 34

C

Cascading Style Sheets (CSS) 197

CERITD 182

CK theory 187

classification 13, 56, 60-61, 86, 95, 97, 110, 120, 172, 174, 177, 239, 242

cloud computing 240

clustering 23, 95, 100, 120, 206

clusterization 179

cognitive dimensions 55, 68

cohesion 20, 58, 61, 121, 214, 218

collaborations 2-4, 7, 33, 39, 41, 45, 47, 51, 53-54, 57-58, 70, 115-117, 119, 136-137, 150, 152-153, 164-165, 167, 185, 189, 193, 204

Collaborative Innovation Networks (COINs) 54, 70, 73

Collaborative Interest Networks (CINs) 54, 73

Collaborative Knowledge Network (CKN) 54, 62-65, 67, 70, 73

Collaborative Learning Networks (CLNs) 54, 73

Collaborative Online Laboratories (COL) 136-141, 147, 149-150

Collaborative Remote Laboratory 136, 138, 141-143

Collaborative Virtual Laboratory 136, 138

collective intelligence 41, 62, 162

communities of creation 47, 52, 71, 73

Communities of Inquiry (CoI) 42, 46

Community Identification 214-215, 218, 223-224

community lifecycle 65, 68, 73

community of interest 42, 52, 69, 192

Community of Practice (CoP) 29, 31, 41, 52, 75-79, 85-86, 95, 103-104, 106, 109-110, 114-118, 120

Community-University Research Alliances (CURA) 12

computer-assisted translations 153-154, 159

Computer-Mediated Communication (CMC) 131-132, 209, 217-219, 222, 224, 226, 230, 233-235

Computer-Supported Collaborative Learning (CSCL) 136-137, 141, 143, 152

Computer Supported Cooperative Work (CSCW) 69, 151-152, 160, 188, 225

concepts space 173, 186

concordance 154, 156-161

configurations 35, 142, 148, 163, 165-166, 169-175, 178, 184-186, 190, 204

W